I0090634

A MARXIST READING OF YOUNG BAUDRILLARD

THROUGHOUT HIS ORDERED MASKS

A MARXIST READING OF YOUNG BAUDRILLARD

THROUGHOUT HIS ORDERED MASKS

by Zhang Yibing

Translated by He Huiming

Edited by Cem Kizilcec

CANUT INTERNATIONAL PUBLISHERS

Istanbul ▪ Berlin ▪ London ▪ Santiago

Published in 2009 by The Commercial Press

The English version is published in cooperation with China Renmin University Press.
Original Chinese Copyright © 2009, First Chinese Edition
ISBN: 978-7-100-06705-8

Canut International Publishers
Published by Canut International Publishers
Canut Intl. Turkey, Balipaşa Cad. 155a, Tel : +90-212-5124356, Istanbul, Turkey
Canut Intl. Germany, Heerstr. 49, D-47053, Duisburg, Germany
Canut Intl. UK, 12a Guernsay Road, London E11 4BJ, England
Web: http://www.leftreader.com
E-Mail: canut@leftreader.com

Copyright © 2014 of the First English Edition

All rights reserved. No part of this book may be used or reproduced in any manner whatsoever without the written permission of the publisher.

A Marxist Reading of Young Baudrillard. Throughout His Ordered Masks, July 2014

English Paperback Edition:

ISBN: 978-605-4923-04-5

English Digital Edition:

ISBN: 978-605-4923-00-7

From Baudrillard:

Disappearance of the object into its system

Disappearance of production into its mirror

Disappearance of the real into the simulacrum

Disappearance of the Other into its double

Disappearance of the majorities into their silence

Disappearance of Evil into its transparency

Disappearance of seduction into the orgy

Disappearance of crime into its perfection

Disappearance of memory into commemoration

Disappearance of illusion into its end and, finally,

Disappearance of the illusionist himself, on stage, in the full glare of the lights. The illusionist, having displayed all his art, cannot but make himself disappear (without knowing how)

Jean Baudrillard. *Cool Memories IV*: 1995-2000

CONTENTS

Publisher's Note   11
Preface   13

INTRODUCTION

WAS BAUDRILLARD A MARXIST BEFORE?.................................47

1 Mauss's Symbolic Exchange and the Grassroots Romanticism.............48
2 Bataille's Non-useful Philosophy of Grassrootism.........................54
3 *The System of Objects*: Symbolic Relation to be Absent from
Functional Gestell and Series Mode..60
4 Hidden Logic Support in *The Consumer Society*.........................**73**

PART ONE

**THE SECRET OF THE SIGN: THE ILLUSION THAT MATE-
RIAL EXISTENCE TRANSFORMING INTO A BUTTERFLY
– A CRITICAL READING OF JEAN BAUDRILLARD'S**
FOR A CRITIQUE OF THE POLITICAL ECONOMY OF THE SIGN

CHAPTER I

THE SIGN CODE IN THE DIFFERENTIAL PRACTICE
OF THE OBJECT..97

1 The Utility of the Object and the Social Value of the Sign.............98
2 The Codified Society: The Differential Practice of Objects...........104
3 Social Distinction and the Illusion of Consumption that
Hides Class Antagonism..113

CHAPTER II

ILLUSORY NEEDS BEHIND PSEUDO-CONSUMPTION.........119

1 The Consumable Thing is not the Thing Itself.........................120
2 Degradation from the Symbolic Exchange into the Sign Value........124
3 False Consumption as a Differential Exchange System................134

CHAPTER III

FROM COMMODITY FETISHISM TO SIGNIFIER FETISHISM...145

1 What is Marx's Fetishism Critique?...................................146
2 The "Original Sin" and Salvation of Marx's Fetishism................151
3 Theoretical Aberration from Commodity Fetishism to Signifier
Fetishism...157

CHAPTER IV

"REVOLUTION" OF THE POLITICAL ECONOMY OF THE SIGN...167

1 The Differential Production in the Modern art Signature............168
2 The Art Auction: The Academic Delivery Room of the Political
Economy of the Sign............173
3 Who Can Criticize Contemporary Capitalist Ideology?............182

CHAPTER V

THE COMPLEX LOGICAL STRUCTURE OF THE NEW
ECONOMICS............189

1 The Symbolic Exchange of Authenticity in the Four Different
Social Logics............190
2 The Charming Conversion Formula of Multi-Logics............194

CHAPTER VI

A METAPHYSICAL CRITIQUE OF THE USE VALUE............199

1 To Criticize the Lost Use Value in Marx's Critical Logic............200
2 The Metaphysics of Use Value............207
3 Use Value Fetishism—More Mysterious?............211

CHAPTER VII

FOR A CRITIQUE OF THE POLITICAL ECONOMY OF
THE SIGN AND IDEOLOGIES............219

1 The Ideology Being as a Secret Form............220
2 Critiques on the Metaphysics of Referential Signs............226
3 To Resume Symbolic Exchange: Surpassing the Value and the Sign....233

PART TWO
FROM APE TO MAN, A SUBVERSIVE PERSPECTIVE
CRITICAL READING OF JEAN BAUDRILLARD'S
THE MIRROR OF PRODUCTION

INTRODUCTION

CHAPTER VIII

MARXISM: TRANSGRESSION OF HISTORICAL MATERIALISM..245

1 The Mirror of Production: What does the Young Baudrillard
object to?............245
2 Rejection of the Gestalt of Historical Materialism............253
3 Methodological Root Cause: Transhistoricized History............259

CHAPTER IX

ONTOLOGY OF PRODUCTION:
I PRODUCE, THEREFORE HISTORY IS 267

1 Mis-criticism of Use Value and "Exchange Value" 268
2 Theoretical Stick of Symbolic Exchange in Primitive Societies 271
3 Down with the Utilitarian Ontology of Production 276
4 Re-questioning the Marxist Criticism of the
Capitalist Mode of Production 286

CHAPTER X

CRITIQUE OF LABOUR IDEOLOGY 291

1 Metaphysical Evil of Labour:
The Concrete vs. the Abstract; Quality vs. Quantity 292
2 Guilt of the Productive Labour 299
3 Good Labour and Beautiful Non-labour 304

CHAPTER XI

MARX AND THE DOMINATION OF NATURE 309

1 Conception of Enslaving Nature in Enlightenment 310
2 "Half-revolution" of Marxist View of Nature 312
3 Big Law and the Big Necessity of Nature 316

CHAPTER XII

MARX AND ETHNOCENTRISM 321

1 The Big History and the Big Dialectics 322
2 Categories of Analysis and Ideology 325
3 Is the Anatomy of Man a Key to the Anatomy of Ape? 329
4 Historical Materialism and West-centrism 334

CHAPTER XIII

RIDDLE OF MONKEY ANATOMY AND APE ANALYSIS 337

1 New Dialectical Interpretation of the Master and the Slave 338
2 Difference between the Artisan's Work and the Useful Labour 341
3 The Logical Anatomies of Man, Monkey and Ape 344

CHAPTER XIV

HISTORICAL MATERIALISM AND EUCLIDEAN
GEOMETRY OF HISTORY 349

1 Legitimacy of Articulating the Archaic History with a
Contemporary Discourse 350
2 Does Historical Materialism Have the Universality of Science? 353
3 Outdated Economic Root of Historical Materialism 356
4 Origin and New Revolution of *The Political Economy of the Sign* 360

PART THREE

FROM THE SIGN TO THE MORTAL SIMULATION—
A CRITICAL READING OF *SYMBOLIC EXCHANGE AND DEATH*

DEATH AGAINST DEATH: UNDERSTANDING
BAUDRILLARD AS A THEORETICAL TERRORIST........369

CHAPTER XV

STRUCTURAL VALUE—
A REPLACEMENT FOR QUALITATIVE VALUE........389

1 What is the Structural Revolution of Value?........390
2 How does the Age of Production end?........398
3 The Labour that has been Emptied by Codes........404

CHAPTER XVI

NON-PRODUCTIVE LABOUR AND SUFFOCATION OF
SOCIAL REVOLTS........411

1 Production Transfers to Non-production........412
2 Lowering Labour to Services and Liberation of Free Time........416
3 Disappearance of Workers and Workplace........420
4 Hollowization of Currency and Struggles in the Illusion........425

CHAPTER XVII

SIMULATION AND RESISTANCE AGAINST THE
CONTEMPORARY SYMBOLIC DOMINANCE OF CAPITAL.429

1 The Obscene Presence of Capital Logic in Simulation........430
2 Simulation at the Second Level........435
3 Symbolic Exchange: The Only Way Out for the Resistance
against Contemporary Capital Logic........438

CHAPTER XVIII

SIMULACRA AND SIMULATION:
VISTA OF THE BOURGEOIS KINGDOM........443

1 The Counterfeit: Hierarchical Transgression of Signs and
Simulacra of Nature........444
2 Production with No Prototype and Reproduction of Series........448
3 Simulations: Pattern Formation and Differential Code Modulation.454
4 The Violence of Code Domination and Pale Speculation to Death..466

CONCLUSION

SEDUCTION, DEATH AND DISAPPEARANCE........471

Bibliography........483
About the Author........487

PUBLISHER'S NOTE

After *Lenin Revisited* and *Althusser Revisited*, we publish a further textological study by Zhang Yibing, which sharply confronts Baudrillard, who was once an extremely popular postmodern thinker. After supervising several doctoral dissertations on Baudrillard, Zhang noticed a deeper level of theoretical logic in the *The Mirror of Production*. This was also a period when Chinese academia made important breakthroughs in their research into Western Marxism and Marx's concept of history. In August 2007, a seminar on Baudrillard's academic thoughts was held in Shenyang. In October, the same year Douglas Kellner, the famous Baudrillard researcher, visited Nanjing University and attended an International Symposium on Jean Baudrillard held by Center for Studies of Marxist Social Theory. In this context, Zhang was disappointed to notice critical blank spaces and ambiguity in Baudrillard research, and felt the need to create a countertrend. This is the story of how this meticulous, polemical work was produced and published. Zhang belongs to the third generation of Marxist philosophers in China, is renowned for his textological researches, and has developed a unique reading methodology which is his hallmark.

The book mainly reads the three works of early Baudrillard, and challenges current research into his philosophical journey. Zhang also reads Baudrillard's other works to fully situate him theoretically, asserting that Baudrillard cannot be classified within postmodernism or neo-Marxism in any period.

Since the end of 1960s, Baudrillard wrote three important works, *For a Critique of Political Economy of the Sign*, *The Mirror of Production* and *Symbolic Exchange and Death*, which furiously attacked Marx, aiming to refute historical materialism and deconstruct Marxian theory of labour value. Especially *The Mirror of Production* was prepared as a heavy artillery for the deconstruction and disordering of the logic of Marxist theories from the interior, which was ignored by many Marxist researchers. What was the real thought situating and historical context of the shift in his critique, and how was symbolic exchange combined with death? The author with sharp insight discovers Young Baudrillard's thinking trapped by the logic of symbolic exchange based on grassroots' romanticism (radicalism) of Mauss-Bataille, then keenly follows the secret of transformation process in his critical logic, his passage from the dissolution of the ideographic material to the symbolic value of coding structure, then to the quasi-real existence without a model, and finally the symbolic miscoding of death becomes the hopeless waiting for Baudrillard's tentative salvation of the world. This is a death trilogy, which occurs in Baudrillard's academic scenery and in which the real existence is murdered. The thinking of late Baudrillard is a discourse like virus and paranoia. This kind of logical violence of theoretical terrorism has become an absurd modern academic caricature in the excessive rational interpretation. In this book the reader will also find Zhang's innovative interpretation and updating of Marx's historical materialism. He argues that this discovery of Marx's cannot be grasped and enriched unless its two aspects—general and specific—are clearly demarcated, among which the latter aspect focuses on capitalism and transition from capitalism to communism.

We hope this publication will add to benign exchanges among Marxist researchers from all over the world. Finally, we thank Renmin University Press and its editors for their collaboration in producing an accurate translation, and especially to our dear translator Professor Yang Liu for her precision.

Atiye Ugur Humes
April 2014, London

PREFACE

In this book, we deal with the extremely popular Jean Baudrillard.[1]

---

1 Jean Baudrillard (July, 1929-March, 2007), the famous contemporary French thinker, was born into a common family in Reims, a remote area of Northeast France. His grandfather was an ordinary farmer, and his parents were normal civil servants. Therefore, Baudrillard did not possess deep-rooted elitism in his early mind. This fact might also psychologically explain his later acceptance of the Bataille-Mauss grass-roots radicalism. After graduating from high school, he failed in the entrance examination of the Paris Higher Normal School, and was even unable to be admitted to a university through common procedures. In his own words, his enrollment was done "in a tortuous way." Failure to obtain a teacher's certificate deepened his hatred to the mainstream Western culture. Thus, in the early 1960s, Baudrillard simply relied on his language talent to teach German in a middle school. At the same time, he began to encounter Mauss's anthropological view and note Bataille's philosophy. In 1966, Baudrillard attended Roland Barthes's seminar in l'École Pratique des Hautes Études; meanwhile, he completed his doctoral thesis Le Système des objets (The System of Objects) under the supervision of the famous Western Marxist Lefebvre. In the same year, he served as an assistant at the University of Paris V and later he taught sociology for nearly 20 years at the Université de Paris-X Nanterre. In 1986, Baudrillard began teaching at the Université de Paris-IX Dauphine. He retired from Dauphine in 1990. His ex-wife was Lucile Baudrillard. They have two children: Gilles Baudrillard and Anne Baudrillard. In 1995, Baudrillard married Martine Dupuis, photo editor of a magazine, a marriage obviously connected with Baudrillard's interest in photography. From the beginning of the late 1960s, he established close relationship with and published lots of essays in the journals Utopie and Tra-verses, two heterodox radical publications of the left-wing. Subsequently, Baudrillard published a series of important academic works in succession and established his fame as an academic master. Judged from his academic

Baudrillard died not long ago, an event which undoubtedly attracted attention from the outside world.[2] Usually, he is considered as a great master of "Postmodernism," and even praised as the "supertheorist of a new postmodernity."[3] Despite his passing, his great influence on international academics is still profound and comprehensive.

Needless to say, Baudrillard is one of the most important figures among radical post-modern thinkers of Europe. However, in my view, there are always some misunderstandings as to his status in the history of Western thought: Firstly, it is believed that he was once a "Neo-Marxist" in Western Europe. In fact, he *never* embraces Marxism, or more precisely, his academic presence was acquired by betraying his teachers' leftist position. A retrospective look at the "post-1968" period in Europe shows that this betrayal coincided with the emergence of *post-Marxism*[4]. At the same time, post-modern thought came in to being as a whole. Secondly, he is regarded as a great master of "Postmodernism"; but I hold that Baudrillard is not a *post-modernist*[5] in the strict sense. Indeed, he not only tenaciously opposes the entirety of modernity but also spares no effort to *radically criticize and reject all post-modern spectacles*. Therefore, the

---

career, he is not an orthodox academic scholar. His writing style is relatively free, and he paid little attention to references and bibliographies in his later years. However, we have to admit the explosive power of creativity and extraordinary depths of the thinking displayed in his texts. In addition, his thought displays extreme variety and nonlinear thickness. In his own words, he was a "pataphysician at twenty—situationist at thirty—utopian at forty—transversal at fifty—viral and metaleptic at sixty—the whole of my history." (*Cool Memories II 1987-1990*, p. 131) His representative works: *The System of Objects* (1968), *The Consumer Society: Myths and Structures* (1970), *For a Critique of the Political Economy of the Sign* (1972), *The Mirror of Production* (1973), *Symbolic Exchange and Death* (1976), *Seduction* (1979), *Simulacra and Simulation* (1981), *The Other, by himself* (1987), *Cool Memories* (Five volumes 1986-2004), *The Illusion of the End* (1992), *The Transparency of Evil* (1990).

2   Jean Baudrillard died of illness on March 6, 2007. In August of that year, a seminar on Baudrillard's academic thoughts was held in Shenyang, China. In October, Kellner, the famous international expert on Baudrillard, visited Nanjing University and attended International Symposium on Jean Baudrillard held by Center for Studies of Marxist Social Theory at Nanjing University.

3   Steven Best, Douglas Kellner. *Postmodern Theory: Critical Interrogations*. Macmillan, 1991, p. 111.

4   See my essay: "Western Marxism, Post-Marxism and Late Marxism" in *Journal of Fujian Tribune*, 2000. 4.

5   Postmodernism has no "principles" as it disposes of all theoretical logic structures. Therefore, it can only be translated into postmodern thoughts or postmodern theories.

view that Baudrillard can be evaluated as "post-modernist" is unscientific. In my opinion, the otherness theory framework, which was so long ingrained in the young Baudrillard's mirror image, is in fact the theory of symbolic exchange. The theory was founded by the French sociologist Marcel Mauss in his aboriginal anthropological studies. It was later expounded widely in the sense of culture by the French philosopher George Bataille.[6] My view is that the demonizing logic, *Mauss-Bataille academic logic*, fundamentally resists human civilization. We might as well define it as *grassroots romanticism* of cultural throwback (I shall make a detailed explanation of this concept later), so that the following analysis will be proceeded. In addition, it should be pointed out that Baudrillard's logic dramatically differs from others' *affirmative conclusion* of postmodernism, such that of as Jacques Derrida and Jean Lyotard. In fact, post-modern thought is the *simulation object* that Baudrillard castigates in the ironical context.[7] Thirdly, the *non-homogeneous* problem, which is the crucial Baudrillard's concept, also lacks an accurate recognition. Amongst current academic research on Baudrillard's thoughts, I find that most theorists readily endow some similar concepts (symbolic exchange, series, and authenticity) with homogeneity when they discuss these concepts used by Baudrillard at different stages. This approach is actually ahistorical, and will inevitably lead to the homogeneous committing violence against Baudrillard's ever-changing theoretic logic.

Here, I would like to briefly discuss the first above-mentioned misunderstanding, which closely connects with the theme of this book. The belief that Baudrillard was once a Marxist is incorrect. I will face Baudrillard's deep questioning and critique on Marxism, and then, I will identify the historical understandings in his deep academic paradigm.

---

6   Kellner is also aware of it. However, he only refers to it as the thought background from *The Mirror of Production to Symbolic Exchange and Death*. He also mentions that Baudrillard is influenced by Jarry's pataphysical desire to exterminate meaning. Please refer to: Douglas Kellner. *Jean Baudrillard in the Fin-de-Millennium, Baudrillard: A Critical Reader*. Basil Blackwell Ltd. 1994, p. 6.

7   Mike Gane holds the similar concept, too. Therefore, Kellner's critique of Gane actually makes no sense. Scholars who describe post-modernism are not necessary post-modernists. As for Kellner's concept, please refer to Kellner, Douglas. *Jean Baudrillard in the Fin-de-Millennium, Baudrillard: A Critical Reader*. Wiley-Blackwell Ltd. 1994, p. 11.

Conventional Western researchers of Baudrillard simply refer to his early theoretical development within the framework of *neo-Marxism*. For example, Mark Poster implies that before 1973, "Baudrillard's critique of the capitalist commodity economy can still be viewed as within the general framework of Marxist political economy and structuralism."[8] Similar opinions are held by Steve Best and Douglas Kellner.[9] After reviewing several noticeable Chinese sources, I came to realize that most Chinese researchers seem to accept the above assertion, too. However, after a careful reading of Baudrillard's early works, *The System of Objects*[10] and *The Consumer Society*, and especially other works written before 1973, I cannot help doubting this consensus judgment.

Was there a real Marxist Baudrillard? According to my present research, the answer is no. After careful analysis, the reason why the majority draws this false conclusion is that "Baudrillard consistently criticizes capitalism." However, the logical relation that is clear to be seen is also liable to cause theoretical strabismus: *Criticizing capitalism is not equal to Marxism.* Baudrillard *never* becomes a real Marxist! Even in the beginning stages of constituting his theoretical logic, his theoretical position is post-Marxism. The symbolic textual event at that time was his first book, *The System of Objects*, published in 1968,[11] the year of demarcation in the history of European leftist academia. Early in the mid-1960s, Baudrillard's three teachers, Henri Lefebvre, Roland Barthes, and Guy Debord did not belong in the traditional *Western Marxist* context. Although Barthes belonged to the European left in his later years, he was never a Marxist. In

---

8   Mark Poster. *Jean Baudrillard, Selected Writings, An Introduction.* Stanford University Press, 1988, p. 6-8.
9   Douglas Kellner. *Jean Baudrillard in the Fin-de-Millennium, Baudrillard: A Critical Reader.* 1994, 5. Kellner even claims that semiology is used to be a supplement to Marxism. Best's points can be found in the book. In October, 2007, I exchanged my views with professor Kellner face to face. He did not oppose my point directly.
10   Published in 1968, *Le Système des Objets* does not discuss the object or natural material beyond people. It aims to probe into non-natural objects which have already been in the world of instrumental "circumspection" (Heidegger). In our words, the non-natural object is the artificial material system in social existence—object. Actually the object group in a specific meaning emerges after industrialness. Therefore, the title of the book, I think, should be translated into "客体的系统". (In the Chinese version of *Baudrillard: A Critical Reader*, the translator correctly uses the title). Considering the standards of quotation, I retain the title used by the translator in my book.

addition, Lefebvre's and Debord's theoretical position also transcended Marxism at that time.[11] We should bear in mind this significant
point. It means that when the young Baudrillard builds his mirror image at the beginning, the Other theory dominating the generation of
his initial thoughts belongs to post-Marxism. It should also be noticed
that Baudrillard's theoretical tendency towards post-Marxism is only
a *transitional* residence of temporary theory for his logical modelling
at this time. Moreover, post-Marxism is not the same as Marxism.[12]

In the next place, my judgment is that in his early works *The System
of Objects* and *The Consumer Society*, Baudrillard converts his teachers' critique of the latest capitalist changes into an abstract philosophical reflection. In *The Consumer Society* especially, he merely offers
a popular and hyperbolic portrayal of the *dominant* phenomenon in
contemporary society, of which Lefebvre and Debord had already
been aware (Lefebvre calls it the bureaucratic society of controlled
consumption,[13] and Debord regards it as the consumer society with
spectacle control as the dominant structure). It should be noted that
Baudrillard does not base his theoretical standpoint of *otherness* on
historical materialism. Instead, he employs what Lefebvre taught
him, the *symbolic being* of ancient life, unpolluted by utilitarian logic.
Therefore, during the process of generating the theoretical questions
in the two texts, Marx's historical phenomenology appears with a per-
functory and unconvincing presence, if it is present at all. It is my submission that young Baudrillard's real standpoint of his initial context
is Marcel Mauss and Bataille's conception of *grassrootism* centred on
the primitive (tribal) gift-exchange relations and non-utilitarian consumption. However, the appearance of the important otherness theory
is sporadic in his early theoretical situating, such as that found in *The
System of Objects* and *The Consumer Society*.

---

11   Lefebvre begins to criticize Marx's productivism in *Everyday Life in the Modern
World*, written in 1967. In *The Society of the Spectacle*, Debord uses spectacle
production to replace commodity production. It is the beginning of post-Marxism texts.
Therefore, I have reason to make the judgment that the source of young Baudrillard's
logic is not found in the logical structure of Western Marxism.
12   See my essay: "Post-Marxism is not Marxism"in *Journal of Nanjing University*, 2003, 2.
13   Henri Lefebvre. *Everyday Life in the Modern World*. Continuum International
Publishing Group, 2002, p. 68.

From the perspective of deep narrative logic, *For a Critique of the Political Economy of the Sign, The Mirror of Production*, as well as *Symbolic Exchange and Death* are an academic trilogy declaring that Baudrillard's authentic being (symbolic exchange) has been perfectly murdered. It announces his standpoint as being against Marxism. Simultaneously, from standpoint of the development of Baudrillard's thoughts, it is also the critical period during which he converts his own theoretical modelling into original mind.

For a Critique of the Political Economy of the Sign,[14] published in 1972, could be regarded as the first rebellion against Marxism in the context of post-Marxism. Admittedly, the book is one of the most important books among Baudrillard's early academic works and is also the first step in the "murder trilogy." In the first two chapters of the book, Baudrillard transcends extremely from the idealistic "society of spectacle" to the nothingness sign kingdom by semiologically rewriting Debord's "society of spectacle." At the same time, the structure of material production in society, which is the prerequisite element emphasized by Karl Heinrich Marx, is totally replaced by sign production and abstract differential social relations. As a result, when identifying the nature of contemporary capitalism, he transcends from "the consumer society" to "sign society." In the third chapter, Baudrillard bids farewell to Marxism, becoming the direct opponent of Marx's social critiques, political economy, and historical materialism. By this point, great changes have arisen from his logical situating. He proposes a critical logic which concentrates on the *symbolic labour of different signifiers* and *symbolic value*. In addition, he begins to directly criticize Marx's labour value (mainly use value) and economic fetishism.[15]

---

14   The Chinese version was translated by Doctor Xia Ying, published by Nanjing University Press, 2009.

15   Poster believes Baudrillard still remains Marxist in his *For A Critique of the Political Economy of the Sign* and uses semiology to examine the general principle that Marx adopts to analyze commodity. Baudrillard never fought against Marx until he finished *The Mirror of Production*. I will prove that Poster's assumption is wrong. It is in *For A Critique of the Political Economy of the Sign* that Baudrillard begins to deny Marx's historical materialism. Poster's view can be found in: Poster, Mark. *The Second Media Age*. Cambridge: Polity Press, 1995. Kellner, Douglas. (ed.), *Baudrillard: A Critical Reader*, Oxford, Wiley-Blackwell, 1994.

Shortly thereafter, in *The Mirror of Production*, which was published in the following year, Marx's historical materialism becomes his target. This text is the second step in Baudrillard's murder trilogy of authentic being. It is true that he still holds a vestige of *post-Marxian* ideas, but *The Mirror of Production* establishes his position as a thorough anti-Marxist theorist. Baudrillard's opposition to Marx is not simply the result of his bourgeois standpoint but arises because he believes Marx's critique on capitalism is incomplete: Marx still falls a victim to the capitalist material foundation and the entire Western civilization that creates this foundation. In Baudrillard's view, besides the economic relations of corrupted bourgeois and political structure, the real culprit is the *material mode of production* per se which is easily let go by Marx.

Capitalism is merely the highest level of this historical *utilitarianism*. According to Baudrillard, Marx universalizes the economic framework of capitalism, generalizes labour and production, use value and the mode of production that only emerge in the system of exchange value to "the general mode of human production." Therefore, Marx seriously objects to the capitalist mode of production and exposes the exploitative nature of capital, but he is unaware that the discourse of the philosophy of history centred on the *useful* production of labour is still the coded product of the unconscious in the bourgeois system of value exchange. For Marx, the reason why we are human beings owes to production: *I produce, therefore I am.* This is the real intention of "the mirror of production." According to Baudrillard in *The Mirror of Production*, man acquires an imago from the Smith-Marx mirror and then creates an illusionary utilitarian world, a self-reference of the effective subject. The essence of the image is the *utilitarian logic of value*; hence, the production of the mirror can be developed into *the mirror of political economy, the mirror of labour,* and *the mirror of history*. Baudrillard believes that the recessive nature of historical materialism and capitalism are homogeneous. However, Marx neutralizes the productive force(s) by extending it to the foundation of general social existence and progress while being unable to realize it is this utility system of production that generates the entire utilitarian coordinate of values. Therefore, Baudrillard thinks Marx's criticism of the capitalist mode of production not only fails to solve the problem once and for all, but also obscures the deep truth of the matter to the extent that the radical revolution digresses. Subsequently, Marx fails to make critical changes to the capital logic: He is against the very capitalist economic relations but only creates an "ideological phantasm that capital has itself elaborated."

Baudrillard refutes this "I-produce-therefore-history-is ontology", Marxism, and even all of the radical discourses of false *producibility* of the post-Marxian trend. At this point, it is clear that he denies all social existence and historical movement established on the basis of shaping material production, rejects the ordering social development of progressive history, and refuses to view man as the producer (labour power). In a word, Baudrillard is strongly opposed to the logic of utility shaping and to the development of material productive forces as man's end. Judging from the common knowledge of contemporary Western thought, he wants to abandon *productivism*. That is the reason why he is frightening. As a defector from Western Marxism and a participant in the French translation of *The German Ideology*, Baudrillard is different from other external Marxist enemies who simply attack the historical patterns and ideological fantasy derived from Marxism. He attempts at a direct and accurate blasting of the principal pillars that sustain Marxist historical materialism–the basic theory of material production and the logic of historical phenomenology. Thus, Baudrillard's challenging questions are by no means trivial to Marxist historical materialism. He becomes destined to be Marx's theoretical antagonist.

The third book, *Symbolic Exchange and Death*, written in 1976, shows that logical detournement seems to happen again in Baudrillard's mind—his *original* theoretical situating finally comes into being. In the first two books, he mainly regards the symbolic exchange as the logical scale, illustrating that Marx's historical materialism based on the mode of material production is an unconscious conspiracy with bourgeois ideology. However, from the beginning of this book, he starts with the new changes in contemporary capitalism, stating that Marx's labour and production concepts are out of date. At this stage, the crucial concept used to draw social existence of contemporary capitalism—*simulation*—appears. Moreover, *authenticity* as a basic category lacking ontology begins to act as the pivot for his situating and logic of critique. Thus, Baudrillard begins to use the theory of *simulacra and simulation* to reinterpret the logical existence of contemporary capitalism. Qualitative analysis of contemporary capitalism shows that he transcends from "the consumer society" to "sign society," and then to super-realistic simulation society. It seems to me that Baudrillard at this time is directly influenced by the late Lacanian thought, although this deep influence is mostly exerted quietly through misrecognition. Taking a comprehensive view of Baudrillard's grand "murder trilogy," we can see that it is at this step that he moves directly to the death of the authentic being. It is here that Baudrillard rejects publicly the scientific socialist theory of Marxism. He compares his thought to "theoretical terrorism" and proposes a political alternative schema of *symbolic subversion*. "Burn down the sign" and "death against death." During the symbolic "revolution in the depths of soul," everything is substituted by imagination. Therefore, the actual revolution against capitalist control finally transforms into a conceptual rebellion of idealism.

Baudrillard continues to produce a large number of new concepts and analytical frameworks paying close attention to the most significant changes in contemporary Western society; hence, he becomes the centre of attention with his radical negative perspective and post-modern critique in the Western academic world. Here, I have to remind the reader that Baudrillard is not a post-modernist. He is simply a solitary thinker, persistent in his own grassroots romanticism and yet reaching a distant realm along the pointed dimension of human thinking, a domain beyond even post-modernism. Some new concepts proposed by him in the late 1970s, such as the crucial categories "simulation," "surreal world," and "seduction," etc., all expose the nature of slavery of the latest post-modern ideology. In fact, it is interesting that Baudrillard himself feels uncomfortable about the popular misinterpretation of him as a "post-modern" "authority of reference." He publicly expresses that he has nothing to do with "post-modernism." To him, it is quite absurd for his critical analysis of contemporary society to be casually "patched up at hindsight" and labelled as "post-modern."[16] For this reason, if we extol Baudrillard as a post-modern theorist, then we shall simply miss him.

Another problem requiring explanation is that my research approach has changed in this book, namely moved to a new platform for the *intellectual situating theory*. On this issue, I make a detailed explanation in *Lenin Revisited*.[17] Here, I only extract a few relative segments of situating as my explanation of my methodology: In my opinion, the essence of any theory or academic thought is not a concrete logical framework like Newton's substantive framework of time and space. It is rather the historical constituting in the context of complicated and ever-changing thoughts and *contexts*. This situating theory is a non-Paradigm, without even a specifically dead or petrified framework. It is a functional questioning and thinking, which usually behaves as a *fragile, dogged question reconstructed at any time and a temporary stance*. The theory is intertwined with *logical rays*,[18] *theoretical circuits*,[19] and *discourse détournement*,[20] which carry the multiple vectors of time. To constitute the intellectual situating theory, the subject usually resorts to the basic theoretic model consciously or unconsciously and immediately activates the *academic memory of this convex point*[21]. Then it is suddenly consti-

16   See Lin Zhiming's Introduction to *The System of Objects*. Shanghai Century Publishing Group Co., Ltd., 2001, p. 9.
17   See my Introduction to *Lenin Revisited. A Post-textological Reading of Philosophical Notes*. Jiangsu People's Publishing House, 2008. English version published by Canut Publishers, Berlin/London, 2011
18   Logical rays is a concept I newly created. The word ray refers to electromagnetic waves that cannot be observed by human eyes, such as infrared rays, X rays, etc. Here, logic ray denotes the hidden intention that cannot appear in the logic space. It can be used to penetrate through the surface and thus find the hidden objects in a research effort.
19   Theoretical circuit is a also new concept of mine. Circuit originally means a complete path along which an electric current flows. Generally, it is also called a closed circuit. Theoretical circuit here is used to describe a closed thought existing in theoretical identification. Closed thought can be contrasted with open thought.
20   Détournement is an important concept of French situationist Debord. It originally means the thought revolution which breaks through the domination of traditional spectacle. It usually achieved in artistic situations. Here, it is used to identify the uncommon conversion of different thought contexts or sub-cognitive structure. Debord's idea on détournement can be referred to: Debord, Guy. *The Society of the Spectacle*, Trans. Donald Nickleson-Smith, New York: Zone Books, 1994.
21   Academic memory is also a concept I have newly created, which refers to other thinkers' academic resources remaining in a thinkers' minds. It generally can be rendered as the *academic memory of the convex point, complex academic memory cluster*, and *other problematics*, etc.

tuted through the specific theoretical circuit. However, the different logical rays of the subject's unconsciousness and suspicious questions are the real driving force behind the changes and revolutions of situating theory. Meanwhile, this non-linear logical circuit will be achieved by the whole Gestalt transformation, and new constituting logic will again form the new intellectual situating in the moment.

I have come to realize that the generation of the mirror of thought is complicated to every original thinker, but I find a general mode among the common paradigms in the history of thought. Almost all the formation process of each thinker's theoretical logic transforms from *mirror-image in otherness to the spontaneous ordering of thought,*[22] and then to *his/her original intellectual situating phase.*

Mirror-image in otherness means that, a thinker's intellectual situating is the dominant discourse of his/her academic reflection. It mainly relies on the other academic logic (text) which presents as *the mirror-image of other*[23] and acquires or appropriates this logic consciously or unconsciously. Generally speaking, the other intellectual situating constitutes intentional or sub-intentional supporting components by one or several *inactivated* theoretical resources (academic memory cluster) and the otherness theoretical questions; hence a specific thought will be activated. Borrowing and rewriting Julia Kristeva's discourse, I define it as *simply an academic intertextuality.* The relationship between the theory of production and the subject is that the subject is usually structurally dominated and conceptually anchored by the otherness theoretic *framework.* However, the subject's thought appears as a simple reproduction or closed theoretical circuit, thus generating a certain producibility and relatively independent theory. Fundamentally speaking, the activated intellectual mirror at this time is still an unconscious identification of mirror image. It is more complicated that the academic memory in the other thinking space often reappears in the form of *imaginative* theoretical

---

22   In this book, intellectual situating will be changed into intellectual *ordering.*

23   Lacan's concept: According to Lacan, other can be divided into the small other and big Other. The former represents the ontological misconception of an ego's mirror projection at the beginning stage of establishing the ego's identification. The latter is the construction that the whole language and symbolic systems interrogates the personal identification. Please see my book: *The Impossible Truth of Being: Mirror of Lacan's Philosophy,* The Commercial Press, 2006.

misunderstanding. In general, in the context of this imaginative mis-understanding, the signifier is inconsistent with the signified. I found that the thinker usually constitutes his other logic during his nascent academic development, as with Lenin's early philosophy thought studied in this book. By viewing the young Lenin's thought and re-search on social and economic development and political struggle, we discover that he becomes a mature Marxist very early on. On the other hand, his early understanding of philosophy is based more on the *other* cognitive structure. It can be said that his concept depends on the philosophy of Georgi Plekhanov and Joseph Dietzgen, etc. The same situation also occurs when Lenin studies Hegelian phi-losophy in his early stage. Georgi Plekhanov's philosophy thought is always in the structure of the *other*. Although a few thoughts of him are original, Plekhanov misunderstands Marx, for example with re-gard to geographical determinism. What's more, within the domain of medieval theology and the framework of Stalinist dogmatism, the other structure becomes the sole existence of the thought, in which the thought is stagnant and dead.

Additionally, *the spontaneous ordering of the thought* is a transi-tional stage in which a thinker begins to mature in his/her thoughts. During this period, the thinker often begins to get rid of the domi-nance of the Other and thinks independently. Indeed, it is also the result of deep intertextuality. However, in most contexts, the thinker will convert the other structure, formerly as the outer mirror, into academic production "for us." With regard to the relationship be-tween the theory in production and the subject, I can say the subject will negatively produce more active constructions. Therefore, the constructions will force the current theoretical resources to serve the context of the new thought more frequently. Its closed theoretical circuit and simple reproduction of the other thinking space are also challenged by the new thought. It is necessary that the subject con-verts theoretical logic into the creative theory of *production*. Thus, the theory in production "for us" and the open theoretical circuit become the basic content and operational mode of situating. For ex-ample, around 1844 the young Marx's thought was actually simul-taneously influenced by multiple other thinkers, including Georg Wilhelm Friedrich Hegel and Ludwig Andreas Feuerbach, whose minds were active in his deep logic. These thoughts also included the young Friedrich Engels and Moses Hess who were in direct dialogue with Marx. The classical economics in a negative context was also included. It is not difficult to find that the young Marx never simply succumbs to any other constructions. He is always trying to transform other thoughts into his own logical component. Labour alienation theory is definitely the achievement of his spontaneous situating through intertextuality at a deeper level. Although the young Marx's critique of capitalism depended on the proletarian standpoint, his theoretical questions were still related to the other, that is, Feuerbach's humanistic alienation logic. This is a deeper question.

The original intellectual situating means that the thinker constitutes his own theoretical logic and thinking space through his/her original theory in production. Needless to say, this situation appears more at the stage of theoretical maturity. At this point, the thinker critically begins to go beyond his former other framework, treating the predecessor's pseudo-solution as the other illusion. As a result, the academic memory succeeds in freeing itself from the unconscious mirror identity, from misrecognition, and falsity. The memory is often activated by conscious deformation and metonymies. Subsequently the thinker promotes the former thoughts through a totally new discourse system or spontaneous theoretic questions. This success of his original intellectual situating announces a great revolution in his thought. After this revolution, the thinking history may even be adapted or rewritten in the process of a new theoretical circuit. Of course, absolutely original thought never exists from the view of post-modernism. Therefore, this so-called original intellectual situating is basically considered as higher intertextual thoughtsweaving, and integration (Barthes). In fact, I find that some of the greatest original theories occur at the stage of logical integration. For instance, one has Plato's realm of ideas after Socrates, Immanuel Kant's transcendental epistemology after David Hume, Hegel's absolute concept after Johann Gottlieb Fichte and Friedrich Wilhelm Joseph Schelling, Marx's historical materialism was founded between 1845 and 1858 after Hegel, Ludwig Andreas von Feuerbach, and David Ricardo, Martin Heidegger's ontology after Søren Aabye Kierkegaard and Edmund Husserl, etc.

Admittedly, when one considers the whole process of a think-er's development, the thought situating transforming wholly into different situatings may occur at any period of the generation of thought. However, the most important conversion is still the Gestalt transformation from mirror-image in otherness to the spontaneous ordering of thought. This conversion is a process from quantita-tive changes to qualitative changes. The other which situates con-tinuously gives place to the spontaneous thought. Thus the thinker transforms his/her passive position into an active construction and independent thought process. Of course, only a few original think-ers are able to establish their original theory of production in the end. Most scholars will always remain in the framework of the *other*.

This new point should be regarded as my latest *interpretative mode for analyzing thoughts history* at present.[24]

Actually, during my recent research into situating,[25] I have real-ized that *Lenin Revisted* is incomplete in many areas in terms of situating. Although I have published dissertations on (thought) his-torical situating, the narrative logic of the way of thinking still needs to be further improved. Therefore, I will publish some new disser-tations successively to complement my explanation from different perspectives. Here I merely point out that situating theory is a philo-sophical way of thinking *based on* the *contemporary interpretation* of Marx's historical materialism. The situating is the top component of historical ontology rather than an ontological weltanschauung. In the contemporary interpretation of Marx's historical materialism, I would like to use four categories to reinterpret historical materialism through situating. First, the subject's labour shaping used to shape his material existence and himself. Second, the subject and the shaped object's systematic *configurating* in a certain functional field. Third, production *ordering* of the thingness and social systematism. The subject's production and his social activities order the thingness and

24   See my introduction to *Lenin Revisited. A Post-textological Reading of His Philosophical Notes*. Jiangsu People's Publishing House, 2008. English version by Canut Intl. Publishers, London 2011.
25   See my essays: "Problems, Ways, Methods: Reflections on New Academic Heights in Marxist Philosophical Studies" in *Academic Monthly*, 2007, 5. "Historical Materialism and Historical Situating" in *Journal Historical Research*, 2008, 1.

social systematic in specific historical conditions. Fourth, structure *modelling* used to functionally construct and deconstruct daily life and also social existence by men's social practice, personal behaviours and language activities. Fourthly, the *situating* of the real life and thought presents at the top level as I mentioned.[26]

Labour *shaping* is proposed by Marx in *1857-1858 Economics Manuscripts*, in which Marx explains the process of production. It is used specifically to identify the labour activities of *subjective objectification*. I have already given explanations for it in *Back to Marx*. In the context of Marx' thought, Marx desires to *return to* subjective labour from material production. Additionally, material production based on objective orientation can be seen in the general historical materialism of *The German Ideology* (1845-1846)[27]. Therefore, subjective labour is considered "as a living labour capacity."[28] Marx realizes at this point that material production is the basis of social existence and social change. However, the objects of labour and tools perform a negative act in the process of material production. The core driving force is labour's shaping of people's intentional and subjective activities. As a matter of fact, *man's labour activity* is recognized as the *fundamental position* where material production creates social history. In my opinion, this is the *logical starting point* of Marx's *special historical materialism*. From the view of philosophy, Marx *starts again from the subjective dimension* which is the real and historical origin of his historical phenomenology. It is important to note that in the *1844 Manuscripts* labour activity is not the

---

26   It may be easily seen that I add the suffix "ING" to all five relevant English words. Firstly, they are obviously influenced by Heidegger's Being. Secondly, I am directly inspired by Andrew Pickering, the contemporary sociologist of science and a famous American scholar. Pickering uses words such as Modelling in *The Mangle of Practice: Time, Agency, and Science*. Refer to: Pickering, Andrew. *The Mangle of Practice: Time, Agency, and Science*. Trans. Xing Dongmei, Nanjing University Press, 2004.

27   When confronting the structure of materialized labour, which is capitalistic and complicated, Marx suddenly realizes that it is problematic to directly criticize it from the perspective of production. Production is only the materialized labour of objectivity. As the subjective activity, labour relation is historically subverted and alienated. This alienation is not the essential labour alienation as grasped in *1844 Manuscripts of Economics and Philosophy*. Instead it refers to the subversion and metamorphosis of living labour in the real economic relations.

28   John E. Elliott. *Marx and Engels on Economics, Politics, and Society: Essential Readings with Editorial Commentary*. Goodyear Pub. Co., 1981, p. 151.

idealized nature of man *"that should exist"* but *"does not"*. Labour activity exists objectively in the entire production of social reality.[29]

According to Marx, "Labour is the living, form-giving fire; it is the transitoriness of things, their temporality, as their formation by living time."[30] Here "formation" as Marx mentions, refers to *transitoriness* and *temporality* gained by material production through man's labour. This new form differs from natural existence. However, man's labour activity itself fails to achieve material shaping independently. Material shaping can only be accomplished through the connection of tools and labour in the specific production process. Thus, shaping is always a purposeful material production initiated by labour. The so-called shaping refers to the production and reproduction process in which man's labour activities change the existence of material objects "for us." It is impossible to create material; however, the social and historical forms of material existence are continuously changed by labour production. *Man's labour provides the natural substance with something of social existence "for us" (a certain social and historical needs),[31] rather than creating material*

---

29   In *Back to Marx: The Philosophical Discourse in the Context of Economics*, I concluded the logic of Marx from *1844 Manuscripts of Economics* and *Philosophy to Economic Manuscripts of 1857-1858*: From the view of philosophy, Marx' thought *starts from humanistic labour regulations to practice, from production and then back to scientific labour regulations*. In other words, the logic transforms *from the value subject to the historical object, and then to the historical subject*. The diagram is as follows:

1. *1844 Manuscripts of Economics and Philosophy*: Labour alienation Koseli paragraf(genus (speciesessence) → Return to humanistic view of alienation, subject, value critique based on ethics.

2. *On an Outline about Feuerbach (Theses of 1845)*: Practice → Man's historical nature → Reality: Perceptual activities, practical materialism, and realistic critique by revolution.

3. *The German Ideology* (1845-1846): Production → The social and historical existence → Mode of production: Real Individual, general historical materialism, historical dialectics and critical empiricism based on economics.

4. *Economic Manuscripts of 1857-1858*: Labour (the essence of social relationships)→ Value (class relation) → Money (materialized labour) → *Capital*: special historical materialism, economics, and the *historical phenomenological* critique. See my book: *Back to Marx: The Change of Philosophical Discourse in the Context of Economics*, p. 599, English version published by Göttingen University Press, in 2014.

30   Karl Marx. *Grundrisse: Foundations of the Critique of Political Economy*. Vintage Books, 1973. pp. 360-361.

31   See my book: *Back to Marx: The Change of Philosophical Discourse in the Context of Economics*, p. 630.

itself in the production. To say in Heidegger's romantic words, the object is not allowed to be "thinged" (existence) as the former natural features. It becomes the material existence of man's readiness-to-hand[32] through the ready-to-hand of "Dasein." In fact, this process is a fundamental one of social existence that men acquire the material life through production, as Marx has underlined.

Many years ago I pointed out: "Where Marx finally surpasses the old materialism is that Marx refers to the essence of social life as practice. The basis of social life should be the practical process of man's activity and advancement. It is also the real intention of the continuance of human history. The historical essence is the *mobile creation and duration* of subjective practice, rather than the amount of increase in the object's annual-rings. Therefore, social essence should not only remain at the level of mechanicalness but also should be considered as "an ever-burning fire" looking from the revolutionary and dialectical perspective."[33] Now, this creative "living fire" is labour's shaping. According to Marx, it is only man's labour that subjectively changes the natural being in the production process. Historically speaking, labour's shaping diversifies its appearance: Firstly, agriculture, forestry, and animal husbandry produce and reproduce in the long process of natural economy ages. Man's labour only shapes the outside natural objects simply by the selective preference "for us." For instance, man selects and rejects natural conditions in the natural economy. Thus species are divided into *desirable and undesirable* ones. Desirable species includes poultry, husbanded animals, and cereals. Man also creates clothing to replace animal fur and builds village houses to substitute caves via using his handicrafts *in a bionic way.* More importantly, it is labour that historically changes man's existence mode. This change is the greatest ontological life-shaping, which is also the key point proposed by Engels in his *The Part Played by Labour in the Transition from Ape to Man.*

Secondly, labour's shaping, in the process of industrial production and reproduction, is no more than a selective preference or simply a bionic transformation of material existence. It begins to focus

---

32   Readiness-to-hand, Heidegger's Zuhandensein, is translated as 用在性 in Japan by famous Marxist philosopher Hiromatsu. In China, it is usually translated as 上手性.
33   See my "On Social Practice" in *Jianghai Academic Journal*, 1988, 5.

on the material's *qualitative creation*. The essence of industrial modernity is making the entirety of nature become the object of man's work (Heidegger). Moreover, nature is no more the object imitated in industrial production, but the material dominated and subdued by men. The essence of industrial production is that, labour's shaping creates the material existence beyond nature. Here the innovative ideas in the work process become science; man's handicrafts capacity dealing with thingness operation transforms into technology. Through industrial material production, "social wealth" (William Petty-Adam Smith's labour value) emerges entirely on the basis of man's labour. Commodity-market economy appears based on the division of labour and exchange activities.

In this way, material's production and reproduction driven by labour's shaping is identified by Marx and Engels as the general basis of human history and society. Meanwhile, it is the most basic paradigm of historical materialism established by Marx and Engels. Of course, Marx and Engels have two production concepts at the beginning. That is to say, besides material production, man's own production of himself plays a dominant role in an ancient society. Thus material production only plays a subsidiary role.

Two points need to be noted: Firstly, the production labour in the eyes of Marx is not, as Baudrillard criticizes, the decisive essence of social existence and essence of human subjects. Under any historical conditions, production labour is only the basic premise of society and humanity. Man's survival depends on production labour instead of work. The reason why man's survival rate is higher than that of animals is because of outside effective work. However, after men's entering into antagonistic historical phenomena, the ruling class turns production labour into a steppingstone and living hell for their non-work survival. Secondly, in daily and social life, subjective shaping act without work is the most fundamental behaviour of the life situation. It is also the basic activity of art. The activity of art is a more complex subjective activity.

Relation *configurating* denotes the objective relationship and re-construction (reproduction) between man and object, and man and intersubjectivity.[34] It is the most important ontological foundation explaining that man's existence surpasses that of animals in a *context relationship*. Marx, Heidegger, and Hiromatsu as well as the contemporary Lacan and Baudrillard, all advocate ontology of rela-tions.[35] I also believe that ontology of relations is the crucial thought of Marxist historical materialism which has long been buried by Stalinist dogmatic textbooks. Thought is the result of cooperation be-tween *labour and technique* in production relations. Differing from intentional and subjective labour shaping, the relation configurating more often than not appears as an objective result of structured pas-sivity. It is the field-being of social life as well as the construction of social space. However, relation configurating is a certain histori-cal form that provides a prerequisite for labour shaping and other shapings. It furthermore appears as the *objective condition of social transcendentalism* before man's shaping in each historical period. The relationship between configurating and shaping is the primary relation to the becoming nature of personal activities and the inert structure of social practice that Jean Sartre is concerned with. This relationship is also the basic level of the later debate of *agency and structure* discussed by Anthony Giddens et al.

---

34   I have recently learned about the so-called Space Syntax theory from architecture research. Space syntax is best described as a research program that investigates the relationship between human societies and space from the perspective of the structure of inhabited space in all its diverse forms: buildings, settlements, cities, or even land-scapes (Bafna, 2003). It was conceived by Bill Hillier, Julienne Hanson, and colleagues at The Bartlett, University College London. There is a interesting concept, as "con-figuration," in space syntax theory. Configuration is originally defined as "The form, as of a figure, determined by the arrangement of its parts or elements" (The American Heritage Dictionary of the English Language). However, Hillier defines it as "a set of interdependent relations in which each is determined by its relation to all the oth-ers" (Hillier, Bill. *Space is the Machine: A Configurational Theory of Architecture*. Cambridge, UK. Cambridge University Press, 1996, p. 35). It is an extremely compli-cated paradigm, which denotes the transformation from perceptual material operations to ordering structure.

35   However, Lacan and Baudrillard advocate the negative ontology of relation which is anti-constructivist. Comparatively speaking, Lacan is more radical, as he sees impos-sible relations as the truth of being. Baudrillard rejects functionalized use value and also economic exchanges and claims to return to original symbolic exchanges. As for Lacan, see *The Impossible Truth of Being: Mirror of Lacan's Philosophy*, The Commercial Press, 2006.

To begin with, in the production process, relation configurating initially appears as the labour association and as an objective series of productive results.

In the first place, as mentioned above, labour cannot occur independent of the tools of labour and the object of labour. Labour thereby presents as the *agency* factor in the material production process. More importantly, labour shaping is not only an isolated activity. Labour always occurs in the specific field and space of configurating between man and shaped objects as well as in intersubjective labour relations. Marx and Engels refer to it as the primary form which is usually ignored in the process of labour production. Relation configurating of production is not only the people's social (class) relations in the production process, but above all is ready-to-hand configurating. Configurating is the connection between the for-us function and another function. It is the *field-being* of objective relationships in labour's production process. After the emergence of industrial production, this labour association directly behaves as a complicated division and cooperation of labour. Diachronically speaking, ready-to-hand configurating often transfers and reconstructs itself through the intergenerational experience of labour in the natural economy and through the production and reproduction of handicraft. Later, configurating's recurrence, maintenance, and reconstruction are achieved by technical parameters in contemporary production and reproduction.

The second point is that man and shaped objects are reconstructed as the basis of social existence in a specific functional configurating. The *closely ordered connection* of the specific man and shaped objects is, in fact, the basic component of the direct thingness of social existence. The immediate result is usually revealed systematically by historically shaped objects and the specific historical relations of instruments. The shaped objects are the result of production. In the labour process, one labour shaping is bound to be relative to other shaping activities. Based upon labour shaping, more general social chains are generated to form the most direct world for human survival. Moreover, shaped objects as the productive result are generated from the "for-us" configurating which centres on the value of human existence. They also build a surrounding material world surpassing natural existence by *closely linking to another*. It is the world, as Heidegger says, "surrounded" by activities ready-to-hand and things ready-to-hand. Or, it is the so-called functional object system (the system of objects) further developed by Baudrillard. The "ready-to-hand" material world behaves as natural objects after selective preference and processing in natural economy, while in the reified industrial and economic world, it is the economic system of artificial objects all over. This point is deeply exposed by Baudrillard in *The System of Objects*.[36]

There is no doubt that the emergence and reconstruction of configurating in the process of labour and production shaping is a long historical process. In the early stages of material production, the configurating of labour's shaping is achieved by thingness' incremental relation, while in the later period of modern industry, labour's shaping transforms from specific operation to technical *configurating*. At present, it is the virtual configurating and coding process in computer systems. Transformation from general shaping to *technical configurating* is a great stride forward in the labour production process. It is a complex and historical transformation. Related to this transformation, shaped objects in different historical periods as a matter of course differ from tool system's ordering. On this basis, other type of social shapings and configuratings emerge.

Relation configurating, then, is also the major construction form of social life. This is the signification of Marx's social relations of production and contemporary economic relations. Marx's social relations of production are based on the above labour activities and relation configurating of shaped objects. It must be specifically pointed out that the *object* in social existence defined by Marx's historical materialism is far from continuous material entity in social life (including historically shaped objects, reified tool systems, and other social objective adjuncts). The object is the *field-being of objective relationship* emerging from people's history. There is no denying the fact that Feuerbach and Hess are unscientific when they regard communication as human species nature. However, people's inter-communications and coexistence are indeed the critical approaches

---

36   Baudrillard, Jean. *The System of Objects*. Trans. James Benedict. Radical Thinkers, p. 3. London [u.a.]: Verso, 2005.

to constructing social life. Especially in an economic social form, people's relations are inverted to the objects' relations in product and market structure. The inverted relations deepen the people's mis-recognition toward reified objects in that social form.

More than twenty years ago, I proposed a rather abstract general concept—the ordering of social practice. I believed at that time: "Proposing the category of social practice field does not mean that this field-being is regarded as something of initiative basis. It means further identifying the more important interaction process of subject and object in a microscopic view, compared with material entity in social existence. It also identifies *objective functional network* of human practice in social existence. Therefore, the so-called social practice field refers to mutual construction between the subject and object in social practice. The objective and effective entirety created by the subject's resonance is a practice field in reality."[37] My point here should be seen as a further development of those ideas mentioned above.

Production *ordering* concept corresponds with Marx's *concept of material productive forces.*. . Actually, several years ago I opposed the way in which Marx's concept of material productive forces and material production was misrecognized as *physical factors of sub-stantiality*, namely, three physical factors,–workers, work tools, and the subject of work–comprise productivity. My opposition stems from the fact that the textbook system of Stalinist doctrines mistakenly appropriates the three factors of production process in Marx's *Capital* to explain productivity.[38] In fact, in Marx's view, the *productive forces/productivity* concept is not one of physical factors of sub-stantiality at the beginning. Instead, it is the *functional level* concept brought out in the production process. Different from the subjective labour shaping and distinct from the relations configuring, productivity always refers to the level of material production. The said level is *brought out objectively* in a certain process of material production in society. In some sense, the productivity functionally and histori-cally abstracts the process of material production operated by la-bour's shaping and the relations configuring in reality. This point is

---

37   See my article: *On Social Practice.* Jianghai Academic Journal, 1988, 5.
38   *Ibid.*

the same as Marx's touching on the *productive forces/productivity* category of Friedrich List and Hess et al in his early work.

The theory of powers (Germ. Produktivkraft) of production proposed by Friedrich List (1837-1841) shows that the ability to produce wealth is more important than wealth itself, "because the forces of production are the tree on which wealth grows, and because the tree which bears the fruit is of greater value than the fruit itself."[39] Friedrich List himself says that Jean-Antoine Chaptal is the first one to realize the importance of productive force in *De l'industrie française.*[40] This work represents the first time, actually, that the *productivity concept* gets rid of the *physical view* of social basis, establishing the functional rules of social basis. Friedrich List is insightful in that he perceives that material production and economic developments in different countries have differences in productivity. This recognition is the foundation for his opposition to unequal exchanges between the developed countries and the developing ones, and moreover for his proposing trade protections. Hess's idea is also very interesting. After identifying men's communication as men's nature in reality, Hess then regards men's mutual cooperation as his social nature; communication is a form for man to achieve and bring about his own strength and nature, as well as for him to achieve *productivity*. However, his is an inaccurate statement of relations configurating inasmuch as he mainly attaches importance to *intersubjective* relations. He totally ignores relations configurating between people and the object as well as the shaped objects. From 1843 to 1844, Hess said: "The stronger their intercourse, the stronger also is their creative power and as long as their intercourse is restricted so too is their creative power."[41] If, according to List, the productivity concept is only manifested simply as an abstract and objective category; then in Hess's opinion, productivity is the cumulative *ontology of relations* of men's cooperation. Marx is influenced to some extent by those two points.

---

39   List, Friedrich. *The National System of Political Economy.* Cosimo, Inc., 2006, p. 59.
40   See: Chaptal, Jean-Antoine. *De l'industrie française*, Ant. Aug. Renouard. 1819.
41   Hess, Moses. *The Essence of Money.* Trans. Adam Buick. Rheinische Jarhrbücher zur gesellschaftlichen Reform, Darmstadt, 1845.

Marx's productivity concept is generated from creative practice (*On an Outline about Feuerbach*, in short *Theses*). He further establishes material production as the basic prerequisite for the *first level* of social-historical existence. This is the first step that Marx and Engels establish the general historical materialism in *The German Ideology* (1845-1846). It can be seen that Marx refers to men's "common activities as the productivity" when he first identifies the *productive forces/productivity* concept. He is obviously writing in reference to Hess. According to the *general historical materialism* of Marx and Engels, *productive forces* are the driving force of historical movement and development.

More than twenty years ago, I also directly identified the so-called practical construction. I mentioned at that time: According to the new horizon of Marx's philosophy, *productive forces* is men's creative activity of transforming nature. Productive force is a specific ability and level in which people use tools (the extension of his natural organs) to intentionally transform natural object "for-us." Here the essence of productivity is the *subject*'s ability to *create material*, rather than the object of productive result or rather than the intermediate tools of productivity. Well, what is the objective creative ability starting from the subject? In my opinion, *it is the vector order of social existence as man historically constructs specific material existence by special practice*.[42] Now, it appears that in Marx's opinion, the productivity concept is List's comprehensive social productivity centred on the functional level of modern industrial production (Even culture and education is included in the *productive forces*). Then to this concept is added people's common active productivity defined by Hess et al (which originates from Adam Smith's theory of labour division). Productivity therefore is integrated to display the productive and creative ability of *specific order* in modern society. However, in Marx's general historical materialism (1845-1846), productive forces concept is defined as specific orderly relations created by material production in common historical existence and movement.

---

42   See my essay: "Practical Construction" in *Fujian Tribune*. 1991. 1.

Different from subjective labour shaping and subjective activity relations as well as the configurating of shaping objects, production ordering is a specific coding and functional order. It behaves vigorously in the whole social production process. Or, it can be seen as the orderly sources of negative entropy maintaining social existence and erasing the disorderly sources of positive entropy. Positive entropy always interiorly falls down to natural existence. Ordering in social historical existence is an integrative creating ability dominated by labour shaping. This ability is rich, along with the complicated social production. Marx in the middle and later periods of his economic research, as I note, considers *productive forces* as the creating ability displayed by comprehensive factors in the production process. Today, the generation of production ordering, which is the orderly relations of specific social existence, transcends more and more from reified production to scientific and technological practice.

Structure *modelling* is a contemporary rewriting of the most crucial category the mode of production in Marx's historical materialism. At first, I rewrite the mode of production as the *scheme of practice* to break up the petrified entities' understandings on Marx's important paradigm. For Marx, orderly relations between man and nature (productive forces), and the specific configurating of inter-subjective relations (production relations), are the historical essential structure in the process of social and historical development. Productive forces ordering and configurating of production relations are the *ordering ability* and *orderly functional structure* in men's practice. They are not isolated material entities. The shaped material entities (including the economic consequences of configurating) are only adjuncts to productive forces and production relations. They are the same as what Marx brings up in his discussion of the society's superstructure and its subsidiary facilities. The mode of production, which is the historical and specific orderly structure, is obviously *subjective*. In other words, the basis and dominated factors of social and historical development is an active ordering structure of social practice. The ordering structure is constructed in reality under a certain historical condition, rather than subjective motivation, or objects without man, or abstract human activities. At that time,

I called it the *scheme of practice*.[43] The scheme of social practice is a *dominant functional structure* in the field of social practice. It is also the structural basis of specific integrated practices that happen in reality. The scheme of practice is the *constraint structure* in social history. It appears, as we say, as the relations constituting objective human activities; however, it is a functional structure and not an entity or an entity's adjunct. It (the mode of production) is not substantiality external to human survival (structure). It is an *ordered structure*. When traditional Marxist philosophy explains the production relations and the mode of production, it makes the same mistake as Sir Isaac Newton did. The existence of a material entity is regarded as an independent framework. Such an interpretation is totally inconsistent with Marx's original intention! For Marx, the scheme of practice is the "practical relationships based on action" and people are not by "finding themselves" in a relationship but by behaving actively."[44] Therefore, practice is bound to be a creative activity with structure and has its (practice) objective reality, thus it is the ontology of social existence. At this point, it may be easier for us to understand Marx's expression, such as "society does not consist of individuals, but expresses the sum of interrelation"[45] and "the relations within which these individuals stand."[46] The scheme of practice is a functional structure integrated into practice. It is the *construction* that continuously creates *negative entropy* of social existence and also historical evolution. In the course of social history, material entities do not make history, and neither do men, in a biological sense. It is the human society which is actively engaged in social activities that create history.[47] The above thoughts represent what I wrote 20 years ago. I chose to use Jean Piaget's scheme at that time to avoid the substantive understanding and non-subjectification of the category production mode. I was influenced by structuralism.

---

43   In his texts, Marx uses words such as "forms of communication" and "mode of production". Mainly, he wants to show that dynamic and functional structure consist of social activities. As structure and form are usually related with statics, I choose the "scheme". Scheme always denotes an inner function and non-entity structure formed in a dynamic process. On this point, I am inspired by Jean Piaget's action-scheme.

44   McLellan, David. *Karl Marx. Selected Writings*. Oxford University Press, 1977, p. 581.

45   Karl Marx, Martin Nicolaus. *Grundrisse: Foundations of the Critique of Political Economy*. Penguin Classics, 1993, p. 265.

46   *Ibid.*, p. 265.

47   See my "Practical Scheme" in *Journal Seeking Truth*, 1989. 5.

Therefore, there are many structural marks in my thought, despite the fact that I try to establish the production mode as a non-solidified and dynamic structure.

The term modelling I appropriated from Andrew Pickering, but I now believe that it is proper to refer to modelling as the mode of production. Therefore, a mode which is generated instantly and functionally can more accurately display Marx's mode of production. Of course, modelling also appears in a more complex logic construction as well.

Finally, as I have put forward, there are social and historical situating as well as intellectual situating. In my latest understanding of intellectual situating, I mainly consider some micromechanisms of logical situating, such as the relations within convexity[48] and the concave point in the conception of ideology. I use convexity to describe the visual point of view and intelligible vision in the process of cognitive activity and theoretical logic. Conversely, the concave point is invisible and also it is situated in a blind zone. Furthermore, in the process of logical construction, a new intellectual situating of the Gestalt finally comes into being from the general words shaping the orderly increase of conceptual creation (negative entropy), and to the modelling of a certain theoretical production. It seems to be consistent with the emergence of historical situating. Consequently, the thought framework of my former situating theory will change to some extent as follows. At the early stage of a thinker's mirror-image in otherness, he only remains at the level of shaping words, appropriating them thoughtlessly, and considering his usage and identification of the other's theory. While constructing his own theory, the thinker begins to treat the other's theory as the organic logical component to create orderly logic modelling. It is only at the stage of innovative thinking that he can achieve the new level of discourse situating. The more interesting thing I observe is that there

---

48   The *convexity* concept was introduced into my research via contemporary architecture. It is originally a mathematical concept. An object is convex if for any pair of points within the object, any point on the straight line segment that joins them is also within this object. Therefore, convex is a small-sized space that does not include a dent. In a cognitive sense, any point within convex can see the whole convex. It indicates that all people in the same convex can watch each other and therefore they can understand and interact fully and stably.

is a heterogeneous logic appearing in Western post-modern thinkers, namely, the *non-shaping, disordering, and deconstruction* of anti-constructivism. Lacan, Jacques Derrida, and Michel Foucault are all the same in this way, while Baudrillard's logic almost inverts the whole historical materialism.

Based on the above understanding, I feel that a new discovery will be made when we use this new research mode to go deep into Baudrillard's early thought. Strictly speaking, all of Baudrillard's works are *in a critical position* when viewed in the face of contemporary capitalism and the entirety of human social history. This is one of the most valuable spirits to be found in his academic writings. However, Baudrillard's works that really belong to post-Marxian school of trend are *The System of Objects, The Consumer Society*, and *For a Critique of the Political Economy of the Sign*. As for his own intellectual situating, the framework of *mirror-image in otherness* plays an important role in these three texts: On the surface of discourse, it contains Roland Barthes, Henri Lefebvre, Guy Debord and Ferdinand de Saussure; but at the level of deeper logic, it includes Martin Heidegger, Jacques Lacan, and occasionally Thorstein Veblen.[49] Mauss-Bataille of course is the real basis to Baudrillard's logical situating. In my opinion, however, in the entire process of Baudrillard's intellectual situating, we can scarcely find a level which is totally dominated by other's thought. From the beginning, his academic appearance is the spontaneity of conceptual situating. When it comes to *Symbolic Exchange and Death*,

---

49   Thorstein Bunde Veblen (1857-1929) was an American economist and the founder of institutionalism. He was born in Cato, Wisconsin, of Norwegian American parents who had immigrated from Norway. In 1874, he attended Carleton College and studied with John Bates Clark. Later, he studied philosophy at Johns Hopkins University. As he failed to win a scholarship, Veblen went to Yale University. He took his Ph.D. in 1884. In 1891, he taught at Cornell University. He served as an assistant professor in Stanford University in 1906. In 1911, Veblen joined the faculty of the University of Missouri. He began to work in the United States Food Administration in 1918. In 1924, he refused an offer to be the president of the American Economic Association. In early 1927, Veblen retired and settled down in California and died there at the age of 72. Major works of Thorstein Veblen: *The Theory of the Leisure Class* (1899), *The Theory of Business Enterprise* (1904), *The Place of Science in Modern Civilization and Other Essays* (1919), *Absentee Ownership and Business Enterprise in Recent Times: The Case of America* (1923). In Baudrillard's texts, we can see that Baudrillard's *For a Critique of the Political Economy of the Sign* is mainly influenced by Veblen.

Baudrillard displays his original situating by the paradigm of simu-lacra and simulation. In other words, Baudrillard's thoughts were largely the intertextual montage of other theories in his early works. For example, the hybridity from Heidegger, Barthes and Lefebvre in *The System of Objects*; the symbiosis of Marx and Debord in *The Consumer Society*; the coexistence of Saussure and Marx in *For a Critique of the Political Economy of the Sign*; and finally Mauss-Bataille's concept of symbolic exchange formed his real logical basis. Basically, the activation of these academic memories is in-tegrated into Baudrillard's *spontaneous* theoretical platform. *The Mirror of Production* is a transitional text which *bids farewell to post-Marxism*. Baudrillard highlights a new radical discourse by directly criticizing Marx. In his theoretical logic, Mauss-Bataille's concept of symbolic exchange is convex in a redemptive way. Symbolic exchange confronts Marx's historical materialism, which is the object of adjudication. Also in this book, Baudrillard begins to directly utilize the Lacanian theory; however, this academic memory of Lacan is intentionally misinterpreted from the beginning. As the mirror-image in otherness, Lacan here becomes something of imagi-nary form of outside academy in a metonymic sense. In *Symbolic Exchange and Death*, Lacan's problematic is internal, demonstrating the real death of ontology. However, the impossible and traumatic authenticity again metonymically becomes the having-been sym-bolic exchange. More importantly, *Symbolic Exchange and Death* is the context in which Baudrillard develops his original situating. It is the first time that he constructs his logical space of originality. He fabricates the new picture of the development of contemporary capi-talism by series of new signifier and the signified discourses, such as simulacra, simulation, generation from models, etc. It is a significant logical détournement in the real sense. After that, Baudrillard finally establishes his own status of thought in academic circles.

Another important problem needs to be noted. Ontologically speaking, Baudrillard derives deeply from Heidegger's *ontology of relations*, rather than starting from the substantive individual. It is true that he here identifies the situating of men's symbolic exchange as fundamental to men's real being. Therefore, when the econom-ic kingdom of capitalism crazily pursues materialistic interests as in present society, he as well as Lacan would be in favour of *anti-constructivism* and *negative ontology*. He drives out alienation from men's relations to the field of objects' *pseudo-relations*. He also denies the illusion of human nature in reality which is the sum of functional economic relations. So, in the process of our discussion, we will first encounter *functional object and its chain-link-system*, and how men's symbolic relations distort into the functionalized objects criticized by Baudrillard in *The System of Objects*.

In *The Consumer Society*, functional object chains begin to transform into producing want for merchandise display. Advertising has produced *pseudo-symbolic situating* which is constructed by men and others at first. *For a Critique of the Political Economy of the Sign* is an important process in which Baudrillard further evaporates functionalized objects into signified codes. When criticizing Marx's use value, he for the first time proposes the loss of symbolic exchange in men's ontological existence. *The Mirror of Production* also provides the battleground for denying the *logic of violent conquest* for anthropocentrism. When criticizing Marxist historical materialism, he also reversely constructs the real being of symbol exchange. *Symbolic Exchange and Death* is the most dangerous battle, in which Baudrillard defends his ontology of symbolic exchange. It is dangerous because he identifies the simulation world of capitalism today as the greatest *pseudo-symbolic situating*. It is this simulation logic which is more real than the real that buries the symbolic exchange. The simulation substitutes the functional chain of objects for men's false symbolic code, succeeding in preventing the appearance of real symbolic exchange. Thus, human existence will forever fall under the control of code and seduction.

Finally, I should particularly emphasize that the connotation of numerous similar concepts used by Baudrillard is not exactly homogeneous in the different historical periods and the contexts of his thought development. His thought is an ever-changing and in-depth process. I always oppose logical *homogeneity* in the research of history of academic thought. For instance, Mauss-Bataille's concept of symbolic exchange—the most important keyword in Baudrillard's logic– runs through the entire process of his thought development. However, in his early thought (*The System of Objects*, etc.), symbolic exchange is resolved. On the one hand, it appears close to Lévi-Strauss's symbolism, and on the other it then transforms into symbolic value (*The Consumer Society*). Gift exchange establishes another intellectual context. Symbolic exchange does not appear as Mauss-Bataille's prototype until at the stage where his spontaneous thought formed (in his *For a Critique of the Political Economy of the Sign*).

After the stage of establishing his original thought (*Symbolic Exchange and Death*), symbolic exchange appears in the manner of death. Other examples where the *series* concept is represented by the reproduction of production appear in *The System of Objects*; by the consumer goods in a chainlike series in *The Consumer Society*; by the self-proclaimed style of contemporary art in *For a Critique of the Political Economy of the Sign*; and by the productive symbol as the second existence of the entire capitalist simulacra in his *Symbolic Exchange and Death*. The authenticity concept, in the context of his earliest texts, refers to symbol and symbolic exchange, while in Chapter two of *Symbolic Exchange and Death*, it refers in particular to the natural being opposing the presentation in the imitated relations of simulacra. Furthermore, in *The Perfect Crime*, it becomes the dead existence without Gestell in ontology. From the genetic clues of these important paradigms—difference, simulacra, simulation, and model—we can find the historical changes running from his earlier to his later periods. It is this complex thought ordering that we should pay attention to and carefully define in our interpretations.

It stands to reason that I should focus on Baudrillard's three early works, namely, *The System of Objects*, *The Consumer Society* and *For a Critique of the Political Economy of the Sign*, when viewing from the requirements of foreign Marxist research in China. However, I have shifted my focus to the latter for several reasons. Firstly, Yang Haifeng's doctoral dissertation, which I have supervised, offers valuable ideas towards Baudrillard's previous thought, constructing a rather solid and deeper academic platform.[50] Secondly, in my opinion, Baudrillard's *For a Critique of the Political Economy*

50   Yang Haifeng's *Towards Post-Marx: From Mirror of Production to Mirror of Symbols*. Central Compilation & Translation Press, 2004.

of the Sign and *The Mirror of Production* pose a truly serious threat to Marxism, and furthermore, his *Symbolic Exchange and Death* (mainly Chapter One) is the logical extension of *The Mirror of Production*, so I therefore believe that I should simultaneously include these three books within the scope of my research. Thirdly, the reason why I chose this *critical* dimension is that, though there are many critics of Baudrillard's academic research, most of them fail to respond to Baudrillard's denial and accusation of Marxism. On this point, I basically agree with Kellner's view that, "Many studies of Baudrillard have themselves skimmed the surface of Baudrillard's texts, failing to interrogate their use and abuse, or the contributions and limitations of his writing."[51] As a Chinese Marxist, I hope to face this important theoretical enemy and defend the dignity of historical materialism in the following theoretical argument.

In order to clarify the real logic that supports those important texts, I think it is necessary to expend some effort discussing Mauss-Bataille's grassroots romanticism and Baudrillard's two early books, *The System of Objects* and *The Consumer Society*. Afterwards, we can then smoothly enter into the context of *For a Critique of the Political Economy of the Sign* and *The Mirror of Production*. This section therefore constitutes the preface to my book. The book is then divided into three parts. The first part, comprised of seven chapters, interprets *For a Critique of the Political Economy of the Sign* in detail. The second part, also seven chapters long, focuses on the response and critique to *The Mirror of Production*. The last part III of my book contains the least content, with only an introduction and four chapters. It mainly discusses chapter one and later sections of chapter two in the *Symbolic Exchange and Death*. Since Baudrillard's discussion of some background contexts for the logical ordering related to our interpretation is dispersed amongst his diary texts especially in his *Cool Memories*, I will also bring some important content of *Cool Memories* into the discussion to serve as analytical clues.[52]

---

51   Kellner, Douglas. (ed.), *Baudrillard: A Critical Reader*. Oxford: Wiley-Blackwell, 1994, p. 3.
52   Baudrillard, Jean. *Cool Memories* (5 Volumes). Verso, 1990-2004.

There is no denying that I am deeply aware of the depth and logical penetration of Baudrillard's thought as I write this book. It is difficult to respond to Baudrillard's critique of Marxism. Moreover, Baudrillard touches many economic, social, and cultural phenomena unfolding in contemporary Europe. My analysis, therefore, is not necessarily correct and accurate. Of course, we can generally charge that Baudrillard simply denies Marx's critique of capitalism as incorrect. However, this effort takes effect on the condition that we as Chinese Marxists, on the basis of Marxist historical materialism, give our own answers when making critical surveys on various political, economic, and cultural problems in contemporary capitalism, which is of course the project that "Cognizant Research of Contemporary Capitalism" seeks to undertake.[53]

More importantly, I fully expect that this polemical writing criticizing Baudrillard is an effort no different than casting a minnow in order to catch a whale, in order that more Chinese Marxists will stand up to respond to the various challenges confronting Marxism. Let our independent theories resound in the world![54]

Zhang Yibing
At Nanjing University on May 6, 2008
Modified in Nanjing during the 2009 Spring Festival

---

53   "Cognizant Research of Contemporary Capitalism" is one creative platform for national social science research which is part of the current project titled as Creating High-Caliber Universities in the Sphere of Marxist Discipline at Nanjing University. As the initial result of this project, the first draft of *The History of Understanding Capitalism* (6 volumes), edited by me, has been finished. At present, the book is in the process of discussion and revision. It is expected to be published by Jiangsu People's Publishing House in 2009.

54   In 2007, Slavoj Zizek and Bob Jessop paid a visit to me, and I discussed my critical research on Baudrillard with them. They took a lively interest in my research. After understanding my basic principles and main ideas, have praised for my efforts.

INTRODUCTION

WAS BAUDRILLARD A MARXIST BEFORE?

The Young Baudrillard rose to fame with *The System of Objects*, *The Consumer Society* and *For a Critique of the Political Economy of the Sign*. They are usually classified by overseas researchers as the neo-Marxist text because Baudrillard is anyhow criticizing today's capitalism. Nevertheless, it is a hasty conclusion that cannot hold up after careful reconsideration. If we penetrate behind the lines of the text, it is not difficult to find that the real logic of the text is neither Marxist ideas nor the critical thinking of his left-wing teachers, like Lefebvre, Barthes and Debord. It is but Mauss-Bataille's thought of symbolic exchange. In this section, we are going to have a general discussion about the Mauss-Bataille thought at first, and then clarify the basic clues of Baudrillard's discourse in the early works to pave the way for the critique of *The Mirror of Production*.

1 MAUSS'S SYMBOLIC EXCHANGE AND THE GRASSROOTS ROMANTICISM

Strangely, in all the available biographies of the young Baudrillard, there does not seem to be sufficient attention to the important influence of the mid-20th century French anthropological-sociological thinking on the development of Baudrillard's thought. In my opinion, people, especially the western researchers, are absorbed in the trendy "post-modern" ideas of his late period, while ignorant of the original discourse framework hidden in his various creative logical platforms. Therefore, Mauss's social anthropological concepts and the ensuing Bataille's philosophy, the most influential and important factor in the development of the young Baudrillard's thought is but eclipsed by the popular discourse and kept far away from people's attention. Now, I want to start from Marcel Mauss's anthropological discoveries about primitive societies achieved through his fieldwork and then investigate the inherent correlation among them.

Nephew of the eminent sociologist Émile Durkheim,[1] Marcel Mauss[2] had a favourite condition to pursue his studies of sociology and anthropology. He inherited many Durkheim's sociological doctrines. In his early studies, he was also under the guidance of other sociologists, such as Claude Lévi-Strauss and Antoine Meillet. This experience benefited him much in studying methodology and Sanskrit, laying a sound foundation for his anthropological field research later. Mauss began from the first hand investigation of the lives of the primitive tribes. His most important contribution to

---

1   Emile Durkheim (1858-1917), renowned contemporary sociologist of France.
2   Marcel Mauss (1872-1950), the famous French anthropologist and sociologist. He was born to a Jewish family in Epinal. His father was a small embroidery workshop owner while his mother is sister of the eminent socialist Émile Durkheim. After high school graduation in 1890, he was not admitted to Ecole Normale Super Paris but studied philosophy at Bordeaux, where he followed Durkheim and became his assistant. At the same time from 1891, he registered for the study of law. Tow years later, his learning was interrupted by military service abroad. In 1895, Mauss passed the national qualification exam for teachers of philosophy and then studied and worked in Ecole Pratique des Hautes Etudes. In 1898, Mauss founded Année sociologique with Durkheim, and began "L'École de L'Année Sociologique" in France. In 1930, he took up the chair of Sociology at the Collège de France. In 1938, he was elected dean of the religion and science section in EPHA. He died in 1950 at the age of 78. His works include *The Nation* (1920), *The Gift* (1925), *Sociology and Anthropology* (1950) and *Works (Vol. 1-3)* (1968-1969).

anthropology is to abandon the conservative construction of primitive cultures through modern western discourse. Instead, he infiltrated himself into the real life of primitive tribes and depths of the primitive culture, acquired many completely new explanations of the field investigations, created a new academic platform for French sociological and anthropological studies, and affected a whole generation of French thinkers. We should pay attention to the following aspects of Mauss's achievement.

First, the whole symbolic culture dominates the material existence in primitive social life. In 1896, Mauss published his first important paper, *A General Theory of Magic*.[3] By observation of the primitive tribes, Mauss initiated his unique thought from the social role of magic. After examining the indigenous peoples of Australia, the Melanesians and Iroquois in the North Pacific region and the Mexican tribes, Mauss found that magic almost permeated every corner of the tribal life, be it primitive techniques, arts, or mystical religious ceremonies. Everywhere was seen the power of magic. "Association with evil as an aspect of magical rites always provides humanity with a rough general notion of magic."[4] Various rites were centred on a supernatural power in order to structure all the material existence of man. Different from the religious tendency towards the abstract, magic usually draws to the concrete. Mauss drew three laws on magic: "contiguity, similarity and opposition." He stated that the essence of magic is to pursue the usage of ascertaining man, things and concepts as well as the specific, general or common power. Magic seeks a vigorous and shapeless *totality of symbolic relations* to attain the control of interpretations and constructions of life. Thus, Mauss made the important assertion that in primitive life "the whole adds up to much more than the number of its parts."[5] (Claude Lévi-Strauss highly praised this opinion.) In primitive tribes, things such as "nature," "Mana"[6] and "power" belong to a symbolic totality that offers real meanings to man, objects and various social phenomena

---

3   It was co-written with Henri Humbert.
4   Mauss, Marcel, and Robert Brain. *A General Theory of Magic*. London: Routledge & Kegan Paul, 1972, p. 27.
5   *Ibid.*, p. 107.
6   An important concept with divine power discovered by Mauss in his fieldwork about the Melanesians.

and turns the material existence into *being*. Mauss discovered "the sacred"[7] positioned as the object of worship in primitive societies. At least to the primitive people, the sacred is not a hallucination, but a more "real social entity"[8] and generally structures the existence of the primitive life. (Mauss's conception has a deep influence on Bataille.) Mauss further valorised this symbolic relation as the most real being, only obscured by numerous material signs of today's society. (According to Lévi-Strauss, as early as 1924, Mauss said that the social life is in "a world of symbols,"[9] which also accounts for Marshall Sahlins' logic of symbolic culture governing the praxis.)

Second, the structure of *reciprocal symbolic exchange* in primitive societies. In *The Gift* (1925), Mauss discovered a "trading humanly nature" by the original people, which he named the *gift-exchange* relation. It is very different from the utilitarian economic relation that dominates today's society. Mauss drew conclusion from his analysis of Indian tribes in the North Pacific region, especially, the phenomenon of "potlatch" between Tlingit and Haida tribes. The so-called "potlatch" is a modern name, which means the hosts endeavour to demonstrate their wealth through mutual invitations of eating. Mauss perceptively found that during the potlatch between these two tribes, people attached no importance to the eating itself but aimed to realize a process of gift exchange, for instance, they wantonly squandered and destroyed things during their enthusiastic gift exchanges. In their eyes, everything had a certain spiritual power, called "hau".

In the process of gift exchanges, the state of responsibility for objects and the received objects were not rigid. Even if one did not receive the gift, "hau" still belonged to him. Therefore, the act of receiving the gift actually corresponded to a symbolic essence and spirituality. That was why "hau" had to be returned to where it came.[10] Mauss believed the potlatch is very similar to the con-

---

7   Mauss, Marcel, and Robert Brain. *A General Theory of Magic.* London: Routledge & Kegan Paul, 1972, p. 11.
8   See the appendix of *A General Theory of Magic* in *Sociology and Anthropology* translated by Yu Biping Shanghai Translation Publishing House, 2003, p. 104.
9   Claude Lévi-Strauss. "Introduction to Sociology and Anthropology." Trans. Yu Biping. *Sociology and Anthropology.* Shanghai Translation Publishing House, 2003, p. 5.
10   Mauss, Marcel. *The Gift: Forms and Functions of Exchange in Archaic Societies.* Trans. Ian Cunnison. Glencoe: Free Press, 1954, p. 9.

sumption and destruction in sacrificial ceremonies, only in different names of man and God but for the same purpose of mutual peace and co-existence. Mauss also found another kind of potlatch, the Kula, "the system of gift exchange" in larger scale, in which, the general sense of "wealth" circulation was brought to a halt and replaced by "killing" the exchanged gifts. This exchange turned out to be more of a *symbolic* rite, during which people exchanged their soul and meanings, and the gift became the sacré. Unlike the ubiquitous market exchange today, the primitive people not only avoid possessing the sacred thing but also revere it and prepare to waste anything for it. This symbolic exchange produces a continual, reciprocal and equal communication and circulation. It forms the basic structure that supports the entire social activities.

Finally, Mauss drew from his anthropological research an important *judgment of value* that the relation of primitive symbolic exchange is the cure for modern social diseases. (It is the conclusion also to the ecstasy of Bataille and Baudrillard.) Mauss believed that the primitive system of symbolic exchange possesses a "common sociological value" for our society today. It can explain the historiography of human societies and should be restored as "the way to better administrative procedures for our societies."[11] According to Mauss, it is only a recent event in Western society for man to become an "economic animal (Marx)." (Michel Foucault echoed it later.) "Homo economicus is not behind us, but before, like the moral man, the man of duty, the scientific man and the reasonable man. For a long time man was something quite different; and it is not so long now since he became a machine—a calculating machine."[12] In his opinion, only recently, people begin to chase fame and wealth, while in the most Epicureanistic ethics of ancient times, people pursue goodness and happiness instead of material interest. Mauss then visualized a beautiful future, in which he attempted to substitute the primitive relation of symbolic exchange for today's utilitarian value exchange. "The producer-exchanger feels now as he has always felt—but this time he feels it more acutely—that he is giving something of himself, his time and his life."[13] Mauss was happy that "it

11   *Ibid.*, p. 69.
12   *Ibid.*, p. 74.
13   *Ibid.*, p. 75.

can be seen at work already in certain economic groups and in the hearts of the masses who often enough know their own interest and the common interest better than their leaders do."[14]

This idea at last gives birth to what I call the *grassroots romanticism*. It is well known that in traditional humanistic logic the idealized man's authenticity is based on an abstract value assumption. The contradiction between the *must existence* ("ought") and the non-logical *bad reality* ("is") generates a tremendous critical tension. For instance, Rousseau's ideal natural status of man before degeneration and Feuerbach's inalienated natural species being of man hollowed by divine attributes are well known. Therefore, Mauss's opinion does not belong to the traditional humanistic discourse. In his mind he has formed a logical mode in which the primitive tribal life (the past) is employed to judge the social reality (the present). Obviously, this notion stems from the under-developed primitive societies. Moreover, Mauss assumes the *ontological base* of the primitive existence and the *authentic ought* of the sortal being. Without doubt, it should be included in romanticism. And it differs from the classic romanticism centered on theological critique occurred in late Middle Ages. I hereby refer to it as the grassroots romanticism. This *backward* logic did appear in previous history, for example, the Confucian vision of self-abnegation and etiquette-restoration, which regards a historical past as a gauge of value to measure the present reality. Mauss's ontological vision of the past is an important achievement in the fieldwork of modern anthropology and its theoretical value can never be overestimated. If extended to the theoretical level of social reform, it can be called practopianism, in contrast to the fantastic utopianism. However, the real situation of the primitive tribal life is not as beautiful as in Mauss's poetical description. Those who could attend the potlatch were confined to a few chiefs and even women were taken as consumptions in the free exchange of gifts. Earlier, Marx commented that such a life was "natural and restricted."[15] At first glance, the primitive life is not poisoned by the capitalist exchange-value, and from the perspective of symbolic exchange process, it generally "seems personal." After all, it was a

---

14   *Ibid.*, p. 76.
15   Karl Marx and Frederick Engels. *Collected Works*, Vol. 28. London: Lawrence & Wishart, 1986, p. 100.

finding on the early state of social life. Hence, when the eminent anthropologist Mauss jumps out of his research field and idealistically appoints this primitive tribal life as the authentic being of human modernity, he becomes what Lenin calls a "poor philosopher." The reason why Mauss's concept is first treated here is that it later becomes a theoretical tool to criticize Marxist historical materialism by such people as the young Baudrillard and Sahlins, whom I am going to deal with in the following part. In addition, it is still popular in certain fields, such as anthropology and sociology.

It should be recognized that Mauss's impact on the French academia is enormous, which is reflected through many other theorists. For instance, in the field of philosophy, there is Bataille; in sociology, there are Lévi-Strauss, who, based on Mauss's theory, proposed the structural anthropology that emphasizes the symbolic system, and his successor, Sahlins[16]; in sociology, Pierre Bourdieu first combined Mauss's concept with Marxist economy and put forward such concepts as "cultural capital" and "social capital." Later, Mauss

---

16   Marshall David Sahlins (1930-) was born in Chicago, Illinois on December 27, 1930. He is a prominent American anthropologist. He received both a Bachelor's and Master's degree at the University of Michigan in 1951 and 1952. He then earned his Ph.D. of anthropology at Columbia University in 1954. He returned to teach at the University of Michigan from 1956 to 1973. After it, he moved to the University of Chicago, where he is today the Charles F. Grey Distinguished Service Professor of Anthropology Emeritus. In 1976, he was admitted to the American Academy of Arts and Sciences. His major works include: *Social Stratification in Polynesia* (1958), *Evolution and Culture* (ed., 1960), *Moala: Culture and Nature on a Fijian Island* (1962), *Culture and Practical Reason* (1976), *Historical Metaphors and Mythical Realities* (1981), *Islands of History* (1985), *Cosmologies of Capitalism* (1988), *Anahulu: The Anthropology of History in the Kingdom of Hawaii* (co-authored with Patrick Kerch) (1992), *How "Natives" Think: About Captain Cook, for Example* (1995), *The Sadness of Sweetness* (1996). As early as in the 1960s, Sahlins gradually gave up the traditional concept of historical evolution and accepted the so-called cultural schema neoevolutionism. In the mid-1970s, based on Mauss's anthropology, he turned his critique to the economic anthropology, that is, to employ contemporary western culture, especially, employ economics in the illustration of primitive societies or non-western cultures. In 1976, he published the *Culture and Practical Reason*. In his opinion, the symbolic cultural logic is rather a deep supporting structure for social existence and movements. In this book, Sahlins quoted much from Marx's literature, with profound and accurate understanding. By comparison, Baudrillard's *Mirror of Production* is a simple negation of Marxist historical materialism. Because Sahlins's text is later than the *Mirror of Production*. I would not have a comprehensive discussion here but selectively employ contents of Sahlin's book to help illustrate the thought of the young Baudrillard.

was faithfully followed by Baudrillard[17] and others. As a matter of fact, Mauss's thought was well accepted wherever it spread in the French academia. His fame reached the summit in the 1980s, when a handful of French sociologists launched a famous interdisciplinary Movement of Anti-Utilitarianism in Social Science, in a word, "MAUSS."[18]

Next, we are to examine Bataille's philosophical concept because Baudrillard's early theoretical logic derives more directly from him.

2 BATAILLE'S NON-USEFUL PHILOSOPHY OF GRASSROOTISM

George Bataille (1879-1962) is a very important contemporary French thinker.[19] (My book, *The Impossible Truth of Being: Mirror of Lacan's Philosophy*, has already touched upon Bataille's philosophical thought.[20]) As early as in the mid-1920s in his communication with the surrealists, Bataille distanced himself from their elitism. He supported the "vulgar" heterogeneity of the famous pornography writer Marquis de Sade. (It is reasonable to believe that Bataille's philosophy is engaged with an anti-elitist grassrootism from the very beginning.) At that time, Bataille already focused on the non-useful secular "excretion" in a society of possession and utilitarianism as well as the heterogeneous religious life.[21]

---

17   The young Baudrillard did not agree to Bourdieu's interpretation of Mauss.

18   In French, It is "Mouvement anti-utilitariste dans les sciences sociales." In short, "MAUSS."

19   Georges Bataille (1897-1962) was born in Billom in France, Sept. 10th, 1897. In his 17, he was baptized as a Catholic. After the outbreak of World War I, he was recruited to the army and retired due to illness in the same year. In 1918, he past the university entrance examination and studied at the École Nationale des Chartes in the following years. After graduation in 1922, he was given the position of librarian in Bibliothèque Nationale. He then founded a series of journals, *Documents* in 1929, *Acephale* in 1936. He died in Paris in June 8th, 1962. His major works include *The Solar Anus* (1931), *The Notion of Expenditure* (1933), *The Inner Experience* (1943), *The Accursed Share* (Vols. I&II, 1949-1951), and *On Nietzsche* (1945).

20   See *The Impossible Truth of Being: Mirror of Lacan's Philosophy* (The Commercial Press, 2006).

21   See Georges Bataille's "The Use Value of D.A.F. Sade" translated by Allan Stoekl, with Carl R. Lovitt and Donald M. Leslie, Jr. Excerpted from the book *Visions of Excess: Selected Writings, 1927-1939*, Minneapolis: UMP, 1985.

In 1925, Mauss published *The Gift*, a desired treasure for Bataille, who soon devoted himself to the popular anthropological and sociological research of primitive tribal lives. In 1933, another book *Notion of Expenditure* was printed, which was Bataille's metaphysical summary of Mauss's theory. In 1937, Bataille, together with others, established "The College of Sociology." They honoured Mauss as their spiritual leader and attempted to develop his anthropological and sociological achievements into a new philosophy to criticize social reality. (To their disappointment, Mauss moderately gave his support, and even openly expressed his opposition to over-philosophize and over-politicize his own theory.) Bataille then discussed the subject in *The Limitations of Usefulness* (1945, draft), *The Accursed Share Vol. III* (1945-1954), *Hegel, Death and Sacrifice* (1955). These writings composed his most important philosophical thoughts. (It is also the logical pillar behind the critical theory proposed by the arrogant young Baudrillard.) Next, I am going to have a general discussion about Bataille.

First, his division between the *profane world* and the *sacred world*. The sacred thing is Mauss's deferential call for the non-actual existence indicated by the symbolic exchange relation in primitive life. Bataille expands the concept to philosophy. (He confirms the division of the binary world as "one of the conclusive findings of social anthropology."[22]) In his early research of Sade, Bataille put forward the division between the "profane" reality with utilitarian possession as the scale of existence and the religious reality with the useless excretion as measurement. He believed in the "division of social facts into religious facts (prohibitions, obligations and the realization of sacred action) on one hand and profane facts (civil, political, juridical, industrial, and commercial organization) on the other."[23] In his later studies, Bataille went further to state that the secular world is at the same time a *materialized* world of homogeneity, where the material production and reproduction is put on a fundamental position as the only standard to arrogantly determine this world. (It is the logical start for Marxist historical materialism. Later, the young Baudrillard

---

22   Bataille, Georges. "The Psychological Structure of Fascism." *Visions of Excess: Selected Writings, 1927-1939*. Trans. Allan Stoekl. Theory and History of Literature, V. 14. Minneapolis: University of Minnesota Press, 1985, p. 144.
23   *Ibid.*, p. 94.

hounded this negative theoretical point.) In such a utilitarian profane world, any item is linked to another by human-defined means and purpose. This linkage goes on and on, composing a systematic material world of utility. (Here is easily seen what Heidegger defines the "ready-to-hand" material world. It is also here earth is turned into the earthly world.[24]) In such a world, man's thought and practice only caters for the requirement of material utility. "The object sets its prime task to protect its 'value of utility' from destruction and sustain it in a certain way."[25] Thus, the utilitarian world makes human character "an abstract and interchangeable entity."[26] (Bataille's idea has a direct impact on Baudrillard's *System of Objects*.)

In Bataille's view, the production and possession oriented *progressive* world is a *projected* world. (Bataille believes this is a historical progressive logic of rationalism posited by Descartes.[27]) The so-called project refers to people's labour and creative activities under the guidance of rationality. And their purpose is not immediate pleasure but a *delayed* expectation. (This project/plan is the ontological base of late Sartre's idealization of Marxism.) Unlike other animals that indulge in current pleasure, human beings temporarily give up the present satisfaction and willingly postpone it because they believe their ongoing labour is for the fruitful result in the future. People grow out of the direct animal existence and live for the delayed utilitarian value. Hence, anything that does not help achieve the objective or harvest the desired result will be estimated meaningless and ruthlessly abandoned. (Obviously, the profane world here is the actual society based on material production that the young Baudrillard loathed.) Bataille thinks that sacred things stand in contrast to this utilitarian secular world. They, unlike the palpable and useful items, stem from the resistance against this world and the secular time.[28] They essentially

---

24   See Heidegger, Martin, and David Farrell Krell. *Nietzsche*. San Francisco: Harper & Row, 1979.
25   Yuasa, Hiroo. *Georges Bataille: Consumption*. Trans. Zhao Hanying: Hebei Educational Publishing House, 2001. 155.
26   Bataille, Georges. "The Psychological Structure of Fascism." *Visions of Excess: Selected Writings, 1927-1939*. Trans. Allan Stoekl. Theory and History of Literature, V. 14. Minneapolis: University of Minnesota Press, 1985, p. 138.
27   Bataille, Georges. "Pain" Trans. Wu Qiong. *Eroticism, Expenditure and General Economics*. Ed. Wang Min'an: Jilin People's Publishing House, 2003, p. 49.
28   See Bataille's *History of Eroticism* (Trans. Liu Hui: The Commercial Press, 2003, p. 187).

allude to filth, sex and death of the profane world, where man escapes time and dedicates his life to expenditure.[29] "The *heterogeneous* world includes everything resulting from *non-productivist* expenditure (sacred things themselves form part of this whole)."[30] In comparison with Mauss's anthological thought, Bataille's discussion is ontological. He turns Mauss's hypothesis of grassroots romanticism into an anti-actual *philosophy of grassrootism.*

Second, Bataille's confirmation of the *non-productive expenditure schema.* According to Mauss, the primitive tribes see the non-utilitarian expenditure happen in sacrifice, potlatch and other large-scale symbolic exchanges, which compose the social structure that supports the tribal life. Bataille's notion of expenditure is, first of all, inheritance of Sade's "excretion" in contrary to the industrial utilitarianism. In *The Use Value of D.A.F. Sade*, Bataille says, the weird but attractive thing in ordinary people's eyes is nothing else but his cognition of excrement and the ensuing pleasure.[31] Unlike the utilitarian possession in today's production realm, man undergoes an authentic existential pleasure of escaping homogeneity during the physical excretion of the waste. The same experience repeats in other situations such as sex abuse, sight of dead body and puke as well as the time of facing truth and sacredness. Bataille even assumed the "identical nature" "of God and excrement."[32] Based on Mauss's theory, Bataille extends the non-utilitarian sacred "excretion" to an *ontological* concept of expenditure. (In the second part of *The Notion of Expenditure*, Bataille details Mauss's discussion of the potlatch phenomenon.[33]) As stated by the non-useful excretion

---

29   *Ibid.*
30   Bataille, Georges. "The Psychological Structure of Fascism." *Visions of Excess: Selected Writings, 1927-1939*. Trans. Allan Stoekl. Theory and History of Literature, V. 14. Minneapolis: University of Minnesota Press, 1985, p. 142.
31   Lacan wrote Kant with Sade, but it was not included in the Chinese version of Selected Works of Lacan. Bataille wrote *The Use Vale of D.A.F. Sade: An Open Letter to My Current Comrades.* (Bataille, Georges. *Eroticism, Expenditure and General Economics.* Ed. Wang Min'an: Jilin People's Publishing House, 2003. 1.)
32   Bataille, Georges. "The Use Value of D.A.F. Sade." *Visions of Excess: Selected Writings, 1927-1939*. Trans. Allan Stoekl. Theory and History of Literature, V. 14. Minneapolis: University of Minnesota Press, 1985, p. 102.
33   See Bataille's "The Notion of Expenditure." *Visions of Excess: Selected Writings, 1927-1939*. Trans. Allan Stoekl. Theory and History of Literature, V. 14. Minneapolis: University of Minnesota Press, 1985.

logic, the essence of expenditure is non-productivist and non-utilitarian. Through the primitive sacrificial ceremony, Bataille discerns a pure destructive "exhaustion," a material consumption that is separated from the utilitarian utility in real social life. This consumption of abandonment, destruction, loss and emptiness symbolizes a certain God-oriented spiritual function that is external to man's material existence. Therefore, in Bataille's opinion, the non-productivist expenditure breaks the project logic and makes the existence recover its original glow by negating the utilitarian utility. (The utility is man's insult at the object through production, if adapting Heidegger's words, the "thing not thinged.") In this regard, Bataille says expenditure can refer to luxury, mourning, war, cults, the construction of sumptuary monuments, games, spectacles, arts, perverse sexual activity (i.e., deflected from genital finality)—all these represent activities which, at least in primitive circumstances, have no end beyond themselves.[34]

This definition clearly exceeds Mauss's anthropological scope. Bataille believes that "in the market economy, the processes of exchange have an acquisitive sense."[35] In contrast to the productivist possession and acquisition during the value exchange, expenditure is a non-utilitarian and -useful action. It concerns man's entire inner life instead of his material existence.[36] To illustrate it, Bataille employs the example of the pyramid: In the eyes of the profit, pyramid building is a big mistake; instead, people could well have dug a hole and then filled it.[37] However, for the ancient Egyptians, the pyramid was the symbol of the shining sun. They firmly believed that the pyramids, although useless in today's secular world, could transform death into radiance, the endless existence.[38] The pursuit of divine attributes is prevalent. (If Bataille's thought would be actualized, it

34   *Ibid.*, p. 118.
35   *Ibid.*, p. 123.
36   Bataille, Georges. *History of Eroticism.* Trans. Liu Hui: The Commercial Press, 2003, p. 181.
37   Bataille, Georges. "General Economics." Trans. Wang Min'an. *Eroticism, Expenditure and General Economics.* Ed. Wang Min'an: Jilin People's Publishing House, 2003, p. 167.
38   Bataille, Georges. *Eroticism, Expenditure and General Economics.* Jilin People's Publishing House. Ed. Wang Min'an, 2003, p. 236.

might stage the scene in Andrei Platonov's *City of Gradov*[39] or the Chinese Cultural Revolution, where people denied material interest, completely stopped the utilitarian production, indifferently saw the weeds growing in the cornfield, blindly shot the so-called bourgeois, or passionately performed the "Loyalty Dance." With incredible enthusiasm, people joined the symbolic revolutionary activities and happily allowed the detestable economy end in collapse. The miserable result is not difficult to imagine.)

Third, coexistence of the *general economics* with divinity. Bataille bases his philosophy on religious feelings, which differs him from Mauss. In the guiding light of the religious lamp, Bataille does not have Mauss's practopian complex of recovering the primitive life. In my understanding, the so-called general economics is the *road to the sacred world* in his mind. To Bataille, the secular capitalist society implements a *limited* special economy in pursuit of mundane utilitarianism while he admires and yearns for general economics with the yardstick of "non-acquisition." Bataille thinks that the capitalist possessive economy based on utilitarianism is a kind of special, socially alienated existing form and the most general authentic being is just incarnated in the "glory" existence of endless expenditure, like the shining sun never asking for returns.[40] Bataille appeals that it is indeed man's authentic mode of being and the meaning for God's existence because the essence of religion lies in man's transcendence of material possession. Apotheosization of God is then associated with de-apotheosization of human life.[41] Only in the bright city of God can we acquire the divine existence of non-productivist expenditure. In this connection, Bataille thinks that beauty is nothing and the artist is *nothing* of the material world.[42]

---

39   *Gradov City* was written by the former Soviet Union writer Andrei Platonov during 1927-1928 but was delayed to be published until 1978. The Chinese translation was done by Gu Yang in 1997.
40   Bataille, Georges. "General Economics." Trans. Wang Min'an. *Eroticism, Expenditure and General Economics*. Ed. Wang Min'an: Jilin People's Publishing House, 2003, p. 151.
41   Bataille, Georges. "Origin and Reform of Capitalism." Trans. Wu Qiong. *Eroticism, Expenditure and General Economics*. Ed. Wang Min'an: Jilin People's Publishing House, 2003, p. 171.
42   Bataille, Georges. *Eroticism, Expenditure and General Economics*. Ed. Wang Min'an: Jilin People's Publishing House, 2003, p. 265.

"God is NOTHING."[43] In fact, the true, the good, the beautiful and the divine of the sacred world become the anticipated Nothing and *désoeuverment*. Due to the absence of the object, God is not an actual and useful presence but "death" in the profane world of utilitarianism. It should be admitted that Bataille aims for the City of God from the primitive grassroots Existenz. This is his essential difference from Mauss.

Bataille has two other points that are worth our attention. First, although he noticed the sacred thing and non-utilitarian expenditure in Mauss's theory, he did not over-emphasize Mauss's symbolic exchange thought. In comparison, the idea of symbolic exchange was frequently echoed by Lévi-Strauss and Sahlins in their anthropological studies, as well as the young Baudrillard to found his philosophical ontology. Second, Bataille did not turn his critique against Karl Marx. In his early years, he admitted that Marx was "justified"[44] in his criticism of capitalism about the question of state and class. Later, in his talk about the whole secular world based on material production, he repeatedly confirmed Marx's idea of "going back to one's real being" through negating the material reality and thus believed it would open a new chapter for human liberation.[45] Like Sartre, Bataille also commended Marx's decisive impact on our era, although he at the same time pointed out that Marx's communist ideal is still preconditioned by material wealth. These ideas just pave the way for young Baudrillard's avant-garde critique of Marxism.

3 *THE SYSTEM OF OBJECTS*: SYMBOLIC RELATION TO BE ABSENT FROM FUNCTIONAL GESTELL AND SERIES MODE

We are now ready to deal with the two important works of the young Baudrillard: *The System of Objects* (*Le système des objets*, 1968) and *The Consumer Society* (*La société de consommation*, 1970). There have been sufficient explorations of their historical

43   *Ibid.*, p. 217.
44   Bataille, Georges. "The Psychological Structure of Fascism." *Visions of Excess: Selected Writings, 1927-1939*. Trans. Allan Stoekl. Theory and History of Literature, V. 14. Minneapolis: University of Minnesota Press, 1985, p. 139.
45   Bataille, Georges. "Origin and Reform of Capitalism." Trans. Wu Qiong. *Eroticism, Expenditure and General Economics*. Ed. Wang Min'an: Jilin People's Publishing House, 2003, p. 180.

context and theoretical convex (academic memory cluster), including, for instance, theoretical premises by Lefebvre, Barthes, and Debord. There is also clear distillation of the basic thoughts in the texts.[46] Therefore, these subjects will not be repeated here. In fact, it interests me that previous studies are so drawn to such aspects of Baudrillard's thought as consumer-oriented view, spectacle-presentation, semiology, etc. Another important logical structure may well have been overlooked in previous books. *Hidden but dominant in two books, Mauss-Bataille problematic concept* is gradually constructed by the young Baudrillard. In the following analysis, we will first discuss the functionality and paradox of symbolic relation in *The System of Objects*.

The first is the ontology by which the orderly objects system is linked and constructed by the *utility framework* prevalent in contemporary capitalist society. Differing from others' opinions, I believe that in *The System of Objects*, the young Baudrillard's ontological concept stems from Heidegger's ready-to-hand "circumspection." In the vista of the reified world, it is obvious that the object does not refer to natural existence in general. It is the rich objects produced by human beings, namely the object produced by the subject for us (therefore, the system of objects is actually the *objective* system shaped and manufactured by people). According to Heidegger, objects and people go beyond authentic being in *ready-to-hand* reification, to become the petrified entities in the world. (Hiromatsu translates Zuhandensein into readiness-to-hand, an actuality manifested by people's use. This is a profoundly free translation. By contrast, he translates Vorhanden into presence-at-hand. The reified capitalist society is based on industrial production, which was discovered by Marx. If Heidegger is to dialectically interpret the reified capitalist society as the metaphysical ontology, Baudrillard again restitutes the abstract ontology to the profane world.) It is in the thought space of Heidegger's logical situating that Baudrillard discerns the secret of the daily life of the capitalist system. The secret is that the *functional utility chain* gradually becomes the basic existence of objects. Baudrillard calls it "the scientificalized and structuralized process of

---

46   Yang Haifeng's *Towards Post-Marx: From Mirror of Production to Mirror of Symbols*. Central Compilation & Translation Press, 2004.

objects."[47] (He uses the example of automobile cylinder in Gilbert Simondon's *On the Mode of Existence of Technical Objects*.) It is not that he supposes there is a vista of the objective world beyond men. On the contrary, he regards the entire social existence as the objects system and the orderly field of humanity. The system and the field are constructed by special capitalist Gestell. If, according to Mauss, it symbolizes the construction of life meaning in primitive tribes, it herein represents the functional orderly system of scientific and technological productions. Baudrillard believes that technology gives us a rigorous account of objects. It is in the orderly system of functionality that the objective presence of everything can acquire the ontological situation. Every transition from one system to another, better-integrated system; every commutation within an already structured system; every functional synthesis, all precipitate the emergence of meaning.[48] (It is easy to see that this concept is an explanation which Marx uses to positively describe the development of the capitalist economic and structural system in *Manuscripts of 1857-1858*) Behold, Baudrillard here takes a negative attitude towards the functional field of objects. (Douglas Kellner is insightful in spotting this convexity.[49] No doubt, such logic also derives from his academic memory of late Heidegger's criticism of technology, his romantic conversion of Heidegger's "das ding dingt." Mark Gottdiener deems that Baudrillard appropriates the concept of the planning critic Francoise Choay.[50]) As expected, Baudrillard says, in such a structuralized system, "objects are generally isolated as to their function, and it is the user who is responsible, as his needs dictate, for their coexistence in a functional context."[51] For instance, the functional order of a coffee grinder is to link coffee beans, people's need for caffeine, and powdered coffee into a structuralized objective system, the system *for us*. He is clearly dissatisfied with the system of objects' existence practiced and shaped by the

47   Baudrillard, Jean. *The System of Objects*. Trans. James Benedict. Radical Thinkers, 3. London [u.a.]: Verso, 2005, p. 3.
48   *Ibid.*, p. 5.
49   Kellner, Douglas. "Introduction: Jean Baudrillard in Fin-de-Millenium." *Baudrillard: A Critical Reader* (Jiangsu People's Publishing House, 2005. Page 6)
50   Kellner, (ed.) *Baudrillard: A Critical Reader*, Oxford: Wiley-Blackwell, 1994, p. 31.
51   Baudrillard, Jean. *The System of Objects*. Trans. James Benedict. Radical Thinkers, 3. London [u.a.]: Verso, 2005, p. 6.

anthropocentric discourse. Here, his mood is in accordance with the late Heidegger. (In Gottdiener's view, the discussion of the object in this book can be regarded as Baudrillard's exemplary exercise in mateialist semiotics.[52] I propose that Baudrillard's discussion in fact does not relate to semiology, let alone materialism. More precisely, Baudrillard's thought at this time can still be incorporated into radical social critiques, revealing a few ideas from Heidegger and post-Marxist thinking.)

Secondly, the functional existence of commodity betrays the *situating of symbolic relation* in traditional life. In fact, the opening stance of *The System of Objects* toward furniture layout seems to take the early patriarchal Bourgeois tradition as the initial reference to criticize the functionality of precious family furniture and items. The essence of the traditional furniture layout lies in building an invisible "entity of moral order," and is also an idealized situating of objective existence. (Please note that Baudrillard herein concentrates not on the material existence of family furniture itself, but on the objects' functional structure in the field of human existence. In the later *For a Critique of the Political Economy of the Sign*, he refers to the objects' functional structure as the differential practice of objects.) "To personify human relationships," he says, borrowing his teachers' Marxist terminology.[53]

I think this statement is not wrong in and of itself. However, I find other important other evidence in Baudrillard's consideration of the traditional ordering structure of objects and space, the "symbolic relation." (The symbolic relation is the first stage of Baudrillard's symbolic concept. Symbolic exchange itself at this point is divided into two aspects: Symbol herein and gift exchange. There is no doubt that symbolic relation mentioned here by Baudrillard is close to Claude Lévi-Strauss's symbolic concept.[54] But he fails to realize that Lévi-Strauss's symbolic concept differs from Mauss's original context.) Through the presence of objects, Baudrillard believes, the traditional furniture layout embodies and symbolizes a deep

52   Douglas Kellner. *Baudrillard: A Critical Reader*.Basil Blackwell Ltd. 1994, p. 30.
53   Baudrillard, Jean. *The System of Objects*. Trans. James Benedict. Radical Thinkers, 3. London [u.a.]: Verso, 2005, p. 14.
54   See my *The Impossible Truth of Being: Mirror of Lacan's Philosophy*. The Commercial Press, 2006, p. 170-171.

emotional relationship of family spirit. With the change of life, the current capitalist home furnishings break the traditional "density" structure. The object has been greatly functionalized and modern age furniture strides toward a completely fresh, utility-oriented system. (For example, in the furniture layout of traditional Chinese life, the layout of table and chairs represents the authority of the older generation, forming the family relations in a central scroll. Furniture today, however, manifests primarily the function and fashion of outer formation.) Speaking of which, the young Baudrillard seems to passionately lament: Why?

If, as Heidegger states, objects and people all surpass the authentic being through readiness-to-hand, then, in Baudrillard's eyes, the modern system of objects chooses its orderly organization to shroud the "symbolic values, and along with them use values."[55] (At that moment, Baudrillard still regards the use value as an *original* material attribute, an ideal much less radical than that of his *Mirror of Production* later. At the same time, symbol, the *basis of ontology*, cannot be valued because value itself is the object corresponding to the subject's utility relations.) He states that in today's structure of objects,

> These objects are no longer endowed with a "soul," nor do they invade us with their symbolic presence: the relationship has become an objective one, founded on disposition and play. The value this relationship takes on is no longer of an instinctive or a psychological but, rather, of a tactical kind.[56]

It is noticeable that Baudrillard still takes the original use value as the foundation of *symbolic value*, with a more important symbolic relation here. (In my opinion, the young Baudrillard is very similar to Marshall Sahlins at this moment, to regard symbolic relation as the basis of practical survival.) The conventional structure of objects is poetic in people's life. Their objectivity adopts closed and mutually responsive objects to stage an associated scene, that is, the system of symbolic family *relations*. This is a poetic field embracing people. (Different from Heidegger, young Baudrillard considers the symbol which is the basis of originality as a *relation situation of modelling*,

55   Baudrillard, Jean. *The System of Objects*. Trans. James Benedict. Radical Thinkers, 3. London [u.a.]: Verso, 2005, p. 19.
56   *Ibid.*, p. 19.

instead of as an isolated situation.) This system is accompanied by a whole set of poetic and metaphoric symbols. "So, with meaning and value deriving from the hereditary transmission of substances under the jurisdiction of form, the world is experienced as given (as it always is in the unconscious and in childhood)."[57] (It is clear to us that this non-utilitarian and non-reciprocal *gift* belongs to Mauss. However, in Baudrillard's thought situation, the gift is independent and symbolic. Moreover, Baudrillard misinterprets that it only exists in man's early life and unconscious state. Thus, it is totally different from Mauss's *having-been* signified in the primitive tribes. We can even go so far as to say that the signifier and the signified of Mauss's gift concept is disjointed in the framework of young Baudrillard. The discourse details are very interesting.) The object in our lives exists in an "anthropomorphic" presence. As a result of the present functionalized and shaped objects in the contemporary capitalist society, "the notion of a world [is] no longer given but instead pro-duced–mastered, manipulated, inventoried, controlled: a world, in short, that has to be constructed."[58] (This is still the late Heidegger's logic that objects are schemed and mastered by men.) Hence, once full of numerous functionalized objects, "rooms now have traded in the symbols of family for signs of social relationship."[59] As a result, the poetic field of I-Thou fades away from the objects' structure, and the objects' existence becomes the function of I-It. Baudrillard sadly comments, "we have thus moved from the depth of a vertical field to the extension of a horizontal one."[60] The vertical relation here is the reciprocal relationship between Dasein and Being mentioned by Heidegger (Martin Buber's relationship between I and Thou). And the horizontal relation is the eradicated ordinary relations of Dasein and the object, as well as Being-there (Dasein) and Being-in-the-world. (More specifically, this point is later developed in *Symbolic Exchange and Death*, where the transition of vertical relation to hor-izontal relation refers to the transformation of the "law of commod-ity value," with reference frame, to the semiotic "structural law of commodity value," which is without reference frame. The detailed

---

57   *Ibid.*, p. 67.
58   *Ibid.*, p. 28.
59   *Ibid.*, p. 48.
60   *Ibid.*, p. 53.

analysis on this issue can be seen in part two of this book.) Now the object behaves "as humble and receptive supporting actor, as a sort of psychological slave or confidant"[61] and "man is not at home amid pure functionality."[62] The speaking of the young Baudrillard is permeated with Heidegger-Holderlin's deep homesickness. Man is not at home in existence, but in the endless panic entangled with functional and orderly objective system.

Kellner once commented that *The System of Objects* contains two theoretical logics: "The analyses presuppose the theory of the commodification of everyday life under capitalism advanced by Marxists like Lukács and by semiological theories in which objects are interpreted as signs that are organized into systems of signification."[63] In fact, the critique of commercialization of capitalist society derives not from Lukács, but directly from Marx. Besides, the application of semiology in this book of Baudrillard can only be considered as an initial attempt. (In my opinion, Kellner fails to capture the deeper thought ordering, as we have disclosed it here; Heidegger's ontology; and deeper the Mauss-Bataille's thought of symbolic exchange. Only, in this book, Baudrillard's understanding and application proceeding towards the latter are not accurate and profound.)

Baudrillard proclaims that the system of objects in capitalism betrays the symbolic relation. The most crucial point is to know what exactly the real meaning of the *symbol* is. Let us define it through discourse analysis of the text. In the second part of the text, "Structures of Atmosphere," Baudrillard even includes an independent section, "The End of the Symbolic Dimension" to illustrate the loss of symbolic value in conventional arts. (It is the first time he uses the word "end." We will find that the "*end*" will become the key word of his critical logic. In addition, the extreme word "death" is not yet used

---

61   *Ibid.*, p. 26.
62   *Ibid.*, p. 84.
63   Steven Best, Douglas Kellner. *Postmodern Theory: Critical Interrogations.* Macmillan, 1991, p. 113. As an aside, the most important concept in the book is mistranslated, namely, the crucial *symbol* and *sign*. The translator translates symbolic society and symbolic exchange into sign society and sign exchange. And the title of the first section in this chapter becomes "From sign society to production society" and the title of the second section becomes "Sign exchange, micropolitics and cultural revolution." The mistranslation will not emerge here. It totally misinterprets Baudrillard's original intention.

here.). Men with traditional handcrafts link each other with gestures and form a symbolic "theatre," where items play various roles while "gestures and physical effort are also the vectors of a whole phallic symbolism, as deployed, for example, in such notions as penetration, resistance, moulding or rubbing."[64] This is an artistic situating! For instance, gestures of farmers and handicraftsmen seem to construct a living performance in the process of transplanting rice seedlings and harvesting in traditional farming, traditional wine making, potting, and weaving. While in assembly line, the objects represent life and situation does not exist, only remaining faceless, fragile, professional, and functional actions. (It should be particularly noted that, in Baudrillard's original understanding, the symbolic concept is displayed as the situation of relational and particular presence. The situation is constructed by people's interactions in social life. Hereinbefore furniture layout representing family relations and phallic symbolism of traditional handcrafts are all the same. In my understanding, such is an inaccurate image and imaginary situating towards Mauss's symbolism. In some sense, the young Baudrillard's symbolic situation is more akin to Walter Benjamin's aura, which disappears in the modern industrial process.) However, in the modern system of technical production, the traditional symbolic relation of gestures completely retires. Technology creates, through imitation, an "artificial intelligence world" where only functionality and symbols dangle. The symbolic value that represents man's qualitative existence disappears. This is a fundamental transformation of situation.

At the same stroke the symbolic relationship likewise disappears. What emerges from the realm of signs is a nature continuously dominated, an abstract, worked-upon nature, rescued from time and anxiety, which the sign is constantly converting into culture. This nature has been systematized: it is not so much nature as naturalness (or, equally well, "culturalness"). Such naturalness is thus the corollary of all functionality and the connotation of the modern system of 'atmosphere.'[65]

---

64   Baudrillard, Jean. *The System of Objects*. Trans. James Benedict. Radical Thinkers, 3. London [u.a.]: Verso, 2005, p. 57.
65   *Ibid.*, p. 68.

Baudrillard repeatedly maintains that the present existence of the life world has lost the symbolic relationship. Consequently, man's existence is no longer authentic and nature is not the real nature. (This point is related to his view of nature advocated in *The Mirror of Production*. In addition, this point is the death of the existence in *Symbolic Exchange and Death*, or, it is the starting point where Baudrillard begins to construct the murder of existence.)

It needs to be further clarified what exactly the young Baudrillard means with his symbolic *value* in *The System of Objects*. The discourse analysis on antique objects had let me to realize that Baudrillard offers a rather clear explanation. In Baudrillard's eyes, "the antique may be said, though it serves no obvious purpose, to serve a purpose nevertheless at a deeper level." The reason why antiques are precious is their important use of the *uselessness*.[66] (A parroting of Bataille.) Theirs is a *symbolic* situation of divine existence. For example, the primitive's rude tools or an emperor's mausoleum discovered by archaeology do not function directly in our practical life at present. However, we are enabled by them to achieve divinity across time and space. In contrast to the vulgar utility of today's functionalized objects, the antique means complete fulfilment, and the demand to which antiques respond is the demand for definitive or fully realized being. If the functionalized object is "devoid of being,"[67] the existence of the antique as such should be used in "perfective aspect." Hence "that which is founded upon itself, that which is 'authentic'."[68] (The later Heidegger calls it *"das ding dingt."*) The antique in fact cannot avoid the historical shaping and orderly coding of human life. But compared to the present artifacts, the shaping and ordering appear extensive and naive. Baudrillard can't help chanting passionately,

> *Like the holy relic, whose function it secularizes, the antique object reorganizes the world in a dispersive fashion which is quite antithetical to the extensive nature of functional organization— such organization being the very thing, in fact, from which it seeks to protect the profound and no doubt vital lack of realism of the inner self.*[69]

---

66 *Ibid.*, p. 79. Here the translator uses Zhuangzi's words to literally translate Baudrillard's discourse. – The author
67 *Ibid.*, p. 79.
68 *Ibid.*, p. 79.
69 *Ibid.*, p. 84.

YOUNG BAUDRILLARD THROUGHOUT HIS ORDERED MASKS   69

It is still the poetic situating of discourse. Romanticism is always akin to falling into a reverie. Baudrillard goes on to affirm that the older the object, the closer it brings us to an earlier age, to 'divinity', to nature, to primitive knowledge, and so forth.[70] Being close to the *earlier* age is the throwback of the practopian complex Baudrillard borrows from Mauss. Unsurprisingly, here is clearly seen *Mauss-Bataille logic.* (When the young Baudrillard uses this independent symbolic concept, his understandings move forward. However, in the discussion about the symbolic value of antiques, it can be seen that Baudrillard only has a vague and imaginary understanding of this idea despite Mauss-Bataille's influence on him.) Now, things become relatively clear—the theory used to attack the capitalist system in *The System of Objects* is not Marxism at all. The theories are the nostalgic Heidegger's ontology and Mauss-Bataille grassroots romanticism. In other words, it is true that Baudrillard steadily hates the capitalist utility-utilitarian system. His alternative is not a progressive reform but an impossible return to the past.

Another crucial detail needs considering in *The System of Objects*. It is the *model*[71] and *series* productions of commodities which Baudrillard later used to describe objects' generation in contemporary society. In the book, he begins to distinguish pre-industrial "period" objects and products' relationship generated by model and series productions in our modern system.[72] (This is the first point at which Baudrillard generates series concepts. Of course, those concepts do not consist of his entire logical modelling at this time—as we know, in the later *Symbolic Exchange and Death*, model and series productions are further divided into the second level, *production*, and the third level, *simulation*, in the capitalist three levels

---

70   *Ibid.*, p. 80.
71   In *The System of Objects*, modèle is translated into paradigm in Chinese translation version. In my opinion, it never expresses the meaning of paradigm from *The System of Objects* to *Symbolic Exchange and Death*. In the original context of The System of Objects, modèle denotes that the traditional and personalized production has changed into a process. In the process, model and series produce the same goods, which are featureless and homely. In *Symbolic Exchange and Death*, modèle means generative model of simulation. Its context has transformed into the coding structure. Therefore, it is better to be translated into paradigm in Chinese. Of course, Baudrillard's modèle is not in the context of Pickering's modelling.
72   Baudrillard, Jean. *The System of Objects*. Trans. James Benedict. Radical Thinkers, 3. London [u.a.]: Verso, 2005, p. 148.

of simulacra—but they activate the original situating of the late Baudrillard's thought.) At this point, Baudrillard uses concepts of model and series as the basic cognitive paradigm to observe contemporary society. Interestingly, if Baudrillard's former discussions still focus on the specific ordering structure of shaping objects in human life, he here begins to analyze the generation structure of the objects.

According to Baudrillard, in pre-industrial society, objects produced by handicraft possess working characters and shaping styles which are impossible to get rid of. For instance, the style of a Louis XV table crafted by a carpenter in the 18th century will differ from that of one in a farmhouse. There is a differential "abyss" that cannot be ignored. Today, however, we are able to *serially produce* numerous completely undifferentiated tables imitating the style of Louis XV. (These are what David Riesman calls marginal differences, according to Baudrillard.[73])

I am reminded of Baudrillard's associate Jean Paul Sartre, who derogatorily uses the series to illustrate individual negative coexistence in the first chapter of *Critique of Dialectical Reason*.[74] Later, the series becomes the second level of simulacra in Symbolic Exchange and Death.) However, Baudrillard fails to notice that the fundamental basis of the transformation is the conversion from labour's subjective shaping to the non-subjective duplication of industrial production—the other pseudo-shaping. He only lets people see the result of series production. In his opinion, most people in society are unconsciously surrounded by these series objects. However, people at their heart tend to choose those models and products lived by the few. (The model here is clearly not the generative mode that presents later as simulation.) Model products refer only to the differential products which derived from *pseudo-aristocracy*. It is impossible for them to be owned by the majority. The model and series, however, are in the same transformation.

Models themselves have quit their former isolated, caste-like existence; they are themselves now open to serial distribution... the model is internalized by those who are involved with serial

73   *Ibid.*, p. 152.
74   See Section 6 of Chapter V in *A Deep Plough of Texts (Vol. 1)*. Renmin University Press, 2008. (Chinese Version)

objects, while the series is intimated, negated, transcended and lived in a contradictory manner by those who have to do with models. The socially immanent tendency whereby the series hews ever more narrowly to the model, while the model is continually being diffused into the series, has set up a perpetual dynamic which is in fact the very ideology of our society.[75]

It has risen to the height of the ideological control. However, the relationship between model and series is not the same as that of pattern and imitation. For example, the model is just like essence. Essence derives division and complexity from the group to achieve series. On the contrary, the model is precisely concluded from the series. "Model is ubiquitous in the series." It is the nuanced and specific difference produced intentionally in series objects. The above may seem difficult to understand, so an example can be used to explain Baudrillard's concept of the model. The series of Digital Single Lens Reflex (DSLR) cameras, produced by Japanese Nikon Corporation, are intentionally distinguished by a specific nuance (such as pixel, monitor size) from D80 to D40 (every pattern is even further differentiated into D40 and D40X, etc.) "where each item in a collection is marked by a relative difference which momentarily lends it a privileged status—the status, in effect, of a model."[76] (Marketing strategies for almost all contemporary electronic products (cameras, DV camcorders, MP3, MP4 and cell phones, etc.) work this way) This artificial difference is the model Baudrillard refers to. Baudrillard deems that "for only models change; series merely follow upon one another in the wake of a model with which they can never catch up. That is where their true unreality lies."[77] Admittedly, Baudrillard deeply exposes the essence of fashion goods in contemporary capitalist society. (Obviously, the relations between series and models here are different from the same concepts as he defines them later in terms of simulacra and simulation. By the same token, the difference he derogatorily uses is heterogeneous with respect to the *affirmative* difference. The affirmative difference is used to mark the postmodern core by the other postmodernists of the same era, such as Derrida and Deleuze's differance and difference.)

75   Baudrillard, Jean. *The System of Objects.* Verso, 1996, p. 139.
76   *Ibid.*, p. 144.
77   *Ibid.*, p. 152.

It is at this point that he exposes that the essence of models and series artificially *shortens the life of objects.*

BUT THE OBJECT CANNOT BE ALLOWED TO ESCAPE FROM EPHEMERALITY OR FROM FASHION. This is the fundamental characteristic of the series: the objects that compose it are weakened on a systematic basis. In a world of (relative) affluence, the shoddiness of objects replaces the scarcity of objects as the expression of poverty. The series is forcefully imposed for a brief cross-section of time; its universe is distinctly perishable. THE OBJECT CANNOT BE ALLOWED TO ESCAPE DEATH.[78]

The character of objects produced in the consumption series today are no more durable or permanent than those once shaped by traditional production. Series production aims to let the objects die immediately. The span of their existence is a presupposed brief cross-section of time. The shaping here is the trick of death, in an attempt to enable people to buy and consume goods again as soon as possible. What a brilliant analysis it is—this process is the essence of goods models and series in contemporary capitalism. The production of models and series must lead to fresh consumption. In fact, it is not difficult to find in the last chapter of *The System of Objects* that Baudrillard has already recognized the process. The process is that modern capitalist society walks towards the world of consumption. In this consumption world, the desired consumption precedes shaping production and also accumulation. It is the activity consisting of the systematic manipulation of signs that becomes the most important existent structure.[79]

Baudrillard finds that contemporary capitalism manipulates a concave complicity. Modern consumers are spontaneously absorbed in an obligatory requirement. They *unrestrainedly* purchase so that production will be endless. This finding is the starting point of his later logic, in fact, *consumption determines production.* In his view, the hidden secrets show that advertising manipulated by signs is also an accomplice. It performs as the credit of political logic. The logic of advertising is unconscious in that "persuasion is hidden," and its function "assails us relentlessly." In essence, advertising is itself is less a determinant of consumption than an object of consumption.[80]

78   *Ibid.*, p. 147.
79   Baudrillard, Jean. *The System of Objects.* Trans. James Benedict. *Radical Thinkers*, 3. London [u.a.]: Verso, 2005, p. 218.
80   Baudrillard, Jean. *The System of Objects.* Verso, 1996, p. 173.

People consume the violent shaping (brain-washed) sense in the visible concave point in the advertising, and sense is modelled by the sign links. When we consume advertising, sense unconsciously refers to the models and series goods for sale. (An important theme exposed in his next book *The Consumer Society*.)

The System of Objects is derivative of others' thought constructions in its overall logic. However, we have to acknowledge that the young Baudrillard shows his outstanding originality once he appears in European academic circles. The academic value of his research is obvious, except for the fact that he intentionally criticizes Marx in order to raise his own position. As it turns out, academic memories in his thought storage do not appear via simple appropriation. Their quotes, as used by Baudrillard, are mostly autonomous and generative activation of convexity. Such is the distinct characteristic of his entire thought ordering space.

4 HIDDEN LOGIC SUPPORT IN *THE CONSUMER SOCIETY*

Later, in *The Consumer Society*, Baudrillard's analysis of the system of objects transforms to research on the structure of commodity circulation, especially *people's servile position* in the consumption activities of contemporary capitalist society. This transition is one *from the object to people*. (I note that from this book on he sets foot on economics. But his logical position shows little change from the beginning. He does not directly call it the symbolic value again. Instead, he refers to the resisting standpoint that deconstructs consumption logic as the "natural ecological laws," vis-à-vis "the law of exchange-value."[81] However, this theoretical standpoint disappears immediately afterwards.) According to Baudrillard, people living in contemporary capitalist society are surrounded by objects and become more and more functional. This position is clearly the logical continuation of *The System of Objects*. He says:

> We live by object time: by this I mean that we live at the pace of objects, live to the rhythm of their ceaseless succession. Today, it is we who watch them as they are born, grow to maturity and die, whereas in all previous civilizations it was timeless objects, instruments or monuments which outlived the generations of human beings.[82]

81   Baudrillard, Jean, Chris Turner, and George Ritzer. *The Consumer Society: Myths and Structures*. Theory, Culture & Society. London: Sage Publications Ltd, 1998, p. 26.
82   *Ibid.*, p. 25.

This is a very interesting contrast. As we have known, objects are Heidegger's ready-to-hand orderly world shaped and woven by people's utility. As the result of human activities, objects created by humans cannot serve the people but surround and besiege them in the opposite manner. (This statement seems to be similar to *commodity enslavement* in Marx and Engels's *The German Ideology*. Baudrillard seems to agree with Marx at this time, as he says that dominance is the law of exchange-value rather than natural ecological laws.) It sounds as though he is still describing the objective shaping objects in *The System of Objects*. However, the above description is but an introduction. The new question is what he really wants to discuss. Baudrillard quotes Marx's statement regarding commodity's images in the process of circulation. Then he suddenly turns to emphasize the guidance and dominance of people's deep desires by the brilliant shop windows of commodity. (This is also the important social critique that Benjamin starts with, and Baudrillard's teacher Debord thus puts forward the concept of *spectacle*. In *The Society of the Spectacle*, Debord proposes that in the abstract system of contemporary capitalist society, commodity's showy appearance and demonstrative spectacle are more important than its practical use value.) Obviously, in *The System of Objects*, Baudrillard still pays attention to the world ordering of the basic functionalized object. In *The Society of the Spectacle*, he begins to think about the new social domains of *consumption* and consumables. This is an important theoretical shift. Of course, the real subject of consumption research is less the object than the consumer. However, they are the unfortunate *consumers* ruled and enslaved by the new type of bourgeoisie. It is clear that Lefebvre and Debord had already profoundly researched consumption's outstanding status in social existence, but Baudrillard reconsiders this status in the higher metaphysical level. To this end, he even asserts, "We are at the point where consumption is laying hold of the whole of life."[83] That consumption controls the entire life of contemporary people is the most important initial definition that he gives to consumer society.

---

83   *Ibid.*, p. 27.

In fact, in the latter half of *The System of Objects*, Baudrillard begins to consider consumption. He moves from concentration on the shaped objective system to *the relation between consumer and commodity*. More precisely, man-the consumer is controlled and exploited in the consumption structure. If *The System of Objects* mainly exposes the orderly functional structure in the world, it is still a topic discussed in terms of metaphysical *ontology*. *The Consumer Society*, however, tries to explain the new domination and enslavement relations of present economic life: The relation between the consumer and the object is no longer the relationship between man and objects' *use function*. The relationship has become a coercive one between man and the orderly consumables, which performs as "a set of objects." We can see Baudrillard illustrates this point in the following ways:

The first illustration is the *meaning of chains* in modern consumption control. Baudrillard argues: "And this changes the consumer's relation to the object: he no longer relates to a particular object in its specific utility, but to a set of objects in its total signification." What does he mean? At first glance this statement is difficult to understand. In fact, Baudrillard at this time is no longer concerned with the functional structure of objects' ontology in *The System of Objects*. Instead, he identifies the new shaped and enslaved objects in consumption. He takes Parly 2, "the largest business centre in Europe," as an example. Parly 2 is a shopping mall made up of hundreds of shops and recreation areas, where people can buy all of their daily consumer goods. However, he views Parly 2 in a different light. Apart from the specific use of the appliances, Baudrillard finds another deep meaning which we generally ignored when considering of consumer goods:

> *The shop-window, the advertisement, the manufacturer and the brand name, which here plays a crucial role, impose a coherent, collective vision, as though they were an almost indissociable totality, a series. This is, then, no longer a sequence of mere objects, but a chain of signifiers, in so far as all of these signify one another reciprocally as part of a more complex super-object, drawing the consumer into a series of more complex motivations.*[84]

---

84   *Ibid.*, p. 27.

In *The System of Objects*, Baudrillard researches the object's ontology "surrounded" in the utility Gestell of people's functionality.
He at this point seems to be discussing consumption in terms of economics. However, from within the economic relations he exposes
a kind of a *mutual referent of fresh order* which is invisible in the
consumption structure. (This order is actually the higher form of
Heidegger's ready-to-hand orderly relations. It is the *critique of metaphysical phenomenology behind economics*.) Baudrillard means
that in the process of capitalist consumption, goods' convex display
is magnificent and dazzling. In lofty the aesthetics and structural
advertising of psychology, goods are imbued with the allure of the
brand, which demonstrates status and success. Then goods generate what Debord calls the conspicuous spectacle-presentation, the
sub-conscious rule, and domination of people's deep mental modelling. However, Baudrillard's new discoveries are more profound
than Benjamin and Debord's, inasmuch as this control has become
a motivation control of the goods chain. When you purchase a high
grade product, this product will form a closely modelling chain of
desire and temptation with other same grade products. Such products are a chain of signifiers with convexity that mutually implies
one another, so as to control and dominate people's desire. For example, when you buy a luxury car (convex desire A), the car implies that it connects with a villa with garage; the villa undoubtedly
suggests a whole set of high-grade decorations (convex desire C)
and so forth in a limitless consumption chain and obligatory series.
My understanding is that it is the fraudulent pseudo-desires situation
generated by the consumption structure in market economy at present. In the consumption field, people are forced to consume and are
tied by the invisible convex chains. It should be pointed out that the
enforcement here is not a *sensual* thing *outside*, but seduction within
consumption! The enforcement is carried out by the volunteer who
is seduced by illusion.

Here, the *series* appears again. (It is the second stage at which
Baudrillard generates series concept.) However, this series is no
longer the "reproduction" logic of production in *The System of
Objects*. It refers to the mandatory logic among the consumer goods
that we have just discussed. Series begins to change here, which

means that consumers are unconsciously dominated and move *logically* from one object to another.[85] One voluntarily purchases product A, and B, then C. It is the desire logic that one should fulfill one's "own value" and become one of the "successful people." (Actually, mandatory consumption logic strongly activates the chain effect in Chinese (consumers) minds with opulent vacation imagery (Golden Week and Long Vacation) and collective metaphors. Interestingly, in the present field of Chinese cultural critique today, consumption "alienation" is the only exception without critique.)

Secondly, consumption is manipulated and produced by code. In Baudrillard's view, *consumer series* in the consumption structure of contemporary capitalist society necessarily means orderly reference among *a whole set of consumer goods*. The fundamental and dominant thing is the implicit structural meaning and sign value produced by sign discourse (style, prestige, luxury, power, and status). Therefore, he believes that in consumption, consumers' needs are directed not so much towards objects as towards values, and their satisfaction initially has the sense of signing up to those values.[86] In other words, it is a kind of symbolic code meaning that is more attractive to people rather than the objects themselves. (Hereto Mark Poster says that according to Baudrillard, "the signifiers themselves, not the products, had become objects of consumption that drew their power and fascination from being structured into a code."[87]) As a result, today's consumption is less real consumption than the consumption of the meaning system. Consumers are not individuals and the real individual is deleted (The same $ as Lacan says). Also in this sense, Baudrillard declares, *"The subject of consumption is the order of signs."*[88] More precisely, the governor of consumption creates order for code. (In my opinion, the academic memory of semiology here becomes the logic convexity and is really activated and incorporated into his intellectual situating. Different from Debord, the consumption logic is more general code logic than spectacle-presentation logic outside or the simple logic of displaying and seeing.

---

85   *Ibid.*, p. 27.
86   *Ibid.*, p. 70.
87   Douglas Kellner. *Baudrillard: A Critical Reader*. Basil Blackwell Ltd. 1994, p. 76.
88   Baudrillard, Jean, Chris Turner, and George Ritzer. *The Consumer Society: Myths and Structures*. Theory, Culture & Society. London: Sage Publications Ltd, 1998, p. 192.

It is at this point that Baudrillard begins to own his new ideas on the entirety of contemporary capitalism, namely the capitalist rule based upon the *political economy of the sign*. Poster responds that Baudrillard for the first time subordinates semiology to critical theory.[89] It does make sense. More precisely, it is the first time that semiology belongs to social critical theories because the sign has already become subjective critical logic in Lacan's view.) The meaning and symbolism of sign production is the secret of consumption control in contemporary capitalism, and the logic of consumption can be defined as a manipulation of signs."[90] Therefore, "more and more basic aspects of our contemporary societies fall under a logic of significations, an analysis of codes and symbolic systems."[91] If we rewrite Lacan's "the unconscious is the discourse of the Other" here, then the consumption dominated by unconscious control is the result of the power discourse of symbolic code system (the Other) in capitalism. (Please note that in *The System of Objects*, Baudrillard specifically discusses the transformation from the traditional symbolic existence to the functionalized object. While analyzing the consumption structure, he again identifies the transformation from the functionalized object to meaning and symbolic relation in the consumption structure. This change is very interesting. Of course, the symbol here is a bad one, or a pseudo-symbol, which is a snake luring people towards the desirable illusion. The pseudo-symbol hereafter is referred to as symbolic exchange value. To avoid misunderstandings, Baudrillard carefully adds an explanation, "It cannot become primitive society," which refers to the primitive lives of Mauss-Bataille's symbolic exchange.) Here the pseudo-symbol is the consumed imaginary and artificial myth. Man consumes this myth as he consumes object."[92] The symbolic structure of myth determines that the relation situating of social life is the common concept that Mauss and Lévi-Strauss hold. But Baudrillard's myth here is also the pseudo-situating produced by ideology.

---

89 Douglas Kellner. *Baudrillard: A Critical Reader*. Basil Blackwell Ltd. 1994, p. 76.
90 Baudrillard, Jean, Chris Turner, and George Ritzer. *The Consumer Society: Myths and Structures*. Theory, Culture & Society. London: Sage Publications Ltd, 1998, p. 114.
91 *Ibid.*, p. 33.
92 *Ibid.*, p. 75.

In Baudrillard's view, this new consumption logic is the most important ideology in the contemporary consumer society, the consumption ideology.

> *It is, rather, by training them in the unconscious discipline of a code, and competitive cooperation at the level of that code; it is not by creating more creature comforts, but by getting them to play by the rules of the game. This is how consumption can on its own substitute for all ideologies and, in the long run, take over alone the role of integrating the whole of society, as hierarchical or religious rituals did in primitive societies.*[93]

The above-mentioned is one of the most important statements in Baudrillard's book. It is also the theoretical commanding height in his spontaneous intellectual situating. Just like the primitive myth and religious narrative in the Middle Ages, divine illusion on the other bank sustains the function of "integrated" ideology in the life of modelling. Today's consumer myth also constructs integrated ideology in our life. The difference is that while traditional myth governs life through thingness and etiquette, consumption logic enables people to play the consumer game, which they inwardly desire to play through their imaginary code relation. The game spontaneously generates an integrated "unconscious discipline" by competitive purchase in order to "catch up with each other." Thus, consumption logic rules in a concave place. There is no doubt that consumer ideology has become the most effective way that the ruling class carries out *non-mandatory identity* at present society. This is a very profound social criticism. (I often wonder whether, in *The System of Objects* and *The Consumer Society*, Baudrillard reaches the deepest realm of contemporary social critical theories. Unfortunately, this valuable criticism begins to loosen and deform when he moves onwards to establish his independent thought modelling space. Especially, when he opposes historical materialism, his intentional theory and artificial logic actually undermine the seriousness of his thought.)

Thirdly, social classes are divided by the consumption. Baudrillard points out, "One of the basic mechanisms of consumption is this formal autonomization of groups, classes, and castes (and the individual)."[94] Such is a very strange argument. What does the

---

93   *Ibid.*, p. 94.
94   *Ibid.*, p. 138.

formal autonomization mean? In his view, in consumption in contemporary capitalism, "you never consume the object in itself (in its use-value); you are always manipulating objects (in the broadest sense) as signs which distinguish you either by affiliating you to your own group taken as an ideal reference or by marking you off from your group by reference to a group of higher status."[95] It is the further interpretation of meaningful chains constructed by goods' mutual implication and reference. To buy a product is mainly not to use its function but rather is a symbolic convex display. "XX is affordable to me," means you can enter a higher social group through the convex sign meaning of the product brand. Meanwhile, to purchase the high grade product is a process by which one differs himself/herself from the lower group. For example, one in China today purchases a BMW automobile to indicate that he is in the so-called "successful people" class and rids himself of the status as a common person at the bottom of society. Recently an interesting event took place in Nanjing that illustrates Baudrillard's opinion. (Not long ago in the highway near Nanjing, an "auto club" motorcade (Group A) made up of more than 20 modified Mazda 6 driven by Nanjing citizens encountered a Hummer H2 SUV with a Changzhou license plate (Group B). Perhaps while of overtaking cars or giving way, several Mazda 6 cars surrounded the Hummer, using the motorcade to bring the Hummer's speed down to 30 km/h on the highway. The whole process lasted up to 10 minutes. The event later garnered public attention when the owner of a Mazda 6 posted digital video of the event on the internet. Of course, the major netizens denounced the behaviour of the Mazda 6 owners. According to Baudrillard's logic, this event can be regarded as the confrontation of differential convex presentation between two totally different consumer groups. Group A, the owners of Mazda 6s (which cost about 200,000 RMB) belong to the lower middle class, while group B, the owner of Hummer, obviously belongs to an upper class. The event reflects the mental confrontation between two convex sign meanings: jealousy and envy coupled with deep desire as well as apparent "resentment.")

---

95   *Ibid.*, p. 61.

In Baudrillard's view, consumption in contemporary capitalist society is in fact an exchange system amongst differential codes. It is through consumption that people acquire this kind of specific sign identity. When you consume, you can have "the same code in common, of sharing the same signs which make all the members of that group different from a particular other group."[96] As Baudrillard says, people will definitely catch sight of *consumer series* in consumption. More importantly,

> *Consuming is something one never does alone (this is the illusion of the consumer, meticulously sustained by the whole of the ideological discourse on consumption). One enters, rather, into a generalized system of exchange and production of coded values where, in spite of themselves, all consumers are involved with all others.*[97]

In the process of consumption, no one exists in a pure and isolated condition of product purchasing and consuming. Consumption is the orderly code of status and identity, and code is at the same time class division. Poster once explained that Baudrillard has developed a theory to make intelligible one of the fascinating and perplexing aspects of advanced industrial society: the proliferation of communications through the media.[98] Everyone is, in spite of himself, referred to one another, and reflects one another in the orderly model of consumption. As we mentioned above, the Mazda 6 and Hummer H2 generate class divisions due to mutual reflection of the other. (The so-called code value is later defined again as sign value or symbolic exchange value in *For a Critique of the Political Economy of the Sign*.) Thus, Baudrillard believes that the consumption area has become a *structured social field*. The specific structure is class divisions. Need itself is also constructed as "*series class*." These distinctions are very intuitive to Baudrillard. He starts with people's smoking Kent and Marlboro, analyzing in detail the unconscious desire which is concealed in people's innermost concave place:

> *You have a classy girl and an Alfa-Romeo 2600 Sprint? Just add 'Green Water' cologne and the trinity is complete: your status as a true aristocrat of the post-industrial age is secure. Or put*

---

96   *Ibid.*, p. 92.
97   *Ibid.*, p. 78.
98   Baudrillard Jean, Poster Mark. *Selected Writings*. Stanford University Press, 2001, p. 1.

*the same earthenware tiles in your kitchen as Françoise Hardy
or the same built-in gas hob as Brigitte Bardot. Or use a toaster
which makes you initialled toast, or put charcoal 'aux herbes
de Provence' in your barbecue. Of course, the 'marginal' differences themselves are part of a subtle hierarchy.[99]*

It seems that people may be equal when confronting the "use value" of product. However, in front of the deeply hierarchical product
which performs as the sign and difference, no equality can be found
amongst people. Differential sign consumption aims to produce survival hierarchy. (In *For a Critique of the Political Economy of the
Sign*, Baudrillard identifies it as "the Veblen effect, that is, I am buying this because it is more expensive, in which the economic (quantitative) is converted into sign-difference. Sign-difference leads to
the people's existential difference in reality. According to Thorstein
Veblen, conspicuous consumption of valuable goods is a mean of
reputability to the gentleman of leisure."[100])

After incisive critical analysis of contemporary capitalist consumption, Baudrillard further discusses the function of advertising
upon consumption control. This discussion is another important part
of the research in *The Consumer Society*. (His social critical thought
began in the last part of *The System of Objects*.) Following the consumer logic above, he says that in fact, people are the consuming
subjects. "There is no 'mass of consumers' and no need emerges
spontaneously from the grassroots consumer: needs have no chance
of appearing in the 'standard package' of needs if they have not already been part of the 'select package'."[101] That is to say, the consuming subjects (mass of consumers) who are the produced illusionary ones appear to be none when shopping independently. Then what
are they made of? *Advertising.*

*The strategic value of advertising—and also its trick—is precise-
ly this: that it targets everyone in their relation to others, in their
hankerings after reified social prestige. It is never addressed to
a lone individual, but is aimed at human beings in their differential relations and, even when it seems to tap into their 'deep'*

99   Baudrillard, Jean, Chris Turner, and George Ritzer. *The Consumer Society: Myths and Structures*. Theory, Culture & Society. London: Sage Publications Ltd, 1998, p. 90.
100   Thorstein Veblen. *The Theory of the Leisure Class*. Forgotten Books, 1965, p. 46.
101   Baudrillard, Jean, Chris Turner, and George Ritzer. *The Consumer Society: Myths and Structures*. Theory, Culture & Society. London: Sage Publications Ltd, 1998, p. 62.

motivations. It always does so in spectacular fashion. That is to say, it always calls in their friends and relations, the group, and society, all hierarchically ordered within the process of reading and interpretation, the process of 'setting-off' or 'showing-off' [faire-valoir] which it sets in train.[102]

Baudrillard's critical thought on advertising should be regarded as the most profound view amongst social critical theories of advertising since the "consumer alienation" idea proposed by the Frankfurt School. Lacan presents here first. Because people are always desirous of other people's desired objects,[103] the strategy of advertising is to produce a myth of materialized society which everyone accepts. The other mirror produced by advertising is to interest those who want to "succeed" with the implied status and class divisions (BMW, luxurious house, and lasting bodily youthfulness), not individually. (In fact, this process is precisely what is unfolding around us now.) Others' desires consist of everyone's desire in deep motivation. The secret of advertising is that it *controls the deep situation* of this desire. Therefore, Baudrillard intends to say that the use value of the object has never been consumed in the consumption of contemporary capitalism. People only consume a kind of "consumed imaginary," which is the illusion of *symbolic value* produced by weird advertising. This consumption is *pseudo-situating*. Obviously, Baudrillard also specifically interprets the implied enforcement and sign control of the above consumer relations.

Baudrillard believes that the essence of advertising is symbolic and illusionary. It is clear that symbol here is not positive. It is an alienated form of authentic being. (In *Symbolic Exchange and Death*, the appearance of authentic being is identified as *simulation* that is more real than the real.) Additionally, symbolic illusion does not act directly as a convex phenomotive in advertising. It controls people's *subconscious* desires. Therefore, "it is not only the mirage of rich objects, but also the assurance to the constantly motiveless miracles." The mirage (illusion) is the pseudo-situating. (Gérard Lagneau's words are specially quoted in the reference by Baudrillard, "Advertising is the wrapping up of an unbearable economic logic

---

102   *Ibid.*, p. 64.
103   See my monograph: *The Impossible Truth of Being: Mirror of Lacan's Philosophy*, Beijing: Commercial Press, 2005.

in the thousand seductive artifices of 'exemption from payment,' which negate it the better to allow it to operate."[104] Meanwhile, he also mentions the contribution of Vance Packard's *The Hidden Persuaders* and Ernest Dichter's *The Strategy of Desire.*[105]) In the open conspiracy of advertising, according to Baudrillard, non-motivation is the largest motivation, non-enforcement is the greatest enforcement, and non-oppression is the greatest oppression. In other words, "all these things are gently extorted from you."[106] Such is one of the secrets that bourgeois rule.

All the artful moves of advertising tend in this direction. See how discreet it is everywhere, how benevolent, self-effacing and disinterested. An hour's radio programme against a one-minute 'ad' for its product. Four pages of poetic prose and the company trademark placed shame-facedly at the foot of a page.[107]

Ordinary people never realize that the strategic target is *unconscious temptation*, rather than people's self-consciousness. Advertising as a whole has no meaning. It merely conveys significations.[108] (John O'Toole firstly used "persuasion"[109] when he mentioned the definition of advertising in 1904.) The trick of advertising is to practice deception and open conspiracy, which mentions trademark quickly in a low profile way. Literary discourse and artificial shame are the effective way used by advertising to rape subconscious psychology in the concave part. Another important strategy of advertising, Baudrillard says, is "the ideology of the gift." That is to say, in the form of reductions, discounts, and free gifts, etc.,[110] one is persuaded unconsciously to buy what one really does not need, is indulged in this kind of service free of charge, and "benefits" (when winning a prize outright). In fact, advanced advertising intends to

---

104   Baudrillard, Jean, Chris Turner, and George Ritzer. *The Consumer Society: Myths and Structures.* Theory, Culture & Society. London: Sage Publications Ltd, 1998, p. 202.
105   *Ibid.*, p. 71.
106   Baudrillard, Jean. *Cool Memories II, 1987-1990.* Trans. Chris Turner. Duke University Press, 1996, p. i.
107   Baudrillard, Jean, Chris Turner, and George Ritzer. *The Consumer Society: Myths and Structures.* Theory, Culture & Society. London: Sage Publications Ltd, 1998, p. 165.
108   *Ibid.*, p. 88.
109   Clark, Eric. *The Want Makers: The World of Advertising: How They Make You Buy.* Viking, 1989, p. 39.
110   Baudrillard, Jean, Chris Turner, and George Ritzer. *The Consumer Society: Myths and Structures.* Theory, Culture & Society. London: Sage Publications Ltd, 1998, p. 164.

control people in the pseudo-situating unconsciously. "Advertising is neither to be understood by the people, nor people to learn, but people should hope that, in this sense, it is a prophetic discourse." (Clark once pointed out: "There is the theory that advertisements work on people on a kind of drip principle without conscious attention being given to them."[111] For example, the beauty turning around and smiling gently in Hennessy XO parfume advertisements or the man projecting desirous eyes in the advertisements for Lexus brand car are both a kind of implied concave temptation. The drip principle is used so that the implied temptation is shown several times in a single TV episode. There are two to three episodes in a single night, and from twenty to thirty episodes to hundreds of episodes in a serial TV drama. The picture of tempting aesthetics and desirous situations thus dominate people's subconscious psychological structures by means of limitless repetition. When one enters a shop, one will subconsciously buy the specific commodities in the desirous pseudo-situating. Thus, the hidden domination of advertising just happens. Researchers enter the picture to help to determine the kind of sounds that will best penetrate people's consciousness; it has been found that the human voice has most effect when it is pitched in the frequency range between two and six kilohertz.[112])

In the advertising industry, the object is designed as pseudo-events first, and then it becomes the real event of daily life through the consumer's endorsement of its discourse.[113] In the modelling activity of a *tautological* narrative pattern, the boundary line between situating and pseudo-situating is thoroughly wiped out—advertising can be compared to the spell which creates pseudo-desires. (In *For a Critique of the Political Economy of the Sign*, "tautology" becomes the main pattern of the contemporary bourgeois ideology.) Under the tautological command of such a spell, pseudo-situating desire quietly and coercively substitutes the authentic being. Sadly, it is impossible to resist this spell even if we have realized this point. Horkheimer and Adorno identify the fact that advertising today has

---

111   Eric Clark. *The Want Makers: The World of Advertising: How They Make You Buy*. Viking, 1989, p. 63.
112   *Ibid.*, p. 100.
113   Baudrillard, Jean, Chris Turner, and George Ritzer. *The Consumer Society: Myths and Structures*. Theory, Culture & Society. London: Sage Publications Ltd, 1998, p. 127.

won a fundamental victory, because "of the compulsive imitation by consumers of cultural commodities which, at the same time, they recognize as false."[114] In fact, this phenomenon is constantly at work around us. (I often mention in my class that one should never consider as fools those manufacturers who invest hundreds of millions in television advertising costs. All advertising costs are integrated into the cost of goods, which means we who purchase these goods unconsciously are the real idiots.) Another example is that advertising control constructs a specially ordered classification: The masculine model is the model of particularity, while in the feminine model, women are enjoined to take pleasure for themselves; the masculine choice is 'agonistic,' while women are only called on to gratify themselves in order to better to be able to enter as objects into the masculine competition (enjoying themselves in order to be the more enjoyable).[115] (In China, the famous French fashion magazine *Elle* is enjoying popularity an article from it is used by Baudrillard to elaborate how those want makers, driven by capitalists, tell women the secret keys to beautiful bodies. His analysis is brilliant.)

It is the ubiquity of advertising today that forges "*total consumption.*"

Through a complicity, an immanent, immediate collusion at the level of the message, but above all at the level of the medium itself and the code. Every image, every advertisement imposes a consensus—that between all the individuals potentially called upon to decipher it, that is to say, called on, by decoding the message, to subscribe automatically to the code in which it has been couched.[116]

Advertisement acts "*from one sign to the other, from one object to the other, from one consumer to the other.*"[117] Total consumption and identity further interpret what he asserts above the orderly consumption chain. (Clearly, this idea is the further logical development of Heidegger's ready-to-hand world view (namely the link of object's functional being), which is used metonymically in *The System of Objects*. At the same time, Saussure's academic memory of cross-section of time among signs is constantly highlighted.)

---

114   Max Horkheimer, Theodor W. Adorno, Gunzelin Schmid Noerr. *Dialectic of Enlightenment: Philosophical Fragments*. Stanford University Press, 2002, p. 136.
115   Baudrillard, Jean, Chris Turner, and George Ritzer. *The Consumer Society: Myths and Structures*. Theory, Culture & Society. London: Sage Publications Ltd, 1998, p. 96-97.
116   *Ibid.*, p. 125.
117   *Ibid.*, p. 125.

Finally, Baudrillard claims that capitalism's total consumption, created by advertising, is "the world of the pseudo-event, of pseudo-history and pseudo-culture," and "a world of events, history, culture and ideas not produced from shifting, contradictory, real experience, but *produced as artifacts from elements of the code and the technical manipulation of the medium.*"[118] (The pseudo-event, pseudo-history artifacts, and authentic being history remind us of Karol Kosik's pseudo-concrete world and concrete collectivity.[119]) Therefore, advertising "means the rule of pseudo-events."

In my opinion, advertisement creates pseudo-life situating, or pseudo-desires situating. Many years ago, Horkheimer and Adorno said that advertising is the elixir of life.[120] Baudrillard further explains that advertising is the death of real event, real history, and real culture. (Notice that it is also the first time he touches upon the important theme that the authentic being is "murdered." Although Baudrillard carelessly puts forward *judgment on true and false,* we fail to understand what he really means when he casually says "the changing, contradictory and really experienced events, culture, and thoughts. The real being is dying, but slowly outlined and shaped in his symbolic exchange relations." In *Cool Memories IV,* he writes: "The effort to publicize the truth leads to the denial of truth itself."[121])

Of course, product advertising is not the only thing accounting for the creation of pseudo-events. Mass media as the carrier of advertising is a sort of accomplice to the murder of the authentic being. (In making this statement Baudrillard for the first time begins to criticize mass media, which is one of the most important critiques that the late Baudrillard possesses. We can easily find that this critique is the theoretical circuit of critical reflection that originated in his teacher Debord's *The Society of the Spectacle.*) According to Baudrillard, the "truth" shaped by mass media such as newspapers and magazines, videos, and popular presses, appears on the premise that "*I was not there.*" "It is the truer than true which counts or, in

---

118   *Ibid.*, p. 125.
119   See Chapter IV in *A Deep Plough of Texts.* People's University Press, 2004.
120   Max Horkheimer, Theodor W. Adorno, Gunzelin Schmid Noerr. *Dialectic of Enlightenment: Philosophical Fragments.* Stanford University Press, 2002, p. 131.
121   Baudrillard Jean. *Cool Memories IV: 1995-2000.* Trans. Chris Turner. Verso, 2003, p. 20.

other words, the fact of being there without being there. Or, to put it yet another way, the fantasy." What mass communications gives us is not reality, but the dizzying whirl of reality.[122] Therefore he states in a hyperbolic way: The TV: every image is an ephemeral vanishing act.[123] He asserts that in mass media,

> *A message-consumption message, a message of segmentation and spectacularization, of misrecognition of the world and fore-grounding of information as a commodity, of glorification of content as sign. In short, it performs a conditioning function (in the advertising sense of the term: in this sense, advertising is the 'mass' medium par excellence, and its schemata leave their stamp on all the other media) and a function of misrecognition.[124]*

Obviously, mass media, which is not advertising itself, is consumption in another sense. Television images, promotional information, and ideological signs shape a real being consisting of blood, murder, and tragedy in a place *where nothing happens.* (In *Cool Memories IV*, Baudrillard writes: "Information is not knowledge, it is making-known, and this has its counterpart in making-out-that-one-knows-in pretend knowledge. Propaganda, ideology, and advertising are not belief, but making-believe, which has its response in making-out-that-one-believes-in pretend belief. Television is not seeing, it is making-see, the corresponding reaction being to make out that one sees-pretend seeing. We are prisoners of facticity: of making-see, making-believe, making-out, etc. We are no longer the direct agents of our acts and thoughts. We are merely heteromobile vehicles, who have set their vital functions to automatic pilot and become indifferent to themselves."[125]) Thanks to mass media, we 'consume' our tranquillity, a pseudo tranquillity that exists under the construction of ideology. Its tranquillity requires perpetual *consumed violence* for its own exaltation. Moreover, the violence is stronger than any others. That violence is characterized by the fact that it is aimless and objectless

---

122   Baudrillard, Jean, Chris Turner, and George Ritzer. *The Consumer Society: Myths and Structures.* Theory, Culture & Society. London: Sage Publications Ltd, 1998, p. 34.
123   Baudrillard, Jean. *Cool Memories: 1980-1985.* Trans. Chris Turner. Verso, 1990, p. 67.
124   Baudrillard, Jean, Chris Turner, and George Ritzer. *The Consumer Society: Myths and Structures.* Theory, Culture & Society. London: Sage Publications Ltd, 1998, p. 123.
125   Baudrillard, Jean. *Cool Memories IV: 1995-2000.* Trans. Chris Turner. Verso, 2003, p. 33.

and therefore impossible to control. He identifies that this violence seems unspeakable to us, absurd, diabolical.[126]

In fact, it is also the coding and modelling of ideology. Based on this argument, Baudrillard draws the conclusion: "The characteristic, therefore, of our 'consumer society': This is the denial of the real on the basis of an avid and repeated apprehending of its signs."[127] We still do not know what the truth really is.

In *The Consumer Society*, the more important theoretical assertion is: Social production has been replaced by consumer society. Baudrillard believes that the traditional legend of the producer has given way to the consumer. This assertion in fact has another implication, that is, that the basic structure and foundation have moved from *Producer-Driven* towards *Consumer-Led* structure in contemporary capitalist society, which is the real argument that this book depends on.

First of all, qualification of material production and shaping is reversed in contemporary consumer society: "The production today exists depending not on the use value or durability but *on its death*, instead. As the commodity is to speed up death, the price of commodity will be definitely accelerated. Producing goods is in order to kill goods early."

Now, we know that the order of production only survives by paying the price of this extermination, this perpetual calculated 'suicide' of the mass of objects, and that this operation is based on technological 'sabotage' or organized obsolescence under cover of fashion. Advertising achieves the marvellous feat of consuming a substantial budget with the sole aim not of adding to the use-value of objects, but of subtracting value from them, of detracting from their time-value by subordinating them to their fashion-value and to ever earlier replacement.[128]

With regards to the point that the commodity is predestined to die, we have faced its theoretical convexity and focus in the last part of *The System of Objects*. Here Baudrillard only emphasizes that the relation between production and consumption is being reversed. The

---

126   Baudrillard, Jean, Chris Turner, and George Ritzer. *The Consumer Society: Myths and Structures*. Theory, Culture & Society. London: Sage Publications Ltd, 1998, p. 34, p. 35, p. 174, p. 175.
127   *Ibid.*, p. 34.
128   *Ibid.*, p. 46.

purpose of production and shaping is for the death of the commodity in consumption, not for functional utility. *Fashion logic* is a "built-in obsolescence"[129] game aimed at the consumer. At present, it is easy for us to see that people's daily lives are dominated by fashion. Fashion magazines are found throughout newsstands, airplanes and hotels; catwalk show appears on television every day; stars' lives are described in literature and movies and in TV dramas. All of the above force people to constantly purchase new but dying fashions by the other logic of desire.

In addition, "technical faults" and intentional *technical damage* ordered and produced by capitalists fundamentally take the place of production. (Raoul Vaneigem says: "The harder you run after time, the faster time goes: this is the law of consumption."[130]) Today, the defects intentionally built into commodities are not really problems related to quality. They are rather the convex deficiency highlighted in the differential relations of commodities. For example, before the Audi A6 was officially launched in Germany, a short-lived "pseudo A6" with 2.6L displacement appeared before the Audi 100 and 200 left the market. This pseudo model and its interior trim were a transitional improvement over traditional Audi 100. Its convex appearance was intended only to show off the advantages of the to-be officially launched new Audi A6. The result of technical damage unconsciously impels one to update fashionable goods. What a tragic-comic reality! (*For a Critique of the Political Economy of the Sign* further discusses the issue.) In this sense, Baudrillard believes that "the truth of consumption is that it is not a function of enjoyment, but a function of production."[131] Consumption replaces production, and it becomes production! (Later, he also points out the mortality of immaterial commodities. Art is becoming ephemeral, not in order to express the ephemeral nature of life, but to adapt itself to the ephemeral nature of the market.[132])

---

129   *Ibid.*, p. 100.
130   Vaneigem, Raoul. *The Revolution of Everyday Life*. Trans. Donald Nicholson-Smith. Rebel Press, 2001. p 155.
131   Baudrillard, Jean, Chris Turner, and George Ritzer. *The Consumer Society: Myths and Structures*. Theory, Culture & Society. London: Sage Publications Ltd, 1998, p. 78.
132   Baudrillard, Jean. *Cool Memories II, 1987-1990*. Trans. Chris Turner. Duke University Press, 1996, p. 51.

In the transitional part of Chapters One and Two, Baudrillard merely gives us a presentation of various problems extant in consumer society. At the end of the first section in Chapter two, we encounter an old friend, Marshall Sahlins, with his famous *Original Affluent Society*. This appearance triggers a new logical ordering. There is no doubt that Sahlins's main ideas are deeply influenced by Mauss. Baudrillard fully agrees with Sahlins's concept that in capitalist *productivity-oriented* society, needs are turned into "the very needs of the order of production, not the 'needs' of man."[133] (It should be noted that Baudrillard borrows the "productivity-oriented" concept from Sahlins. Here lies an important logical turn. In *The Mirror of Production*, he changes the concept into a vicious slogan against historical materialism.) In Baudrillard's eyes, Australian primitive tribes live an "affluent" life. People there have never possessed objects or material worries. They do not have our political economic concept of utility. They readily discard and consume anything they want. (In the following discussion, Baudrillard says that the primitive society does not have today's idea of time, like "time is money." To them, time is only the rhythm of existence, symbolic, unable to be abstracted or substantialized.[134] Further, in this symbolic-value dominated existence, "gold and money are excrement." Gold and money have the non-utilitarian "sacrificial function of excrement."[135] It is here that Mauss-Bataille's otherness problematic theory begins to become the most important thing in Baudrillard's theoretical and logical modelling.)

Baudrillard bemoans that the most valuable treasure in the primitive life is not material wealth but a *symbolic* social relation, which, unlike the chaotic and blind utilitarian possession of objects, is "transparent and reciprocal."[136]

In the economy of the gift and symbolic exchange, a small and always finite quantity of goods is sufficient to create general wealth since those goods pass constantly from one person to the other. Wealth has its basis not in goods, but in the concrete exchange

133   Baudrillard, Jean, Chris Turner, and George Ritzer. *The Consumer Society: Myths and Structures*. Theory, Culture & Society. London: Sage Publications Ltd, 1998, p. 66.
134   *Ibid.*, p. 153.
135   *Ibid.*, p. 155.
136   *Ibid.*, p. 11.

between persons. It is, therefore, unlimited since the cycle of ex-change is endless, even among a limited number of individuals, with each moment of the exchange cycle adding to the value of the object exchanged.[137]

What value? The symbolic value. (Here we come to the second stage of Baudrillard's symbolic concept. At this point, his under-standings on Mauss's symbolic exchange are obviously not very ac-curate. Actually, as symbolic relationships are not the *value*, symbol-ic exchange and gift then are not the *economy*! Therefore, this convex activation of academic memory is clearly a kind of misunderstand-ing in the young Baudrillard's thought construction. For Mauss-Bataille's logic, symbolic value itself is a *logical paradox*. Later, in *For a Critique of the Political Economy of the Sign*, Baudrillard puts forward symbolic exchange value in a negative sense, that is, "sign and value." However, the important thing is that he takes a crucial step here as he begins to *homogeneously* understand sym-bolic exchange. Interestingly, Baudrillard has not directly connected symbol with the authentic being, which is reversed by the consumer relations in his logic.) It is from this important reference point that Baudrillard begins his critique of "consumer society." His theoretic foundation or logical circuit is not Marxism. In his negation of the legitimacy of consumer society, Baudrillard does not adopt histori-cal materialism to criticize the capitalist exploitation system. On the contrary, he bases his theoretical framework on Mauss-Bataille's grassroots romanticism.

Baudrillard reveals the essence of the consumption logic as a symbolic manipulation with the following words:

The symbolic values of creation and the symbolic relation of inwardness are absent from it: it is all in externals. The object loses its objective finality and its function; it becomes a term in a much greater combinatory, in sets of objects in which it has a merely relational value. Moreover, it loses its symbolic meaning, its millennial anthropomorphic status, and tends to peter out into a discourse of connotations which are also simply relative to one another within the framework of a totalitarian cultural system (that is to say, a system which is able to integrate all significa-tions whatever their provenance).[138]

---

137   *Ibid.*, p. 67.
138   *Ibid.*, p. 155.

In other words, reactionary consumer pseudo-situating deprives man and object of real symbolic value; accordingly, people and objects are degraded to a useful exchange of values. Baudrillard takes sexual desire as an example, "once its total, symbolic exchange function has been deconstructed and lost, sexuality collapses into the dual use-value/exchange-value schema," and becomes a false consumption of sex fantasy.[139] (Please note that here we see the first instance where use value is placed into a negative context by Baudrillard, which is a logical foreshadowing for his criticizing use value in his *For a Critique of the Political Economy of the Sign*.)

In the last chapter of the book, a discussion of leisure, Baudrillard finally lets Bataille join the stage. He goes directly to late Bataille's *Accursed Share* and fetches the "gift exchange" found by Mauss. In his eyes, the real free time is the *exchange of meanings and symbols*, and the value of existence lies "in its very destruction, in being sacrificed."[140] At this time he still hopes that the consumer society in the white mass can be broken by the kind of May Storm of 1968 seen in France, and restored to a meaningful situation of human existence.

It is the *theoretical other* that supports the real logic of early Baudrillard's discourse in these two important works. As we know, *critiques against capitalism do not necessarily belong to Marxism.* They can also be rejections of the *capitalism* from a theological perspective, such as Blaise Pascal's, or anti-capitalist speculations based on oriental populism, as with Narodnik Nikolay Konstantinovich Mikhaylovsky. It is only in appearance that the young Baudrillard follows his leftist teachers in the critique of the capitalist system of objects and consumer society, with a slight adornment of post-Marxian thought. What lies at the core is Mauss-Bataille's grassroots romanticism. (The *reversed disordering logic*, to Baudrillard, is really self-conscious. In *Cool Memories IV*, he clearly identifies the so-called the almost timeless curvature of the space of ideas which obeys neither chronology nor history: "To reread the world of ideas against the grain of the ideology of the Enlightenment, the ideology of a chronological order of events."[141])

---

139   *Ibid.*, p. 150.
140   *Ibid.*, p. 157.
141   Baudrillard Jean. *Cool Memories IV: 1995-2000.* Trans. Chris Turner. Verso, 2003, p. 85.

In fact is that the young Baudrillard follows Mauss' (Sahlins')-Bataille's concepts from the very start of his theory building. Although he pays some superficial attention to Marxism in *The System of Objects* and *The Consumer Society*, it is only a background account made to pay respect to his teachers. The essence of Baudrillard's theory is a grassroots romanticism that is qualitatively and essentially different from Marxism. After *For a Critique of the Political Economy of the Sign*, which is a direct transcendence of Marxist political economy, the young Baudrillard quickly changes his post-Marxian position to one which is the opposite of Marxism. With the arrival of *The Mirror of Production*, Baudrillard has grown into an important theoretical opponent of Marxism. Unlike the late Lefebvre and Debord, or even Foucault, Deleuze, Derrida, and Pierre Bourdieu, Baudrillard since the 1970s never possessed any favourable impression about Marx, and he worships Mauss-Bataille's grassroots romanticism, sparing no effort in using the symbolic exchange of primitive societies to dethrone Marxism and the entirety of modern life. In my opinion, this self-righteous and absurd fantasy is doomed to fail.

PART ONE

THE SECRET OF THE SIGN: THE ILLUSION THAT MATERIAL EXISTENCE TRANSFORMING INTO A BUTTERFLY – A CRITICAL READING OF JEAN BAUDRILLARD'S *FOR A CRITIQUE OF THE POLITICAL ECONOMY OF THE SIGN*

CHAPTER I

The Sign Code in the Differential Practice of the Object

CHAPTER II

Illusory Needs behind Pseudo-consumption

CHAPTER III

From Commodity Fetishism to Signifier Fetishism

CHAPTER IV

"Revolution" of the Political Economy of the Sign

CHAPTER V

The Complex Logical Structure of the New Economics

CHAPTER VI

A Metaphysical Critique of the Use Value

CHAPTER VII

For a Critique of the Political Economy of the Sign and Ideologies

CHAPTER I

THE SIGN CODE IN THE DIFFERENTIAL PRACTICE OF THE OBJECT

From the shaping of the object to the sign code, Baudrillard must have taken a very difficult way in his theoretical exploration, changing his conceptual modelling several times. That process is almost a logical drama of "Transforming into a Butterfly" on the stage of sociology and semiotics, displaying a vivid transition of the objective social existence into the sign code. Baudrillard first chooses to perform the transformation of the differential practice of the object into the code of signs in social life. In fact, his trick is originally intended for the evolution of the objective object into the functional sign, during which he can also develop and reinterpret the logics in his previous *System of Objects* and *Consumer Society*. Unfortunately, he fails to understand that the human mode of dealing with the object is above all an integral part of the objective *ordering* system with specific significances in the actual existence of people, instead of a simplified subjective representation of the sign. In my opinion, Baudrillard's symbolic semiotics is essentially an idealistic mistake. After all, the sign only composes one of the elements for the subjective situating.

1 THE UTILITY OF THE OBJECT AND THE SOCIAL VALUE OF THE SIGN

Baudrillard's expansion to the new field dates back to an essay written in 1969: "Sign-Function and Class Logic," which becomes the first chapter of *For a Critique of the Political Economy of the Sign* later. (After careful investigation, the essay is found to be a year away from the publication of *The Consumer Society*. I believe that Baudrillard must have got some novel ideas in his composition at that time so he placed it as the first chapter in *For a Critique of the Political Economy of the Sign*.) In the essay, Baudrillard intends to criticize or falsify "the ideology of consumption" by "the surpassing of a spontaneous vision of objects in terms of needs and the hypothesis of the priority of their use value."[1] (The idea of "the ideology of consumption" is put forward in the later part of *The Consumer Society*, indicating their intertextual relationship.) Here, it is obvious that Baudrillard continues the discussion in *The System of Objects* and *The Consumer Society* but his falsifying tentacles now silently touch Marx. This time, it is the basis of use value that he wants to directly deny. (He has penetrated the non-functional logic of the mirror image proposed by Marcel Mauss and Georges Bataille as the utilitarian shaping and ordering exactly lead to the death of symbolic situating, which is a conspicuous logical rupture as well as an important turn in Baudrillard's understanding of symbolism.)

Thus, Baudrillard puts forward a new idea: The utilitarian function of the object results not from its own utility but from the *code of a specific social sign.*

> *Far from the primary status of the object being a pragmatic one which would subsequently come to overdetermine a social value of the sign, it is the sign exchange value (valeur d'echange signe) which is fundamental—use value is often no more than a practical guarantee (or even a rationalization pure and simple).*[2]

In the context of *The System of Objects*, we know that the object mentioned by Baudrillard is not a common natural thing but that being shaped and sent to the ordered social structure of the Heideggerian

---

1   Baudrillard, Jean. *For a Critique of the Political Economy of the Sign*. Trans. Charles Levin. St. Louis, MO.: Telos Press, 1981, p. 29.
2   *Ibid.*, p. 29.

In-der-Welt-sein (being-in-the-world), that is, the enframed thing centred on human existence. (As noted earlier, Heidegger's readiness-to-hand, called "用在性" by Hiromatsu Wataru, leads the object and Dasein to reified seiende/entity and existential alienation.) It can be felt that the more Baudrillard meets the object, the more he hates the specific utility of it. With the continual attempt to discover some new situation from the object's function in the circle of human life, he does make a crucial step forward. While the use value of the object is still treated as the carrier of symbolic relation in *The System of Objects* one year ago, it is reversed into an "exchange value" of the sign now. (In a deeper context, it is precisely the real beginning of his walk out of Marx as use value is nothing else but the basis of exchange value in Marxist economic theory.) As a result, *symbolic exchange* is singled out as the foundation for Baudrillard's philosophy, or, as the *authenticity* of the historical existence of human beings. Finally, Baudrillard finds the existential root of his own authenticity. (It just demonstrates the logic of otherness in a hidden grassroot humanism mentioned before. But Baudrillard immediately lays his cards here. Hence, if Mauss-Bataille as an academic memory cluster is the theoretical other, Baudrillard's compliance with the other is not an unconscious reflex but a deliberate and willing action. More importantly, Baudrillard is the first thinker to employ this logic for a profound reflection on the social life of contemporary capitalism. He nearly translates Bataille's metaphysical thought via the language of sociology.)

Next, Baudrillard naturally turns to exploring the situating meaning of the non-utilitarian Kula and Potlatch described in Mauss's *Gift*. (Here, he relies on Bronislaw Malinowski's anthropological field research of the aboriginal tribes in the Trobriands to delineate the social relation between the economic function, which already begins to divide, and the sign function. In fact, he pays more attention to the "symbolic exchange system." At this point, Baudrillard's interpretation of Mauss gets more accurate and comprehensive than that in *The System of Objects*.) In his view, the *non-economic* system of "social benefit" (prestation sociale) in the aboriginal tribes contains the social function of disseminating prestige and demonstrating hierarchy. (His explanation, however, is not correct since the aboriginal tribes do not have the same "prestige" and "hierarchy" as those of today.) When the symbolic exchange system disappears, contemporary society keeps or reproduces a novel *value* relation *comparable* to symbolic exchange besides the economic exchange value system, namely, the "symbolic" "exchange value" and the values of "social benefit," rivalry and class division. (It can be counted as the third stage of Baudrillard's modelling process of symbolic exchange, when symbolic *value* is no more positive, replaced by a negative pseudo-symbol, the modern deformation of the real symbolic exchange. It can be counted as a courageous self-criticism by Baudrillard. In addition, there is another textual detail that deserves attention: the positive *symbolic value* that emerges in *The Consumer Society* one year later, which, I speculate, might be rewritten to be included in For a Critique of the Political Economy of the Sign again; otherwise, a logical paradox would have occurred.) At the same time, these values belong to some consumption, irrelevant with human utility. Baudrillard cites an example: the "conspicuous consumption," discussed in *The Theory of the Leisure Class* by Thorstein Veblen, so as to illustrate reputation and social status. In this consumption, the object has got rid of specific utility to enter the new situating level of functional simulacrum. (Simulacrum here is still regarded as a common concept, not assuming the ontological category later defined in the context of *Symbolic Exchange and Death*.)

At this point, a new *quasi-spontaneity* begins to take shape in Baudrillard's logical modelling, where there are three social relation systems as follows. Firstly, Mauss-Bataille's symbolic exchange in aboriginal tribes. It initiates the identification for his logical ontology and basic problematic as a theoretical other, in which the object is a useless gift in the context of human existence. Secondly, the ordered economic system of use value and exchange value. It is well known as Marx's major analytical target, that is, the capitalist mode of production, which creates an economic domain by ordering and which made people addicted to the mysterious and abstract wealth of symbol–exchange value while ignoring use value. It should be pointed out that the exchange value here appears to be falsified. Thirdly, the *pseudo-symbolic* exchange value in today's life, which shakes off the object's utility and symbolizes more than exchange, usually connected with the pseudo-situating of the non-economic social significance, reputation and status. (It is obviously related to the academic memory of Veblen's convexity. In the following discussion, the second relation is again divided into two parts: the logic of use value and the logic of exchange value. Thus, Baudrillard gives a summary of four logics of social relations.) The third relation is the convex identification in contemporary capitalist social existence.

However, Baudrillard cannot figure out what is exactly in this pseudo-symbolic relation this time. What is certain to him might be: The *actuality* of the object shaped in the capitalist production transforms to an abstract *existence of signification*. This is a deceptive situating of social life. Baudrillard adds that here is the paradox and uncertainty of the object itself.

> So, under this paradoxical determination, objects are not the locus of the satisfaction of needs, but of a symbolic labour, of a "production" in both senses of the term: pro-ducers—they are fabricated, but they are also produced as a proof. They are the locus of consecration of an effort, of an uninterrupted performance, of a stress for achievement, aiming always at providing the continual and tangible proof of social value.[3]

There are two original concepts worthy of notice here: One is the symbolic labour and the other is the "proof" coexistent with production. (The former is not only a mixture in the logic of other but also a result of *intertextuality* between Marx and Mauss. Of course, both of these academic memories become the convex idea in their metonymic crossing.) Compared with the traditional labour, the symbolic labour here produces not useful shaped objects but the *signs of production* (symbols). (Baudrillard has not been as extreme as he does in *The Mirror of Production* years later because he is still using such concepts as "labour" and "production.") Clearly, the symbolic labour is fundamentally different from the working and shaping of the object that produces use value, while the alleged "proof" refers to a "continual and tangible" identification of some social value. Both of them are outside the system of use value and "exchange value" connected with needs; they are but used to pave the way for the later

---

3   *Ibid.*, p. 33.

development of the sign/value system. Baudrillard's identification, in my view, does make sense here except that he overstates the problem. It is true that the non-functional requirement and non-physical reputation exist today but they are not the real essence of social life in contemporary capitalist society. The reason why this essay is put in the beginning of *For a Critique of the Political Economy of the Sign* is to set up a mark for the theoretical source of his new thought.

Baudrillard's profoundness is not limited to define the code of the sign from the *other* side of the utilitarian object. It is not a direct transformation from the shaping of the object to the conceptual sign but an examination of the *non-physical* symbolic meaning of the object from the ordered function system itself, which accounts for his uniqueness against common linguistic semiotics. It should also be mentioned that Baudrillard's logical path starts not from the object relation (Marx's economic relationship) directly to the *presentational spectacle centred on a vista* but instead from the object's own *mode of practice* innately to the symbolic meaning that represents situation via the object, and then from this modelling sense to the object's non-physical symbolic meaning, which is different from the opinion of his teacher Guy Debord. (If interpreted in my discourse of situating, it is a transition from the *scene of the object relation* to a deeper and more dominant *scene of convex situation*.

But how can the object represent its own non-physical symbolic situation? Baudrillard finds the so-called differential practice (pratique) of the object: "It is certain that objects are the carriers of indexed social significations."[4] Thus, it can be seen that the practice of objects constitutes "a code" in Baudrillard's theoretical modelling at this moment.[5] (This practice will be discussed in detail later.) Meanwhile, there must be a medium: the functional simulacrum of the object. (At its initial stage, the conception of simulacrum has not entered Baudrillard's crucial academic category.) The simulacrum here refers to the substitution of the utility and order of the object by symbolic function. It constitutes a code, which then constitutes different ideographic discourses, behind which must be some grammatical structure of the *class*. Obviously, it displays a theoretical

---

4   *Ibid.*, p. 37.
5   *Ibid.*, p. 37.

tendency. At this moment, Baudrillard's theoretical modelling begins to abound with popular concepts of linguistics and discourse theory: "This discourse always expresses in this very syntax a neurosis of mobility, of inertia or of social regression."[6] Furthermore, a code of objects "is never spoken as such in any case (although it hides a strict social logic), but is always restored and manipulated according to a logic peculiar to each social situation."[7] Please note that the sign here is more of a *differential* signification represented by the object and its differential practice than an abstract linguistic mark of a concept. (It is the second time for Baudrillard's logical validation of the concept of differentiation after *The System of Objects*, which is not yet the anti-homogeneous uniqueness in the postmodernist context. Besides, it seems to me that Baudrillard changes his method of argument, employing *ideographic signs to govern objects* the other way around instead of simply transforming from the object to the ideographic signs in Chapter Ten, "Design and Environment," the last part of *For a Critique of the Political Economy of the Sign*. As he says, "The object only begins truly to exist at the time of its formal liberation as a sign function."[8] Baudrillard regards the emergence of the Bauhaus design school of the early 20th century in German as the inception of historical generation. For him, it is from the Bauhaus that we can have the "revolution of the object." In other words, before Bauhaus there is not the object. "It is the Bauhaus that institutes this universal semantization of the environment in which everything becomes the object of a calculus of function and of signification. Total functionality, total semiurgy."[9] From then on, everything becomes the object while the object becomes was the form of everything in functional structure. In this sense, the Bauhaus triggers another revolution after the Industrial Revolution and unintentionally marks the point of division where the political economy of the sign is born.)

In fact, the transformation from shaped objects to ideographic signs, as Baudrillard argues here, is truly the important way of qualitative ascending in social existence. He also correctly perceives the

---

6 *Ibid.*, p. 37.
7 *Ibid.*, p. 38.
8 *Ibid.*, p. 185.
9 *Ibid.*, p. 185.

new changes in contemporary capitalist society. However, his way of analyzing the problem lacks of an actual *historical* dimension and an internal logic, which produces a fatal defect on the fundamental base of his profound thinking.

So far, a new impression of Baudrillard takes shape in my mind. His brilliance lies in that he discreetly brings together various discourses of other, such as those of Saussure, Marx, Heidegger, Foucault and Debord. Prima facie, they do not take an independent appearance in the book, but the academic memories present them all in a faceless mode. (In *Cool Memories I*, Baudrillard admits "having subtly drawn my energy from the energy of others according to a mental law of derivation."[10]) The reactivation of the convexity of the integrated academic memories constitutes the base of Baudrillard's new ideas and the theoretical loop of his productivity. However, Baudrillard is unable to create his own discourse system of signifier and signified independently at this point. The road of a theoretical modelling before him is still long.

2 THE CODIFIED SOCIETY: THE DIFFERENTIAL PRACTICE OF OBJECTS

Thus, the differential practice of the object becomes the focus of Baudrillard's next analysis. (I think it just continues his previous theoretical thinking on the calculus of function of the shaped objects in *The System of Objects*. Deep in Baudrillard's mind, the academic memory of Heidegger is always in a convex state that is repeatedly activated.) Then what on earth is the differential practice of objects from Baudrillard's point of view? In my opinion, it means *a special mode of ordered presence in terms of how people acquire, utilize and fiddle with objects*, which is both Heidegger's secular readiness-to-hand and an instrumental variant of Marx's concept of practice, with an important difference here: It is no longer the shaping in the production process, but the practical mode of circulation, distribution and consumption (of the shaped object itself). However, for Baudrillard, the heterogeneous practice of objects (the presence of readiness-to-hand) has generated a new relationship of symbolic

---

10   Baudrillard, Jean. *Cool Memories I*. Trans. Chris Turner. London; New York: Verso, 1990, p. 38.

signs, and society has been reconstructed by the new order generated from the code. (Here, Baudrillard seems to create a new signification system, which is of course based on the activated academic memory of the semiotic and ideological critics of fashion by Roland Barthes.)

In order to elaborate his new viewpoint within the context of the discussion, Baudrillard starts with Francis Stuart Chapin's systematic studies on objects. We can see that Chapin, to whom Baudrillard referred, also links the object to the social status of human beings. But Chapin believes that the so-called social status is "the position occupied by an individual or family according to the dominant standards of cultural goods, of net revenues, of material goods and of participation in group activities of the collectivity."[11] Baudrillard does not agree. He criticizes Chapin's opinion for being "characterized by the most naive empiricism" because social strata are not simply defined with the *possession (distribution)* of "a balance-sheet of objects." In a pretentious tone, he says that Chapin's theory is obviously out-of-date as he fails to bring semiological elements and discourse analysis into his theory, in particular, Chapin leaves the analysis of the syntax of objects behind. (Here you can see how proud Baudrillard is by the discourse of other proposed by Saussure and Lévi-Strauss. It is not Baudrillard's original theory to reconstruct the mirror of social criticism with a semiological discourse for his teacher Roland Barthes has done a lot of research before.) Baudrillard gives the instruction that for people today, social distinction has "passed from possession, pure and simple, to the organization and the social usage (pratique) of objects," and the index of social strata had taken form in "a more subtle semiology of the environment and of everyday practices."[12] The development from the simple possession of wealth (objects) to the practice of objects, from the richness of objects to the semiology of signification analysis in the practice of survival consists of the new idea that Baudrillard takes pride in.

> The problem then will be on the one hand to make a coherence emerge between the relative position of a given object, or ensemble of objects on the vertical scale, and on the other hand the type of organization of the context in which it is found and the type

---

11   Baudrillard, Jean. *For a Critique of the Political Economy of the Sign.* Trans. Charles Levin. St. Louis, MO.: Telos Press, 1981, p. 34.

12   *Ibid.*, p. 34.

of practices connected with it. The hypothesis of coherence will not necessarily be justified: there are barbarisms, lapses not only in the formal discourse but in the social discourse of objects. It is not only a question then, of noting them in the structural analysis, but of interpreting them in terms of logic and of social contradictions.[13]

Traditional sociologists must feel confused about the above words, which are probably used to mean that people's practice bring objects into an intersectional and complicated modelling of relations: One is a vertical structure, called by Baudrillard as "a semiological analysis"; the other is a horizontal relation structure, namely, the series of "topoanalysis." These two relations structure the stratification standard of modern society. (Such analysis seems unmatched to Saussure's classic semiotics. The previously clear boundaries between synchronism and diachronism become vague by Baudrillard's intertextual "innovation" here. After a careful investigation, I do not think he forms a complete logical circuit here.)

Nevertheless, Baudrillard feels good about himself. He believes that his thought directly exposes a *profound social discourse of objects* represented by their practice. In traditional society, People's status and identity are often symbolized by the sum of objects that they possess, but nowadays humans construct the whole social environment with the practice of objects at hand. And they even directly model the structure of activities in their existence, during which, the practice of objects generates a certain social signification, and gradually transforms into a code situating that is *tacitly understood* by a particular stratum in social existence. "Objects are the carriers of indexed social significations, of a social and cultural hierarchy—and this in the very least of their details: form, material, colours, durability, arrangement in space—in short, it is certain that they constitute a code."[14] Baudrillard takes an attitude different from that in our past common senses. In his eyes, contemporary social life is not the *objective existence* of objects but the situating of social life constructed through practice, signification and various convex codes. He questions, "Is it through these objects, rather than through one's children, friends, clothing, that one indicates a demand for conformity, for

13   *Ibid.*, p. 35.
14   *Ibid.*, p. 37.

security, or rather, what sort of ambition, and through what category of objects?"[15] (Here, Baudrillard is rewriting Marxist historical materialism and Heidegger's ontology. As a result, the objective relations of society and Dasein are thoroughly replaced by Baudrillard's code.)

It is not easy to understand what exactly Baudrillard wants to express here. I would like to take several examples for explanation. With Baudrillard, although there are no born aristocracy and populace in today's social strata of the capitalist society, the stratum cannot be simply defined by the possession of property. For example, some people in China become rich overnight through extraordinary ways, but it does not mean that they can enter a new stratum that they do not belong to. Recently, in the city of Nanjing, a place where I live and the gap between rich and poor is not very obvious, a number of expensive scarlet BMW Z4 Coupes and MINI Coopers roared in the streets. Those fair young ladies alighting from these cars spoke rudely and behaved vulgarly. Most ordinary people in Nanjing nicknamed them the "mistress cars," instead of admiring their possession of such expensive cars. (Of course, not all owners of these cars are mistresses). It is the same with people wearing luxury suits, jewelleries, expensive watches and so on. The decisive factor that enables these people to acquire social status is not the possession and convexity of those things but the mode of utilization ("practice") of them in certain concave points of social life. (In my understanding, whether can the object depend on its real situating determines the innate acquisition of the social status.) Baudrillard wants to illustrate that the object's considerate interdependence on human beings can display a special *tacit* discourse and situating only to people from the same stratum and of the homogeneous life, and it is this discourse of code and modelling that constructs different social structures.

Baudrillard claims that he has found "a code of objects, which is never spoken as such in any case (although it hides a strict social logic), but is always restored and manipulated according to a logic peculiar to each social situation."[16]

---

15   *Ibid.*, p. 37.
16   *Ibid.*, p. 38.

> *Thus objects, their syntax, and their rhetoric refer to social objectives and to a social logic. They speak to us not so much of the user and of technical practices, as of social pretension and resignation, of social mobility and inertia, of acculturation and enculturation, of stratification and of social classification. Through objects, each individual and each group searches out his-her place in an order, all the while trying to jostle this order according to a personal trajectory. Through objects a stratified society speaks and, if like the mass media, objects seem to speak to everyone (there are no longer by right any caste objects), it is in order to keep everyone in a certain place. It tries to place each person into a particular position. In short, under the rubric of objects, under the seal of private property, it is always a continual social process of value which leads the way. And everywhere and always, objects, in addition to utensils, are the terms and the avowal of the social process of value.[17]*

The object, no longer in a simple objective existence, does not even compose an ordered "ready-to-hand" world with the endless links of utilitarian function. Instead, the object has a mandatory relation with a *syntactic structure of the codified society*, which cannot be directly comprehended by human beings. (Later, Baudrillard says it is a "strong symbolic chain, the one through which a victim of the whim of a superior power passes it on to an inferior species, the whole process ending with someone taking it out on a powerless simulacrum, like a toy-and beginning no doubt with an all-powerful simulacrum, like the masked divinities which men themselves invent to justify this wretched chain."[18] So God will tell human beings, "You are the second master on the earth," which is a legal recognition of human enslavement of objects.) In this sense, *the practice of objects in turn determines social existence and models all the social life*, generating social strata and the situating of upper and lower classes. However, it is a profound idea with mistakes.

This crucial practice of objects identifies itself not by a qualitative stipulation of itself by but by a new *systematic differentiation*, which, obviously, contains some new meanings here. In the following part, we might as well read the specific description by Baudrillard.

---

17   *Ibid.*, p. 38.
18   Baudrillard, Jean. *Cool Memories I.* Trans. Chris Turner. London; New York: Verso, 1990, p. 116.

For example, during the collapse of feudal strata, the bourgeoisie cannot change their status according to their wealth. They have to rely on the practice of the object to "translate the immanence of a jurisdiction which in appearance is rejected,"[19] that is, they must own the special convexity of utilitarian things to symbolize their ascendance in social status. (Later, in *Symbolic Exchange and Death*, Baudrillard employs counterfeit, the first level of simulacra, to identify the process that the bourgeoisie change their symbolized status through the counterfeit of signs.) It is also precisely the nature of the non-aristocratic civilian presence. Baudrillard claims that there is a special way that the object manifests itself, symbolizes values, and covertly judges the social classes. Obviously, this is a secret method used by the bourgeoisie to celebrate their victory and obtain the seemingly unreachable social recognition. (Baudrillard believes that in primitive tribes, the special "exhausting" of objects in Kula and various potlatches symbolizes "a provocation, a competition, a challenge. But it is also a rite, destined to evince an order of values, a rule of the game, in order to be integrated by it."[20] This is surely a restatement of Mauss's "spiritual mechanisms," only with Baudrillard's failure to recognize its erroneous recognition. In comparison, the practice of objects in modern capitalist society distorts the signification system into a ridiculous "simulation logic," namely, "a simulation of the bourgeois models of domestic organization."[21] Simulation is also a *pseudo-situating*. Here, term is used in its first categorical application as well as the identification of the bourgeois aesthetic paradigms, however, like simulacrum, both of them have not been realized in the ontological category.) For example, the bourgeoisie are clearly different from the petty bourgeoisie in the spatial structures of their residence. "The bourgeois house is closed upon itself and full like an egg," while "along the same line, the petty bourgeois interior is indicated by congestion."[22] And in terms of house decoration and housekeeping, people from different social strata will choose different decorative styles (a special fixed structure in the practice of objects). (It is not difficult to see that Baudrillard means

---

19   Baudrillard, Jean. *For a Critique of the Political Economy of the Sign*. Trans. Charles Levin. St. Louis, MO.: Telos Press, 1981, p. 40.

20   *Ibid.*, p. 41.

21   *Ibid.*, p. 41.

22   *Ibid.*, p. 41.

not the existential form of the object itself but man's way of dealing with objects.) He points out:

> *The varnished object is satisfying for a vast socio-cultural category because it appears as the synthesis of a conspicuous morality, summarizing the two imperatives of the prestation of prestige (sign exchange value) and of the prestation of merit (productivity and use value), inconsistently on the formal level but according to a closely knit social logic.*[23]

The examples cited by Baudrillard are intended to illustrate that each stratum has its own specific practice of objects in a larger ordered organization model and it is the differential ordering that signifies the unique existence of different social strata in modernity.

In this regard, Baudrillard also performs an interesting analysis of the bygone object, which is already discussed in *The System of Objects*. The bygone, collected and carefully appreciated by people, has lost the traces of industrial production and the pragmatical function that is formerly shaped.

> *For all these reasons the taste for the bygone is characterized by the desire to transcend the dimension of economic success, to consecrate a social success or a privileged position in a redundant, culturalized, symbolic sign. The bygone is, among other things, social success that seeks a legitimacy, a heredity, a "noble" sanction.*[24]

In the process of collecting the bygone, the privileged stratum "were trying to transmute their economic status into inherited grace,"[25] while some intellectuals expressed and simulated the "emblematic of a past prior to industrial production"[26] through the collection of the bygone or old books. This is a typical example to display the "taste" beyond the reality of objects through the differential practice. (The so-called *taste* constructs the strict cultural distinction of signification among the social strata. Taste cannot be obtained through external imitation. It is the tacit discourse of signification and the situating of existence.) Baudrillard says, "Their

---

23   *Ibid.*, p. 45.
24   *Ibid.*, p. 43.
25   *Ibid.*, p. 43.
26   *Ibid.*, p. 44.

social function is first to be distinctive signs, to be objects which will distinguish those who distinguish them."[27] He warns us not to take the practice of objects for granted because it is the beginning of the ordered re-coding of social existence, in which "one must perceive a cultural logic of mobility."[28] In Baudrillard's own opinion, he just needs to make "a semiological analysis of the world of objects."[29]

For the fashionable things and discourse, Baudrillard almost adopts the same method of analysis. (It is an important field of discussion started by Barthes.) Baudrillard holds that the nature of the issue is to tackle "their (objects) status in time, their cycle of erosion and renewal."[30] Different categories of objects in people's arrangement and lives have "a variable longevity," or they "wear out at different rates."[31] There are mainly two elements that greatly affect the life span and durability of objects: One is their actual rate of wearing out, which is determined by the structure and material during shaping; the other is the accelerated obsolescence due to the *changes of fashion.* According to Baudrillard, the second element is more important in today's life, "What is important for us here is this second value and its relation to the respective situation of groups in a stratified and mobile industrial society. How does a given group distinguish itself by a more or less strong adhesion to the ephemeral or to the durable? What are the various responses of different groups on the social scale to fashion's demands for accelerated renewal of objects?"[32] (This issue, already discussed in *The Consumer Society: Myths and Structures*, is re-activated here by Baudrillard in a profound situating, with a changing perspective that is more theoretical.)

We may see that the longevity of objects in the fashion chains mostly relies on the "constraints of social differentiation and prestige"[33] instead of the changes of their natural demands.

---

27   *Ibid.*, p. 48.
28   *Ibid.*, p. 44.
29   *Ibid.*, p. 47.
30   *Ibid.*, p. 49.
31   *Ibid.*, p. 49.
32   *Ibid.*, p. 49.
33   *Ibid.*, p. 49.

Ascending or descending social status must be registered in the continual flux and reflux of distinctive signs. A given class is not lastingly assigned to a given category of objects (or to a given style of clothing): on the contrary, all classes are assigned to change, all assume the necessity of fashion as a value, just as they participate (more or less) in the universal imperative of social mobility. In other words, since objects play the role of exhibitors of social status, and since this status has become potentially mobile, the objects will always simultaneously give evidence not only of an acquired situation this they have always done), but also of the potential mobility of this social status as such objects are registered in the distinctive cycle of fashion.[34]

Baudrillard believes that when people's social status ascends, they would inevitably symbolize the changes through the renewal of objects: "unable to change the apartment, one changes the car."[35] This renewal is based on the symbolic meaning of the code instead of the practical function of objects. (It has gradually become a social trend in today's China, too.) Of course, the renewal of objects is sometimes deliberately manufactured, under whose circumstance the "death" of the object merely depends on artificial renewal rather than their specifically shaped effect. Sometimes, the object "comes to compensate the social inertia of a certain group or individual whose disappointed and thwarted desire for mobility comes to register itself in the artificial mobility of decor."[36] Therefore, "it is even clearer that the accelerated renewal of objects often compensates a disappointed aspiration to cultural and social progress" as man "falls back upon them, and objects often translate, at the very most, his frustrated social aspirations."[37] They are very incisive remarks on the social life of contemporary capitalism. (There is a mirror of other similar to historical phenomenology down the end of Baudrillard's thought. In fact, he has been unconsciously imitating Marx, who directs people to see through the economic and materialized relations to find out the hidden domination and exploitation relations behind them, while Baudrillard follows Debord's theory of mirror image to turn the object into a spectacle, then turn spectacle into a symbolic code, representing the new ruling power. It is an interesting

---

34   *Ibid.*, p. 49.
35   *Ibid.*, p. 50.
36   *Ibid.*, p. 50.
37   *Ibid.*, p. 50.

phenomenon that Marx seems to become the most significant theoretical other in Baudrillard's criticism of capitalism. Perhaps, it is in
this context, that people mistake Baudrillard's thought for Marxism
and even identify it as Marxism, which is but a superficial understanding of him.)

Baudrillard adopts the differential practice of objects, namely,
the renewal of objects in fashion, residence and the bygone collection, to identify certain invisible social signification system and the
unique existential situating of the bourgeoisie. He even believes that
this signification system of objects codifies and differentiates the life
of modern capitalist society on a deeper level.

3 SOCIAL DISTINCTION AND THE ILLUSION OF CONSUMPTION THAT HIDES CLASS ANTAGONISM

Based on Baudrillard's logical thinking, the signification analysis of an object or the purpose of semiological analysis, has another
important sociological function: the *social stratification* or *social
distinction*. (It is a typical sociological issue.) "So, the paradigmatic
oppositions…are not only the instruments of a semiological analysis
of the world of objects, but are also social discriminants, characteristics which are not only formally distinct but socially distinctive."[38]
In order to find "a more differentiated hierarchical classification"[39]
in the present pyramid structure of society, Baudrillard insists that
the sociological analysis is not just an analysis of logics but should
be an *ideological analysis of politics*. It is correct. Baudrillard says,

> *In other words, the distinguishing function (distinctive) of objects
> (as well as of other systems of signs relevant to consumption) is
> fundamentally registered within (or flows into) a discriminating
> function: thus the logical analysis (in tactical terms of stratifica-
> tion) must also open onto a political analysis (in terms of class
> strategy).*[40]

---

38   Baudrillard, Jean. *For a Critique of the Political Economy of the Sign.* Trans.
Charles Levin. St. Louis, MO.: Telos Press, 1981, p. 47.
39   *Ibid.*, p. 52.
40   *Ibid.*, p. 53.

These words only complicate the issue. To illustrate this matter, Baudrillard manages to distinguish two different ways of practice: One is the realistic practice of shaped objects that we have already known; the other is the *ritualistic* practice of objects. In my understanding, if the former is the intention expressed in the process of dealing with objects; the latter is the path to social integration and recognition. (At the beginning of this book, Baudrillard identifies the latter as a "proof" in parallel with production.) Baudrillard claims, "It is the social theory of the sign-object that we wish to dwell on here, in the perspective of consumption."[41] Here, he employs the "practice" of "TV-object," an example very familiar to people, as the main target of analysis.

Baudrillard presumes, in previous sociological studies, people's main concern on television is images and media discourse, while ignoring the fact that people's buying TV is not just out of their interest in image information and the needs of entertainment. He cites Stuart Mill's view, identifying that behind the possession of an object, there is a socialized function: proof.

> *As a certificate of citizenship, the TV is a token of recognition, of integration, of social legitimacy. At this level of almost unconscious response it is the object that is in question, not its objective function—and it no longer has an objective function, but a proof function. It is a social exhibitor and is given values as such: it is exposed and overexposed.[42]*

The implication is that, as a shaped object, TV's function of information transmission and entertainment is only external; it also has another layer of profoundness in nature, namely, the possession of TV as an index "of social membership." It is a very interesting proposal. (After all, it was a phenomenon in Europe in 1970s, the television Baudrillard mentions has apparently lost such function as social stratification today.) Baudrillard says, "The TV object is sanctified as such apart from its function as communication, that one indulges in systematic, non-selective viewing."[43] It is true that people can freely criticize the boring content and fancy forms of television programs but they are inevitably involved in a passive

---

41   *Ibid.*, p. 54.
42   *Ibid.*, p. 54.
43   Ibid., p. 55.

and compromising style at the same time, which proves the ritualistic practice of objects proposed by Baudrillard. In this process,
people are always in "a more profound social constraint—that of
symbolic prestation, of legitimation, of social credence, of *mana*."[44]
So he states in a hyperbolic way that every scene in television is a
progressive coma without tomorrow. In this way, the "TV-object"
"refers to a socio-economic imperative of revenue production, to the
object as capital,"[45] which strikingly contrasts with the positive description of mass media by Marshall McLuhan. (This view easily
reminds one of Debord's critique on McLuhan in his *Society of the
Spectacle*. But the academic memory of this convex point is more
radically activated here.)

It is not difficult to find that during the discussion on the TV-
object, Baudrillard's logical focus unconsciously wanders in an instant absent-mindedness. I have a new concept to explain this phenomenon: *logical strabismus*. (It happens in a situation where saying
A is actually meaning B.) He first uses the television-object to illustrate a "proof" in social stratification. As he runs on, his thinking
migrates to the *subordination* and assimilation of the consumption
culture during the practice of objects in society.

It is that of a resigned and accultured class *whose demand for
culture*, following a relative social promotion, is *conjured in objects
and their worship* or at least in a cultural compromise governed by
the economic and magical constraints of the collectivity. It is the
face and very definition of consumption.[46]

Baudrillard is good at the critique of consumption. But here he
regards consumption as the ideological fantasy that hides social antagonism. From his point of view, in the illusions created by the
bourgeoisie, "it is absurd to speak of a consumer society as if consumption were a system of universal values appropriate to all men because of being founded upon the satisfaction of individual needs."[47]
What is more insidious is that the bourgeoisie present consumption
as "a democratic social function," even creating such illusions as

---

44 *Ibid.*, p. 56.
45 *Ibid.*, p. 56.
46 *Ibid.*, p. 56.
47 *Ibid.*, p. 62.

"(the leitmotiv of the ideologies of consumption) that its function is to correct the social inequalities of a stratified society."[48] In fact, consumption, as a system of universal values, is just another means to cover class antagonism and the control of society. Moreover, there is a slave morality hiding in the concave point. Therefore, it is in this way that consumption is and will be "an element of the strategy of power in any society, past or future."[49]

For Baudrillard, the attitude of traditional sociology towards consumption is quite disappointing.

> *Here sociology is most of the time both a dupe and an accomplice: it takes the ideology of consumption for consumption itself. Pretending to believe that objects and consumption (as formerly moral principles or religion) have the same meaning from top to bottom of the social scale, it accredits the universal myth of status and on this basis goes on sociologizing, pondering, stratifying and correlating things at statistics' whim.*[50]

Baudrillard is apparently criticizing the reflectionless positivistic path represented by the American sociology. Because in this positivistic study of consumption, sociologists only face the change of needs in consumption based on different statistical data. However, is consumption in contemporary capitalist society really a universal necessity? Baudrillard takes the strategic concept of Europeanization as an example for illustration. He first cites "the *Reader's Digest Selection* survey of "the consumers' Europe: 221,750,000 consumers (Common Market and Great Britain)"[51] carried out in 1967. According to the survey, the EC residents appeared to represent "a homogeneous group crossing all borders," having "a common model of consumption."[52] The indicators of social stratification are: "luxury equipment (dishwasher, tape recorder, camera, etc.), luxury foods, comfortable living quarters, toiletries for women, basic household equipment (television, refrigerator, washing machine, etc.), cleaning products, everyday food, male toiletries and intellectual curiosity (voyages abroad, speaking a foreign language)!"[53] According to

---

48   *Ibid.*, p. 58.
49   *Ibid.*, p. 62.
50   *Ibid.*, p. 62.
51   *Ibid.*, p. 58.
52   *Ibid.*, p. 58.
53   *Ibid.*, p. 59.

this system of consumption index, people are divided into groups of A's or non-A's. Baudrillard keenly discovers that the political, social, economic and cultural *differentiation* disappears without leaving a trace in the system of positivistic indices, only replaced by the same mechanical consumption. In the eyes of statistians, the antagonism between classes is conjured away, and the radical difference between the "company president and ordinary salaried employees" is wiped out, or, there is not any actual social distinction but a grand illusion of "middle class."

> *From top to bottom of the scale, no one is inexorably cut off by distance. There are no more extremes, no more tension: the formal frontier between the A's and the non-A's is there only to better prime the aspiration toward the higher level and the illusion of a general regrouping to take place sooner or later in the paradise of A.*[54]

When the logic of social contradiction vanishes, all the homogenous consumers fantasize about transferring to group A from group non-A as soon as possible. (I am afraid this is also the common phenomenon that coexists in China's economical and sociological study of consumption today.) And Baudrillard insightfully points out, with the cover of harmonious and universal illusions of consumption, there is a deeper and stronger intention of control, that is, the European bourgeois strategy of solidarity in global competition. "This very real solidarity disguises itself in the formal solidarity of the consuming masses (so much the more formal in that its indices, the goods of consumption, are more 'concrete'). European Community is materialized and spatialized, revealing itself in the living room and ice cream."[55] The will of the big bourgeoisie in Europe is realized through the commonest living consumption, being objectified and modelled in food consumption such as ice cream and in every other detail of living consumption. However, statistics in the sociological positivistic study often generate an ideological cover since the real social stratification and class antagonism are hidden. Therefore, we must "search beyond figures, statistics and the study itself, for what it does not wish to express, for what it wishes to hide. Its secret is that consumption, with its false social appearance, veils

54 *Ibid.*, p. 60.
55 *Ibid.*, p. 59.

the true political strategy, and is thus one of the essential elements of this strategy."[56] This is still Baudrillard's phenomenological critique of society.

Baudrillard believes that the ideology of consumption itself contains a slave morality, because people are generally immersed in "enjoyment, immoral and irresponsibility."[57] In fact, in such consumption of food, drink, clothing and housing that appears to have no value orientations, the strongest slave morality of the bourgeoisie is generated and imposed on people at every moment. Baudrillard is very insightful here. Apparently, from the direct clue of his theoretical situating, these views are quite close to the Frankfurt School's cultural criticism of capitalism in the 1950s and 1960s instead of simply depending on Marxism. (However, at the end of Chapter One, we cannot find the least trace of Saussure's and Bataille's otherness. Does Baudrillard really take the discourse of Marxism or Western Marxism? Let us set this mystery aside for the time being. We shall deal with it in detail later.)

56   *Ibid.*, p. 61.
57   *Ibid.*, p. 62.

CHAPTER II

ILLUSORY NEEDS BEHIND PSEUDO-CONSUMPTION

Baudrillard's critiques of the consumer relations of the capitalist economic structure is undoubtedly the most profound and influential theories to appear since Marxism and also the Frankfurt School. If Hegel's *Phenomenology of Mind* transforms objects' idealism into direct misrecognition and falsity, then Baudrillard criticizes the bourgeois consumption concept so as to wipe out the consumable things as they exist in people's common sense. In his view, the object in the market economy's consumer relations substitutes the death of authentic being for people's needs. Needs and desires derived from barter are only ideologically shaped illusions. In pseudo-situating, consumers as well as consumer needs disappear, and so too do consumable things. Everything is reduced to the illusion and pseudo-mirror in the differential system of sign and symbol. Thus, capitalist "consumer society" transforms into "sign society." Baudrillard later even coins a slogan, "Sign is the highest level of commodity development." Although the general direction of Baudrillard's theoretical critique is correct, he ultimately fundamentally takes the wrong path.

1 THE CONSUMABLE THING IS NOT THE THING ITSELF

In the previous chapter, Baudrillard's reflections on "the consumer society" aim at roughly describing people's general practice on objects in daily life. Then he describes the mutual waxing and waning back and forth between the utility of shaped objects and signs. However, in Chapter Two, *The Ideological Genesis of Needs* (1969),[1] he makes a further theoretical deduction regarding the logical process in which object transforms into sign. This time, he focuses on the *consumer illusion*, which dominates the life of the bourgeoisie. His own theoretical modelling takes an even greater step forward, but it is a step closer to idealism. (In addition to Debord's critical inquiry into modern consumption, Lacan's academic memories of pseudo-desires begin to quietly play a supportive role.)

On the platform of academic theoretical research, Baudrillard always comes straight to the point. According to his critiques, humans living in capitalist commodity-market society today indulge in the "exciting satisfaction created by consumption." This satisfaction is directly attached to the object. We already know that the so-called matter here refers to people in the mad chase of consuming various goods. However, Baudrillard says:

> *We believe in "Consumption": we believe in a real subject, motivated by needs and confronted by real objects as sources of satisfaction. It is a thoroughly vulgar metaphysic. And contemporary psychology, sociology and economic science are all complicit in the fiasco. So the time has come to deconstruct all the assumptive notions involved—object, need, aspiration, consumption itself.[2]*

In the context of Heidegger, Baudrillard's "metaphysic" is a derogatory term. In this special metaphysical consumption, the consumer goods that people desire and the possession of these goods are identified as *pseudo-life situating* on the subjective illusion. All the "real subjects," as well as objects, consumption, needs, and expectations have become the object of Baudrillard's deconstruction. Differing from his teacher Debord, Baudrillard randomly

---

1   First published in *Cahiers Internationaux de Sociologie*, 1969.
2   Baudrillard, Jean. *For a Critique of the Political Economy of the Sign*. Trans. Charles Levin. Telos Press Publishing, 1981, p. 63.

deconstructs the *ready-to-hand world*, which is a differentially *interlocked* consumption. Debord merely identifies the transition from the goods kingdom to the spectacle kingdom. This radical step is a kind of Lacanian deformation on Baudrillard's original thought logic and theoretical modelling.

In the previous article, we read Baudrillard's new opinion on objects; therefore, it is not surprising to re-encounter these sentences:

> The **empirical** *"object"* is a **myth (mythe)**. How often it has been wished away! But the object is nothing. It is nothing but the different types of relations and significations that converge, contradict themselves, and twist around it, as such—the hidden logic that not only arranges this bundle of relations, but directs the manifest discourse that overlays and occludes it.[3]

Here Baudrillard appropriates Lacan's thinking. Hegel's thoughts play a supportive role in a deeper context. Hegel's *Phenomenology of Mind* comes straight to the point that "object," in terms of intuitive experience, is a constructed false image. Lacan radically changes this image into nothingness. However, Hegel still admits the individual presence of limited "passion." Lacan states that individual subject is the mirror-image of pseudo-other nothingness, based upon ontology. Thus the open space of ontology is constructed by the symbol (according to Lacan symbol itself is the nothingness and the corpse of being.[4]). As a result, life is all along an alienated illusion and trick. (Baudrillard disagrees with Lacan's symbolic concept, only linking negatively Lacan's falsification of the symbolic concept with his own symbolic exchange value. He absorbs Lacan's the very critical concept, that is, "the desire of the Other's desire." After all, the latter is the discourse through which Alexandre Kojève interprets Hegel.[5] This concept is a new complex thought in the third stage of Baudrillard's symbolic concept.) The academic memory activated in his mind shows that Lacan's logical problematic is no more a closed theoretical circuit.[6] He audaciously uses Lacanian logic to openly criticize consumer relations and consumable things in the capitalist social life.

---

3   *Ibid.*, p. 63.
4   See Chapter 5 in my *Impossible Truth of Being: Mirror of Lacan's Philosophy.* Commercial Press, 2005.
5   *Ibid.*, Chapter 9.
6   *Ibid.*

Therefore, it is possible that objects in human life are a kind of "cultural existence," according to Baudrillard. The essence of shaped objects is the transformation of meaning into non-objects while the essence of consumer goods is a signified logic (Logique des Significations). In this sense, the object is spoken of as functionally decontextualized.[7] Of course, the concept so-called *"the name of the object is not the object itself"* can be also understood in the context of late Heidegger's das ding dingt (exists-as-thing). However, Baudrillard is obviously getting rid of Heidegger's hidden moral education, totally turning to the deconstruction logic of symbolic relationships. There is another intertextual simile. As with Lacan, Baudrillard embraces his *negative ontology of relation*. But he incorporates Lacan's falsification of individual's ontology of relations into the negative deconstruction of consumer goods. As I once mentioned, Marx's concept that the essence of the individual is the ensemble of the social relations in reality was rewritten by Lacan, but for whom the essence of the individual is the ensemble of the pseudo mirror and dead symbol relationship between the Other and other. Baudrillard, however, deems that consumer goods are not any more real entities or symbolic exchange of authentic beings. Rather, they are the totality of the differential relationships of consumer pseudo-situating generated from the object's practice and series. The above, of course, is the falsification logic of existence *going to death*. (Surprisingly, although Baudrillard's words here are not many, an extremely complicated process of thought situating has nevertheless been realized. A multitude of other resources such as Heidegger, Lacan, and Marx have all been integrated into a new framework. Overall, Baudrillard's problematics are still a mirror-image in otherness; however, they are not simply the academic memory cluster outside. Reflecting on the mirror-image of others, he forms his own unique critical field. Thus, it becomes possible for him to draw and inspect the essence of the contemporary capitalist consumption. At this time, his deep logical mirror is still Mauss-Bataille's problematics, but he is obviously beginning to possess his own autonomous thinking. He is on the way from other structure to spontaneous intellectual modelling.)

---

7   Baudrillard, Jean. *For a Critique of the Political Economy of the Sign.* Trans. Charles Levin. Telos Press Publishing, 1981, p. 63.

To illustrate his point, Baudrillard takes refrigerators as they used in daily life as an example. (This is second time he gives an example of refrigerator.) He says that when the refrigerator is only used as a machine, ordinary people fail to inspect its deep essence, which is that the refrigerator is not the object. *Not being the object* means that it is *not* the Heidegger's primitive object of *das ding dingt*. Firstly, the refrigerator in use is the object of consumption. Its whole function (content) is "qualified by its exclusive relation with the subject, who then cathects it as if it were his own body (a borderline case)." The name, refrigerator, represents the identification of functional relations. In other words, in the meaning of the natural things' primitive existence, all factors which constitute the refrigerator are absent from the situation of ontology. The refrigerator is the pseudo-image constructed by anthropocentrism's for us relations in the object's fragment. (This idea is romantic and illusionary nonsense. If the object exists as the primitive object, human history would never have begun.) Secondly, as a non-thing object, the refrigerator is an object specified by its trademark (MARQUE[8]), charged with differential connotations of status, prestige, and fashion.[9] This idea is still the conception of non-thing shaping. (The so-called trademark matters very much as it later links the brands of the consumer goods. It is indeed a real problem.) "The 'consumption' of the object occurs in the context of its brand name, which is not a proper name, but a sort of generic Christian name."[10] (In Lacan's words, it is in the name of the capitalization and the Father. In the later *The Mirror of Production*, Baudrillard totally denies every capitalized concept without exception.) Thirdly, the symbolized trademark moves the refrigerator away from material existence and toward a sign identifying position.

---

8   Baudrillard capitalizes the marque in the book. Marque in French has several meanings, including mark, sign, symbol, brand, trademark. It means the object is special as it can be symbolized. Here I translated it into trademark. —The translator.

9   Baudrillard, Jean. *For a Critique of the Political Economy of the Sign.* Trans. Charles Levin. Telos Press Publishing, 1981, p. 64.

10   In the logic of the commodity, all goods or objects become universally commutable. Their (economic) practice occurs through their price. There is no relationship either to the subject or to the world, but only a relation to the market. *Ibid.*, p. 69.

Each social status will be signified by an entire constellation of exchangeable signs. No necessary relation to the subject or the world is involved. There is only a systematic relation obligated to all other signs. And in this combinatory abstraction lie the elements of a code.[11]

Please note that this is also a new point! Connected with the problem discussed in the previous article, the object will also generate a symbolic value besides utility. This point is a new code construction. (Above, the context presents as "explanation" and "production" side by side.) According to Baudrillard, the acquisition of the latter value has nothing to do with the relationship between the object and people (utility). Even "this object does not assume meaning in an operational relation to the world," which means that it is unrelated to the object's Being in the world. "It finds meaning with other objects, in difference, according to a hierarchical code of significations. This alone defines the object of consumption."[12] When the last curtain is pulled back, the object of consumption appears immediately— Baudrillard metaphysically beats around the bush. What he really wants to say is: the object of consumption is *not* the object itself. He takes great pains to operate logical modelling. Firstly he incorporates Lacanian problematics into the social consumption structure, then he identifies that the object of consumption is the pseudo-relationship constructed by the exchange sign. Therefore, the object of consumption is nothingness. The pseudo-situating is not nothingness in the meaning of objective entities, but is positioned in the object's functional relationships. In this sense, the object of consumption is an important step towards the death of the object.

2 DEGRADATION FROM THE SYMBOLIC EXCHANGE INTO THE SIGN VALUE

Here, in order to elaborate his theoretical innovations, Baudrillard first positively turns to the Other theory that is his lifeblood—Mauss-Bataille's grassroots romanticism. Thus, the symbolic exchange, the *true* existence relationship between human beings, at last directly becomes a logical convexity. (This is the main theory at the third stage of the understanding of symbols. Another explanation should

---

11   *Ibid.*, p. 68.
12   *Ibid.*, p. 64.

be made that in Baudrillard's thought modelling here, the symbolic exchange originating from Mauss-Bataille is heterogeneous to the Lacanian symbolic field of signs, because the former is a true existence, while the latter is a construction of the pseudo-subject Big Other. This language symbol system's ideological inquiry about subjects, in Baudrillard is probing into the consumption structure, directly manifests as the pseudo symbolic value controlling and manufacturing consumption. If the symbolic exchange is real, then the symbolic exchange value (sign value) will be the pseudo-reality generating from the sign exchange in contemporary capitalist society, and it is also the predecessor of the concept simulation proposed by Baudrillard afterwards with a very complex logic modelling and transformation relationship. Later, Baudrillard often, in this *having-been* sense, talks about the murder and death of reality (Réel = symbolic exchange).) In Baudrillard's view, a gift is not an ordinary object in gift exchange in the primitive tribes revealed by Marcel Mauss, as it can neither be divorced from the specific relationship where the exchange happens, nor the transferred part in exchange—symbolic presence (the divine "hau" found by Mauss), and more importantly, it "has neither use value nor (economic) exchange value." In this connection, gifts are arbitrary. (Obviously, this arbitrariness is Baudrillard's own activated academic memory, namely his theoretical transformation of the arbitrariness of Ferdinand de Saussure's signifier and signified.) However, as a material carrier of gifts different from the arbitrariness of language symbols, "the material of symbolic exchange, the objects given, are not autonomous, hence not codifiable as signs. Since they do not depend on economic exchange, they are not amenable to systematization as commodities and exchange value."[13] In comparison to Georges Bataille's philosophy abstract, Baudrillard's instruction on symbolic exchange here seems to be a closer approximation to a sociological interpretation. However, he still says in a pretentious tone:

> *What constitutes the object as value in symbolic exchange is that one separates himself from it in order to give it, to throw it at the feet of the other, under the gaze of the other (ob-jicere); one divests himself as if of a part of himself—an act which is significant in itself as the basis, simultaneously, of both the mutual*

---

13   *Ibid.*, p. 64.

presence of the terms of the relationship, and their mutual ab-
sence (their distance). The ambivalence of all symbolic exchange
material (looks, objects, dreams, excrement) derives from this:
the gift is a medium of relation and distance; it is always love
and aggression.[14]

These instructions on the theory of symbolic exchange may constitute the most important and thorough theoretical interpretation of
Mauss that I have ever seen after Bataille. Obviously, Baudrillard
specially sets out an important property for the symbolic exchange,
namely *a property of uncertainty with infinite possibility*. (In the
notes specifically made for this passage, Baudrillard cites the symbolic and uncertain exchange relationship that may come from
Lévi-Strauss, while, interestingly, he does not recognize that Lévi-
Strauss's concept of symbolism is built on criticism and negation of
Mauss's theory. I notice that in the subsequent text Baudrillard adds
more and more notes with much more detail.)

In the overall logic, Baudrillard first establishes the symbolic exchange relationship as the gauge of theoretical logic (the true "ought
to"), then begins to describe the alienation and degradation of objects from the true symbolic exchange to the sign value of *symbolism of evil*, which is actually one of the most difficult items to understand in Baudrillard's theory. Symbolic exchange refers to the
ideal true existence of human beings, which is a good symbolism in
Baudrillard's mind, while the entire consumption structure under the
control of codes in today's society simply appears as a sign value exchange relationship in approximation to symbol. However, this exchange relationship is the symbolism of evil, because the symbolic
sign presence here is just the Lacanian death of being. It should be
noted, particularly that here also is the real beginning of true existence's (symbolic exchange) Murder Trilogy by Baudrillard, where
an important link in Baudrillard's logical concave has been omit-
ted: during the transformation from symbolic exchange to utilitarian labour shaping, the use value of material shaping only starts to
give way to the code modelling in exchange value in the ordered
economic structure of modern capitalism. (Here, we can clearly

---

14   Thus the structure of exchange (cf. Lévi-Strauss) is never that of simple reciprocity. It is not two simple terms, but two ambivalent terms that exchange, and the exchange
establishes their relationship as ambivalent. *Ibid.*, p. 65.

recognize the dominant role of the mirror-image in Otherness by Mauss-Bataille, which also is the most important theoretical circuit at a deep level in Baudrillard's theoretical ordering. Meanwhile in his understanding of Mauss-Bataille, Baudrillard has reunified the disjointed signifier and signified, and comes to realize that *symbolic exchange is not the economy, and symbols cannot be valued*. He has indeed done things beyond the ability of Mauss-Bataille—that is, he critically examines the entire capitalist consumer society with symbolic exchange as the gauge of value. In this connection, in the space of Baudrillard's Other thought, there is also a certain part of autonomous thinking.)

Baudrillard points out that in the modern consumption relationship, or, when the exchange of objects is no longer a gift-like "purely transitive," the object may become the sign. (It should be noted that this is the symbolization occurring in the commodity exchange instead of the previous function-code of objects displayed in the practice of people's general livings, and the originally denigrated link of shaping-utilitarian object now directly disappears.) Here, the object "becomes autonomous, intransitive, and opaque." The original symbolic relationship constituting the scene of *true* existence in gift exchange has been completely abandoned, and the symbolic exchange in the modern consumption structure is a new symbolism of *evil* with the function of constructing a deceptive pseudo-situating. According to Baudrillard's theory, Mauss's social relationship appearing in gift exchange is *transparent*, however,

> In the commodity, on the other hand, we perceive the opacity of social relations of production and the reality of the division of labour. What is revealed in the contemporary profusion of sign objects, objects of consumption, is precisely this opacity, the total constraint of the code that governs social value: it is the specific weight of signs that regulates the social logic of exchange? In the commodity, on the other hand, we perceive the opacity of social relations of production and the reality of the division of labour. What is revealed in the contemporary profusion of sign objects, objects of consumption, is precisely this opacity, **the total constraint of the code** that governs social value: it is the specific weight of signs that regulates the social logic of exchange.[15]

---

15   *Ibid.*, p. 65-66.

There are two levels of issues here: first, the object is opaque in the commodity exchange, the relationship between objects is the reversal of the relations between human beings according to Marx's theory, and this is a fetish illusion. Second, in the present consumption relationship, the opaqueness of the object is deformed into the sign object (L'objet-signe), creating the charming object of desire. (Compared with the mysterious table standing upside down described by Marx, Baudrillard here just shifts to the perspective of semiotic argument.) Baudrillard believes that "the sign object only refers to the absence of relation itself," and this is understandable in Lacan's sense, but there are ambiguities in the exact relationship of absence referred to by Baudrillard himself. Literally, his words seem to identify in the commodity exchange the object, which "is appropriated, withheld and manipulated by individual subjects as a sign, that is, as coded difference. Here lies the object of consumption. And it is always of and from a reified, abolished social relationship that is 'signified' in a code." In accordance with his previous definition, this "social relationship" occupied by the code should be the direct communication and situating of symbolic meaning between human beings.

> *The object-become-sign no longer gathers its meaning in the concrete relationship between two people. It assumes its meaning in its differential relation to other signs. Somewhat like Lévi-Strauss's myths, sign-objects exchange among themselves. Thus, only when objects are autonomized as differential signs and thereby rendered systematizable can one speak of consumption and of objects of consumption.[16]*

Perhaps Baudrillard intends to illustrate that in the consumption relationship of contemporary capitalist society, the object has lost its original direct communication of meaning among human beings seen in the originally true symbolic exchange, and now generates a new semantic scene, which is neither from the object nor from the human beings, but comes from the differential relationship between the object as the consumption sign and other sign objects. (An explanation should be made that although Baudrillard keeps asserting that his ideas are different from linguistics, in fact the differential sign theory in this structure was after all invented by Saussure. The referent composed of signifier and signified in language signs by

---

16 *Ibid.*, p. 66.

Saussure does not point to the target, but depends on the differential relationship in the language sign system. Here, convexity of the concept difference has obviously ascended.) Baudrillard clearly regards the differential sign situation of the symbolism of evil constructed by objects in the consumption relationship as the essence of modern consumption. The essence of "the consumer society" is the sign kingdom.

Thus, Baudrillard identifies consumption as *"a logic of the sign and of difference."*[17] (This is still the metonymic reactivation of the academic memory of Saussure.) In Baudrillard's eyes, this important new logic is entangled with other social relationships and difficult to identify, and hence he makes a significant demarcation, namely the so-called distinguishment of four logics in the contemporary social life:

> *1. A functional logic of use value; 2. An economic logic of exchange value; 3. A logic of symbolic exchange; 4. A logic of sign value. The first is a logic of practical operations, the second one of equivalence, the third, ambivalence, and the fourth, difference. Or again: a logic of utility, a logic of the market, a logic of the gift, and a logic of status. Organized in accordance with one of the above groupings, the object assumes respectively the status of an instrument, a commodity, a symbol, or a sign. Only the last of these defines the specific field of consumption.*[18]

If Baudrillard only unconsciously discusses the three types of social relations in the previous article, then here he consciously extracts *four logics* from the modelling of capitalist social relationships. As this view is indeed a very important, I quote the full text of Baudrillard's elucidation of the four logics. I think that this statement can be regarded as the most critical *point of autonomy* in the early turning of Baudrillard's thought, because it is *the abrupt emergence of new thought situating*, where Baudrillard commences in constructing his own independent problematic theory. Different groups of academic memories coming from Karl Marx, Saussure, and Mauss-Bataille once again are all reconstructed by Baudrillard here, and he further constructs his own critical logic facing life in contemporary capitalist society. It is also in this logic reconstruction

17   *Ibid.*, p. 66.
18   *Ibid.*, p. 66.

that a new theoretical circuit is generated in Baudrillard's thinking, initiating the transformation from the original space of mirror-image in Otherness to the space of autonomous thought. In my opinion, this is *the first significant Gestalt transformation* in the Baudrillard's theory and thought ordering. (The second thought situating of Baudrillard appears in *Symbolic Exchange and Death*, in which Baudrillard achieves the real theoretical innovation and logical détournement, completing the original situating of thought. We will specifically discuss it in this regard in the next section of the book.)

It is easy to see that in Baudrillard's four logics, the symbolic exchange of gifts is the philosophical ontology of the self-conscious otherness or *the suspending of true value*, and we already know that it still derives from the mirror-image of Mauss-Bataille's grassroots romanticism so adored by Baudrillard. The other three logics are to be falsified, because they all belong to an important step of symbolic exchange's walk towards death: first, the logic of market deriving from the "exchange value" is a capitalistic paradigm that has been falsified by Marx, where Baudrillard obviously agrees with Marx's criticism and where he just identifies that it also could no longer be regarded as the critical prism in today's capitalist consumer society. Second, Marx does not negate the logic of pragmatical production shaping determined by the use value, and this is incisively questioned by Baudrillard, and later *to be* completely negated by him. (This negation is undertaken subsequently in the *Mirror of Production*.) Third, the logic of status (difference) symbolized by the *symbolic value* is a new critical logic where Baudrillard faces today's capitalist life, and it is also his logical orientation towards the essence of consumption relationship. However, the other three logics are intertwined with each other in the real capitalist consumption relationship, and they possess a different status in Baudrillard's heart. The first logic discovered by Marx, namely the logic of markets based on economic exchange value, is recognized by Baudrillard. The second logic, namely the pragmatical logic based on the use value, was overlooked by Marx, while Baudrillard vaunts it as his own unique discovery, because only after the deformation of symbolic existence into functional usefulness can shaped objects enter the market. Furthermore, the essence of exchange value has already become the symbolic abstract—the closer to the contemporary, the more domi-nance that the status (difference) of symbolic value obtains. The third logic elicited by the sign, a theoretical discovery made by Baudrillard by means of Saussure's theory, is the focus of discussion in this book and of the criticism of the political economy of the sign, and as it is the most important part of Baudrillard's autonomous thought, he specially identifies: "only the last of these defines the specific field of consumption."

Here, Baudrillard takes different rings as an example to illustrate this complex logical structure. Wedding rings are the same as any or-dinary rings in terms of material existence, but once having entered the marriage situating between people, these rings are immediately constructed as a symbolic gift, and their presence will lose any secu-lar pragmatical value, thereafter only symbolizing the non-utilitarian marriage between the couple. "The symbolic object is made to last and to witness in its duration the permanence of the relationship." A person wears a wedding ring for the symbol and suggestion of marriage rather than for elegance, and the non-utilitarian symbolic relationship always constructs the life situations between the couple, while in the consumption relationship, the ring as a general con-sumption object does not symbolizes a particular relationship: "It is a non-singular object, a personal gratification, a sign in the eyes of others. I can wear several of them. I can substitute them. The ordi-nary ring takes part in the play of my accessories and the constella-tion of fashion. It is an object of consumption."[19] It is apparent that objects of consumption *are not objects*, so rings in the fashion sense are signs among the numerous different relationships. (In fact, when a Chinese girl wears a fashionable ring on her left index finger, it is a symbolic suggestion of her singlehood, which could construct a new love situation.) Therefore, all the objects, if breaking away from their own symbolism and "succumbing to the differential and reified connotations of fashion logic," will become objects of consumption (objet de consummation). "The definition of an object of consump-tion is entirely independent of objects themselves and exclusively a function of the logic of significations."

---

19   *Ibid.*, p. 66.

> *An object is not an object of consumption unless it is released from its psychic determinations as symbol; from its functional determinations as instrument; from its commercial determinations as product; and is thus liberated as a sign to be recaptured by the formal logic of fashion, i.e., by the logic of differentiation.*[20]

Baudrillard completes his logical magic here. After some operations, the reality of thingness becomes the signification, and *objects transform into signs*. In fact, we can also see that the so-called transformation from objects to signs by Baudrillard does not refer to the actual situations in our daily life where the thingness of objects disappeared, but simply means that compared with the relationship of the human subjects, the differential logic or series relations of fashion modes are displayed as *dominant convex* faces after objects of consumption break away from the former three logics. I think that Baudrillard's idealist mistakes are gradually generated in the over-interpreted transgression judgment, which, in Lenin's words, "exaggerate the curve in the cognitive structure into the line". The mistake is also the "one-sided deepness" paradigm of the so-called modern Western rationality. (Here, there is a point worthy of notice in the thought construction, that is, a "psychological" dimension has been added to the concept of the symbol.)

Therefore, when Baudrillard inappropriately defines the object in the so-called four logics as the consumption symbol, he reinforces this "great" discovery from several perspectives. (Here we find the real basis that he later relies on in order to criticize Marx's historical materialism.) Baudrillard says that in this sense the key issue is, instead of the shaped object itself, "of the codes that it puts into play (sign systems and distinctive material)" with a dominant role in the presence of the object of consumption. (We can see that the so-called logic of code is neither a simple reproduction of Saussure's linguistic system, nor a general appropriation of Lacan's symbolic field dominance, but rather another successful reactivation and ordered reconstruction of academic memory by Baudrillard.)

If there is no particular operation of codes in Baudrillard's theoretical system, then there is no object of consumption. (Later, he makes an important extension of this cause-effect logic, that is, *if there is no*

---

20   *Ibid.*, p. 67.

exchange value, then there is no use value. Baudrillard uses this extension in his accusation against Marx. In this way, the relations among
the four logics are reconstructed, because the second logic relies on
the first one. In other words, it is the exchange value system that determines and generates the use value, or the logic of the market generates the pragmatical logic. This result follows thought his thought's
evolution inevitably.) Baudrillard believes that the logic of code here
is a new *Big* Social Order, which "demands not only the renewal of
distinctive material, but the obligatory registration of individuals on
the scale of status, through the mediation of their group and as a function of their relations with other groups."[21] (Here, the concept of Big
is used derogatorily by Baudrillard, and in the subsequent *Mirror of
Production* he also criticizes Marx's concepts of "the Big History,"
"the Big Nature" and so on. This criticism also belongs to the poststudy context originating from the logical falsification of the concept of
Big by the German philosopher Stirner in the 19th century.)[22] This new
social order is by Baudrillard called the *differential symbolic hierarchy*,
and he clearly identifies the individual's acceptance of it, that is, "the
interiorization by the individual of signs in general (i.e., of the norms,
values, and social imperatives that signs are) constitutes the fundamental, decisive form of social control—more so even than acquiescence
to ideological norms."[23] (This change is the most significant qualitative change from the consumer society to the sign kingdom.) Differing
from Louis Althusser's theory of ideological inquiry, Baudrillard discusses the social control of human beings with consumption modelling in the sphere of economics or sociology instead of talking about
the bourgeois domination from the perspective of discourse control or
psychological domination. However, consumption control in real life is
achieved through the sign code, and it is on this point that Baudrillard
sees eye to eye with Althusser. The shocking thing is that Baudrillard,
like Althusser, incisively exposes the fact that the force of this new
form of social control is much stronger than that of external ideological
control exerted on human beings in the past.

---

21   *Ibid.*, p. 68.
22   See "Section Three" in the fifth chapter of *Back to Marx: The Philosophical
Discourse in the Context of Economics* (Jiangsu People's Publishing, 1999.). English
version published by Göttingen University Press, in 2014.
23   Baudrillard, Jean. *For a Critique of the Political Economy of the Sign.* Trans.
Charles Levin. Telos Press Publishing, 1981, p. 68.

3 FALSE CONSUMPTION AS A DIFFERENTIAL EXCHANGE SYSTEM

After the deconstruction of the object of consumption, Baudrillard then needs to falsify the consumption itself, because he believes that consumption from the very beginning in the bourgeois society is a scam woven by illusions. We all know that there is a market relationship consisting of consumption subject, need, and consumption object extant in any kind of consumption activity, and previously Baudrillard has sentenced the object of consumption to death (codified), but now he intends to shift his emphasis to the falsification of consumption subject and need.

Baudrillard points out that subject and object are treated as two separate entities in consumption. Need is what connects the two entities. In fact, this relationship is a metaphysical myth. "Subject, object, need: the mythological structure of these three ideas is identical" (This is the activated academic memory of Lévi-Strauss's mythology, where the reality in ancient social life is often situated in a reverse way by the symbolic mythological structure. It is also a critical rewriting of Marcel Mauss's voodoo situating theory.)

First of all, the consumption subject is a pseudo-subject formed by "a gigantic tautology" of ideological situating. (This view is rather similar to Lacan-Althusser's pseudo-subject theory originating in the Big Other inquiry, and in Lacan's context, the subject is constructed by the tautological inquiry of the Big Other; meanwhile, it is also the falsified inversion of Marx's "a sum of all social relation in terms of reality:" human essence is a sum in the form of a ideological tautology, while individual subject, need, and consumption object are all constructed in this illusion.) The concept *tautology* symbolizes a homogeneous "specular" relationship. (This tautology, if exclusive of its derogatory property, is quite similar to the function of the closed *theoretical circuit* in the otherness thought that I have mentioned.) Baudrillard says,

> *The operation amounts to defining the subject by means of the object and the object in terms of the subject. It is a gigantic **tautology** of which the concept of need is the consecration. Metaphysics itself has never done anything else and, in Western thought, **metaphysics and economic science (not to mention***

traditional psychology) demonstrate a profound solidarity, mentally and ideologically, in the way they posit the subject and tautologically resolve its relation to the world.[24]

In Baudrillard's eyes, subject and object are just objects of ordering in this ideological tautology. "Such run-arounds are always the rationalizing ideology of a system of power: the dormant virtue of opium."[25] (Baudrillard's views here may easily remind people of the alienated concept of *the everyday* by Karel Kosík.)[26]

Additionally, demand is also the product of the pseudo-construction of this tautological ideology, because, in Baudrillard's view, demand in consumption is no more than the existing "reproductive finality of the order of production," and not the real needs of human beings. (Lacan says that my desire is actually desirous of other people's desired objects, while in Baudrillard's theory here, the desire of the Other is directly generated from the illusion of consumption in the market. Consumption is dominated by illusion, and maintains production and reproduction.) However, Baudrillard knows the difference between people's physical demand and need; for instance, it is real physical demand a man feels when hungry, a demand which cannot be satisfied by pseudo-symbolic need. "Hunger as such is not signified, it is appeased. Desire, on the other hand, is signified throughout an entire chain of signifiers. On the other hand, the desire is to refer to the entire chain can be symbolic." The need is specific to the desire, where Baudrillard intends to emphasize the produced symbolic need in consumption.

> *People discover **a posteriori** and almost miraculously that they need what is produced and offered at the marketplace (and thus, in order that they should experience this or any particular need, the need must already exist inside people as a virtual postulation). And so it appears that this begging of the question—this forced rationalization—simply masks the **internal finality** of the order of production.[27]*

24 *Ibid.*, p. 71.
25 *Ibid.*, p. 71.
26 See "Section Four" in the fourth chapter of *A Deep Plough: Unscrambling Major Post-marxist Texts* (People's University Press, 2004).
27 Baudrillard, Jean. *For a Critique of the Political Economy of the Sign.* Trans. Charles Levin. Telos Press Publishing, 1981, p. 71.

This statement implies that consumers feel urgent desire for things because they are controlled by a force in an invisible concave, instead of their own actual needs. To be specific, in stores people continuously "discover" many novel consumer goods in the visual convexity (for example, today's Chinese market is flooded with a variety of health care products that enable people to "live longer" and cosmetics which make people "younger," as well as high-end SLR cameras, mobile phones, plasma TVs, and so on to show people's identity and status), and they mistake these goods for their own real needs. However, these goods are actually produced by the embellished capitalist order of production. This *continuous discovery* is produced by advertising and other media spectacles in an endless tautology. "Tautology is at work everywhere." The key point is: in this tautology the capitalist, *"naturalizes the processes of exchange and signification,"* and "a second nature that really exists" comes into existence here, turning embellished need into a "naive anthropological" hypothesis. The fake desire of the Other is tautologically constructed as one's original need that is seemingly real. It goes without saying that consumption constructs a pseudo-reality situation, while we suddenly become "successful" (VIP customers) in it. (What Baudrillard has critically identified actually occurs around us at the present. Some high-end shopping centres, such as Nanjing Golden Eagle Shopping Centre, Deji Plaza, and Jinling Department Store, attract a group of loyal "VIP" consumers. It firmly controls them with discounts, bonus points, and cash back deals, and these "VIP" consumers almost daily receive circulars and text messages about the latest information on products and promotions, up to and including birthday greetings sent by the businessmen who assert, "Your needs are our concerns." This seems to be a naturalized people-oriented concept.) Baudrillard believes that "the entire question of the social and political finality of productivity is repressed" because of "the meretricious legitimacy of needs and satisfactions." I think that Baudrillard is very astute in his analysis as consumption is a kind of politics. (In Lacan's sense, this manifests as "pseudo-needs"[28] constructed by the desire of the Other, while Baudrillard successfully politicizes the "pseudo-needs.")

28 See *The Impossible Truth of Being: Mirror of Lacan's Philosophy*. Commercial Press, 2006. Chapter Nine.

In Baudrillard's eyes, in the "tautological" construction of the pseudo-world of consumption, the most important instrument is *differential* logic, whose fundamental basis is *differential production* in society, which aims at prestige and status. (The prototype academic memory of differential production is Ferdinand de Saussure's differential generation of meaning, although in his theory meaning is not an object referent, but a combination of differential relations among signs. However, we soon discover the traces of Lacan's Other theory here. It is also a new theoretical peak in the development of Baudrillard's concept of difference.) Baudrillard says,

> *There is no doubt that **individuals** (or individuated groups) are consciously or subconsciously in quest of social rank and prestige and, of course, this level of the object should be incorporated into the analysis. But the fundamental level is that of **unconscious structures** that organize the social production of differences.*[29]

In Baudrillard's view, each individual or group in today's consumer society feels compelled to "produce themselves meaningfully in a system of exchange and relationships," even before basic survivals are guaranteed. In this sense, "in a way, the individual is non-existent (like the object of which we spoke at the beginning)."[30] Indeed, we are no longer surprised that here Baudrillard again naturally turns people into nothing, just as he turns his previous objects into signs. (In the context of Lacan, this is also logical and reasonable.) We can predict that the presence of the Lacanian argument will soon reveal itself. Baudrillard says, for human individuals,

> *This language is a social form in relation to which there can properly speaking be no individuals, since it is an exchange structure. This structure amounts to a logic of differentiation on two simultaneous planes: 1. It differentiates the human terms of the exchange into partners, not individuated, but nevertheless distinct, and bound by the rules of exchange. 2. It differentiates the exchange material into distinct and thus **significant** elements. This language is a social form in relation to which there can properly speaking be no individuals, since it is an exchange structure. This structure amounts to a logic of differentiation on two simultaneous planes: 1. It differentiates the human terms*

---

29   Baudrillard, Jean. *For a Critique of the Political Economy of the Sign*. Trans. Charles Levin. Telos Press Publishing, 1981, p. 74.

30   *Ibid.*, p. 75.

of the exchange into partners, not individuated, but neverthe-
less distinct, and bound by the rules of exchange. 2. It differen-
*tiates the exchange material into distinct and thus **significant***
elements.[31]

With Lacan, the so-called structured language system is the
Lacanian *Big Other*, a "structure without individual existence," because human beings are no more than an illusion of mirror-image
projection of the language exchange structure. There are no individual subjects, only differences in the exchange structure, and such
differences refer to the signification relationship in a mutually distinguished series instead of the differences among the shaped thingness. People are just a *negative totality*, or in my words, a pseudo-
situating of this differential relationship. It goes without saying that
Baudrillard's socio-historical viewpoints are completely heterogeneous to Marx's views of *construction* (human essence is the sum of
all social relations); in a certain sense, the former looks like Lacan's
anti-constructivism, namely the viewpoints that human beings are a
pseudo-phase constructed of a signification relationship.

However, in contrast to Lacan's metaphysical psychology or psychoanalysis, Baudrillard's critique indeed points to real social existence. In his eyes, "consumption is exchange," just as in the language
system an individual can talk, but cannot explain the secret of the
formation of the language matrix, "language—not as an absolute,
autonomous system, but as a *structure of exchange* contemporane-
ous with meaning itself, and on which is articulated the individual
intention of speech." (If Saussure, Barthes, and Lacan say, "It isn't I
who utter the words, it's the words which utter me," then here what
Baudrillard says is, "It isn't I who consume goods, it's the goods
which buy me." Besides, Woolf's words also sound somewhat familiar: "It isn't girls who wear clothes, it's clothes that wear girls."
Cartier-Bresson says: "It isn't I who take pictures, it's pictures which
shoot me." In the subsequent *Cool Memories IV*, Baudrillard continues this thinking with the following contradictory expression, "It
isn't the man who drinks the tea, it's the tea which drinks the man.
It isn't you who smoke the pipe, it's the pipe which smokes you.
It's the book which reads me. It's the TV which watches you. It's

---

31   *Ibid.*, p. 75.

the object which thinks us. It's the lens which focuses on us. It's the effect which causes us. It's the language which speaks us. It's time which wastes us. It's money which earns us. It's death which lies in wait for us.")[32] The same thing also happens in consumption:

> *Consumption does not arise from an objective need of the consumer, a final intention of the subject towards the object; rather, there is social production, in a system of exchange, of a material of differences, a code of significations and invidious (statuaire) values. The functionality of goods and individual needs only follows on this, adjusting itself to, rationalizing, and in the same stroke repressing these fundamental structural mechanisms.[33]*

Baudrillard makes it clear that meaning, like the language system, comes from the differential order between the signifier and signified instead of subject or object. (This logical migration follows the identification of Saussure's mirror-image.) In consumption, meaning never comes into existence in economic relations,

> *The origin of meaning is never found in the relation between a subject (given a priori as autonomous and conscious) and an object produced for rational ends—that is, properly, the economic relation, rationalized in terms of choice and calculation. It is to be found, rather, in difference, systematizable in terms of a code (as opposed to private calculation)—a differential structure that establishes the social relation, and not the subject as such.[34]*

Here meaning refers to, instead of conceptual semantics, the one constructed by consumption subject, of need as well as of consumption object and so on. In short, the secret of consumption lies in a specific *system of differential relations*.

To explain his viewpoints, Baudrillard cites Veblen, and claims that Veblen illustrates "how the production of a social classification (class distinctions and statutory rivalry) is the fundamental law" that "arranges" and subordinates all the other logics, whether conscious, rational, ideological, moral, etc. Then, Baudrillard takes leisure time, which is often discussed by Veblen, as an example to illustrate the issue. Baudrillard says generally "leisure may be defined

---

32 Baudrillard, Jean. *Cool Memories IV: 1995-2000*. Trans. Chris Turner. Verso Books, 2003, p. 22.
33 Baudrillard, Jean. *For a Critique of the Political Economy of the Sign*. Trans. Charles Levin. Telos Press Publishing, 1981, p. 75.
34 *Ibid.*, p. 75.

as any consumption of unproductive time," while substantially, leisure is only a specific symbol used by people to verify their social
status. Herein lies the behind-the-scene truth, which is that "no one
needs leisure, but everyone is called upon to provide evidence of his
availability for unproductive labour." (Coincidentally, Guy Ernest
Debord also undertakes a comparatively deep discussion of this
issue.)[35] In leisure time, people actually have no real freedom and
real needs, and they "need" to *do nothing*, which symbolizes a kind
of social value. The real purpose of people's leisure activities in contemporary life is that

> *He must verify the uselessness of his time—temporal surplus as
> sumptuous capital, as wealth. Leisure time, like consumption
> time in general, becomes emphatic, trade-marked social time—
> the dimension of social salvation, productive of value, but not of
> economic survival.*[36]

> *People are divided into different groups according to this divid-
> ing line: people possessing non-production time are deemed to
> be of high status out of the labour field; otherwise, they become
> production workers of the lower status. Baudrillard writes in his
> book that the differential division of the leisure class analyzed by
> Veblen surpasses all the other rules in material exchange and cir-
> culation, and is another type of value, that is, the sign exchange
> value based on the differential relations. In this regard, the sign
> exchange in differential relations surpasses the economic value
> exchange based on the thingness function order and enters the
> exchange structure situated by symbol/value. (It is not difficult to
> find that Baudrillard here regards Veblen as the first scholar to
> focus on people's fame and status through differential relations
> in the sociological studies.)*[37]

---

35   See "Section Two" in the second chapter of *A Deep Plough: Unscrambling Major
Post-marxist Texts* (Renmin University Press, 2008). English version by Canut Intl
Publishers, London, 2010.
36   "Free" time brings together the "right" to work and the "liberty" to consume in
the framework of the same system: it is necessary for time to be "liberated" in order to
become a sign-function and take on social exchange value, whereas labour time, which
is constrained time, possesses only economic exchange value. Cf. Part I of this essay:
one could add a definition of symbolic time to that of the object. It would be that which
is neither economically constrained nor "free" as sign-function, but, that is, inseparable
from the concrete act of exchange—a rhythm. Baudrillard, Jean. *For a Critique of the
Political Economy of the Sign*. Trans. Charles Levin. Telos Press Publishing, 1981, p. 77.
37   Cf. Thorstein B Veblen, *The Theory of the Leisure Class*. Forgotten Books, 2008.
Chapter Three.

Another example is fashion. In various fashionable objects, fundamental is the replacement of symbolic differences among the fashionable items. "Fashion is one of the more inexplicable phenomena, so far as these matters go: its compulsion to innovate signs." The essence of fashion is an arbitrary and incessant production of differential meanings, and "the logical mystery of its cycle" precisely lies in its everlasting symbolic production of self-discrepancy. (In *The System of Objects*, this differential production is called "series." Apparently, the difference concept is becoming more and more important in Baudrillard's logical modelling at this time.) Specifically, in order to beautify themselves, girls always enjoy the transformation in the fashion difference between micro-miniskirts and dresses. However, "beauty" in the fashion is actually an interpretation, in brief "the rationalization—of the fundamental processes of production and reproduction of distinctive material" and they are bound to continuously manufacture the differential "beauty" fantasy in order to make money off of girls.

> *Thus fashion continually fabricates the "beautiful" on the basis of a radical denial of beauty,* **by reducing beauty to the logical equivalent of ugliness**. *It can impose the most eccentric, dysfunctional, ridiculous traits as eminently distinctive. This is where it triumphs—imposing and legitimizing the irrational according to a logic deeper than that of rationality.*[38]

In fact, from the above discussions we can easily see Baudrillard's question: do people's basic needs (besoins primaires) exist in real social life? He believes what anthropology assumes are people's basic needs assumed are actually illusions, or ideological fantasies. In today's social life, what we eat, drink, dress and liveare no longer discretionary things, "no one is free to live on raw roots and fresh water," and the so-called minimal existence is also a sort of compulsory consumption caused by overproduction. Baudrillard says, "The vital minimum today, the minimum of imposed consumption, is the standard package. Beneath this level, you are an outcast. Is loss of status—or social non-existence—less upsetting than hunger?"[39] This remark does make sense.

---

38 Baudrillard, Jean. *For a Critique of the Political Economy of the Sign*. Trans. Charles Levin. Telos Press Publishing, 1981, p. 79.
39 *Ibid.*, p. 81.

In Baudrillard's eyes, in today's society people's basic needs and disposable income have been reduced to "an idea rationalized at the discretion of entrepreneurs and market analysts." For instance, when people buy cars and clothes, they are mostly making non-autonomous choices under the effect of advertising. As Baudrillard remarks, "when the purchase of an automobile or clothing becomes the unconscious substitute for an unrealistic desire for certain living accommodations," how could such purchase be "discretionary?" The so-called "unrealistic desire" is the illusion of desire manufactured by advertising. (We have noticed in *The Consumer Society* Baudrillard's profound reflection on advertising's control over people's consumption.) If you cannot afford a house, you would unconsciously buy other items (cars, TVs) as the substitute, all of which occurs unconsciously and inevitably. It should be acknowledged that this is another incisive analysis made by Baudrillard, who believes that in today's society things disguise themselves as people's basic needs and consumption is essentially "a compulsion to need and a compulsion to consume," and that there are needs and consumption "because the system needs them." Baudrillard ironically says that if this continues, "one can imagine laws sanctioning such constraint one day: an obligation to change cars every two years."[40]

In Baudrillard's eyes, it is under the manufactured illusion of desire that consumers become obsessively crazy—unsatisfied crazy consumption itself can produce an enormous consummativity (consommativité). "Thus it should not be said that 'consumption is entirely a function of production:' rather, *it is consummativity that is a structural mode of productivity*."[41] The reason is that consumption itself is a kind of production, which is no longer a matter of thingness shaping, but a production of a sign (symbol) based on the differential transformation of "sign exchange value." Baudrillard says, "Capital was already, unearthing the individual qua consumer. He was no longer simply the slave as labour power. And in bringing it off, capital was only delivering up a new kind of serf: the individual

---

40   It is so true that consumption is a productive force that, by significant analogy, it is often subsumed under the notion of profit: "Borrowing makes money." "Buy, and you will be rich." It is exalted not as expenditure, but as investment and profitability. *Ibid.*, p. 82.

41   *Ibid.*, p. 84.

as consumption power."[42] According to Baudrillard's view here, if in Marx's time capitalists conducted labour exploitation through material shaping in production, then today, they have found the new differential sign production constructed by individuals in consumption. Consumption is a more important mode of production. In this sense, it in the traditional understanding is no longer the process of producing needs and satisfaction, *"consumption should be defined not only structurally as a system of exchange and of signs, but strategically as a mechanism of power."*[43]

Thus, individuals in today's social life has the simple natural existence, for they cannot autonomously possess their own basic needs—on the contrary, they are just "survivors" produced by the present social system.

> *If he eats, drinks, lives somewhere, reproduces himself, it is because the system requires his self-production in order to reproduce itself: it needs men. If it could function with slaves, there would be no "free" workers. If it could function with asexual mechanical robots, there would be no sexual reproduction.[44] If the system could function without feeding its workers, there would be no bread. It is in this sense that we are all, in the framework of this system, survivors.[45]*

In the past, we said that men were the products of society, but now, men are just produced and reproduced as elements of the capitalist system. In "monopoly capitalist society," "goods, knowledge, technique, culture, men, their relations and their aspirations—everything is reproduced, from the outset, immediately, as an element of the system, as an integrated variable." It should be noted that this production is not the thingness shaping of objects and men as *use value*, because use value *no longer exists in* this system, and production here refers to the existence itself "produced as sign and

---

42　There is no other basis for aid to underdeveloped countries. *Ibid.*, p. 85.

43　*Ibid.*, p. 85.

44　Robots remain the ultimate and ideal phantasm of a future total productivist system. Still better, there is integrated automation. However, cybernetic rationality is devouring itself, for men are necessary for any system of social order and domination. Now, in the final analysis, this amounts nonetheless to the aim of all productivity, which is a political goal. *Ibid.*, p. 86.

45　*Ibid.*, p. 86.

exchange value (relational value of the sign)."[46] This statement is a code configuration. These words are Baudrillard's final conclusion, and he will assert that in today's capitalist consumer society, it is consumption, the largest production, that determines production, and not production defining consumption. Therefore, Baudrillard realizes that he will begin to *surpass Marx*.

It cannot be denied that Baudrillard's critique of the consumption structure in contemporary capitalism is very profound, and contains points worth learning and considering. However, it is a pity that generation of his theoretical logic develops toward the dimension of negating historical materialism; Baudrillard identifies that social existence in contemporary capitalism is dominated by codes rather than the economic exchange structure identified by Marx. Naturally, he will next directly oppose Marx, and aim Marx's critique of capitalistic fetishism, here it is also the foundation for the establishment of Baudrillard's autonomous thought modelling.

---

46 *Ibid.*, p. 87.

CHAPTER III

FROM COMMODITY FETISHISM TO SIGNIFIER FETISHISM

I do not know why Baudrillard especially hates shaped objects. When he thinks that the operation of code in the previous two chapters has successfully resolved and abandoned the "objects" and people extant in consumer society, he seems to construct a new logical situation of critique theory that surpasses that of his teachers. Therefore, he arrogantly begins to criticize an important part of Marxist historical phenomenology—economic fetishism, which is the theoretical basis of radical discourse by Guy Ernest Debord, Roland Barthes et al. First, Baudrillard directly criticizes Marx's commodity fetishism. He is biased against Marx's fetishism critique and regards it as a substantial worship of objectification thingness. However Baudrillard cannot probe into the reification and subversive misconceptions in capitalist economic relations, while this misidentification greatly damages the so-called code fetishism gathering in signifier. I also note that here the external mirror-image of the other is in decline while on the other side the autonomous logic in Baudrillard's theory is becoming stronger. In this chapter, we will analyze Baudrillard's pretentious views.

1 WHAT IS MARX'S FETISHISM CRITIQUE?

Being completely different from the views of his Western Marxist and leftist teachers, Baudrillard always seems to look down upon the dominant role of Marx's views in terms of critical theories in contemporary Western society, and it seems that he must discuss the concave point that people have not addressed: is Marx really so brilliant? This question is also Baudrillard's attempt to finally eliminate the traces of *post-Marxism* in his own mirror-image of otherness. (This unconventional idea leads to Baudrillard's open opposition against Marxism in the subsequent book, *The Mirror of Production*, and is also one of the important factors of his meteoric rise to fame in the radical context of the European "post-68." era) In the third chapter of *A Critique of the Political Economy of the Sign, Fetishism and Ideology: The Restoration of Semiotics*, published by Baudrillard in 1970, he directly criticizes Marx's views of economic fetishism, which obviously clears the path for the appearance of his dubious "sign fetishism." (It is easy to see that the development of Baudrillard's thought is also a continuous transformation process of the academic memory cluster from dependent logic to the object of negation. Consequently he is able to autonomously achieve his own independent thought modelling. However, I think that Baudrillard's opposition against Marx is especially injudicious and ineffective.) In my opinion, what Baudrillard claims is profound is a mess of theory.

Baudrillard says,

> *The concepts of commodity fetishism and money fetishism sketched, for Marx, the lived ideology of capitalist society—the mode of sanctification, fascination and psychological subjection by which individuals internalize the generalized system of exchange value. These concepts outline the whole process whereby the concrete social values of labour and exchange, which the capitalist system denies, abstracts and "alienates," are erected into transcendent ideological values—into a moral agency that regulates all alienated behaviour.[1]*

---

1   Baudrillard, Jean. *For a Critique of the Political Economy of the Sign.* Trans. Charles Levin. Telos Press Publishing, 1981, p. 88.

Quite apparently, Baudrillard makes a dreadful mistake, because his criticism of Marx here is rather far from the expected target. First, Baudrillard's identification here has lost the most important of the three economic fetishisms by Marx, which is the *capital* fetishism, and thus is bound to hold his understandings of Marx's economic fetishism at the superficial level. Second, it is obviously wrong of Baudrillard to regard Marx's phenomenological critique as a subjective submission in the *psychology* sense. We know that Marx's fetishism critique is not simply an ideological one, but first and foremost the identification of reified reality of the relations among people in the *objective* capitalist production mode and its exchange structure, while idealistic fetishism is a subversive reflection of these objective reification relations. Third, despite Marx's borrowing of the traditional term *fetishism*, his theoretical context has become completely heterogeneous to the traditional fetishism, where the "object," like the "matter" in Marx's historical materialism, is an objective economic relation instead of *substantial* object! (The Japanese scholar Hiromatsu is a profound thinker on this point, for he recognizes that Marx's fetishism critique falsifies *the misidentification of relation as object by the bourgeois ideology*, and he paraphrases Marx's concept of material as "reification" in the phenomenological sense. Compared with Hiromatsu, the academic recognition of the self-righteous Baudrillard is rather low.) Fourth, after 1845, Marx no longer uses the alienation logic (*historical outlook of alienation in anthropological sense*) as an important analytical tool in his theoretical logic, nor adopts the *alienation logic* to analyze total social structures and relations, except in the contradictory sense of the specific economic relations, where he sometimes (*Manuscript On Economics From 1857 to 1858* and *Capital*) moderately uses the alienation concept. Baudrillard is wrong at the starting point of the critical logic, so I do not know what he takes pride in.

Baudrillard then claims that he has found that Marx's fetishism is "the successor to a more archaic fetishism and religious mystification ('the opium of the people')." (Here, Baudrillard plays tricks with the concepts used by Marx in the religion critique and property description of fetishism.) He says that his criticism of Marx aims at removing "the icing on the cake of contemporary analysis." The so-called "icing" here in the irony situation refers to some academic identity that enables the cheap concept to appreciate to convexity. In the eyes of Baudrillard, this theoretical "icing," namely Marx's fetishism, is used by all social critics (including his own teachers), cheaply applied to various analyses of empirical phenomena, "object fetishism, automobile fetishism, sex fetishism, vacation fetishism, etc. The whole exercise is precipitated by nothing more sophisticated than a diffuse, exploded and idolatrous vision of the consumption environment."[2] (Does Baudrillard notice that he will subsequently discuss "sign (signifier) fetishism"? Is sign fetishism other than the so-called "icing" plus cheap concept? Baudrillard often fails to notice that he commits self-contradiction.)

Baudrillard says the concept of fetishism itself is "dangerous," because "since the 18th century it has conducted the whole repertoire of occidental Christian and humanist ideology, as orchestrated by colonists, ethnologists and missionaries." (Here, Baudrillard indeed holds the stand of non-West-centrism, and introduces the concept of what is called in cultural studies today *post-colonial* critique, which in the deep thought modelling coincides with his grassroots romanticism deriving from Mauss-Bataille.) In Baudrillard's eyes, fetishism is "the great *fetishist metaphor (metaphore fetichiste)*;" accordingly, he also cites an expression from Boz to verify his argument, "the worship of certain earthly and material objects called fetishes... for which reason I will call it fetishism."[3] (As I mentioned before, Marx's fetishism has become an ad hoc identification of the kingdom constructed by the bourgeois relations in the context of a specific historical phenomenology, and its core is the reified inversion of social relations instead of the objectified worship of thingness.)

I nevertheless have to admit that Baudrillard's analysis of traditional fetishism is more or less profound, because he notices that the historical generation of traditional fetishism is the logical appropriation of divine force appearing in myth and rituals of primitive social existence, where the situating mechanism of the primary divine projection refers to divine force:

---

2   *Ibid.*, p. 88.
3   De Brosses, Du Culte des dieux fetiches (1760). Quoted from Baudrillard, *Jean. For a Critique of the Political Economy of the Sign.* Trans. Charles Levin. Telos Press Publishing, 1981, p. 88.

As a power that is transferred to beings, objects and agencies, it is universal and diffuse, but it crystallizes at strategic points so that its flux can be regulated and diverted by certain groups or individuals for their own benefit. In the light of the "theory," this would be the major objective of all primitive practices, even eating. Thus, in the animist visions, everything happens between the hypostasis of a force, its dangerous transcendence and the capture of this force, which then becomes beneficent.[4]

Obviously, Baudrillard adopts a critical attitude towards this point, and he believes that Westerners use such Christian spiritual idealism to schematize the otherness culture that never exists in Western culture, especially in Western sociology and anthropology, "exorcising the crucial interrogation that these societies inevitably brought to bear on their own civilization."[5] *Here, Baudrillard's valid vindication of the otherness culture is correct and profound; however, his misinterpretation of Marx thereby can hardly be endorsed.*

Baudrillard voices the criticism that the current logic of fetishism, namely the fetishist metaphor, permeates much of contemporary social criticism, and Marxists, as well as anthropologists of liberalism and rationalism, all fall into a trap by appropriating such idea resources. He questions:

What else is intended by the concept of "commodity fetishism" if not the notion of a false consciousness devoted to the worship of exchange value (or, more recently, the fetishism of gadgets or objects, in which individuals are supposed to worship artificial libidinal or prestige values incorporated in the object)? All of this presupposes the existence, somewhere, of a non-alienated consciousness of an object in some "true," objective state: its use value?[6]

This is a question with very complex context, containing logical presupposition of so many heterogeneity clues, which we must clarify one by one; otherwise this rapid-fire question will not be resolved and confronted.

---

4   *Ibid.*, p. 89.
5   Being de facto rationalists, they have often gone so far as to saturate with logical and mythological rationalizations a system of representations that the aborigines knew how to reconcile with more supple objective practices. *Ibid.*, p. 89.
6   *Ibid.*, p. 89.

First of all, Baudrillard believes that Marx's commodity fetishism solely reveals people's worship of "exchange value" in the capitalist society. In my opinion, this is a typical distortion of Marx's theory at the superficial level. In his middle and late economics studies, Marx establishes three fetishisms, none of which directly analyzes the so-called worship of "exchange value." However, Baudrillard fails to understand that the so-called "exchange value" in classical economics is scientifically identified by Marx as some of the external imagery of the work *value* in the exchange process. Even though Marx touches upon the worship of crystallization of the abstract and objective thingness of the general form of value, it is still within the theoretical falsification of the *money* fetishism rather than the commodity fetishism. (I will discuss this point in details in the following critical dialogue of Baudrillard's *The Mirror of Production*.)

Second, the smart aleck Baudrillard poses another question, namely that it seems there is still a *presupposition of suspending of value* in Marx's fetishism, specifically, the logical tension of fetishism coming from a "non-alienated consciousness of an object in some 'true,' objective state," and he further asks whether this true existence is the "use value." (I find that Baudrillard's misidentification here is related to his previous misinterpretation of Marx's views on alienation.)

I think that Baudrillard's seemingly profound falsification here just proves his own fault: first, in the young Marx before 1845, especially in *1844 Manuscripts of Economics and Philosophy*, there is indeed a suspending of value deriving from humanistic alienation logic, namely the unalienated and true essence of labour as people's genus (species) essence[7]. However, in his subversive philosophical revolution against the traditional Western metaphysics beginning in 1845, Marx completely abandons this anthropological view of alienation, and he establishes the three fetishisms in the middle and late economics studies based on his scientific (special) historical materialism*, indicating that the appearance of true "presupposition of

---

7   See the third chapter of *Back to Marx: The Philosophical Discourse in the Context of Economics* (Jiangsu People's Publishing, 1999). English Version published by Göttingen University Press, in 2014.

*) Ed.: Notice author's distinction between Marx's special historical materialism and general historical materialism.

value" is impossible. Baudrillard here knows nothing but pretends to know everything! Second, in the three fetishisms, where are one of the theoretical cores of Marx's historical phenomenology, there are indeed some logical tensions and non-materialized relations of primitive society, referring to *direct* labour, production, and other social relations among people before their lives enter the market exchange process, instead of the "use value" that Baudrillard so strongly disapproves of. Baudrillard is also wrong on this point, and we may infer that any theoretical analysis based on a misinterpretation of Marx's theories could not be correct.

I hold that Baudrillard's negation of Marx's economic fetishism is mostly based on his so-called "new discovery" of "the theory of sign exchange value," and he strives to prove that because the worship of thingness shaping has been replaced by the worship of sign ordering, Marx is therefore apparently "out-of-date." In the following section, we will look at his further instructions.

2 THE "ORIGINAL SIN" AND SALVATION OF MARX'S FETISHISM

Baudrillard continues saying that the fetishism is based on "a rationalist metaphysic that is at the root of the whole system of occidental Christian values," because this "fetishist" metaphor always contains the anthropological subject consciousness and the *reflexive* critique of man's essence. At the same time, Marxism also takes Western rationalism, the anthropological logic, as its "theoretical pillar," and as all the "fetishism" issues are reduced to some kind of "false consciousness" by Marx, namely a certain mechanism occurring in the superstructure, he eliminates "any real chance it has of analyzing the *actual process of ideological labour*."[8] (It should be noted that there is a subtle implicit migration in Baudrillard's logical modelling here: he begins to affirm the positive aspects of fetishism, because he himself wants to apply this "icing" to his theories. This "icing" lays a significant basis for his subsequent identification of code fetishism.) Therefore, Marx's fetishism theory "refuses to analyze the structures and the mode of ideological production

---

8   Baudrillard, Jean. *For a Critique of the Political Economy of the Sign.* Trans. Charles Levin. Telos Press Publishing, 1981, p. 89.

inherent in its own logic, Marxism is condemned (behind the facade of "dialectical" discourse in terms of class struggle) to expanding the reproduction of ideology, and thus of the capitalist system itself."[9] Baudrillard hands down a felony sentence, and he means that Marx's fetishism critique of capitalism is actually an accomplice to bourgeois ideology. This issue is troublesome. (In the previous sections, I have refuted Baudrillard's argument about Marx's fetishism as merely "false consciousness" in the superstructure; here I do not think it is worthwhile to make a fuss with him. Now let us see what he is going to propagandize next.)

Baudrillard believes that fetishism does have value, and its true meaning appears in Freud's mind instead of existing in social criticism. (This is a very interesting turn in the logical situation, which is completely consistent with his subjectively-fried fetishism.) The original fetishism is the cheap Marxist "icing," but now Baudrillard finds that the truth of fetishism is Freud's "jam."

> *The term "fetishism" almost has a life of its own. Instead of functioning as a metalanguage for the magical thinking of others, it turns against those who use it, and surreptitiously exposes their own magical thinking. Apparently only psychoanalysis has escaped this vicious circle, by returning fetishism to its context within a perverse structure that perhaps underlies all desire. Thus circumscribed by its structural definition (articulated through the clinical reality of the fetish object and its manipulation) as a refusal of sex differences, the term no longer shores up magical thinking; it becomes an analytic concept for a theory of perversion.[10]*

It is good that the psychoanalyst Freud can save the "misconceived" Marx from this trap. In accordance with Baudrillard's previous view of regarding fetishism as a psychological issue, Freud's excellence lies in his thorough discussion of people's subjective psychological structure. (However, in the book Symbolic Exchange and Death, Freud, who is favoured by Baudrillard here to criticize Marx, also becomes a victim of Baudrillard's manic "theoretical violence.") Therefore, the inverted and dancing table in Marx's theory is now replaced by the subjective psychological fantasy. (The mysterious

9   *Ibid.*, p. 89-90.
10   *Ibid.*, p. 90.

inverted table as the commodity is just the theoretical signification of commodity fetishism, and as Baudrillard cannot reach the thought situating of money fetishism and capital fetishism at a deeper level, it is like casting pearls before swine.) The essence of the issue lies here. Baudrillard's interpretation of Marxism has always been based on the logical migration of his teachers in the field of Western Marxism and post-Marxism's idealism, so he is just a smart student choosing the wrong method of interpretation, detouring ever more as a result. If Freud were in the right position, then Baudrillard, too.

The equivalent of the psychoanalytic process of perverse struc-
ture at the level of the process of ideological production—that
is, if it proves impossible to articulate the celebrated formula of
"commodity fetishism" as anything other than a mere neologism
(where "fetishism" refers to this alleged magical thinking, and
"commodity" to a structural analysis of capital), then it would
be preferable to drop the term entirely (including its cognate and
derivative ideas).[11]

This is what he really wants to discuss, and here he begins to strip off his mask: Baudrillard aims at the direct betrayal of his Western Marxist and Leftist teachers; however, he no longer mentions the former U.S.S.R's misinterpretation of the Marxism, "I'll tell you a true Marxism." (An important logical intention in the Western Marxism.) Thus, now he just says: let's *abandon Marxism*! This is a secret button in the post-Marxist logic. (I find that Baudrillard's rise to fame and success lies as such in the "post-68" generation's negation of the Marxism that was highly favoured in the 1968 "Red Storm in May" in France; this negation is completed in the subsequent book *The Mirror of Production*.)

After abandoning the logic of Marx's false economic fetishism, how could the new life of fetishism be possible? Or, in other words, how can the theory of fetishism corrupted by Marxists be saved? In Baudrillard's words, there are three "ifs": "If objects are not these reified agencies, endowed with force and mana in which the subject projects himself and is unalienated—if fetishism designates something other than this metaphysic of alienated essence—what is its real process?" Interestingly, Baudrillard rather seriously points out new "directions" for us Marxists lost on the street.

---

11   *Ibid.*, p. 90.

The first secret of success is to abandon thingness and objective projection in fetishism and alienation logic, because these are historical misidentifications of the term "fetishism" caused by "semantic distortion" at the etymological level. Baudrillard says that today fetishism "refers to a force, a supernatural property of the object and hence to a similar magical potential in the subject, through schemas of projection and capture, alienation and reappropriation" (We've already pointed out in the previous section that this appropriation of the alienation logic of humanist genus essence in Marx's economic fetishism theory is wrong.) In the original context, the meaning of the term fetishism is just the opposite: "It is a fabrication, an artifact, a labour of appearances and signs."[12] We have to keep our eyes wide open, because Baudrillard starts his logic tricks here: "fabrication" and "artifact" refer to the utility for people given by the shaping of labour production, and fabrication of shaping is to highlight the "labour of signs," which is the most important keyword he is going to add his own theories. For this purpose, he lists numerous words, aiming at illustrating that the true meaning of the term fetishism is not only material existence in the sense of labour shaping, but also "a cultural sign labour." I think this behaviour indicates Baudrillard's academic dishonesty, because how could the sign labour come into existence in a fetish discourse generated in the pre-culture sign without modern meanings? Wizardly divination? What a ridiculous viewpoint! (When Baudrillard criticizes today's Western sociology and Marxism, his main weapon is to *impose modern context on primitive social existence*, but he himself often unconsciously enters this logical dead end.)

After such theoretical "fabrication" by Baudrillard, he continues by adopting Hegel's logical structure of idealism to eliminate objects; for him, it is not a new technique. He pretends at profundity by writing that in early animism, people forgot that the essence of fetishism is "an object marked by signs," "signs of the hand, of the face, or characters of the cabal, or the figure of some celestial body that, registered in the object, makes it a talisman." Nevertheless, *the essence of objects is actually symbolic signs!* This is the expression that Baudrillard would most like to mark, because this symbol

---

12   *Ibid.*, p. 91.

is divine and good. (This expression might be Hegel's old logic of "there is nothing new under the sun," and the essence of objects is a new version of this idea. However, it does not mean that Baudrillard simply virtualizes objects into signs, because we have seen the complex steps of objects "transforming into a butterfly" in the books *The System of Objects*, *The Consumer Society* and our previous discussions.) For this purpose, however, Baudrillard finds that in today's consumer society fetishism is also in the pursuit of signs:

> *Thus, in the "fetishist" theory of consumption, in the view of marketing strategists as well as of consumers, objects are given and received everywhere as force dispensers (happiness, health, security, prestige, etc.). This magical substance having been spread about so liberally, one forgets that what we are dealing with first is signs: a generalized code of signs, a totally arbitrary code of differences, **and that it is on this basis, and not at all on account of their use values or their innate "virtues" that objects exercise their fascination.**[13]*

> *The fascination of object does not lie in its own real properties or in the use value from shaping, because the object is the symbolic code of signs produced by the manufacturer of consumption desire, and is no more than a matter outside the differential sign relations, and a phase. Nevertheless, the symbolism here is the one of evil that occupies true vacancy! (In fact, we have seen above that Baudrillard, who in his book The Consumer Society at that time still bore post-Marxism in mind, carries out a lot of profound analysis and discussion of the secret of consumption control in modern capitalist society, and there probes into the nature of slavery of modern consumption in the signification code and unmotivated control of ads. This though is very profound. Nonetheless, it is in an illegitimate transgression that Baudrillard leaves the specific context of the consumption phenomenon behind and thereupon begins to talk about the so-called general phenomenological relations between objects and signs.)*

The second secret of success is Baudrillard's intention of establishing the so-called *critique of the political economy of the sign*, whose key word is *signifier fetishism*. Baudrillard says that even if there is a fetishism, then it is one based on the *signifier* instead of the *signified* fetishism in the property sense or of the one of value and entity. (It should be noted that the first important change in his

---

13   *Ibid.*, p. 91.

logical modelling, namely Baudrillard's new *autonomous* logical situating about critique of the political economy of the sign, starts here.)

> *Behind this reinterpretation (which is truly ideological) it is a **fetishism of the signifier**. That is to say that the subject is trapped in the factitious, differential, encoded, systematized aspect of the object. It is not the passion (whether of objects or subjects) for substances that speaks in fetishism, it is the **passion for the code**, which, by governing both objects and subjects, and by subordinating them to itself, delivers them up to abstract manipulation. This is the fundamental articulation of the ideological process: not in the projection of alienated consciousness into various superstructures, but in the generalization at all levels of a structural code.*[14]

Here, Freud's "jam" of fetishism has been replaced by Jacques Lacan's "cheese." Object is nothing; it is just the signifier that has shaken off the signified, and is a fake code carrier in its own differential sign system, besides which, fetishism seems to worship "object." However, the essence of fetishism is *the worship of the signifier of the evil symbolism.* Marx's fetishism "icing" is an illusion of icing and not a real one. What truly dominates and enslaves people and objects is the sign, while in this sign system, Baudrillard, like Lacan, *abandons the signified* and chooses the empty signifier instead. It is in this signifier sign system that objects and people are virtualized, which is the meaning of what he calls "abstract manipulation." (I specifically mention above that one of Baudrillard's abilities is to seamlessly blend his autonomous thought ordering with different academic memories, leaving later readers vaguely feeling that there is some profundity in his explanations, and yet at the same time feeling confused. Such is one of Baudrillard's knacks.)

Therefore, ideology truly rules and dominates people in the omnipresent structural code of signifier sign, instead of Marx's misconception of the alienated superstructure. Baudrillard finally takes a decisive step away from Marx's economic fetishism, a very important step for contemporary idealism. (In the following sections, I will talk about Baudrillard's creation of logical freaks of idealism, like *the simulation ontology*, in the post-modern context.)

---

14   *Ibid.*, p. 92.

3 THEORETICAL ABERRATION FROM COMMODITY FETISHISM TO SIGNIFIER FETISHISM

It is easy to see that when Baudrillard uses such "theoretical reform" to reinterpret Marx's commodity fetishism, everything changes: the fetishism theory is remodelled in a gestalt manner. Baudrillard is not satisfied with traditional Marxists' interpretation of commodity fetishism, including Marx's original theory of commodity fetishism. So in his eyes, everyone is wrong, and the essence of commodity fetishism is not the separation between producers and products of labour,

> *It is rather the (ambivalent) fascination for a **form** (logic of the commodity or system of exchange value), a state of absorption, for better or for worse, in the restrictive logic of a system of abstraction. Something like a desire, a perverse desire, the desire of the code is brought to light here: it is a desire that is related to the systematic nature of signs, drawn towards it, precisely through what this system-like nature negates and bars, by exorcising the contradictions spawned by the process of real labour—just as the perverse psychological structure of the fetishist is organized, in the fetish object, **around a mark, around the abstraction of a mark** that negates, bars and exorcises the difference of the sexes.*[15]

Baudrillard's first sentence seems to make sense. Marx's commodity fetishism refers to people's passion for ***materialization*** that they cannot grasp in the commodity economy. However, this passion is not conscious passion for the "logic of the system of exchange value," because people with a touch of the common sense of the Marxist political economics know that value relation is not an economic structure that can be directly confronted. The latter part of this argument of Baudrillard's should be regarded as a profound theoretical critique for understanding the consumption/production structure in contemporary capitalist society: the capitalist indeed first manufactures the pseudo-desire that is assumed to be people's real need before production, and the process of controlling people's unconscious desire is achieved by the pseudo-situating of the symbolic code of sign (by image and information). In other words, symbolic code control has become a dominant power in today's capitalist

---

15 *Ibid.*, p. 92.

social structure. This argument of Baudrillard's is also the major contribution that he makes in The Consumer Society to the critical theories against contemporary society. However, problems emerge as the code becomes more and more dominant in the consumption structure of contemporary capitalism. Is it necessary to completely negate material production and the objective circulation of commodity exchange, and is it necessary to negate Marx?

My answer to the above questions is obviously "No." As Baudrillard fails to truly understand the logical relations of *general and special* semantics in Marxist historical materialism, when he meets with the image and information of media age at the critical level of special historical age, he reverses the "sign relations," as the *dominant* factor of contemporary social life, into the basis of social existence, and thus negates *the essential position of material production* which is identified as the basis of *general social existence* in Marxist historical materialism. Herein lies the fundamental reason for his subsequent direct negation of historical materialism. Although Baudrillard is also against the sign pseudo-environment's slavery domination over life, this kind of idealistic deconstruction is just a fantastical revolution and criticism, which may be effective in threatening those people lost in the traditional of Stalinist dogmatism and those outsiders who do not understand Marxism, but it is rather absurd in the face of real Marxist scientific theory.

Baudrillard at this time believes that the essence of commodity fetishism is not the sanctification of a particular object or value, and barter trade, in brief, can "be reduced to commutable sign values."[16] Marx's commodity fetishism in the real capitalist system of "exchange value," is "the fetishization of a product emptied of its concrete substance of labour,"[17] a fetishism subjected to "another type of labour, a labour of *signification*, that is, of coded abstraction (the production of differences and of sign values)."

16   In this system, use value becomes obscure and almost unintelligible, though not as an original value which has been lost, but more precisely as a function derived from exchange value. Henceforth, it is exchange value that induces use value (i.e., needs and satisfactions) to work in common with it (ideologically), within the framework of political economy. *Ibid.*, p. 93.
17   In this way labour power as a commodity is itself "fetishized."

Baudrillard makes his intention very clear here: he wants to reinterpret the original meanings of abstract labour and concrete labour in the context of Marx's economics. Now concrete labour becomes the thingness presence of productivity shaping, while abstract labour turns into the code production that manufactures meanings. He is really playing a big logical trick. The historical ad hoc illustrations missing here lie in the issue of whether Baudrillard intends to identify faults in Marx's analysis of the 19th century industrial capitalism, or whether today's new changes of capitalism cause problems to Marxist economics. This issue is beyond our ken. (At this point, Baudrillard's logical thought is more or less paradoxical, but the subsequent books *The Mirror of Production and Symbolic Exchange and Death* precisely complete his negation and criticism of Marx at two logical scales: the former focuses on direct negation of Marx's critique of 19th-century capitalism, and the latter explains that Marx's critique theory is out-of-date with the new changes of contemporary capitalism. I will analyze this specific point in details in the middle and second part of this book.)

Baudrillard proudly claims,

It is an active, collective process of production and reproduction of a code, a system, invested with all the diverted, unbound desire separated out from the process of real labour and transferred onto precisely that which denies the process of real labour. Thus, fetishism is actually attached to the sign object, the object eviscerated of its substance and history, and reduced to the state of marking a difference, epitomizing a whole system of differences.[18]

Why does Baudrillard insist on replacing Marx's commodity fetishism with signifier fetishism? A reasonable explanation is that he thinks today's capitalist society witnesses the appearance of a labour of meaning-generation that is more critical than that extant in Marx's times, a labour also called "abstract labour." (We must remember that in the previous section "abstract labour" is referred to as "symbolic labour" by Baudrillard.) However, this labour is no longer Marx's original *general* labour objectively generating from the sufficient division of labour and the market exchange in the large-scale production of the capitalist modernity, but the abstraction (the nothing

---

18   Ibid., p. 93.

in Lacan's sense) of the labour of so-called coded and differential production. Therefore, it is in signifier fetishism that the shaping object is emptied, and where it loses its substantial existence and history. Additionally, the sign-object, which may exist to represent the nothingness of sign, is nothing only in the sense of sign. Worship of the signifier sign is worshiping the nothing in Lacan's sense. We do not realize that existence in sign is dead and are still in crazy pursuit of the signifier with empty symbolism—the essence of the signifier fetishism is here. We cannot simply say that there is no ground for Baudrillard's analysis here, but he always disturbs thought situations that can be explained more clearly.

Here, Baudrillard finally talks about money fetishism, and in his eyes, money is a sign in comparison with the visible thingness commodity. It is apparent that Baudrillard does not notice that Marx, in *The Manuscript on Economics From 1857 to 1858*, grasped the real meaning of Hegel's "abstraction becoming domination,"[19] where "abstraction" is not only the code of money, but also one of the objective and historical economic relations, for example the abstraction of capital. Baudrillard is not able to truly enter the context of Marx's economics, so many of Marx's critical understandings of the capitalist production mode are merely fiddled with by Baudrillard at the superficial level of convex semantics. Baudrillard justifies his own viewpoints as follows:

> *What is fascinating about money is neither its materiality, nor even that it might be the intercepted equivalent of a certain force (e. g., of labour) or of a certain potential power: it is its systematic nature, the potential enclosed in the material for total commutability of all values, thanks to their definitive abstraction. It is the abstraction, the total artificiality of the sign that one "adores" in money.*[20]

It is apparent that in Baudrillard's view, the concept of money does not belong to economics, because it no longer corresponds to the labour value nor is a general equivalent objectively abstracting

---

19   See "Section One" in the ninth chapter of my *Back to Marx: The Philosophical Discourse in the Context of Economics* (Jiangsu People's Publishing, 1999). English version published by Göttingen University Press, in 2014.

20   Baudrillard, Jean. *For a Critique of the Political Economy of the Sign.* Trans. Charles Levin. Telos Press Publishing, 1981, p. 93.

from the exchange relations, and instead is only a sign system in the symbolism of evil; this code system causes people to worship money. Therefore, because people are obsessed with a perfect sign system instead of being in the pursuit of gold and silver, money fetishism degrades from being a profound analysis of historical phenomenology in Marx's economics into a superficial cultural assertion. Baudrillard's purpose now becomes increasingly clear: he wishes to transform all the true reality and its social relations into sign relations.

In order to enhance and verify his new ideas, Baudrillard also cites a lively example from social life, namely an ideology exhibited by "body and beauty" (to be specific, he speaks of "liberating the body" and "obsession with beauty") in contemporary commodity fetishism. (This example is a semiotic version of the example in the previous chapter of a girl chooses a long or a short skirt in fashion.) Baudrillard says that the essence of today's so-called "beauty" is a kind of "anti-nature," and this sort of anti-nature beauty is precisely "the generalization of sign exchange value to facial and bodily effects." He means that when a girl is under the fitness beauty, she does not really become beautiful, but only causes her face and body to enter a modelling of *sign exchange value*. (It should be noted that the so-called "sign exchange value" is what Baudrillard adopts to replace Marx's "exchange value" (precisely the commodity value).) In this system, "it is the final disqualification of the body, its subjection to a discipline, the total circulation of signs. The body's wildness is veiled by makeup; the drives are assigned to a cycle of fashion." The body itself loses its natural essence, and enters the sign ordering of fashion; what is beautiful is the differential sign instead of the body:

> It is the sign in this beauty, the mark (makeup, symmetry, or calculated asymmetry, etc.), which fascinates; **it is the artifact that is the object of desire.** The signs are there to make the body into a perfect object, a feat that has been accomplished through a long and specific labour of sophistication. Signs perfect the body into an object in which none of its real work (the work of the unconscious or psychic and social labour) can show through. The fascination of this fetishized beauty is the result of this extended process of abstraction, and derives from what it negates and censors through its own character as a system.[21]

---

21   *Ibid.*, p. 94.

What is enchanting is not the shaped (embodied) body and face of a woman, but the symbolic sign meaning in those *artifacts*. Baudrillard lists some artifacts such as "tattoos, stretched lips, the bound feet of Chinese women, eyeshadow, rouge, hair removal, mascara, or bracelets, collars, objects, jewellery, accessories and so on." (This is a salmagundi embracing jewellery of ancient times, symbolization and physical ravage in the enslavement of women in China's feudal society, and also cosmetics in contemporary life. We do not know whether these objects of different properties are simultaneously used by modern capital as codes, but at least we know that even in today's code system the foot-binding of Chinese women is certainly no longer "beautiful." I note that Baudrillard's viewpoint on the foot-binding of Chinese women originates from his teacher Veblen.[22]) Baudrillard believes that today's so-called "beauty," "as a constellation of signs and work upon signs," exhibits the insidious ideology of "monopoly capitalism." Why?

First of all, there is the *non-subjectification* of the body. In this ideology of beauty, the human body is separated from the subject, and thus one has an individual "with a soul or a mind, but a body properly all his own, from which all negativity of desire is eliminated and which functions only as the exhibitor of beauty and happiness."[23] The body in signifier fetishism is no longer a symbol of subjectivity or the physical basis of the soul, but becomes a "beautiful" product manufactured by the pseudo-symbolic sign system instead. (In fact, we often see the result of code manufacturing on TV in the form of artificial Korean beauties which all look monotonously alike.)

Secondly, there is the *fragmentation* of the human body. Baudrillard says, "monopoly capitalism, which is not content to exploit the body as labour power, manages to fragment it, to divide the very expressiveness of the body in labour, in exchange, and in play, recuperating all this as individual needs, hence as productive (consummative) forces under its control."[24] What he means is that

---

22   When Veblen discusses the so-called "conspicuous consumption" in *The Theory of the Leisure Class,* he also refers to girdling among the women in the West and foot binding among the women in China. Cf. Thorstein B Veblen, *The Theory of the Leisure Class.* Forgotten Books, 2008, p. 106-107.

23   Baudrillard, Jean. *For a Critique of the Political Economy of the Sign.* Trans. Charles Levin. Telos Press Publishing, 1981, p. 96.

24   *Ibid.,* p. 97.

people's bodies as they exist in the monopoly capitalism have totally become fragmentations, and in each partial body (for example the anti-nature "beautiful" body), it is manifested as a pseudo need, and ultimately integrated into a body as the consummativity presence.

Here, the insidious ideology exists within "the same process of labour and desire attached to the organization of signs" and takes effect in two aspects: first is the "construction of signification" and second is the facilitating "process of fetishization." Signification refers to the non-id in the sign code; the process of fetishization is the signifier fetishism that appears in this kind of "beauty." The "object" in the fetishism here no longer exists at the physical level, but is the signifier that constructs "beauty" in the ordered modelling of code. In this sense, Baudrillard even says that nudity in pornographic shows is actually a manufactured need instead of a true desire; there are no longer natural sexuality nor symbols of death, only signifier objects "caught up in the differential play of signs." The reason is as follows:

*Symbolic and sexual truth is not in the naive conspicuousness of nudity, but in the **uncovering** of itself (**mise à nu**), insofar as it is the symbolic equivalent of putting to death (**mise à mort**), and thus of the true path of desire, **which is always ambivalent**, love and death simultaneously. Functional modern nudity does not involve this ambivalence at all, nor thus any profound symbolic function, because such nudity reveals a body **entirely positivized by sex**—as a cultural value, as a model of fulfillment, as an emblem, as a morality (or ludic immorality, which is the same thing)—and **not a body divided and split by sex**. The sexualized body, in this case, no longer functions, save on its positive side.[25]*

*The founder Georges Bataille makes his debut here. Nudity is originally a profoundly "good" symbol; love and death have unlimited space of metonymy, while the present nudity is an illusion of the thingness libido losing the symbolism essence. (His teacher Guy Ernest Debord also talks about this issue in the book **The Society of the Spectacle**.)[26]*

---

25 *Ibid.*, p. 97.
26 See "Section Two" in the second chapter of *A Deep Plough: Unscrambling Major Post-marxist Texts*, Vol. 2. (People's University Press, 2008). English version published by Canut Intl.London, 2010.

Here we find that Mauss-Bataille's symbolic relation, which is the logical coordinate of Baudrillard's basic theory, once again appears. Here, Baudrillard more accurately identifies ideology generation, stating, *"this semiological reduction of the symbolic properly constitutes the ideological process."*[27] This statement is another comparison between the symbolism of good and evil. In Baudrillard's mind, people's true existence is a kind of non-utilitarian symbolism full of mana, and the essence of this good symbolism is uncertainty and disorder. However, the code system's invasion causes people to completely lose the original symbolism of their lives. It is the coded and ordered totalization achieved "by internal differentiation and by general homogenization" that has taken the place of people's true symbolism. This is an evil symbolism, namely the abstract signifier relationship, that

> *makes possible this closure, this perfection, this logical mirage that is the effectiveness of ideology. It is the abstract coherence, suturing all contradictions and divisions, that gives ideology its power of fascination (fetishism). This coherence is found in the erotic system as well as in the perverse seduction exercised by the system of exchange value, which is entirely present in even the very smallest of commodities.*[28]

The final conclusion is drawn that fetishism is equivalent to ideology, while ideology is the abstract totalization generating from the sign code, and that "this abstract totalization permits signs to function ideologically, that is, to establish and perpetuate real discriminations and the order of power."[29] Here, the hegemony of core culture is actually a symbolic sign of evil, and today's world is modelled by the symbolism of evil. (After the "9/11" event in the United States, Baudrillard specifically identified the World Trade Centre Twin Towers in New York as the symbol of the evil of America's attempt to establish a "definitive system," leading to "an allergy to all definitive order, to all definitive power is happily universal, and the two towers of the World Trade Centre embodied perfectly."[30] This statement is an assault against the symbolism of evil.)

---

27   Baudrillard, Jean. *For a Critique of the Political Economy of the Sign.* Trans. Charles Levin. Telos Press Publishing, 1981, p. 98.

28   *Ibid.,* p. 101.

29   *Ibid.,* p. 101.

30   Jean Baudrillard, "This is the fourth world war." *Der Spiegel*, January 14, 2002.

I have to admit that Baudrillard's critical analysis of contemporary ideology here, excluding his misinterpretation of and malicious assault against Marx, contains numerous valuable thoughts, and it behooves us to carefully distinguish and contemplate his ideas.

CHAPTER IV

"REVOLUTION" OF THE POLITICAL ECONOMY OF THE SIGN

After Baudrillard makes single-point breakthrough in a series of theoretical issues, including as objects, consumption, and ideology, he finally feels that it is time to announce his own theoretical revolution, that is, a theory of the political economy of the sign which is superior to traditional political economy. This revolution is not only the new critical logic that he adopts to replace Marx's political economics, but also an autonomous theory Baudrillard created in a new logical situation of intertextuality. In his theoretical revolution, the academic memory of semiotics originates with Saussure, while the political economy is based on Marx's ideas. Baudrillard ingeniously analyzes the art signature and the auction process, trying to verify his original differential production relations, which are different from material production in the shaping manner, and then introduces a new theoretical framework for the so-called political economy. Here, the thorough betrayal of his leftist teachers and Marxism finds completion. The above are the basic contents of chapters four and five in his book. (Unique from the previous three chapters which embody three published papers, Baudrillard specially writes the new contents for the book *For a Critique of the Political Economy of the*

Sign. It may be that it is at this time that he realizes a book should be written to systematically illustrate his autonomous thought situation.) In my opinion, Baudrillard's self-righteous theoretical revolution is merely a brainstorm based on extraordinary logical narcissism, and his falsification of Marx's political economy is based on a completely illegitimate misinterpretation of Marx's theory. Hence, it does not withstand theoretical scrutiny at a deeper level.

1 THE DIFFERENTIAL PRODUCTION IN THE MODERN ART SIGNATURE

Baudrillard proclaims his theoretical revolution by starting with deduction in the production process of the so-called modern art. (Obviously, the "realistic motivation" of his theoretical revolution is too weak.) Here, Baudrillard chooses to discuss the production of contemporary works of fine arts. In his eyes, modern painting is not only just a process of painting on the surface of canvas, but also the production of "a signed object." It seems that he always wants to reach thought situations that ordinary people cannot.

First of all, the so-called *signed* object here refers not to the symbolic meaning generated in the artist's painting process, but specifically to the artist's *signature* applied after a work of fine art is finished. (The signature can also be replaced by a seal. Here we find a very peculiar situating perspective, because Baudrillard first chooses the partial modern painting and then concentrates on the signature that is applied of the modern ideology in modern art production.) Baudrillard says that the signature is an important signed event, because although the signature is not a part of the painting itself, the work transforms into a unique object because of this simple symbolic sign. Once a work of fine art has a particular signature or seal,

> then it becomes **a model** to which an extraordinary, differential value is brought by a visible sign. But it is not a meaning value— the meaning peculiar to the painting is not in question here—it is a **differential** value, carried by the ambiguity of a **sign** that does not cause the work to be seen, but to be recognized and evaluated in a system of signs.[1]

---

1   Baudrillard, Jean. *For a Critique of the Political Economy of the Sign.* Trans. Charles Levin. Telos Press Publishing, 1981, p. 102.

There are two key terminologies at work here: one is sign, the other is the differential value constructed by the orderly system of specific signs. (We can see that here again is the appropriation of Saussure's linguistics, that is, that signification generates in the signified and signifier's special presence in a differential language system. There is really no theoretical innovation.) I have found a fatal blind spot and parallax in Baudrillard's theories: his catastrophic generalization of ad hoc events and situations. For example, here, not all of the signatures found on modern art works will bring them so-called "differential value." For example, an obscure artist's signature cannot add additional value to a piece of work, nor enable him to enter the significant differential sign system mentioned by Baudrillard. His identification only takes effect in the generation of famous artists' works, and the famous artist and his work's stepping into the differential sign system are a rather complicated historical process (from obscure to known, to fame, and on to and recognition as a master at last.) I hold that Baudrillard's theoretical thinking is often distant from a careful and comprehensive level.

Secondly, Baudrillard points out that the creation of modern art works itself is fundamentally heterogeneous to that of traditional art, because modern art works no longer face the real world and people's direct lives, and instead display *the differential series of subject-creator himself.* I think that Baudrillard's analysis here is somewhat reasonable, and indeed it may be one of the important modes that modern art presents. For example, Pablo Picasso's and Salvador Dali's paintings, which we find in metropolitan museums or in the Louvre, can be recognized at a single glace, and do not directly face worldly life, nor simulate and approach reality like the works of classical realism do. Instead they subjectively tear the world in a unique signifier and then produce a distinctive difference in the painting style. With regards Picasso's and Dali's works, this unique signifier makes its presence known in the manner of mutually referential series. Baudrillard says that the essence of modern art work is "a succession of moments," "not in its relation to the world but in its relation to the other paintings by the same artist, its meaning being thus tied down to succession and repetition." (The repetition here coincides with Lacan's logic of object inquiry, and also is of the same structure with the more ambitious ideological "tautology" seen in the previous section.)

*They are only able to follow one another in order then to refer, by
virtue of their difference and their discontinuity in time, to a quite
different model, to the **subject-creator himself** in his unlikeness
and his repeated absence. We are no longer in space but in time,
in the realm of difference and no longer of resemblance, in the
series and no longer in the order.*[2]

Here Baudrillard wants to draw out his views, namely the differential sign structure. (Nonetheless, when compared with Baudrillard's
past thought ordering, the concept of differentiation here exhibits
slight changes, and the series concept reaches a new level of theoretical profundity.) If, in René Descartes's time, people's existence
mode was "I think, therefore I am," and in Smith-Marx's time, "I
produce, therefore I am;" now people's existence mode will be *I
differentiate, therefore I am*. It should be specially noted that differentiation is no doubt the crucial point of logic that generates all the
French postmodern streams. For example, differentiation appears as
a key word in Jacques Derrida's and Gilles Deleuze's early philosophy, and we can even claim that *differentiation* initiates the whole
post-modern stream. Nonetheless, differentiation in Baudrillard's
theory here is certainly not a positive thing, and as with Jacques
Lacan, it is established on the negative ontology of relationships, so
that differentiation in Baudrillard's logical modelling is a secret key
to the modern enslaving discourse, and is precisely the target highlighted by his criticism. Consequently, this "I differentiate, therefore
I am" in Lacan's context should be ironically interpreted as *I differentiate, therefore common people are*, besides which, the essence of
differentiation of I (objects) is absence. (Later, we will examine this
point more clearly.)

In Baudrillard's opinion, modern artists paint because they "can
only prove itself untiringly: by this very fact it constitutes a series,"
and he draws the conclusion that, *"it is precisely because the series has become the constitutive dimension of the modern oeuvre
that the inauthenticity of one of the elements of the series becomes
catastrophic."*[3] This stylistic series only refers to the one generating
in the differential sign structures. (It is apparent that here again we
encounter the concept of differential series that we gradually became

---

2   *Ibid.*, p. 104.
3   *Ibid.*, p. 105.

familiar with in the book *The System of Objects*. I have already pointed out that in *The System of Objects*, Baudrillard once distinguished
the aristocracy's innate and proprietary positions from the differential series existence of modern people.[4] The series of consumption emerged in *The Consumer Society*, so the series category here
should be at its third stage of development. In the subsequent book,
Symbolic Exchange and Death, this series concept becomes the piv-
otal description paradigm produced by simulacrum at the second
level. It is obvious that in his academic modelling, Baudrillard constantly adds new understandings and reconstructs original concepts
and ordered semantic fields of categories.) Additionally, Baudrillard
ensures that the legitimate label of differential production can only
be the signature of the artist. The signature "becomes the veritable
caption of our oeuvres. In the absence of fable, of the figures of the
world and of God, it is that which tells us what the work signifies."[5]
The presence of the differential signs occupies the throne of the past
symbolic god. This assertion has great theoretical importance.

Baudrillard discusses the status of the signature in the production
of modern artworks, with the aim of criticizing today's reality, and
he actually tries to reveal a certain dominant logic in the sign society
of modern capitalism. He believes that the example of the signature
unveils the mask hiding the truth that the concave of today's capitalist domination secretly shelters an accomplice game, namely "a
subjective series (authenticity) and an objective series (code, social
consensus, commercial value), through this inflected sign, that the
system of consumption can operate."[6] (Here, Baudrillard deepens
the dual connotations of the series concept: one is the subjective series, namely the series aiming at the authenticity of the object referent; the other is the objective series of the self-entertainment among
signs losing external referents and the mutual relations among consumer goods.) Baudrillard discovers that the critical revolt against
reality in traditional art no longer exists here: "revolt is isolated,
the malediction 'consumed'," and now, "modern works have indeed

---

4 Baudrillard, Jean. *The System of Objects*. Trans. James Benedict. Verso Books,
2006, p. 70.
5 Baudrillard, Jean. *For a Critique of the Political Economy of the Sign*. Trans.
Charles Levin. Telos Press Publishing, 1981, p. 105.
6 *Ibid.*, p. 105.

become everyday objects: although laden with cultural connotations, they pose no problems to their surrounding environments. A
modern painting, pop, abstract, a 'tachiste,' contradicts nothing." In
modern art,

> *it bears witness to our time, it does so neither by direct allusion*
> *nor even in its pure gesture denying a systematized world—it is*
> *in testifying to the* **systematic** *of this full world by means of the*
> **inverse and homologous systematic** *of its empty gesture, a pure*
> *gesture marking an absence.*[7]

This thought situation can hardly be understood, because the traditional art referred to by Baudrillard here is semantically unclear,
and the timelessness causes the context of this discussion to become
a hollow signifier chain. We know that as opposed to medieval va-
cant theology art, realism in the Enlightenment displayed humanity
via Mona Lisa's smile in order to constitute a revolt against the real
feudal force, and furthermore, modernity and post-modern art works
seem to proclaim a radical rebellion through deviation from traditional realism. In Baudrillard's eyes however, Picasso's and Dali's
later works unconsciously verify "the *systematic* of this full world"
of today's bourgeois through differential series production's homo-
logues to the capitalist system. (There are two possibilities: one is
that there is non-historicity in Baudrillard's logic, leading him to
misidentify the meanings of modern artworks without identifying
the entire history of thought; the other is that Baudrillard's critique
here is indeed a more profound logical falsification. Here, we make
the assumption that it is the second thought situation possibility.)

It is in this sense that Baudrillard accuses modern art of being
a "collusion vis-à-vis this contemporary world" and a supporter of
modern bourgeois' consumer society.

> *It plays with it, and is included in the game. It can parody this*
> *world, illustrate it, simulate it, alter it; it never disturbs the order,*
> *which is also its own.*[8]

This critique seems to be quite incisive. Here, we can still see his
teachers' radical blood flowing in Baudrillard academic veins, and he
still wants to criticize and revolt against the real world. Nonetheless,

7   *Ibid.*, p. 108.
8   *Ibid.*, p. 110.

this revolt is no longer in line with the nature of Marxism, or in other words, Baudrillard will adopt the method of the more radical anti-Marxism to criticize this evil bourgeois world. His intention seems incredible.

2 THE ART AUCTION: THE ACADEMIC DELIVERY ROOM OF THE POLITICAL ECONOMY OF THE SIGN

We have already predicted that the new instrument of critique that Baudrillard possesses is *the political economy of the sign*, which is superior to economic value. In the first several chapters of this book, Baudrillard makes plenty of preparation for the birth of this so-called "political economy of the sign." First he magically transfers the exist-ence of shaping objects into signs, then eliminates the materialized needs by the illusion of desire, and finally unveils the mask hiding the Copernican logical declaration: Marx's political economy based on the "exchange value" has become obsolete, and now it is the politi-cal economy of the sign, established by Baudrillard himself, that can really act as a critical weapon against the new realities of capitalism. (Nonetheless, he later claims that without a proper concept, "the po-litical economy of the sign" is just a strategically "temporary use," because the term "political economy" itself is a product of the eco-nomic value system. It should be specifically pointed out that, as po-litical economy to Marx is just the object of critique instead of some-thing of positive construction, then the political economy of the sign is Baudrillard's negative conceptual modelling of the social mecha-nism in the contemporary capitalism rather than his positive logic.) Different from the assertions of Jean Paul Sartre in 1960s and Jacques Derrida in 1990s, Baudrillard no longer says that Marx is a critical banner or a spectre of thought that we cannot surpass, because now he is a leader armed with a magical weapon criticizing the spectre.

Readers will especially want to figure out what precisely is this political economy of the sign which has replaced Marx's scientific critique theories. We find that Baudrillard this time again chooses an unexpected approach: the art auction. (This ordering perspective is still very insular.) He claims that in the painting market and the art auction mentioned above, we are likely to decipher "the articula-tion, and thus the process, of ideological labour" of contemporary

bourgeois culture. We have seen that in the differential series production and signature application of modern painting, Baudrillard
identifies this particular artistic creation as differential sign production, and here, he reinforces this view with the art auction, bringing this argument to a more important theoretical convexity. (In my
judgment, this is precisely the subject construction of his autonomous theoretical modelling, and also a transitional link of mediation
leading Baudrillard to his original ideas.) It is in modern painting
and in the art auction that Baudrillard will cast light for us on a
New World, where new rules of the game generate the "the inter-
change of values, where economic value, sign value and symbolic
value transfuse, can be considered as an ideological matrix—one
of the shrines of the Super-Big *'POLITICAL ECONOMY OF THE
SIGN' (L'ECONOMIE POLITIQUE DU SIGNE)*."[9] (In the text here,
Baudrillard capitalizes all the letters in the term "political economy
of the sign" to announce his theoretical revolution with the direct
convex character shaping. I refer to it as "Super-Big" in order to
distinguish it from the referents which have their first letters capitalized.) Nonetheless, while Baudrillard distinguishes himself from
post-Marxist trends, he is still connected with Marxism, and also admits that the presence of the political economy of the sign resembles
Marx's political economy, because Marx's political economy for
him is at least a useful "icing" which can be applied to his theories.

At the end of this book, Baudrillard once drew a brief conclusion
of the homology between these two sorts of political economy:

> *1. Political economy: Under the cover of utility (needs, use value,
> etc., the anthropological reference of all economic rationality), it
> institutes a coherent logical system, a calculus of productivity in
> which all production is resolved into simple elements, in which
> all products are equivalent in their abstraction. This is the logic
> of the commodity and the system of exchange value.*

> *2. The political economy of the sign: Under the cover of function-
> ality (objective finality, homologous to utility), it institutes a cer-
> tain mode of signification in which all the surrounding signs act
> as simple elements in a logical calculus and refer to each other
> within the framework of the system of sign exchange value.*[10]

9   *Ibid.*, p. 112.
10   *Ibid.*, p. 191.

Firstly, in these two systems, utility in the political economy and functionality in the political economy of sign act as the logical fulcrum or the ultimate "referent," and "exchange value" and signs form the concrete "embodiment" around utility and functionality. This formation displays the similarity between these two political economy systems.

Secondly, these two systems are absolutely heterogeneous. Baudrillard thinks that in general capitalist consumption revealed by Marx, the "exchange value" (money) of economy transforms into the "exchange value" of sign (for instance "prestige") on the legitimate basis of use value, and yet, exchange in the art auction occurs between money and paintings as pure signs. (It should be noted that paintings (as pure signs) mentioned here are precisely the objects with signatures in the differential series structure as redefined by Baudrillard. I have illustrated the ad hocness of such objects with signatures.) Baudrillard says Marx, in his economics studies, overlooks the act of consumption as purchase (transformation from "exchange value" to use value), and that this act of consumption is also a different Super-Big *"EXPENSE" (DÉPENSE)*, the essence of which is the convex value of wealth. In Baudrillard's eyes, this new value surpasses economic "exchange value." (Here, we can see Baudrillard's teacher, Guy Debord's, enacted values of existence.)[11]

> It is that value, deployed beyond exchange value and founded upon the latter's destruction, that **invests the object purchased**, acquired, appropriated, **with its differential sign/value**. It is not the quantity of money that takes on value, as in the economic logic of equivalence, but rather money spent, sacrificed, eaten up according to a logic of difference and challenge. Every act of purchase is thus simultaneously an economic act and a transeconomic act of **the production of differential sign/value**.[12]

Baudrillard is always fond of negating the general with ad hocness, and here the consumption of the auction's special exchange process is employed to deny the economic consumption of general

11   See "Section One" in the second chapter of *A Deep Plough. Unscrambling Major Post-Marxist Texts From Adorno to Zizek*, Vol. 2. (Renmin University Press, 2008.). English version by Canut Intl. Publishers, London, 2010.
12   Baudrillard, Jean. *For a Critique of the Political Economy of the Sign*. Trans. Charles Levin. Telos Press Publishing, 1981, p. 112-113.

commodities. This deduction is invalid and illegitimate. When he says that every act of purchase is also "a transeconomic act of the production of differential sign value," he never considers the rupture which will inevitably appear in the "magical transformation" from the ad hoc situation to the general logic platform. Will all general acts of purchase be the production process of his so-called "differential sign value?" Are daily necessities, such as bread and butter, purchased by ordinary people, the production of differential value? Definitely not. I cannot tell whether the idea indicates Baudrillard's talent or stupidity. Nonetheless, herein lies a key issue: the explicit expense surpassing exchange value, despite its formal similarities to the non-utilitarian "consumption" (Georges Bataille) in symbolic exchange, is still a non-materialized *value*, which is identical to the aberrance of the symbolism of evil referred to by Baudrillard above. The differential sign value is just a new form of value which is generated in the operation of contemporary capitalism. (Now, the utilitarian value in the process of Baudrillard's logic ordering is always a bad thing.)

Baudrillard immediately comes back from general consumption to the ad hoc art auction. He states that a situation comparable to a game, festival, or carnival appears at the auction, where a group of peers compete on the "aristocrat's" stage, and where they wrestle and sacrifice in a gambling-like display in the pursuit of art works which do not meet their real needs. Therefore, the auction "turns consumption into a passion, a fascinating game, something other than functional economic behaviour: it becomes the competitive field of the destruction of economic value for the sake of another type of value."[13] This value is the new *sign exchange value*, completely different from traditional economic "exchange value." (Later, Baudrillard points out that the academic system produces knowledge in similar non-economic "community competition." He says that the national examinations for degrees and teachers' professional titles in France and other European countries are "the social threshold of the caste," and that meanwhile, "knowledge as a universal value transmutes into knowledge as a sign value." Thus, knowledge has become a title similar to that of "aristocrat." It is the

13 *Ibid.*, p. 113.

same in high-level academic congresses, where scholars participate as though they were laying bets in horse racing, and as a result, the academic congress "(of scholars, of intellectuals, of sociologists) as places of transmission, of hereditary reproduction of the intelligentsia and of a privileged community on the basis of an agonistic debauch of signs."[14] If my understanding is correct, this comparison is Baudrillard's activated academic memories of Bourdieu's theories about academic capital and education reproduction, which are directly identified by Baudrillard elsewhere in the book.)

Baudrillard's analysis of the art auction does make sense, because the act of auctioning art is not carried out in accordance with the principles of common barter. He can therefore indeed bring forward the issue of sign exchange value. However, as doing so is not his purpose, Baudrillard's major logical leap causes this ad hoc discussion to again transform into the thought ordering of general assertion. Baudrillard believes that Marx in the 19th century only focused on the production and systematization of economic "exchange value," where there is "transmutation of all values (labour, knowledge, social relations, culture, nature) into economic exchange value. Everything is abstracted and reabsorbed into a world market and in the preeminent role of money as a general equivalent." Nonetheless, what Marx does not recognize is that the economic exchange process of the commodity-market then is also an "immense process of the transmutation of economic exchange value into sign exchange value. This is the process of *CONSUMPTION* considered as a *system of sign exchange value*." (Baudrillard tries hard to show that he is smarter than 19th-century Marxism.

Here again appears the interesting textual phenomenon that I identified previous section, namely, that Baudrillard often regards the "Big" (the first letter is capitalized) concepts as forced modes, and he sometimes adopts discriminative "Super-Big" concepts (all letters are capitalized).) Baudrillard believes that this "consumption" is the transmutation into an invisible sign exchange value instead of transformation in the common sense from the commodity to the use value identified by Marx, namely, the utility consumption of the commodity. Nonetheless, he does not illustrate here whether the object,

14 *Ibid.*, p. 122.

transmuting into the sign exchange value instead of the commodity's use value, refers to the art auction or all the general commodities. If it refers to the latter, then this argument seems obtuse, because most low-end household goods (oil, bread, butter, salt and the like) directly enter the field of "expense" without any transmutation of differential sign exchange value. If it refers to the special art auction, then there is no reason for him to excitedly announce the advent of the "Copernican revolution" involving the entire political economy:

> *At this point, the field of political economy, articulated only through exchange value and use value, explodes and must be entirely reanalyzed as **"generalized political economy"** (ÉCONOMIE POLITIQUE GÉNÉRALISÉE), which implies the production of sign exchange value in the same way and in the same movement as the production of material goods and of economic exchange value. The analysis of the production of signs and of culture thus does not impose itself as exterior, ulterior, and "superstructural" in relation to that of material production; it imposes itself as a **revolution of political economy** itself, generalized by the theoretical and practical irruption of the political economy of the sign.[15]*

In reality, Baudrillard's argument here is probably just a new supplement to Marx's political economy, because *some* trade acts outside of economic exchange are beyond Marx's theoretical logic, and Baudrillard attempts to identify that the rules of trade can be better illustrated by the sign exchange value. He might be right. However, Baudrillard is so ambitious that he proclaims his over-exaggerated new ideas are a grand revolution of political economy. In my opinion, Baudrillard's words are exaggerated, because if any new idea can bring about revolution, then this ideological revolution is without value.

Baudrillard believes that the traditional boundaries of political economy "should be disregarded," and as it will directly lead to "ideological mystification," the differential sign production he identifies cannot be categorized as so-called superstructure analysis in a "culturalist" manner. He asks in a pretentious tone, "what is a signification? In what social relation is it produced? What is the mode of production of signification? Is it the 'capitalist' mode of production?

---

15   *Ibid.*, p. 113-114.

Absurd." A hundred years later, Saussure's discourse, "signification" and the like in linguistics, are beyond Marx's consideration, and they cannot be simply applied to the non-signifying production mode of thingness. Baudrillard's question here is sheer nonsense.

Nonetheless, Baudrillard gives himself another reason:

> Sign values are **produced** by a certain type of social labour. But the production of differences, of differential hierarchical systems, is not to be confused with the extortion of economic surplus value, nor does it result from it. Between the two, another type of labour intervenes which transforms economic value and surplus value into sign value: it is a sumptuary operation, devouring (consummation) and surpassing economic value according to a radically different type of exchange.[16]

Here, there is a lot of new thinking, but it actually confounds Baudrillard's basic theoretical ordering. According to my summary, this new thinking lies in two major aspects: firstly, the sign value is produced by the above-mentioned differential (series) production instead of the material production dominated by the living labour (variable C) of the proletariat shaping favoured by Marx; secondly, there is a type of labour transmuting the generated economic value and surplus value into the labour of sign value, and Baudrillard names it "a sumptuary operation." For example, in the auction, appreciation comes into existence by means of bidding, which surpasses the consumption of economic value. However, new sign value is generated in the consumption.

Nonetheless, I still have some questions about the two above-mentioned aspects. First, if we assume that the differential series production similar to modern painting described by Baudrillard is a new form of production, then called to mind is the series existing in the production of all modern goods, for instance, the differential production of automobiles, household appliances, and cosmetics. The deliberate differential series described by Baudrillard truly exists, and the code of the sign is indeed a key constraint in the production process, representing an improved version of the trick of modern capital logic. However, I am left with the question of whether or not the differential series can be thoroughly *divorced from* the thingness labour and the production process. Does sign operation

---

16   *Ibid.*, p. 115.

radically *negate and replace* fundamental thingness production? These questions are crucial, but Baudrillard does not answer them. Second, whether the auction can become a new type of labour or not depends on Baudrillard's definition of labour. From my point of view, the most basic content of the concept labour must be the subject's creation activities through his own intellect and strength, which causes the object of labour to generate new forms of personal characteristics in the shaping. It is therefore doubtful that the auction constitutes a type of labour. In reality, the essence of the issue lies in the fact that when Baudrillard simply replaces the political economy control with code control, and Marx's political economy with the political economy of the sign, he uses code, such a *dominant* factor in modern capitalism, to negate the political and economic *foundation* of capitalist slavery.[17] When people are just concerned with resistance against the code control, there is not likely to be a complete change in the reality of bourgeois thingness control. We can immediately recognize the question, who is on earth the real accomplice to capitalist control?!

With regard to Baudrillard's casual inference above, he even believes that here there is a *new type of surplus value*. This kind of surplus value must be distinguished from economic value: "It does not create profit, but legitimacy (légitimité)."[18]

> It issues from it through a reworking of economic value. As a result of having forgotten this very specific labour, Marxist analysis today finds itself in the same position with respect to the field of ideology as the bourgeois economists before (and since) Marx vis-à-vis material production: the real source of value and the real process of production are skipped over. It is from neglect of this social labour of sign production that ideology derives its transcendence; signs and culture appear enveloped in "fetishism," a mystery equivalent to, and contemporaneous with that of the commodity.[19]

---

17 I once specially distinguished and discussed the pair of domination and foundation under the category of general historical materialism. Cf. *The Subjective Dimension of Marxist Historical Dialectics* published by Canut Intl. Publishers, London, 2012.
18 Baudrillard, Jean. *For a Critique of the Political Economy of the Sign.* Trans. Charles Levin. Telos Press Publishing, 1981, p. 121.
19 *Ibid.*, p. 115.

I think that plausibly profound but superficial words are the most disgusting feature of the so-called post-modern academic text. Although Baudrillard does not belong to "post-modernism," he has obviously borrowed this "post-68" type of frivolous convex discourse.

Baudrillard tries to illustrate that neglect of the special labour producing the sign in modern social critical theories renders possible the distribution of contemporary ideology, and today the most deceiving part in bourgeois fetishism is the fetishism of the sign (signifier) he identifies. According to Baudrillard, Veblen and Guy Debord are the only two modern thinkers who truly understand his so-called political economy of the sign, because their analysis of modern capitalism is "beyond the 'dialectical materialism' of productive forces, examines the mechanism of *logic of sumptuary values*"; only their analysis reveals the secret of today's social slavery, that is, that this "logic of sumptuary values" through its code "assures and perpetuates the hegemony of the dominant class, and, in a way, shelters the latter, through its 'transubstantiation' of values, from economic revolutions and their social repercussions."[20] If not over-exaggerated at the thought ordering level, this argument does make sense. In Baudrillard's eyes, one of most important aspects in today's capitalist social control is that "a mastery of the transubstantiation of economic exchange value into sign exchange value based on a monopoly of the code is decisive."

> *Dominant classes have always either assured their domination over sign values from the outset (archaic and traditional societies), or endeavoured (in the capitalist bourgeois order) to surpass, to transcend, and to consecrate their economic privilege in a semiotic privilege, because this later stage represents the ultimate stage of domination. This logic, which comes to relay class logic and which is no longer defined by ownership of the means of production but by the mastery of the process of signification; and which activates a mode of production radically different from that of material production (and which for this reason escapes "Marxist" analysis) is found in its entirety, though microscopically, in the art auction.[21]*

---

20 *Ibid.*, p. 115.
21 *Ibid.*, p. 115-116.

It is fortunate that Baudrillard still remembers the art auction. He says that it is in the art auction and market that a new "nucleum of the strategy of values" is discovered and it is "a sort of concrete space-time, strategic moment and matrix in the process of ideology, which latter is always the production of sign value and of coded exchange. This economy of values is a *political* economy."[22] The new political economy has surpassed economic calculation, thus thoroughly subverting the whole theoretical foundation of traditional political economy. This is the revolution of political economy achieved by Baudrillard, where Marx has been re-grasped; additionally, it also recognizes contemporary capitalist ideology which Marx is unable to probe into. Thereby, Baudrillard begins to shift to another battlefield.

3 WHO CAN CRITICIZE CONTEMPORARY CAPITALIST IDEOLOGY?

After the declaration of his revolution in political economy, Baudrillard still needs to continue with his theoretical modelling and argumentation. In the following discussions, Baudrillard again returns to art auctions, where he intends to further explain the difference between sign value and economic "exchange value." This issue is indeed critical.

Baudrillard says that every art auction seems to construct a ceremonial scene on the spot, a scene which looks like an independent kingdom of the exchange of personal character:

> *This personal character of the exchange implies the insularity (unicité) of the place (one cannot participate without being present), and above all, the concrete integrality (unicité) of the process (the time, order, rhythm, tempo are essential elements of the bidding). In the altercation and the out-bidding, each moment depends on the previous one and on the reciprocal relation of partners. Hence there is a specific development, which is different from the abstract time of economic exchange.*[23]

Baudrillard's statement constitutes another appropriation of Ferdinand de Saussure's interdependent differential relations, and in Baudrillard's opinion each person's out-bidding in the auction forms

---

22   *Ibid.*, p. 122.
23   *Ibid.*, p. 116.

a special abstract time completely different from the one present in economic exchange. (This is again a false argument, because according to Marx's theories, there is only the abstract labour time based on sufficient social division in modern production, not abstract time in economic exchange. Baudrillard is typically free with his tongue here.) In the auction, there is no supply and demand as far as traditional economy is concerned; that is, the market assesses the use value of commodities in advance, and "exchange value" will reach its peak value (for instance in the auction of antique products). In the art auction, "at the moment of bidding, exchange value and use value are no longer correlated according to an economic calculus. The anticipated use value (if there is one) does not increase during the auction." Baudrillard means that the art auction occurs outside of use value, and that once use value is excluded from commodities, the "exchange value" cannot be sold either. Therefore, the art auction enters a new symbolic game:

> At once, it ceases to be exchange value and the whole situation is transferred out of the realm of the economic. It does not, however, cease to be an exchange, although it no longer takes the form of supply and demand, but of reciprocal wager. Thus the auction simultaneously institutes:
> - a transmutation of value and of the economic coordinates;
> - another type of social relation.[24]

Baudrillard does not understand that in the aesthetic context, the creation of artwork generates aesthetic ornamental value instead of the use value of shaped objects, but in the fully materialized bourgeois kingdom, all objects without use value, such as academic thought, religious belief, human conscience, aesthetic value, and many social relations, have to inversely manifest as values, and these objects themselves do not possess direct utilitarian use value or the value to enter the market exchange. However, in the commodity-market economy, all in existence is forced by living to deform and be reduced to for-sale objects. (In this regard, in the article *The Essence of Money*, the German socialist philosopher Moses Hess already before Marx vividly explains that in a bourgeois "vendor" society, every heartbeat is done after being sold off.) As Baudrillard

---

24 *Ibid.*, p. 116.

has little knowledge of the history of ideas, he is delighted by his ignorant "new discoveries."

Baudrillard claims that different from the supply and demand of the market, the auction adopts the *placing of bets*, and thereby two new things come into existence: first, the non-economic sign exchange value refers to the sign value generated by people's out-bidding in the art auction; second, a new social relation also refers to the non-economic symbolic relation—Baudrillard names it the "aristocratic" relation. (In China today, this relation is called a circle of *successful people*. What is disguised by Baudrillard is that this non-economic thing is exactly based on the economic nouveau riche. How can they continue the art auction without a lot of money to serve as an economic prop?)

In the art auction, money is spent as *the luxurious value* instead of the "exchange value." (Thorstein Veblen's academic memory is activated here.)

> *There is no longer an equivalence, but an aristocratic parity[25] established between money, which has become a sumptuary material through the loss of its economic exchange value, and the canvas, which has become a sign of prestige (hence an element of the restricted corpus that we call "painting") through the loss of its symbolic value.[26]*

Baudrillard here intends to emphasize that in the luxurious behaviour that one finds in the auction, money is no longer a general equivalent regulating capitalist social relations, and instead forms the *aristocratic interdependence* in a new symbolic field, where a new community comes into being. Contrary to the economic rivalry between individuals on the footing of formal equality in economic

---

25   Cf. the chapter below on Symbolic Value and Aesthetic Function.

26   "The price at which a canvas is sold is not the measure of its value in the same way as for an article of consumption. The price only has meaning at the very instant of sale, by the game of competition in which it is the relative equivalent of the absolute values and significations to which the painting refers." P. Dard and J. Michener, *Etude sure l'Exchange de Valeur*. In fact, it is no longer a price but a wager (enjeu). Moreover, for real players, money won in the game remains marked by it and cannot be spent for useful economic purposes: it must be put back into the game, poured back into it, "burned"–in a way, it is the part maudite of Bataille. Baudrillard, Jean. *For a Critique of the Political Economy of the Sign*. Trans. Charles Levin. Telos Press Publishing, 1981, p. 117.

exchanges, the auction is the "aristocrat's" fête or game, similar to the *duel*, and at this time, it doesn't matter who is the vanquisher. (Veblen, who is favoured by Baudrillard, once talked about the so-called "Takenao spirit" existing in the leisure class, but in ancient times, this "Takenao spirit" was usually achieved by a "duel.")[27]

> *The essential function of the auction is the institution of a community of the privileged who define themselves as such by agonistic speculation upon a restricted corpus of signs. Competition of the aristocratic sort seals their parity (which has nothing to do with the formal equality of economic competition), and thus their collective caste privilege with respect to all others, from whom they are no longer separated merely by their purchasing power, but by the sumptuary and collective act of, the production and exchange of sign values.*[28]

This group is a special situational community, among which the general rules of consumption and purchase have become nullified, so that the new luxury and collecting lead to exchange between the symbolic values. For the privileged, the artworks to be auctioned do not possess practical value, "the unique value of the canvas itself resides in the relation of parity, of statutory privilege, which, as a sign, it maintains with the other terms of the limited corpus of paintings. Hence, the 'elitist' affinity between the amateur and the canvas that psychologically connotes the very sort of value, of exchange and of aristocratic social relation that is instituted by the auction."[29] The fetishism appearing here is not the material object of artworks, but the differentiation of paintings and bygone antiquities, the signature, and "the cycles of its successive owners."

---

27   Cf. Thorstein B Veblen, *The Theory of the Leisure Class*. Forgotten Books, 2008. Chapter Ten.

28   "Within this community there is a traffic of paintings on the basis of a competition among peers, while from the point of view of the global society, paintings are retained in and by this community—that is, the latter functions on the basis of a social discrimination. Yet this community presents itself as open by the competitive aspect of acquisition.... There we are at the frontiers of strategies of domination, where the possibility of individual mobility masks social discrimination." P. Dard and J. Michner, *Etude sur l'Echange de Valeur*. Baudrillard, Jean. *For a Critique of the Political Economy of the Sign*. Trans. Charles Levin. Telos Press Publishing, 1981, p. 117.

29   *Ibid.*, p. 118.

Therefore, Baudrillard believes that the auction is the matrix of modern ideology. This time, ideology derives from the political economy of the sign instead of being modelled in economic production, exchange, and the social relations of politics and legal rights in Marx's sense. Behind this ideology, the new caste is established precisely upon the destruction of traditional economic value; the production of differential signs is the real secret of this ideology. Baudrillard believes that the ubiquitous consumption found in today's capitalist society "is instituted on the exchange model of sign/value and on the basis of the exchange of differences, of a distinctive material and thus of a potential community."[30]

Here, Baudrillard again turns to his general idea that today what people consume is the differential sign rather than the function of the shaped object. "Today differences of the consumption are produced industrially, they are bureaucratically programmed in the form of collective models. They no longer arise in the personal reciprocity of challenge and exchange. Only the mass-mediatized simulacra (simulacre) of competition operate in the statutory rivalry."[31] (This is Baudrillard's second crucial use of the term simulacrum, which still specifically refers to today's media spectacle, and not to his subsequent identification of the unique ordering modes (three levels) of creating the world through the capitalism in the book *Symbolic Exchange and Death*. Even so, the simulacrum Baudrillard mentions here is still a promotion of Debord's spectacle concept, because the spectacle lays emphasis on *representation*, while the simulacrum highlights an internal *structuralized simulation*. Therefore, in this sense, the spectacle is no more than an external form of the simulacrum.) The competition and the fight between individuals in traditional consumption have given way to a more magnificent arena constructed by the mass media. It is through the simulacrum of the image that the mass media is changing the material commodity into various differential situatings with even more "magic of the code," and the sign code is constructing a special dominant situation of suggestive codes and the symbolic consumption game; thus, in an unconscious community, the consumption game without economic value becomes the fête protested by a hidden society. Baudrillard

30   *Ibid.*, p. 119.
31   *Ibid.*, p. 119.

says that this fête, "whatever the economic status and class condition—it acts to the advantage of the dominant class. It is the keystone of domination. It is not automatically dismantled by the revolutionary logic of productive forces, by the 'dialectical' process of capital or by the traditional critique of political economy."[32] In this sense, Baudrillard intends to announce that Marxism and the traditional critique of political economy is dead; today it is Baudrillard himself who has the ability to really dismantle the ideology of contemporary bourgeois culture.

Thus, only a critique of the political economy of the sign can analyze how the present *mode of domination (mode de domination)* is able to regain, integrate and simultaneously take advantage of all the modes of production—not only of the capitalist mode of production, but of all "previous," "archaic" modes of production and exchange, infra—or trans-economic. Only such a critique can analyze how at the very heart of the economic the mode of domination reinvents (or reproduces) the logic and the strategy of signs, of castes, of segregation, and of discrimination; how it reinstates the feudal logic of personal relations or even that of the gift exchange and of reciprocity, or of agonistic exchange—in order simultaneously to thwart and crown the "modern" socio-economic logic of class.[33]

Baudrillard's invention is really omnipotent. He believes that all previous theoretical efforts will join past logical formulas in history, because economic exploitation and political "class domination" are only certain historical stages, and Marxism and other critical theories are but examples of the numerous social pedigree analyses. Today, as society has become a kingdom dominated by signs, the critique of Marx's theories, let alone to adopt these theories to analyze the dominant logic of feudal society and the ancient gift exchange which never enter contemporary economic exchange, becomes weak and turns out to be a complete failure. Thus, Baudrillard proudly tells the world that the only theoretical tool capable of explaining the whole historical process, "can only arise in the critique of the political economy of the sign." His proclamation is really the ravings of the nouveau riche in the field of theories.

---

32   *Ibid.*, p. 119-120.
33   *Ibid.*, p. 120.

CHAPTER V

THE COMPLEX LOGICAL STRUCTURE OF THE NEW ECONOMICS

In the book *For a Critique of the Political Economy of the Sign*, Baudrillard's theoretical argument is well organized from the perspective of logical narration. After a large amount of theoretical preparation and critical falsification, he makes a systemic description and summary of his new "thought revolution" in Chapter Six of the book. In the section "For a General Theory," Baudrillard is not reserved in the words he uses to summarize and discuss his series of opinions, and of course, this time his thought ordering is more profound and complete. It is in this section that Baudrillard first publicly shows his thorough negation of Marx's theory, and he mainly criticizes historical materialism possessing the core theory of material production, basing himself on the use value. Consequently, this section completes his shift from a post-Marxist trend to one of anti-Marxism. At the same time, it plays a significant transitional role in Baudrillard's escape from the domination of the otherness mirror-image and his realization of autonomous thought modelling. Lastly, it lays out sufficient theoretical preparation for his next step, which is towards a new space of original ideas.

1 THE SYMBOLIC EXCHANGE OF AUTHENTICITY IN THE FOUR DIFFERENT SOCIAL LOGICS

Baudrillard's general explanation of the logical modelling of his autonomous theory commences with discussions in Chapter Two, "The Ideological Genesis of Needs," where he clearly identifies four different social logics: the functional logic of use value, the economic logic of "exchange value," the differential logic of sign value, and the logic of symbolic exchange. (It should be noted that we have already explained that the first three of the four different logics belong to Baudrillard's critical targets, while the fourth one, symbolic exchange, is the true logic that he derives from Mauss-Bataille's theory.) In Baudrillard's views, "corresponding to four different principles are: the usefulness of (l'utilité), equivalence (l'équivalence), difference (l'différence), uncertainty (l'ambivalence)."[1] That is, use value is based on utility, "exchange value" originates in equivalence, and sign value arises in difference; meanwhile, the essence of symbolic exchange, which does not belong to value logics, is an unordered infinite metaphor.

In the summary of new logics here, Baudrillard follows up on the context of discussion of the art auction, and draws up a very complex "general conversion table of all values."

Use Value (UV): (Valeur d'usage)

> 1. UV — EcEV
>
> 2. UV — SgEV
>
> 3. UV — SbE

Economic Exchange Value (EcEV): (Valeur d'échange économique)

> 4. EcEV — UV
>
> 5. EcEV — SgEV
>
> 6. EcEV — SbE

Sign Exchange Value (SgEV): (Valeur d'échange/signe)

> 7. SgEV — UV
>
> 8. SgEV — EcEV
>
> 9. SgEV — SbE

---

1   *Ibid.*, p. 123.

Symbolic Exchange (SbE): (Echange symbolique)

10. SbE — UV

11. SbE — EcEV

12. SbE — SgEV[2]

The above is the new logical modelling of Baudrillard's autonomous theory, with a total of four groups (twelve logics), which in my opinion, are more like pretentious logic manufacturings than logical models. Baudrillard also provides the following definitions of this complex conversion table of logics:

The first, "UV — EcEV," is discussed by the traditional political economy (including Marx), that is, the relation between use value and "exchange value" appearing in the material production of commodity in early capitalism; the consumption discussed here is a productive consumption; namely, the commodity is withdrawn from circulation and enters the thingness expenditure of objects. This logic is related to the fourth logic "EcEV — UV," and the traditional commodity consumption transforms "exchange value" into the presence of use value. However, neither of these two logics mentions sign value. Here, sign value is one of the historical targets denounced by Baudrillard in this logical context.

The second, "UV — SgEV," specially refers to the differential sign production process of contemporary capitalism discussed by Baudrillard in the previous part of this book. There is an inverse relation between use value and sign exchange value, because the presence of the latter is precisely based on the destruction of the *utility* of objects. The essence of modern consumption is no longer the thingness function of productive shaping, but turns into a conspicuous consumption *presenting sumptuary value* instead:

> *"Unproductive" consumption (of time as well, in conspicuous idleness and leisure), in fact productive of differences: it is functional difference playing as a statutory difference (semiautomatic vs. entirely automatic washing machine). Here, the advertising process of conferring value transmutes use goods (biens d'usage) into sign values. Here technique and knowledge are divorced from their objective practice and recovered by the "cultural" system of differentiation.*[3]

---

2   *Ibid.*, p. 123.

3   *Ibid.*, p. 124.

Baudrillard is quite good at giving examples, and he means that the functional difference between automatic washing machines and semi-automatic ones used in our daily lives has been transformed into the differential sign value through the pseudo-symbolism of advertisements, manifesting as a difference of *conspicuous status.* That is to say, people using automatic washing machines are distinguished from those using semi-automatic ones, and thus different social strata are formed. (In fact, today this is a common phenomenon in China's consumption of "series differential commodities," such as V12-displacement cars and the normal cars with displacements under V6; detached villas and townhouses; LCD digital televisions and analog ones; multi-band mobile phones and those with less than two frequencies; and so on.) This logic is identical to the fifth logic, "EcEV — SgEV," which highlights the transformation from the "exchange value" to the sign value. Here the commodity form of objects is upgraded to the sign form; economic power is transformed into the symbolic sign power. This transformation is something new that we encounter in Baudrillard's critique context today.

The third logic is "UV — SbE," wherein the symbolic exchange is different from the former two logics. It is the *true* logic of *should-be* confirmed by Baudrillard. As there is only the "consumption" destructing the use value of objects instead of traditional consumption in Mauss-Bataille's context, this logic belongs to gift exchange in the lives and disorderly symbolic exchanges in the festivals of aboriginal tribes. This point is both the most significant point in Baudrillard's logical situating and his mental City of God. The sixth logic, "EcEV — SbE," also explains that symbolic exchange has surpassed existing economic exchange and sign exchange. In this regard, a special definition is offered by Baudrillard that there is no symbolic *value,* but only symbolic exchange; this true exchange is "the radical rupture of the field of value," and defines itself precisely as a world of defunctionalization and disorder *without object, commodity or sign.* (This statement represents Baudrillard's theoretical introspection. Not long ago, he still practiced concepts like the "symbolic value," but now his symbolic exchange theory has essentially matured.)

From the seventh through the ninth logics, Baudrillard illustrates the transformation from the utility of objects to the monopoly of culture—the sign. Ultimately, he believes that people may be liberated on the condition that sign exchange breaks down and is reduced to the heaven of true symbolic exchange The tenth through twelfth logics then explain that people's true symbolic exchange is disguised by three pseudo-situatings, namely the thingness function, the exchange fantasy, and the sign ideology, because

> *they amount to a kind of "cost analysis" of symbolic exchange under the abstract and rational jurisdiction of the various codes of value (use value, exchange value, sign value). For example: the objects involved in reciprocal exchange, whose uninterrupted circulation establishes social relationships, i.e., social meaning, annihilate themselves in this continual exchange without assuming any value of their own (that is, any appropriable value). Once symbolic exchange is broken, this same material is abstracted into utility value, commercial value, statutory value. The symbolic is transformed into the instrumental, either commodity or sign. Any one of the various codes may be specifically involved, but they are all joined in the single form of political economy which is opposed, as a whole, to symbolic exchange.[4]*

In a word, the valueless human symbolic exchange is endowed with thingness value, "exchange value," and symbolic value, and symbolism itself has become a tool for the exchange of value, while symbolism, which in the past could best demonstrate the essence of human existence, is now the most vicious shadow hanging over humankind's true nature. This phenomenon is called *alienation* in the classical philosophy of the past. Here, Baudrillard just gives another illustration of the loss of true relations among people. (In the subsequent book, *Symbolic Exchange and Death*, this loss is identified as the true death; while in *The Perfect Crime*, it is upgraded to "murder.") Therefore, Baudrillard is after all *humanistic*.

In fact, after careful reconsideration, we find that these twelve logics are a logical fabric intentionally woven by Baudrillard, but they do not constitute an intrinsically consistent logical situation. Here, Baudrillard intends to demonstrate that in today's society, there are four kinds of social relations, among which the reduced symbolic

---

4 *Ibid.*, p. 125.

exchange relation is the one that people should uphold. These twelve logics are nonsense, and it is ridiculous that Baudrillard himself has no idea how to continue his theory after the fourth logic.

2 THE CHARMING CONVERSION FORMULA OF MULTI-LOGICS

After fabricating four logics with twelve formulas, which amounts to an unsuccessful thought modelling, Baudrillard again proposes an analogical formula that he assumes to be very important, namely the formula of equivalence between the economic relations of Marx's commodity exchange and sign exchange relations:

sign value is to symbolic exchange what exchange value (economic) is to use value.

I think it is an interesting formula. These two logical ratios are not truly equivalent, but it is really a good idea that Baudrillard attempts to play himself up by putting his new thoughts on the same status as Marx's famous economic logic through this formula. The second part of this formula is Baudrillard's inaccurate statement of Marx's concept of duality of commodities, and the accurate version is *value* (instead of exchange value) and use value; the first part of the formula belongs to his new ideas, which are by now familiar to us, of the exchange value of the pseudo-symbolic sign in contemporary capitalism, and the symbolic exchange as the true social relation.

I find that the key issue lies in Baudrillard's illustration that similar to the relation between "exchange value" and use value, today's sign exchange value is precisely *replaced and distortedly represented* by symbolic exchange. Sign exchange value also takes symbolic meaning as the convex-representing relationship, but it is, instead of being the real symbolic relationship, the slaughter of the symbolic relationship in the name of symbolism. (This is both an in-depth theoretical identification and the preliminary thought clue to his subsequent concept of simulation.) Baudrillard himself says it "follows" the same theoretical procedure as Marx's. (Some scholars thus try to prove that Baudrillard still subjectively intends to develop Marxism, which is actually a misunderstanding.) What is worth contemplating is an analogy made by Baudrillard, namely that the mysterious material, like the use value of the object and the "exchange value" appearing as a commodity, and it is the same with the relation between sign "exchange value" and symbolic exchange that the true mana exchange in symbolic exchange is replaced and deluded by a false sign value similar to symbolic relationship. In Lacan's context, sign value is the usurper of the symbolic exchange relation of death! The meaning of this logical formula is then directly identified in the second formula as follows:

sign value is to exchange value what symbolic exchange is to use value.

Obviously, this new formula is obtained via the sub-item transposition of the previous one and, as I understand and interpret it, it states the issues explicitly. Next, the issue becomes more complicated, and Baudrillard here turns to Saussure, because the sign in this equation will be decomposed into the constituent *signified* and *signifier*. (In the book *Course in General Linguistics*, Saussure makes a similar comparison.)[5] Saussure says, "in place of the sign as global value, it is necessary to make its constituent elements, the signifier and the signified, appear."[6] Thus, the third equation emerges:

exchange value is to use value what the signifier is to the signified.

Here, Baudrillard organizes an "overt conspiracy": the duality of sign is equivalent to the duality of Marx's commodity, and he also mentions above that the so-called theoretical flaw of Marxism is its neglect of the signed process present in the economic exchange of commodity. In other words, Baudrillard here uses sociology to "describe the field of general political economy," namely the political economy of the sign established by him. (Such illegitimate theoretical description will be specially discussed in the following section.)

Baudrillard then reminds us that symbolic exchange is *expelled from the field of value* after the establishment of this equation, and this expulsion proves that the disorder symbolic exchange has surpassed the utilitarian and order value. It should be noted that this

5   Saussure, Ferdinand de. *Course in General Linguistics*. Trans. Wade Baskin. New York: *McGraw-Hill* Book Company, 1965, p. 75.
6   Baudrillard, Jean. *For a Critique of the Political Economy of the Sign*. Trans. Charles Levin. Telos Press Publishing, 1981, p. 127.

point is a logical focus in Baudrillard's book. Namely, it is the definition of heterogeneity between symbolic exchange and all the *value exchange* systems. Baudrillard believes that all the existing value exchange systems deny and repress the symbolic exchange:

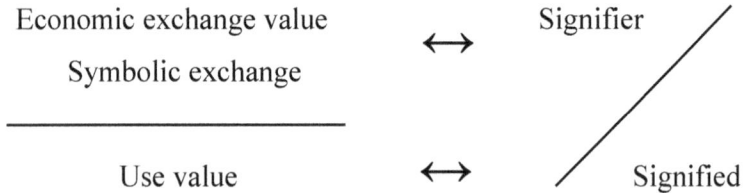

$$\frac{\text{Economic exchange value}}{\text{Symbolic exchange}} \quad \longleftrightarrow \quad \frac{\text{Signifier}}{\text{Signified}}$$

Economic exchange value

Symbolic exchange

⟷   Signifier   /

————————————

Use value   ⟷   /   Signified

The above is the fourth and the most complex theoretical formula, which is Baudrillard's most crucial ontology of autonomous logical modelling. Baudrillard hardly creates an original concept originally with this logical formula, but he does constitute a new thought situation in this theoretical modelling. (Soon, Baudrillard will begin to feel unsatisfied with the construction of his autonomous logical situating with the others' concepts, and instead, he will turn to the original thought situating like simulacra-simulation.) In my opinion, Baudrillard's formula intends to illustrate that the symbolic exchange favoured by him "is a single great opposition between the whole fields of value," and symbolic exchange is precisely "the field of non-value" in a functional economic *entropy field*. Therefore, the identification of the fundamental differences between symbolic exchange and the general political economy (including the political economy of the sign) aims at illustrating that the symbolic exchange is the "the basis of a revolutionary anthropology," which is elaborated by Marxist analysis. But, in the end, the revolution fails due to its inability to completely divorce itself from the traditional political economy system. Baudrillard tries to promote this revolution, and claims that he puts forward three essential tasks with a clear purpose, "beginning from and going beyond Marxist analysis." (Here, we can clearly see how Baudrillard maneuvers from post-Marxism to the anti-Marxism, step by step.) The three tasks are as follows:

The first task is to extend the critique of political economy to "a radical critique of use value" which was "neglected" by Marx. Baudrillard believes this task will reduce the idealism in Marx's anthropological view, and he also intends to undertake a radical critique of "use value fetishism" in Marx's unconsciousness. This task is his direct "attack" against Marxism that is about to commence in the following section.

The second task is to extend his critique of political economy to the critique of "the sign and to systems of signs," and this task is both the second-level criticism and the main purpose of his book. Baudrillard says,

> *the extension is required in order to show how the logic, free play and circulation of signifiers is organized like the logic of the exchange value system; and how the logic of signified is subordinated to it tactically, as that of use value is subordinated to that of exchange value. Finally, we need a critique of signifier-fetishism—an analysis of the sign form in its relation to the commodity form.*[7]

This task is what he works out with painstaking effort in this book, and is the basic thought situation of Baudrillard's third logical equation found above ("exchange value is to use value what the signifier is to the signified.") In Baudrillard's eyes, Marx has merely completed the critical theory of exchange value of commodities, while the critical theories of use value, signifier, and signified remain to be developed by Baudrillard.

The third task is for Baudrillard to directly elaborate the theory of symbolic exchange. This theory, in my opinion, is the worst of his three theories, because we never see Baudrillard systematically and completely articulate the symbolic exchange theory. (Symbolic exchange always presents itself as the negativity of the critical logic, and in the book, *Symbolic Exchange and Death*, it refers to the death of true existence.)

---

7   *Ibid.*, p. 129.

CHAPTER VI

A METAPHYSICAL CRITIQUE OF THE USE VALUE

To criticize use value is the top priority amongst the three main theoretical tasks in *For a Critique of the Political Economy of the Sign* that Baudrillard sets for himself. His most perceptive vision, as it seems, reveals that he knows very well what the most significant constructions of theoretical modelling in Marx's theoretical logic are. Thus, use value becomes the first important concept, when Baudrillard says that it is the foundation of all Marx's historical materialistic concept: mode of production as the core. He convinces himself that negating use value is one of the most crucial strategic links necessary for him to surpass Marx's theoretical logic and methods. The general falsification in his later work, *The Mirror of Production*, thus inevitably appears. This chapter focuses on this argument which Baudrillard puts, which is ridiculous but all the same important. For, in the case that this argument could be proved valid, the whole theoretical mansion of Marxism would be overturned. Is it possible for him to achieve such a victory? I doubt it.

1 TO CRITICIZE THE LOST USE VALUE IN MARX'S CRITICAL LOGIC

Baudrillard understands that to negate Marx is undoubtedly a very fast logic channel that will enable him to take high ground in contemporary western social theory. The first intention of Baudrillard, who thoroughly understands the whole of Marxism, is to criticize the concept of use value. He believes that use value serves as the foundation of Marxist political economy and as the core of all of historical materialism, as the "use value" which shapes the functionality of materials is exactly the purpose of material production. Thus, use value is one of the self-evident logical premises hidden within Marx's theories. As a result, Baudrillard insists that critical analysis has to start with use value, which was unconsciously lost by Marx. (This stance is just a beginning. His comprehensive critiques of Marxist political economy and historical materialism can be found in his book *The Mirror of Production*. The second part of this book will enable us to face his reprehensions in that book.) Baudrillard first repeats Marx's economic views on the duality of commodities here, with the general idea that commodities possess both use value and exchange value. (As we have already mentioned, Baudrillard has no idea that in *Capital* Marx has already discarded the previous unscientific use of the term "exchange value" advocated by the classical economics. Instead, due to his discovery that exchange value is merely the price performance of value in the process of market circulation, Marx initiated use of new expressions, *value and use value*. We will further discuss this item in later sections.) The use value of commodities is concrete and special with its shaped functional attribute as the prerequisite, and different from "exchange value," which is both abstract and general. This statement is invalid. Baudrillard argues that Marx's logic should be understood in a reversed way: *No exchange value, no use value*. He makes this key judgment to show that his ideas differ from that of Marx. (In his book *The Mirror of Production*, this point of view is developed more sufficiently. S. Lash understands this issue incorrectly: he states that "For Baudrillard exchange-value is a simulacrum of use-value; in this a simulacrum is a copy…"[1] I have never found this

1   Lash, Scott & John Urry, *Economics of Signs and Space*. London: Sage, 1994, p. 14.

identification.) In Marx's research of economics, use value has been regarded as the basis of form value, yet why does Baudrillard intend to turn this relationship upside-down?

Firstly, Baudrillard argues that according to Marx it seems that use value has nothing to do with the commodity-market economy. The generation of use value and concrete labour—which is based on the development of material productive forces, is only restricted in space for development in capitalist market economy. We discover that in fact Baudrillard plays two illegitimate logical tricks here: one is to jump into the philosophical logic suddenly from the context of economics; the other is his attempt to switch the concept of use value—which should have situated in the Marxist Economics—to a concept of utility for general objects. In this tricky way, he can say that the "use values" of those objects do not belong to the commodity-market economy, and secondly argues that that the development of productive forces which represents the continuous renewal and increase of these "use values" has just been blocked in the capitalist mode of production. Marx never discusses "use value" beyond the field of economic studies; that is why I define Baudrillard's thinking as an illegitimate logical transgression.

Secondly, Baudrillard points out that Marx denies the capitalist exchange structure by stating: "within it is contained, from this standpoint, the promise of a resurgence beyond the market economy, money and exchange value, in the glorious autonomy of man's simple relation to his work and his products."[2] Objectively speaking, we have never read anything written by Marx stating that use value extends beyond the market economy and exchange value. Obviously, this idea is Baudrillard's logical illusion. In Marx's theories, use value and value are two intrinsic attributes of commodities in the very commodity economy. These two attributes, for the shaped objects, are no doubt *historical* attributes acquired during a certain long history in social development. Baudrillard's ideas are also based on his switch from the economic concept of use value to the general utility of objects. In his critical eyes, Marx views the development of the material productive forces as a realistic foundation to surpass capitalism.

---

2   Baudrillard, Jean, *For a Critique of the Political Economy of the Sign*, Trans. by Charles Levin, St. Louis: Telos, 1981, p. 130.

Baudrillard "*discovers*" that fetishism in Marx's statements commodity is merely a function of "exchange value," which means that the social relations generated by markets are covered up by the attributes of commodities themselves. (To be more accurate, that means that human relations in society reversely perform compared to the relations of objects in market exchange.) However, he says,

> *Use value, in this restrictive analysis of fetishism, appears neither as a social relation nor hence as the locus of fetishization. Utility as such escapes the historical determination of class. It represents an objective, final relation of intrinsic purpose (destination proper), which does not mask itself and whose transparency, as form, defies history (even if its content changes continually with respect to social and cultural determinations)[3].*

As long as we interpret use value as the utility of objects, the original intention of Baudrillard will be clearly revealed. In fact, Baudrillard is blaming Marx for driving objects with "self-oriented" functional utility, constructed by human productive labour, to escape from the conclusiveness of class. In accordance with the situating of the idealized symbolic relationship put forward by Mauss-Bataille, worship of use value is precisely the highest economic fetishism. As a result, Baudrillard claims that this is how "idealism" reveals itself in Marxism, because the use value, which Marx has indiscreetly lost, should not be something good at all. In fact, use value additionally serves as a prior secret theoretical construction of bourgeois ideology – economic fetishism. On this point, I would like to explain that it is not Marx's idealism but actually the super *historical idealism* of Baudrillard himself. Baudrillard's view can only be partially correct on the level of contemporary *ecological-ethics*. The destructive development of nature, in the over-developing of economic productive forces, is wrong. Yet in the 19th century, this sort of abnormal over-production is exactly the result of the "benefit maximization" principle of capitalism, which has been criticized by Marx. (Marx's original words are, "to chase the surplus value crazily.") However, to exaggerate the reasonable concept of ecological ethics to the degree of shaping and reform of nature by all material productive labour is untenable.

---

3   *Ibid.*

Moreover, regarding the relations between value and use value, Marx just explains that values of commodities are based on their use values, which are created by productive labour. His research on the production need/aim of surplus value is conducted from the standpoint of economics and he never intends to discuss the relationship between value and use value philosophically, for these two terms should be used in the specific context of economics and thus are not necessary to be discussed in the field of philosophy. Therefore, Baudrillard's attack on Marx here is without clear aim. (It has come to my attention that the statements by Horkheimer and Adorno in *The Dialectic of Enlightenment* are more accurate and profound than Baudrillard's understandings. They believe that "Even when the art business was in the bloom of youth, use value was not dragged along as a mere appendage by exchange value but was developed as a precondition of the latter, to the social benefit of works of art.")[4]

Baudrillard has no notion of the deeper level of these theoretical situations. He still claims proudly that this critical point of thinking indicates that he is more brilliant than Marx:

> *We have to be more logical than Marx himself—and more radical, in the true sense of the word. For use value—indeed, utility itself—is a fetishized social relation, just like the abstract equivalence of commodities. Use value is an abstraction. It is an abstraction of the system of needs cloaked in the false evidence of a concrete destination and purpose, an intrinsic finality of goods and products. It is just like the abstraction of social labour, which is the basis for the logic of equivalence (exchange value), hiding beneath the "innate" value of commodities.[5]*

Here Baudrillard directly puts an "equal" sign between use value and utility, which perfectly proves that our previous interpretation is valid. Obviously, the focal point of Baudrillard's critical artillery fire lies on the utility of shaped items itself, meaning that the utility of all items can be regarded as being the result of the bourgeois demand system that he specially falsified in previous sections. (As to what Heidegger has said, the readiness-to-hand being has already opened

---

4   Max Horkheimer, Theodor W. Adorno, *Dialectic of Enlightenment*, Trans. by Edmund Jephcott, Stanford: 2002, p. 130.
5   Baudrillard, Jean, *For a Critique of the Political Economy of the Sign*, Trans. by Charles Levin, St. Louis: Telos, 1981, p. 131.

the Gestell quality, which will not enable the natural things to be "thinged.") Therefore, different from Marx, Baudrillard believes that not only exchange value is abstract, but that use value is also an abstraction, namely, a logical abstraction of the bourgeois demand system. In addition, "needs (i.e., the system of needs) are the *equivalents of abstract social labour*: on them is erected *the system of use value*, just as abstract social labour is the basis for the system of exchange value." This idea differs from Marx, who let go of use value via the back door and argued that both use value and exchange value are committed to the capitalist system, "regulated by an identical abstract logic of equivalence, an identical code." Baudrillard holds his opinion that "it is always the systematic abstraction that is fetishized." Thus, the secret that has been ignored by Marx lies right on, "and it is the two fetishizations, reunited—that of use value and that of exchange value—that constitute commodity fetishism."[6] What a really surprising "new discovery"!

I personally take the above statement as nonsense, even though such a discovery seems profound. First of all, in Heidegger's logic of ontology, the readiness-to-hand has already become the forced "objectized" quality of this being, which is heading towards objects, while those heading towards being have to be regarded as foreignizations. It is inevitable in early humanist logic. However, in Baudrillard's attacks on the utility of objects, the basic theory turns out to be the grassroots romanticism of Mauss-Bataille. Baudrillard ridiculously insists that utility is the result of the bourgeois demand system without considering one simple historical fact: in the long period of feudal society in the East—where the Western bourgeois world is nothing but a remote terminology and which he passionately considers as primitive society—the utility of objects shaped by labour did exist. In fact, if we view the utility of objects as an abstraction, it will only be an abstraction of the basic way of living among human beings, not that of the bourgeois way of production. When interpreted as a kind of fetishism, utility should be the worship of Being for one of the mankind's self-characteristics—*the existence for me*. Utility of this character has existed for all of human history. Is Baudrillard able to fight against this utility? Secondly, the

---

6   *Ibid.*

abstraction that Marx used in his economic studies is proved to be the scientific way of abstraction acquired from David Ricardo. The real foundation of this abstraction is profoundly interpreted as the *objective abstraction of social history*. Abstracts concerning common labour, common production, and common value are not subjective abstracts developed in Marx's mind, but rather the objective results of the capitalist mode of production. Marx indeed understood the secrets in the Hegelianism when he found out that in today's social life, "abstracts became the dominant power."[7] Baudrillard, who always uses the concept of "abstract" perfunctorily, never reaches nor understands this mystery of situating the concept of "abstract."

Let us return to discussing Baudrillard's way of thinking. How, in Baudrillard's "smart" opinion, could Marx make such a mistake? The reason is that Marx has assumed the incompatibility (incomparabilité) of use value, while Baudrillard insists on his assumption that use value is comparable. His reasoning is as follows: firstly, utility is the basis of all "exchange values," and useless things have nothing to do with interchangeability. Secondly, if utility is closely tied to the principle of exchange, then equivalent logic may have already entered into the utility; although use value cannot be measured in quantity, things are comparable in the process of exchange. (He argues that the "unique, individualized behaviours" in the symbolic exchange are incomparable with the gifts and thus become the useful universality and the common denominator. Thirdly, universal utility is also the basis of general equivalent. Hence, the use value and "exchange value" share an identical form of logic, "included in each object to the general equivalence of abstract symbols which, it codes Every object is translatable into the general abstract code of equivalence, which is its rationale, its objective law, its meaning—and this is achieved independently of who makes use of it and what purpose it serves. It is functionality which supports it and carries it along as code."[8] This code is exactly the premise of developing the capitalist economics: the foundation of computability. Fourth, Marx has not

7 See Chapter 8, Zhang, Yibing, *Back to Marx: The Change of Philosophical Discourse in the Context of Economics*. English version published by Göttingen University Press in 2014.
8 Baudrillard, Jean, *For a Critique of the Political Economy of the Sign*, Trans by Charles Levin, St. Louis: Telos, 1981, p. 132.

realized that "use value itself can act as a social relationship," just as the economic exchange relationship he has revealed, the producer, rather than a creator, can only exist as an abstract labour. Use value is a necessary component and the foundation of the orderly economic structure of capitalism.

It is really of no use for us to complain about Baudrillard's opinion, for he indeed has no idea that the utility of objects can never equal to use value, which is historical and only makes sense when discussed together with value (in the capitalist era). Marx's calculation of the amount of value is simply for the purpose of economic studies on the relationship between the amount of labour and the amount of surplus value; furthermore, his opinion on the incompatibility of use value only concerns the calculation of the surplus value. Does it make any sense for him to prove the comparability of use value? Can the utility of items be denied simply because it bears comparability?

As a matter of fact, Baudrillard means:

In the system of use value, the consumer never appears as desire and enjoyment, but as abstract social need power (one could say Bedürfniskraft, Bedüfnisvermögen, by analogy with Arbeitskraft, Arbeitsvermögen).[9]

Baudrillard considers a social individual who is facing useful things as a person constructed by the mandatory orderly system of use value (utility function). If Baudrillard has already stated previously that the consumer has been proven to be non-human, he amounts to saying that a person who is useful and has normal functions can also be proved to be non-human. The reason for the existence of that person is to show the internal relationship between the subjective and the economically ordered system, not to be a real human. Then what should a real human be like? Surely a real human should be the ideal found in Baudrillard's Symbolic Exchange, the human who is *not attached to the items, non-scheduled, and dislocated.* So he says that "utility, needs, use value: none of this ever comes to grips with the finality of a subject up against his ambivalent object relations, or with symbolic exchange between subjects."[10] He still

9   *Ibid.*
10   *Ibid.*, p. 133.

bears constantly in mind Mauss-Bataille's undetermined symbolic exchange. The theological life constructed without utilitarian symbolic exchange is the real purpose of the existence of the subjective, which is also the true existence of mankind. Baudrillard's concept of this Bataillian original-but-useless human clearly reveals his intention of opposing the development and progress of the whole history of human civilization.

2 THE METAPHYSICS OF USE VALUE

A theoretical expertise of Baudrillard, as I find it, is his asserting metaphysically by figurative academic discussions. Here he suddenly points out that a history of Western psychology and concepts is indeed a gibbous "history of subjective political economy." The word "subject" refers to the forceful attribute of anthropocentrism while the "political economy" serves as a utility system of the whole exchange value. The key word to label it should be "use value," a term that has been utterly detested by Baudrillard.

> Use value is the expression of a whole metaphysic: that of utility. It registers itself as a kind of moral law (loi morale) at the heart of the object—and it is inscribed there as the finality of the "need" of the subject. It is the transcription at the heart of things of the same moral law (Kantian and Christian) inscribed on the heart of the subject, positivizing it in its essence and instituting it in a final relation (with God, or to some transcendent reality).[11]

We have become too metaphysical. To be more exact, Baudrillard wants to identify the whole history of Western civilization as a history existing *based on the Gestell of human subjective utility.* (As mentioned in the previous section, Heidegger believes that when this being adapts himself to the world by means of instrumental thingness, he will establish a living world around himself with the aim of meeting human needs. This belief is definitely not a neodoxy. Obviously, Baudrillard's mind has been seriously affected by the philosophy of late Heidegger. However, whether he turns a metaphysical meditation into a radical criticism of the real world is legitimate or not remains unknown. Of course, this criticism has been covered with a new academic appearance of Mauss-Bataille.) According to Baudrillard's logical thinking clue here, in this utilitarian world,

11   *Ibid.*

human beings legislate to the nature for the sake of their own needs (Immanuel Kant). The utility of subjects acts not only as the moral imperative in man's world, but also violently becomes the "inner moral imperative" that situates all things (Francis Bacon's "questioning nature"). It also legalizes itself in theological systems ("You are the second master of the planet" in *Bible*) and in the bourgeoisie's' concept, which is metaphysically orderly shaped (historical progress). It strikes me that this perception provides us with nothing new. From the technological criticism of late Heidegger, especially the publishing of *The Dialectic of Enlightenment* by Horkheimer and Adorno, to even the whole of so-called postmodern streams, anti-anthropocentric arguments overflow everywhere. This kind of pseudo-romanticism, as I see it, is indeed useless when separated from objective analyses of real social history, especially from real resistance to real capitalist rule, which is very much like making a fuss over an imaginary illness.

Baudrillard argues that there are two kinds of identical teleology in the metaphysics of use value: one is the teleology self-actualized in the false demands of subjects; the other is the teleology that the objects are situated by utility. In the second one "establishes the object in its truth, as an essence called use value, transparent to itself and to the subject, under the rational banner of utility."[12] (Heidegger said in his later years that the gorgeous Rhine River could never run in a natural way again. Instead, it would be accumulated by human beings and then thrown heavily down so as to meet the "need" of generating electricity. The essence of Rhine was its "use value" that existed for us. Otherwise it would be a disaster and surely be dealt with. Baudrillard's inference here purely belongs to the category of beautiful modern anti-anthropocentric statements based on grassroots romanticism.)

Baudrillard insists that there is nothing other than this utilitarian moral imperative that can definitely affect the *nonlocal* symbolic traits possessed by the inflated human subject and the dominated object. Based on utility, "single purpose replaces the meaning of diversity. It is still the principle of equivalence that dilutes the symbols in a nonlocal way." The single purpose is the orderly use value

---

12   *Ibid.*

for us, while the principle of equivalence is the "exchange value." What we lost is the original symbolic indeterminacy in the existence of human beings and objects. (Please pay attention to Baudrillard's metaphysical assumption here. He believes that the relationship between man and object is substantially a symbolic relationship which is not located in the utilitarian orderly Gestell and thus will be an *indeterminate being*—the being with *infinite varieties of possibilities*. However, men's system of utility forcefully occupies the indeterminate possibility of symbols by means of the single purpose of utility. I personally understand it as Baudrillard's new component to the thinking space of the concept of symbol.) Therefore, on the one hand the object can only establish itself in the functional relation of equivalence—"it establishes the object in a functional equivalence to itself in the single framework of this determined valence: utility"[13]—and as a result, the object enters political economics for its usefulness to man. On the other hand, the subject, by means of its needs and purposes, also becomes an abstract entity that enters into the ordering practice of political economics. These statements serve as metaphors that refer to the two aspects of commodities pointed out by Marx: use value and "exchange value."

However, Marx categorizes use value as not comparable, and at the same time supposes that the functional utility relationship between objects and human beings to be *innocent* naturalness. In this way, "Marxist analysis has contributed to the mythology."[14] (Please note that Baudrillard's frontal attack begins here) Marx says:

> *the relation of the individual to the objects conceived as use values to pass for a concrete and objective—in sum, "natural"—relation between man's needs and the function proper to the object. This is all seen as the opposite of the abstract, reified "alienated" relation which the subject would have toward products as exchange values. The truth of the subject would lie here, in usage, as a concrete sphere of the private relation, as opposed to the social and abstract sphere of the market.[15]*

---

13   *Ibid.*, p. 134.
14   *Ibid.*
15   Consumption itself is only apparently a concrete operation (in opposition to the abstraction of exchange). For what is consumed isn't the product itself, but its utility. Here the economists are right: consumption is not the destruction of products, but the destruction of utility. In the economic cycle, at any rate, it is an abstraction that is

The key words here are "the truth of the subject," which refer to man's dominant position. Baudrillard actually expresses that this kind of control and enslaved power has been forcefully established on objects so as they will be subordinate humanity. Unfortunately, Marx has made a mistake in that he only criticizes the "exchange value" in capitalist economic relations while assuming the natural legitimacy of use value. However, Baudrillard criticizes this point. He interprets Marx's hypothesis as "when one could imagine that if the individual was alienated by the system of exchange value, at least he would return to himself, become himself again in his needs and in the moment of use value,"[16] which he believes is untenable. In contemporary capitalist mass consumption society, all labour inputs are objectified in utility shaping, abstracted in the demand system, and endowed with the "general relation of equivalence." (In his important annotation at the end of this paragraph, Baudrillard again explains the relationship between consumption and consummation. Consumption is not the destruction of utility. As with production, consumption is one of the links in the giant abstract logic of economic exchange structure. What can indeed break this logical cycle would only be the useless consummation that has been identified by

---

produced or consumed as value (exchangeable in one case, useful in another). Nowhere is the "concrete" object or the "concrete" product concerned in the matter (what do these terms mean, anyway?): but, rather, an abstract cycle, a value system engaged in its own production and expanded reproduction. Nor does consumption make sense as a destruction (of "concrete" use value). Consumption is a labour of expanded reproduction of use value as an abstraction, a system, a universal code of utility—just as production is no longer in its present finality the production of "concrete" goods, but the expanded reproduction of the exchange value system. Only consumption (consummation) escapes recycling in the expanded reproduction of the value system— not because it is the destruction of substance, but because it is a transgression of the law and finality of objectss—the abolition of their abstract finality. Where it appears to consume (destroy) products, consumption only consummates their utility. Consumption destroys objects as substance the better to perpetuate this substance as a universal, abstract form—hence, the better to reproduce the value code. Consummation (play, gift, destruction as pure loss, symbolic reciprocity) attacks the code itself, breaks it, and deconstructs it. The symbolic act is the destruction of the value code (exchange and use), not the destruction of objects in themselves. Only this act can be termed "concrete," since it alone breaks and transgresses the abstraction of value. Note by Baudrillard, Jean, *For a Critique of the Political Economy of the Sign*, Trans by Charles Levin, St. Louis: Telos, 1981, p. 134.

16   Baudrillard, Jean, *For a Critique of the Political Economy of the Sign*, Trans by Charles Levin, St. Louis: Telos, 1981, p. 135.

Bataille: the extension of symbolic act to the exchange and use of codes.)

Thus, in Baudrillard's view,

Everything surging from the subject, his body and his desire, is dissociated and catalyzed in terms of needs, more or less specified in advance by objects. All instincts are rationalized, finalized and objectified in needs–hence symbolically cancelled. **All ambivalence is reduced by equivalence.**[17]

Still, it is the real symbolism that makes trouble. Here it seems that Mauss-Bataille's domination of the other has been constantly intensified and made convex. According to Baudrillard, the realness of human beings is the indeterminate symbolic exchange relationship. In the system of utility, all beings have been locked by orderly functionalization, thus making the indeterminate liberty of symbolism leave completely. Therefore, the real root of evil should be this constructive use value, which Marx has lost. Baudrillard even argues that there is some kind of *"use value fetishism"* unconsciously hidden in the criticism made by Marxist political economy. I really doubt this "brilliant" discovery of Baudrillard's.

3 USE VALUE FETISHISM–MORE MYSTERIOUS?

One of Baudrillard's main attractions in this book is his criticism of use value fetishism. We have discussed previously that he demotes economic fetishism while purposes his sign (signifier) fetishism so as to prove the obsolescence of Marx's critical logic. However, here the spearhead of his attack aims directly at Marx's theories, for he knows very well that only in this way can he get the right discourse.

Baudrillard agrees with Marx on the notion that "exchange value" is not the built-in attribute of objects, but rather the expression of a kind of social relation in the capitalist mode of production. What he wants to put forward is that use value should not be a built-in attribute either. Instead, it is "a social regulation (subjectival, objectival, and the relations between them)." (I should say there is nothing wrong about this statement, which is not put forward by Baudrillard, either. According to Marx, both use value and value are unified intrinsic

---

17 *Ibid.*

attributes, which have been generated by the long history of commodities.) Here Baudrillard warns us: "In other words, just as the
logic of the commodity extends itself indifferently to men and things
and makes men (all obedient to the same law) appear only as exchange value—thus the restricted finality of utility imposes itself on
men as surely as on the world of objects."[18] (Problems are revealed
here: Baudrillard also equates the use value of commodities to the
utility of general items, and thus attempts to deny the general utility
of objects to human beings. Obviously this is romanticism and not at
all practical. The denial of men's productive transformation and instrumental utilization of nature is in fact the repudiation of the origin
of human society and history.) He also disagrees with the modern
humanists who believe that "through the functionality, the domestic finality of the exterior world, man is supposed to fulfill himself
qua man."[19] (Heidegger in his later years believed that the functional
Gestell is human fate.) He argued that the humanists had not seen
the fact that men would be dissimilated into commodities and "exchange values" in the commodity exchange system. However, can
men in utilitarian orderly system be themselves? Baudrillard makes
the point mournfully that in the functional utility system, "man is not
so much himself as the most beautiful of these functional and servile
objects."[20] Human beings are still experiencing self-dissimilation!
(Men can neither be considered as themselves, nor as true men. It is
the logical illusion of humanism. It is not enough. When it comes to
Baudrillard, true men become men who serve as the divine situation
in symbolic exchange relationships of Primitive Tribes. This kind
of humanism can be regarded as *grassroot humanism*.) In this way,
Baudrillard still considers the individual structure of man in the use
value system as a false illusion of history, for "as constitutive of the
very structure of the individual—that is, the historical concept of a
social being who, in the rupture of symbolic exchange, autonomizes
himself and rationalizes his desire, his relation to others and to objects, in terms of needs, utility, satisfaction and use value."[21] The
instrumental human life is actually pseudo-situating.

---

18   *Ibid.*, p. 136.
19   *Ibid.*
20   *Ibid.*
21   *Ibid.*

Here, Baudrillard takes a formula—previously mentioned as the third formula—as an example: "exchange value/use value = signifier/signified". This formula is seemingly a logical form of truth value, since Marx always argues that use value has been covered by "exchange value," while Saussure believes that the definite signifier has been denied by floating signifier. However, Baudrillard, who believes himself able to grasp the essential point, points out that on this issue both Marx and Saussure have not discovered the fact that it is exactly the "exchange value" and the signifier that are in a convex dominant position. In my opinion, Baudrillard's point is an extremely complicated and very hard to comprehend multidimensional metonymy.

> *Use value and needs are only an effect of exchange value. Signified (and referent) are only an effect of the signifier (we will return to this point later). Neither is an autonomous reality that either exchange value or the signifier would express or translate in their code. At bottom, they are only **simulation models (modéles de simulation)**, produced by the play of exchange value and of signifiers.*[22]

Here, let us temporarily ignore Baudrillard's concepts of simulation and model, which play a vital role in his original theoretical system, because it is merely a kind of simulation-based signification. Baudrillard's main idea, as I understand it, would be that the use value and the signified, instead of being things to be supported after eliminating exchange relations and floating signifiers, are in fact *results* of a game. (Both of Marx and Saussure have been criticized here. This simulation model is already very close to the simulation regulation that has been set as the third level of simulacrum in his later book *Symbolic Exchange and Death*.) Since "use value and the signified do not constitute an elsewhere with respect to the systems of the other two; they are only their alibis."[23] All that Baudrillard wants to emphasize lies in his viewpoint is that *use value is actually the result of the exchange system.* (Certainly in accordance with this logic the signified should be the result of the signifier's game. This point is also accepted by Lacan, who, however, would describe it as "the signified is the result of the chain of signifiers.")

---

22 *Ibid.*, p. 137.
23 *Ibid.*

Yet it is not widely known that the originality and innocence of use value are among the most dominant ideologies today. Baudrillard claims that thinkers like Marx believe or affirm the inequality of men before bourgeois "exchange value," and the equality of men before use value. Use value thus takes place of the original throne of "exchange value" and becomes God. *Baudrillard's critique here is quite similar to Hillel Steiner's critique of Feuerbach's humanism*[24].

> *Men are not equal with respect to goods taken as exchange value, but they would be equal as regards goods taken as use value. One may dispose of them or not, according to one's class, income, or disposition; but the potentiality for availing oneself of them nevertheless exists for all. Everyone is equally rich in possibilities for happiness and satisfaction. This is the secularization of the potential equality of all men before God: the democracy of "needs." Thus use value, reflected back to the anthropological sphere, reconciles in the universal those who are divided socially by exchange value.*[25]

Baudrillard's ironic statements here inform us that Marx has seen through the formal equality in bourgeois market exchange and dis-covered the substantive inequality of deprived surplus value. Yet by eliminating this intermediary relationship of value can we indeed acquire equality in "use value"? Obviously Baudrillard has given us a negative answer, for he believes that use value is also a false illu-sion. Use value is more deceptive than the "exchange value," he tells us, for "it provides the commodity, inhuman as it is in its abstraction, with a "human" finality.'"[26] The reason, however, is that "the system of use value, on the other hand, involves the resorption without trace of the entire ideological and historical labour process that leads the subject in the first place to think of himself as an individual, defined by his needs and satisfaction, and thus ideally to integrate himself into the structure of the commodity."[27] Therefore, compared to "ex-change value," use value tends to be more cattish, and is thus able to be regarded as the "the crown and sceptre" in capitalist political economics of today. To be more specific, it is the use value neglected

---

24   Zhang, Yibing, *Back to Marx: Philosophical Discourse in the Context of Economics*, Jiangsu People's Publishing: 1999, p. 411-414.
25   Baudrillard, Jean, *For a Critique of the Political Economy of the Sign*, Trans by Charles Levin, St. Louis: Telos, 1981, p. 138.
26   *Ibid.*
27   *Ibid.*

by Marx that serves as the hidden hand behind the domination of capitalism today. Why?

Firstly, use value is the colonial essence in human life permeated by political economics. "He does not rediscover his objects except in what they serve; and he does not rediscover himself except through the expression and satisfaction of his needs—in what he serves."[28] Only through the orderly shaping occupying and using of the functionality of objects can men be self-established as utilitarian beings. Baudrillard views these utilitarian men, however, as *non-human*, materialized men. (Another point that is to be discussed later.)

Secondly, use value is the real strategic value of political economics, for it is use value that "ideologically, (it) seals off the system of production and exchange, thanks to the institution of an idealist anthropology that screens use value and needs from their historical logic in order to inscribe them in a formal eternity: that of utility for objects, that of the useful appropriation of objects by man in need."[29] The *naturalness* of use value (as advocated by Marx's hypothesis) is its most favourite and most successful ideology, because it hides the bourgeois essence. Use value, on the contrary, becomes the general value of men.

Baudrillard proudly informs us that the reason use value fetishism seems to be more profound and mysterious than exchange value fetishism lies right here. As a result, although Marx has already profoundly criticized capitalist political economics, he is "far behind" Baudrillard, since only Baudrillard has found the real secret essence of political economics—use value. Use value, to Baudrillard, is the essence of anthropocentrism and all humanistic ideologies, which are deeply rooted in a process of "naturalization" and "in an unsurpassable original reference."[30] (In his book *The Mirror of Production* Baudrillard defines use as the core of historical materialism.) Therefore, use value (usefulness of shaping) is the only or final value teleology and bourgeois theology in this world, for it exhibits "in the 'ideal' relation of equivalence, harmony, economy and equilibrium that the concept of utility implies."[31]

---

28 *Ibid.*, p. 139.
29 *Ibid.*
30 *Ibid.*
31 *Ibid.*

It operates at all levels: between man and nature, man and objects, man and his body, the self and others. Value becomes absolutely self-evident, "la chose la plus simple." Here the mystery and cunning (of history and of reason) are at their most profound and tenacious.[32]

Baudrillard claims that it should be the last footstone of the capitalist ideology. Use value, even though criticized by Marx incisively, is still covered by a variety of illusions as if in the capitalist mode of production "the finality tarries, and use value, entombed beneath exchange value, like the natural harmony of Earthly Paradise broken by sin and suffering, remains inscribed as an invulnerable essence to be disinterred at the last stage of History, in a promised future redemption."[33]

The above passage informs us that use value has always been the divine primeval value that opposes the evil of exchange value in all liberal illusions directing to the future. All that Baudrillard wants to do here now is to uncover the curtain of ideology obscuring use value.

In fact, based on my understandings, we must go further in seeking Baudrillard's real intention, in order to find the clear target of his attack—objects' *utilities for men* in all human social lives, rather than the use value of *commodities* corresponding with *value* only in the market economy of capitalism. (It seems that Baudrillard has no idea of the reality that if no commodity exchange occurs, then where could use value come from?) His ideas are largely based on the late Heidegger's thinking and Mauss-Bataille's grassroots romanticism. However, there are questions he never carefully considers: if we do not have the *utilitarian transition from the naturalness of objects* generated in the history of labour shaping production to social being, or if we do not have the *reconstructing* of the material system for the ever-growing objective needs based on *the existence for me*, would it be possible for human social history to have developed? Or can we maintain and promote the development of this kind of normal human life? Many years ago I argued that to simply deny the idea of human practice centrism is unreasonable by asking a question: Can man

---

32 *Ibid.*
33 *Ibid.*, p. 141.

be able to eat anything but other animals and plants?[34] The answer would definitely be negative. Today we can even make a detailed inquiry of Baudrillard about a very simple question: is it possible for human beings to use nothing that is useful? Does Baudrillard intend to go back to primitive life completely? Would he let man wear no clothes, build no house to live in, not use anything that has the use value? As a matter of fact, the existence of animals should also be based on negative change towards other species, otherwise they could never survive. Probably Baudrillard thinks much too deeply to notice common sense. Do we really need to list all the evidence lying at hand to fight against him?

As I see, Baudrillard's belief that he is smarter than Marx is and his opposition against the utility of objects causes him to fail to bring the essence of capitalist ideology to light, and rather allows him to conceal the particular historical character of the capitalist mode of production within a pseudo-romanticist's illusion. However, sometimes human beings are unable to deny the utilitarian being of objects for themselves that serves as their own basis of survival, and thus it amounts to a desperate belief in the invincibility of the bourgeois world. This may be the real function of ideology of all radical words. It must be the fiercer rape of ideology behind the desperation and silence in the impossibility.

---

34   Zhang, Yibing, "In and Out of Men's Egocentrism" in *Philosophy Trends*, 1996, 6.

CHAPTER VII

FOR A CRITIQUE OF THE POLITICAL ECONOMY OF THE SIGN AND IDEOLOGIES

The most theoretically significant chapters in Baudrillard's *For A Critique of the Political Economy of the Sign* are Chapters Six, Seven, and Eight, for these three chapters comprehensively illustrate his neodoxy. Chapter Eight, entitled "Toward a Critique of the Political Economy of the Sign," especially allows Baudrillard to further specify his "Political Economy of the Sign." In this chapter, Baudrillard mainly analyzed forms of commodities and signs—their homogeny, and the process of moving towards the codes of the contemporary capitalist social life. More importantly, Baudrillard flatters himself for being the one who reveals the real "secret" of the generation of contemporary bourgeois ideology. His arguments are as follows.

1 THE IDEOLOGY BEING AS A SECRET FORM

Baudrillard tells us that the *Political Economy of the Sign* that he identified has a logical structure similar to the political economy announced by Marx having the essence of capitalist commodity production. (With the thinking mode he uses for the time being, Baudrillard prefers to refer to Marx's theories.) The system of "exchange value" and use value corresponds respectively with the commodity value and format of objects, similarly, the signifier and signified respectively explain the value and format of sign. (Baudrillard is really very good at imagining and diverting theories, yet not in an accurate way, because to say that the signified equals the format of the sign is obviously illogical.)

Baudrillard tells us that in these comparable two systems lies a hidden logical assumption, which is that "in both cases, this (internal) relation is established as a hierarchical function between a dominant form and an alibi (or satellite) form, which is the logical crowning and ideological completion of the first."[1] Here the dominant form should refer to the use value in commodities' attributes and to the signified in signs. It is clear that Baudrillard is about to commence presenting his brilliant ideas on ideologies. In short, his idea is about *the ideological falsification of the mysterious form.*

In Baudrillard's opinion, in traditional ideological researches, ideologies tend to be attributed incorrectly to concepts of the ruling class, as opposed to the economic reality. They are represented as *concrete details* of cultural thought:

> *Thus, ideology (of such-and-such a group, or the dominant class) always appears as the overblown discourse of some great theme, content, or value (patriotism, morality, humanism, happiness, consumption, the family) whose **allegorical** power somehow insinuates itself into consciousnesses (this has never been explained) in order to integrate them. These become, in turn, the contents of thought that come into play in real situations. In sum, ideology appears as a sort of cultural surf frothing on the beachhead of the economy.[2]*

---

1   Baudrillard, Jean, *For a Critique of the Political Economy of the Sign*, Trans by Charles Levin, St. Louis: Telos, 1981, p. 143.
2   *Ibid.*, p. 144.

Seemingly this is another attack aimed at Marx. Baudrillard always attracts attention due to his unique views. In previous research, he tells us, ideology is always identified as a great illusion, which has concrete contents that governs the thoughts of people so that it will maintain affirmation of the political and economic relations in real society. As he sees it, the real function of ideology can lie anywhere but for within its content, and namely in a mysterious form we can hardly see through. Baudrillard therefore argues that ideology is "actually that *very form* that traverses both the production of signs and material production." For this reason, he even praises Marx, stating that "Marx demonstrated that the objectivity of material production did not reside in its materiality, but in its *form*. In fact, this is the point of departure for all critical theory."[3] (We can suppose that he correctly understands the decisive role Marx's modelling "forms" about mode of production and relations of production played on the *unsubstantial* social being premised by material production. However, it is nothing related to objectiveness. Seldom, if ever, would Baudrillard confirm Marx's ideas, yet merely to show greater foresight.) Baudrillard points out that the key problem of *perspective ideology* belongs to this logic clue: the objectiveness of ideology "does not reside in its 'ideality,'" that is, in a realist metaphysic of thought contents, but in its form." (His viewpoint here reminds us of the arguments on the "mysterious form" of social symptoms made by Slavoj Zizek in his book *The Sublime Object of Ideology*.)[4]

Baudrillard, writes: The biggest problem of traditional ideology studies lies in the fact that people tend to identify the ideology as a certain *content*, which is "as form, but as content, as given, transcendent value—a sort of *mana* that attaches itself to several global representations that magically impregnate those floating and mystified subjectivities called 'consciousnesses.'"[5]

According to Baudrillard, however, the path leading to correct understanding of the mysterious essence of ideology is not the content it shows, but its *invisible* form. "In fact, ideology is the process

---

3 *Ibid.*
4 Zhang, Yibing, *A Deep Plough: Unscrambling Major Post-marxist Texts*, Canut Intl. Publishers, 2011, See Part on Zizek.
5 Baudrillard, Jean, *For a Critique of the Political Economy of the Sign*, Trans by Charles Levin, St. Louis: Telos, 1981, p. 144.

of reducing and abstracting symbolic material into a form. But this reductive abstraction is given immediately as value (autonomous), as content (transcendent), and as a representation of consciousness (signified)."[6]

This statement can be regarded as one of his crucial expressions on the essence of ideology. What does it mean then? He gives us examples, such as Marx's analysis of commodities in *Capital*, which show that the mysteriousness of commodities rests not with its own physical properties that can be shaped, but with its abstract mysterious form. People have no idea that "it is the same process that lends the commodity an appearance of autonomous value and transcendent reality—this same process that involves the misunderstanding of the form of the commodity and of the abstraction of social labour that it operates." We have to admit that here his understanding is basically correct and profound. (His analyses are fundamentally consistent with Zizek, as well.) Accurately speaking, the mysteriousness of commodities does not equal its concrete efficiency being shaped. Instead, it equals its value form as a social labour abstract. It must be admitted that the starting point of his thinking, which follows Marx's analytical logic, is definitely profound. Baudrillard tells us:

> *It is the cunning of form to veil itself continually in the evidence of content. It is the cunning of the code to veil itself and to produce itself in the obviousness of value. It is in the "materiality" of content that form consumes its abstraction and reproduces itself as form. That is its peculiar magic.[7]*

Herein emerges a problem. Baudrillard in this section misinterprets Marx's analysis of the duality of commodities (use value and value) and makes a false analogy to equate use value and value to content and form. However, the final purpose of this logical game is to draw forth his sign relations. (Later we will find that he wants to propose the concept that *the mystery of form is the artificial symbolic sign*.) Baudrillard immediately argues that Marx is no doubt profound, but not profound enough. "And if the bourgeois vulgate enshrines it in this transcendence precisely in order to exalt it as *culture*, the Marxist vulgate embalms it in the very same transcendence

---

6   *Ibid.*, p. 144-145.
7   Ibid., p. 145.

in order to denounce it as *ideology*. But the two scriptures rejoin in the same magical thinking."[8]

As I understand it, Baudrillard's transcendence here is *non-intuitionism* with a form of bourgeois culture (with no physical property) and also a form of the enslaving of the invisible ideology denied by Marx. Both of the forms are subjectifications. Baudrillard views such problems as existing solely in the binary split model of modern thinking methods, such as in the discreteness between subject and object, economic base and superstructure, and also exploitation and dissimilation.

Baudrillard takes the relations between exploitation and dissimilation as an example and says that in these relations people always hold different opinions towards which the foundation should be. (Just like what young Marx did in his *Economic and Philosophic Manuscripts of 1844*.) However, such arguments make no sense in "the highest stage of capitalism" today, for the arguments should be based on the split between commodity distribution with physical property and symbolic discourse with meaningfulness.

> *All this is absurd. Not for the first time, the confusion arises from an artificial separation—this time of the sign and the commodity, which are not analyzed in their form, but posed instead as contents (the one of signification, the other of production). Whence emerges the distinction between an "exploitation" of labour power and an "alienation by signs." As if the commodity and the system of material production "signified" nothing! As if signs and culture were not immediately abstract social production at the level of the code and models, in a generalized exchange system of values.*[9]

Baudrillard intends to tell us that ideology does not lie unitarily in a particular part of binary split. In fact, it is probably the only kind of form that penetrates into *all fields of social production*. "Ideology seizes all production, material or symbolic, in the same process of abstraction, reduction, general equivalence and exploitation." Why does he say so?

---

8 "The critical disclosure of human needs and its control are thereby concentrated on the mystique of the uncondition elevation of human consumption". The original note by Baudrillard. Baudrillard, Jean, *For a Critique of the Political Economy of the Sign*, Trans by Charles Levin, St. Louis: Telos, 1981, p. 145.
9 Baudrillard, Jean, *For a Critique of the Political Economy of the Sign*, Trans by Charles Levin, St. Louis: Telos, 1981, p. 146.

The first reason is that the logic of commodities and political economy are essentially: modelling of code. (After beating about the bush, Baudrillard finally presents his own words.) If what he wants to demonstrate in the previous discussion is that exchange value determines use value, here he intends to explain that the whole process of commodity exchange cannot do without symbolic logic. In fact, "exchange value" as communicating discourse and the use value as "rational decoding and distinctive social use" must be knitted in "the abstract equation of signifier and signified, in the differential combinatory of signs" so that they will be able to have access to market exchange and market distribution in reality. Baudrillard believes that he sees more than Marx did in the 19th century. Yet the fact is that we have found no particular rules set by him regarding the formulation above, because situations in which commodity exchange is affected by the manipulation of code are something new, and exist only in contemporary process of capitalist economy. Obviously, for Marx at that time, comments like Baudrillard's above would be empty.

Secondly, the structure of the sign is the essence and at the very heart of the commodity form. (This should be the key point of his logical trick here, which, however, with no restriction of historical dimensions.) Baudrillard abstracts the commodity as a form with mystery before he identifies the essence of this very form as the structure of the sign. Therefore, the essence of commodity has been defined as the sign.

> It is because the structure of the sign is **at the very heart of the commodity form** that the commodity can take on, immediately, the effect of signification—not epiphenomenally, in excess of itself, as "message" or connotation—but because its very form establishes it as **a total medium, as a system of communication** administering all social exchange. Like the sign form, the commodity is a code managing the exchange of values. It makes little difference whether the contents of material production or the immaterial contents of signification are involved; it is the code that is determinant: the rules of the interplay of signifiers and exchange value.[10]

---

10   *Ibid.*, p. 146.

In this way, the commodity then changes from being an objective social economic relation as promulgated by Marx, into a weird pseudo-symbolic code relation. If in the first part of his book Baudrillard has magically changed objects into signs, here he absurdly changes the relations. I take this change as the most significant step in his logic games related to historical idealism.

Now Baudrillard says proudly that only signs can serve as the real entrance for us to understand all social beings, for only signs enable us to rationalize and normalize exchanges between humans. The nature of social life is to be realized in "the law of the code and the signifier that informs and determines (to the point of) 'reality.'" Therefore, the kind of alienated logic that tries to criticize capitalism is a metaphysical result of subjective consciousness, since signs are not among those consciousnesses, alienated from realistic material beings. On the other hand, social communication in primitive society was not accomplished via the system of mythologies raised by Claude Lévi-Strauss. It seems to be an objective description of consciousness. "A parallel confusion arises in the view of 'primitive' myths as false stories or histories that consciousnesses recount to themselves. Here the pregnant effects of mythic contents are held to bind society together (through the 'cohesion' of belief systems). In fact, these myths make up a code of signs that exchange among themselves, integrating the group through the very process of their circulation." (It is absolutely nonsensical to claim that primitive society had what we call signs today; even Baudrillard himself objects to such thinking when he acts strongly against the forceful cultural dominance on history today.)

Surely in the capitalist "mass consumption society" of today, "defines precisely *the stage where the commodity is immediately produced as a sign, as sign value, and where signs (culture) are produced as commodities.*"[11] This sentence, which is italicized in the original text, seems to represent all that Baudrillard wants to express. That is to say, the essence of commodity production today is the production of pseudo-symbolic sign value. He believes that "nothing produced or exchanged today (objects, services, bodies, sex, culture, knowledge, etc.) can be decoded exclusively as a sign,

---

11 *Ibid.*, p. 147.

nor solely measured as a commodity." Thus, commodity today is no longer realized by certain forms (economic "exchange value" or cultural characters). It is complicated for "use value, exchange value and sign value converge in a complex mode that describes the most general form of political economy." This complex mode of political economy is certainly the mode of political economy of signs that Baudrillard puts forward.

2 CRITIQUES ON THE METAPHYSICS OF REFERENTIAL SIGNS

Previously we have discussed that Baudrillard firmly believes that both structures of the exchange value of signs and commodity value have homo-organicity. He also admits that Marx's political economy initiated the critical logic of commodity fetishism and that Barthes' *Tel Quel* initiated the critical logic of sign fetishism. However, both of them belong in a kind of production mode with *reference objects*. Baudrillard states "that the abstraction of the exchange value system is sustained by the effect of concrete reality and of objective purpose exhaled by use value and needs. This is the strategic logic of the commodity; its second term acts as the satellite and alibi for the first."[12] To be more direct, the use value of commodity should be the imagined basis of "exchange value." (Of course this is to testify on the basis of a sense of denial.) Baudrillard thinks that the logical strategy of the exchange of sign value is like that as well, and that Marx's and Barthes' critical introspections do not gone beyond this logical ordering to a deeper level.

Baudrillard believes that the random relation between signifier and signified in Saussure's linguistic semiotics may possibly bring us to a new space in which to understand the problems. He claims that it is correct to say that the randomicity in structures of language and code submits to the differentiation in their own unique structures. Take the word "apple" for instance; it does not directly refer to apples in reality but merely a random, differentiated combination in the English writing system. Therefore, in Saussure's random collocation of signifier and signified "positive, rational, exchangeable value, all virtualities of meaning are shorn in the cut of structure"

---

12   *Ibid.*, p. 148.

of *all concrete references* have been dispelled in this differentiated structure. This statement is basically correct as well. The key point of Saussure's semiotics is to enable the language sign to completely rid itself of objective reference, and the randomicity is referred to the indefinitely associative relation of signifier and signified in the structure of language sign system. Baudrillard holds the opinion that this randomicity should have been closer to the relation of *symbolic exchange*. The reason is that in the combination of signifier and signified, sense appears in a way of indefinite symbol, "a signifier may refer to many signifieds, or vice versa." Sense would be a continuous and infinite process of metonymies and thus constitutes the indefiniteness in symbolic exchange. (In his logical situating, the formation of sign exchange value in today's capitalism lies precisely in this indefinite and symbolic dilution and reversed value. Later, he identifies it as imagined simulacrums and simulation.) Baudrillard says:

> Only ambivalence (as a rupture of value, of another side or beyond of sign value, and as the emergence of the symbolic) sustains a challenge to the legibility, the false transparency of the sign; only ambivalence questions the evidence of the use value of the sign (rational decoding) and of its exchange value (the discourse of communication). It **brings the political economy of the sign to a standstill**; it dissolves the respective definitions of Sr and Sd.[13]

He wants to complete his argument here, which is that the indefinite symbolic relation as an invincible logic weapon can indeed dispel all the realistic relations of value. It cannot only put the political economy of the sign to an end, but it can also end all political economies. In other words, the reformed Saussure can simultaneously defeat both Marx and Barthes, who have criticized commodity fetishism and sign fetishism. (This should be a view that can hardly be fully understood. We can see that Baudrillard's indefinite symbol is confirmed logically by the symbolic relation of signification (in Saussure's semiotics). However, he regards this symbol as the only supporting point of humans' real being, and criticizes and fights against the physical world of value today by using this non-objective, non-functional ordering method of symbolic exchange between

---

13   *Ibid.*, p. 150.

man and man, man and object. I do not think his actions constitute a reasonable diversion of theories.)

Yet Baudrillard finds that in the later development of linguistics, the principle of randomicity has been furtively falsified. The so-called "the mirage of the Referent" appears again. The guilty party is Emile Benveniste. Baudrillard points out that in Benveniste's book *Problems of General Linguistics* (Miami, 1971), Saussure's random relation, which is based on the accidental collocation of signified and signifier, has been changed into an inevitable relevance of the sign and reality. Benveniste declares: "For the speaking subject, there is complete adequation between language and reality. The sign recovers and commands reality; better still, it is that reality..."[14] This declaration really infuriates Baudrillard. He claims that Benveniste is a "poor speaker" and criticizes his false understanding of the random relation in Saussure's semiotics, which leads to an incorrect change: the indefinite symbol that is not related to object becomes a physical sense again, mixed up with real references. Baudrillard considers this point of view as a horrible dualistic illusion about the division of the sign and the world, which is "the logic of equivalence, abstraction, discreteness and projection of the sign engulfs the Rft as surely as it does the Sd." To be clearer, he wants to say that the sign reflects the objective world and becomes a metaphysical illusion of all perceptive logic of Western science in the modern times.

Baudrillard believes that the truth is simply inverted:

> *This "world" that the sign "evokes" (the better to distance itself from it) is nothing but the effect of the sign under the shadow of the sign, and a "pantographic" extension of the sign. Even better: this world is quite simply the Sd — Rft. As we have seen, the Sd — Rft is a single and compact thing, an identity of content that acts as the moving shadow of the Sr. It is the reality effect in which the play of signifiers comes to fruition and deludes the world.[15]*

---

14   Benveniste, Emile. *Problems of General Linguistics*, Miami, 1971. See Baudrillard, Jean, *For a Critique of the Political Economy of the Sign*, Trans by Charles Levin, St. Louis: Telos, 1981, p. 152.
15   Baudrillard, Jean, *For a Critique of the Political Economy of the Sign*, translated by Xia Ying, Nanjing University Press, 2009, p. 152.

The "world" here is certainly not the common objective material being, but the "object in phenomenon" as Edmund Husserl put it, nor the "living world" of human beings, nor the order world around us established on the basis of production of shaping labour, nor even the world constructed by Heidegger's ready to hand. But according to Baudrillard, the consumption world of modern capitalism surrounding us has become a construction of the sign. (His teacher Guy Debord calls it landscape construction. Here the concrete landscape has transferred into the sign, which is more abstract. In the previous discussions, we have already gotten to know the real meaning identified by Baudrilard's theory.)

Moreover, Baudrillard also states that the logic of this relation of signification and that of political economy are isostructural. In political economy, things appear as references are called needs. The use value, however, becomes the objective essence of humanism. This should be a *super big* need, just like that big referent in Benveniste's semiotics. He says: "*Need, motivation*: one never escapes this circle. Each term conceals the same metaphysical wile." Needs are always to be first examined in Baudrillard's critical thinking.

> Needs are not the actuating (**mouvante**) and original expression of a subject, but the functional reduction of the subject by the system of use value in solidarity with that of exchange value. Similarly, the referent does not constitute an autonomous concrete reality at all; it is only the extrapolation of the excision (**decoupage**) established by the logic of the sign onto the world of things (onto the phenomenological universe of perception). It is the world such as it is seen and interpreted through the sign— that is, **virtually excised and excisable** at pleasure.[16]

Baudrillard believes that this real need, which is capitalized, does not exist at all. If we are able to find "reality," "this is because it has already been designated, abstracted and rationalized by the separation (decoupage) which establishes it in this equivalence to itself." Thus, the discovery of truth is an ideological logic game in and of itself. (This is the second time that Baudrillard directly discusses reality. The first time he was arguing about the death of reality in the codes of advertisements and media. We will see that in his though process, the problem of reality is going to become more and more

16   *Ibid.*, p. 155.

significant.) The referent Benveniste puts in via the back door "has no other value than that of the signified, of which it wants to be the substantial reference in vivo, and which it only succeeds in extending *in abstracto*."[17]

Please pay attention to another note here: Baudrillard quotes an expression of Lefebvre's (also one of his teachers) on "referents," which is that the referent is not reality but just an imagination of reality in the pseudo-situating of the sign.

> *The referent is not reality (i.e., an object whose existence I can test, or control): we relate to it as real, but this intentionality is precisely an act of mind that **belies its reality**, which makes a fiction, an artificial construction out of it.[18]*

The above is a very extreme and metaphysical statement. The referent is no longer a perceptual object, but an imaginary false reality constructed by the sign. This kind of pseudo-reality becomes the *real* being in man's "belief" and "illusion." Obviously this statement

---

17   The portrait of the *en dur* only conveys a realistic fetish, while fetish for material objects all end up as idealist fetish. (For more discussion on the en dur, see Lefebvre, N.R.F., Feb 1970, 1ˢᵗ edition: "A referent is not real…and was only our mental reflection of the reality. It is a reference that is dominated by the referred reality, and therefore cannot be considered in relationships that can be referred to, as the linguistics do. Based on the concept of reference, I see referents as the concrete paths to the world.") But the mixture of materialism and idealism is rooted in the integration of Western metaphysics, and has laid the foundation for the study of signs. The feature of the Lefebvre's theory lies in the fact that reality could regenerate itself behind the study of signs so as to formulate a more effective semiotic strategy despite its critique. Therefore the metaphysical trap of the semiotics cannot be evaded without posing challenge to the self-explanation of semiotics. Lefebvre believed that "The referent is not reality (i.e., an object whose existence I can test, or control): we relate to it as real, but this intentionality is precisely an act of mind that belies its reality, which makes a fiction, an artificial construction out of it." Thus, in a kind of flight in advance, the referent is drained of its reality, becomes again a simulacrum, behind which, however, the tangible object immediately re-emerges. Thus, the articulation of the sign can gear down in infinite regress, while continually reinventing the real as its beyond and its consecration. At bottom, the sign is haunted by the nostalgia of transcending its own convention, its arbitrariness; in a way, it is obsessed with the idea of total motivation. Thus it alludes to the real as its beyond and its abolition. But it can't "jump outside its own shadow": for it is the sign itself that produces and reproduces this real, which is only its horizon—not its transcendence. Reality is the phantasm by means of which the sign is indefinitely preserved from the symbolic deconstruction that haunts it (Baudrillard's original note). Baudrillard, Jean, *For a Critique of the Political Economy of the Sign*, Trans by Charles Levin, St. Louis: Telos, 1981, p. 155.

18   Lefebvre, N.R.F., Feb 1970, 1ˢᵗ edition. See Baudrillard, Jean, *For a Critique of the Political Economy of the Sign*, Trans by Charles Levin, St. Louis: Telos, 1981, p. 155, note 1.

of Lefebvre's has enlightened Baudrillard. (I do sense that his expressions will later enable the autonomic logic situating to step further towards an innovation, which should be the relation between *simulacrum and reality*.)

> *Thus, in a kind of flight in advance, the referent is drained of its reality, becomes again a simulacrum, behind which, however, the tangible object immediately re-emerges. Thus, the articulation of the sign can gear down in infinite regress, while continually reinventing the real as its beyond and its consecration. At bottom, the sign is haunted by the nostalgia of transcending its own convention, its arbitrariness; in a way, it is obsessed with the idea of total* **motivation***. Thus it alludes to the real as its beyond and its abolition. But it cannot "jump outside its own shadow": for it is the sign itself that produces and reproduces this real, which is only its* **horizon***—not its transcendence. Reality is the phantasm by means of which the sign is indefinitely preserved from the symbolic deconstruction that haunts it.*[19]

We have to bear in mind that a large number of the words and expressions used by Baudrillard here are not understandable with common sense. Reality is not objective material existence anymore; truth is not the real being behind the false; and even the referent is not the reflective relation of materialism. All things have been re-ordered by the logic of the sign. The sign does not refer to any object but to itself only. Therefore what look like traditional referents no longer possess reality. Instead, they are just simulacrums constructed by the sign. However, it is indeed in reality that the simulacrums have generated reality that surpasses reality. This reality, which is constructed through the reference of the sign, is not actually the real symbolic relation, but the real death. (I consider that this idea which appeared in the notes as the most significant innovation space in Baudrillard's whole book, as this kind of new logical situating intention will become the direct foundation of his original thoughts in his next book, *Symbolic Exchange and Death*.)

Later on Baudrillard points out that in the logic of commodity exchange the situation is the same. "The commodity (UV/EV) in fact conceals a formal homogeneity in which use value, regulated by the system of exchange value, confers on the latter its "naturalist"

---

19 Baudrillard, Jean, *For a Critique of the Political Economy of the Sign*, Trans by Charles Levin, St. Louis: Telos, 1981, p. 155, note 1.

guarantee." He insists on a point of view in which use value is actually the result of commodity exchange system instead of the natural premise and foundation of "exchange value." Therefore,

> There is a metaphysic of the Sd — Rft, homologous with that of needs and use value. The Sd — Rft is taken for an original reality, a substance of value and recurring finality through the supporting play of signifiers (cf. the analysis of **Tel Quel**[20], in particular Derrida). Similarly, use value is given as origin and purpose (**finalité**), and needs as the basic motor of the economic—the cycle of exchange value appearing here as a necessary detour, but incompatible with true finalities.[21]

Now his criticism comes to Derrida. On account of Baudrillard's intention to eliminate reality and objectiveness, he believes that any association with objectiveness and objects is irremissible. In the study of the sign in linguistics all that have references would be false images for "reality" itself is "nothing more than a coded form," just as in commodity researches where the use value is a function of "denotation" for object. It has been worked out systematically by the "exchange value" system. Thus Baudrillard says, "denotation or use value; objectivity or utility: it is always the complicity of the real with the code under the sign of evidence which generates these categories."[22] The real masters behind it are signifier and "exchange value." We never know that "it is the rational abstraction of the system of exchange value and of the play of signifiers which commands the whole." Baudrillard also says: "Far from being the objective term to which connotation is opposed as an ideological term, denotation is thus (since it naturalizes the very process of ideology) *the most ideological term*—ideological to the second degree."[23] However, what would be Derrida's role in this issue?

---

20   *Tel Quel* was the name of an influential avant-garde magazine founded in 1960 in Paris by Philippe Sollers and Jean-Edern Hallier.—Translator's note.

21   Baudrillard, Jean, *For a Critique of the Political Economy of the Sign*, Trans by Charles Levin, St. Louis: Telos, 1981, p. 157.

22   *Ibid.*, p. 158.

23   *Ibid.*, p. 159.

3 TO RESUME SYMBOLIC EXCHANGE: SURPASSING THE VALUE AND THE SIGN

Baudrillard has found that in the philosophical discourses of Derrida et al (which are usually identified as things related to "post-structuralism") a sort of illusion has appeared, which tries to surpass the sign system. For example, with his theory of deconstruction Derrida's tries to reach the real moment of a certain real being in deconstructing the structure of the sign by the *difference* of meaning and the erasing of the concretionary being. Baudrillard considers this attempt unsuccessful because

> *its phantasm is that of a total resurrection of the "real" in an immediate and transparent intuition, which establishes the economy of the sign (of the Sr) and of the code in order to release the Signifieds (subjects, history, nature, contradictions) in their actuating, dialectical, authentic truth.[24]*

We have to admit that Baudrillard's understanding is profound, for the truth that he understands thoroughly is: all the real presences can be games of ideology, thus any criticism or extension aimed at a certain concrete referent will not be thorough because the liberated signified inevitably embodies a meaning which has given a certain sense, "ethical and metaphysical status" and cannot do without "idealism of referent (idéalisme du referent)." Derrida's deconstruction is also like this. He believes that we can find the original meaning of being in the traces that are *different* and disseminated, and that to criticize the signifier in the name of the signified or to use the games of signifiers to replace the real ideals will never work. Baudrillard says that just as with Marx's illusion of trying to rescue use value from the "exchange value," the problem would be that Derrida has never realized "use value in its relation to exchange value:"

> *This is precisely the idealism and transcendental humanism of contents which we discover again in the attempt to rescue the Sd (Rft) from the terrorism of the Sr. The velleity of emancipating and liberating the "real" leaves intact the entire ideology of signification—just as the ideology of political economy is preserved* **in toto** *in the ideal autonomization of use value.[25]*

---

24   *Ibid.*, p. 160.
25   *Ibid.*

Baudrillard believes that nowadays this kind of radical "post-modern" critical concept has been generated in different fields. Men can hardly gain insight into the essence of this concept to find that it is merely a "bourgeois system of individualist values." At last, "this vision is developed largely in the critique of the abstraction of systems and codes in the name of authentic values (which are largely derived from the bourgeois system of individualist values). It amounts to a long sermon denouncing the alienation of the system, which becomes, with the expansion of this very system, a kind of universal discourse." Therefore, postmodern discourses are also under the control of the capitalist system.

Of course Baudrillard wants to tell the whole world that only his infinite symbolic exchange system can really eliminate all things in the ideology of the sign and value system. A real revolution! In other words, in order to break the capitalist "circle of exchange value" we have to "restore symbolic exchange in a paradoxical sense, exactly opposed to the current accepted use." "This revolution is not about liberating objects and their value, but the relation of exchange." (Mauss-Bataille is present again.) Because only:

> *In symbolic exchange, however, the object, or the full value that it was, returns again to nothing (consider the ambivalence of the Latin term res[26]). It is that something which, through being given and returned, is, as such, annulled, and marks in its presence or absence the movement of the relationship. The "object," this **res nulla**, has absolutely no use value, it is good for nothing. Thus, only that which assumes its meaning through continual reciprocal exchange eludes exchange value, in the gift and counter-gift, in the ambivalence of an open relationship, and never in **a final relation of value**.[27]*

Baudrillard's revolution is to make all the values (=usefulness) become nothing. The relationships between men or men and objects no longer possess the value orientation that is complicated with orderly economic utility. Instead, the relationship will get back to the original infinite symbolic exchange that is in disorder. He gives us examples to illustrate this point:

---

26   In Latin, both res and objectus refer to objects, while the latter has such connotations as concreteness and conflict.—Translator's note.
27   Baudrillard, Jean, *For a Critique of the Political Economy of the Sign*, Trans by Charles Levin, St. Louis: Telos, 1981, p. 212.

*What is neither sold nor taken, but only given and returned, no one "needs". The exchanges of looks, the present which comes and goes, are like the air people breathe in and out. This is the metabolism of exchange, prodigality, festival—and also of destruction (which returns to non-value what production has erected, valorized). In this domain, value isn't even recognized. **And desire is not fulfilled there in the phantasm of value.**[28]*

No doubt, this theory is really a *mana*-imbued fairyland. However, Baudrillard never thinks about how he could survive if everything became nothing. What will he use to take photos? What about the air and the sunshine?

Baudrillard never addresses these common issues. He still concentrates on his great "revolution," and he strongly believes that in the kingdom which has been dominated by the sign, the slogans of liberation and criticism will never get rid of the shadow of the sign if they are some kind of reality, referent or the final value that are present for all the definite signified will be structuralized by the sign. He states that *the process of signification is, at bottom, nothing but a gigantic simulation model of meaning.* The hidden fact is that all concrete signifiers (such as reality, communism, and the Great Harmony of the world) are merely simulacrums of symbolism. The thing is that when the liberated expectation still stays in the referents of the sign, it will always be imaginary. Baudrillard claims that: "Only total revolution, theoretical and practical, can restore the symbolic in the demise of the sign and of value. Even signs must burn."[29] To burn the pseudo-symbolic sign and to restore the symbolic, give it a dose of the feelings of the French "Red May Storm" of 1968.

More interestingly, in order to illustrate this point, Baudrillard seriously quotes some formulations from Lacan. Lacan's formulation of semiotics, which turned Saussure's formulation up-side-down, precisely reveals a symbolic function of pre-semiotics, which is "the process of reducing and abolishing meaning (or non-meaning: ambivalence)."

Lacan's formulation of the linguistic sign reveals the true meaning of this line: S/s. It becomes the line (barrier) of repression itself— no longer that which articulates, but that which censors—and

---

28 *Ibid.*, p. 207.
29 *Ibid.*, p. 163.

thus the locus of transgression. This line highlights what the sign denies, that upon which the sign establishes itself negatively, and of which it is only, in its positive institution, the symptom.[30]

The sign, which occupies the spare space of symbolism, has been denied, yet the symbolism is present in this negation to the concrete signifiers. Lacan is taken advantage of by Baudrillard here. He actually cares nothing about Lacan's original meaning but to figure out the indefinite symbolism he needs to borrow from Lacan's analyses on semiotics.

Rather, it is to conceive it as that which, denied by the sign, in turn denies the sign's form, and can never have any place within it. It is a non-place and non-value in opposition to the sign. Barred (barrée) and deleted (rayée) by the sign, it is a symbolic ambivalence that only re-emerges fully in the total resolution of the sign, in the explosion of the sign and of value. The symbolic is not inscribed anywhere. It is not what comes to be registered beneath the repression barrier (line), the Lacanian Sd. It is rather what tears all Srs and Sds to pieces, since it is what dismantles their pairing off (appareillage) and their simultaneous carving out (découpe).[31]

Although Lacan believes that the truth is always reached in the misinterpretations and he never expects correct reductive understanding to his thoughts, I personally think it necessary to understand his thoughts in a way that is basically acceptable, not to disobey its fundamental meaning, and, of course, not to call black white. Baudrillard usually acts in a deliberately mystifying way in his books, though he in fact seems childish next to Lacan. Baudrillard only thinks about his indefinite symbolic relation of pre-semiotics while understanding nothing about the whole logical structure of Lacan's theory, let alone the underlying context of symbolic semiotics that belongs to Lacan's second important research field and the purpose of the discussion and criticism of Lacan's semiotics—announcing the illegitimacy of all the symbols.

We are aware of that being is also the logical extension of Mauss's concept of symbolism. Claude Lévi-Strauss' identification argues mainly about thoughts, which refers to those in the early

---

30   *Ibid.*, p. 161, note 1.
31   *Ibid.*

days of the development of human primitive thoughts when rational regulations were far from occupying the dominant position. The thoughts are "images" without concepts, which are symbolic signifiers used to identify the relation between men and the world—"*la pensée sauvage*."[32] The core of these non-ideational thoughts could be a "symbolic system," which takes images as the principal thing. Unlike Baudrillard, who shows little wisdom in following Bataille and directly changes the symbolism of pre-semiotics into the logical base of some kind of authenticity, Lacan actually views symbolism as the essence of the language sign system. According to him, the whole symbolic field is a miserable world where individuals are raped and enslaved by the Other—the symbolic sign system. Therefore when Baudrillard quotes Lacan's semiotics, a ridiculous logical dislocation immediately appears. Moreover, differing from Baudrillard's illusion, which expects the restoration of symbolic exchange, Lacan's philosophy aims at eliminating all the "made" possibilities, let alone to set frame to the world today by using some sort of gift exchange system and symbolic relation that should have occurred only in primitive society. His diversion of Lacan's theory is so foolish that it would make Lacan—the Other—roll in his grave.

---

32   Many commentators has translated the name of this work by Lévi-Strauss as "The Savage Mind." However, judging from the context, what the author focused was a kind of primitive thought reflected in the Totem System. Therefore, "The Untamed Mind" should be a better translation. See Sturrock, John. *Structuralism and Since*, Liaoning Education Press, 1998, p. 11-12; also Lévi-Strauss, Claude. *The Savage Mind*, The Commercial Press, 1987, p. 249.

PART TWO

FROM APE TO MAN, A SUBVERSIVE PERSPECTIVE – CRITICAL READING OF JEAN BAUDRILLARD'S *THE MIRROR OF PRODUCTION*

CHAPTER VIII

Marxism: Transgression of Historical Materialism

CHAPTER IX

Ontology of Production: I produce, therefore history is

CHAPTER X

Critique of Labour Ideology

CHAPTER XI

Marx and the Domination of Nature

CHAPTER XII

Marx and Ethnocentrism

CHAPTER XIII

Riddle of Monkey Anatomy and Ape Analysis

CHAPTER XIV

Historical Materialism and Euclidean Geometry of History

INTRODUCTION

Soon after *For A Critique of the Political Economy of the Sign* was published, Baudrillard wrote another important academic book, *Mirror of Production* in 1973. Due to his satisfaction of negating Marx in the previous works, Baudrillard seemed to feel it was necessary to have a comprehensive critique and negation of Marx's *historical materialism*, the methodological "guide," which has never truly dominated the social critical construction of the contemporary leftists. Hence, he would make his deep thought known. From the perspective of Baudrillard's own logic, it is his independent thinking, and the display of the second step of his "murder trilogy" of the symbol exchange of the real being of humanities. As a matter of fact, in the end of *For A Critique of the Political Economy of the Sign*, Baudrillard puts forward a question: Is Marxism still legal? Can Marx's theory of material production in historical materialism be "saved"? To Baudrillard, the answers are negative. Moreover, he opposes the fine technical repatching by Althusser's disciples. Baudrillard says the radical way is nowhere else but to overthrow of Marx's theoretical system in *The Mirror of Production*. Now, Baudrillard intends to explain that the death of symbol exchange starts with Marx's *logic of production*, which truly accounts for the *utilitarian logic* constructing today's world reality.

242   A MARXIST READING OF YOUNG BAUDRILLARD

Since the first reading of Baudrillard's *Mirror of Production*, I have been harboring the anger that is difficult to subdue in my heart. Baudrillard, the savvy and talented elf, is generally regarded a great postmodernist avant-garde. Unexpectedly, he proves to be the most profound and dangerous theoretical enemy of Marxism we have ever seen. His attack on Marxism, especially, on historical materialism in *The Mirror of Production,* is without doubt the most vicious but comprehensive critique in contemporary history. It is true that Marx has many enemies across the **bourgeois camp. Since the birth of Marxism,** criticism and condemnation against it have never stopped. However, in comparison with these outside clamors, Baudrillard's philosophical outset extends from the *inner logic* of Marxism. As a disciple of the western Marxist master Henri Lefebvre and a participant in the French translation of the *The German Ideology*, Baudrillard has a deep understanding of historical materialism in many aspects. Therefore, his accusation of historical materialism and Marxism as a whole is almost lethally fundamental. Unlike most Marxist critics who give shallow talks like a dragonfly skimming the water surface but miss the real target, Baudrillard's criticism seems to be developed to a quite destructive level, which we cannot be more serious to deal with. In this connection, he is quite similar to the Frankfurt School deserter, Jürgen Habermas,[1] and to some extent, even goes far beyond him. In short, Baudrillard is much more profound and precise than his stupid predecessors, whose abuses are mere bluffings directed at the pseudo-image of Stalinist dogmatism but unable to shake the real Marxism itself at all. Baudrillard grasps the two basic Marxist concepts, the material production and the mode of production, from which he goes on to negate the basic standpoints, concepts and the methodology of the whole Marxist system. Thus, all the core concepts of historical materialism and the basic logic of Marxist political economy seem to be completely brought within the range of Baudrillard's critical fire. If he had succeeded, the building of Marxist historical materialism that has weathered 160 years would have collapsed. To avoid the misfortune, we are obligatory to face Baudrillard and accept his challenge.

---

1   The young Habermas finished his *Legitimation Crisis* (1975) in 1973, which is another important inner-logic critique of Marxism. Unlike Baudrillard's choice of a pseudo-romantic return to primitive situation, Habermas straightly towards Capitalism.

Early in 1973, Baudrillard's *The Mirror of Production* was pub-lished. Regrettably, in the past 30 years, little attention has been paid to it by most international left-wing scholars, few of whom really ex-plore the theoretical truth of the text except some abstract and empty rejections in the name of criticism.[2] Ironically, in other fields such as anthropology and sociology,[3] *The Mirror of Production* is acclaimed as an important philosophical achievement. Even more disappoint-ing is the situation in China. No counterattack essay has been seen since its Chinese translation appeared nearly two years ago. How puzzling is it? Where are those slogan-shouting "theoretical leftists" and bombastic claimants who always chant "perfect Marxism?" Why don't the orthodox old guards stand out to face Baudrillard and make high-keyed refutations? Over 30 years ago, Baudrillard threw down the gauntlet with his *The Mirror of Production* before all the Marxists, while this side has been almost silent. I am compelled to put off things in hand and tackle this important theoretical enemy. In fact, it also explains why I chose to write this book in the beginning.

This part will focus on the discussion of the basic logical struc-ture of *The Mirror of Production* by Young Baudrillard, in particular, of his comprehensive questioning of historical materialism. Judging from the contents of Baudrillard's *The Mirror of Production*, he spends most of the time on Chapters 1 and 5, which will naturally become the special points in my discussion.

---

2   No essay in a 1994 reader of Baudrillard has a serious discussion of *The Mirror of Production*. See *Baudrillard: A Critical Reader* (Jiangsu People's Publishing House, 2006).
3   As far as I know, *The Mirror of Production* is enlisted in the sociological reference of many overseas universities.

CHAPTER VIII

MARXISM: TRANSGRESSION OF HISTORICAL MATERIALISM

1 THE MIRROR OF PRODUCTION: WHAT DOES THE YOUNG BAUDRILLARD OBJECT TO?

"A spectre haunts the revolutionary imagination: the phantom of production. Everywhere it sustains an unbridled romanticism of productivity."[1] Baudrillard opens his preface with a parody of the celebrated statement from *The Communist Manifesto*. This sentence has been dealt with in numerous critiques and adapted to various theoretical contexts—Kelso and Adler's *Capitalist Manifesto*, neo-humanistic texts of ex-communist Eastern Europe, and even today's post-modernist thought, for example, Derrida's *Spectres of Marx*. However, it is different this time in Baudrillard's adaptation, which menacingly points toward the very heart of Marxism. "Revolutionary imagination" is used as a metaphor to present all radical discourses that criticize capitalism. Baudrillard attempts to identify that right

---

1   Baudrillard, Jean. *The Mirror of Production*. Trans. Mark Poster. St. Louis: Telos Press, 1975, p. 17.

before those seemingly radical revolutionary expectations there hides a wild dragon called "romanticism of productivity," whose initiator is nobody else but Marx the revolutionary. However, he admits that this dragon is set free *unconsciously* by Marx.

Baudrillard's real target is Marxist historical materialism that transcends all the old ideologies along with the ensuing critical theory of the entire capitalist social historical mode of production. (I once mentioned that the critical logic aiming the mode of production is an important qualitative logic to define late capitalist thoughts.)[2] In Baudrillard's eyes, he seems to pinch the Achilles heel of Marx the giant. He says,

> *The critical theory of the **mode** of production does not touch the principle of production. All the concepts it articulates describe only the dialectical and historical genealogy of the **contents** of production, leaving production as a **form** intact. This form reemerges, idealized, behind the critique of the capitalist mode of production. Through a strange contagion, this form of production only reinforces revolutionary discourse as a language of productivity. From the liberation of productive forces in the unlimited "textual productivity" of **Tel Quel** to Deleuze's factory-machine productivity of the unconscious (including the "labour" of the unconscious), no revolution can place itself under any other sign.[3]*

Without my preparatory discussion of Mauss-Bataille's non-productive thought, a common reader would find it rather abrupt and thus hard to enter Baudrillard's textual context here. In fact, what Baudrillard wants to say is this: Despite criticism of the capitalist mode of production, Marx is never able to touch the ontological foundation on which the capitalism relies, namely, the *logic of production*; despite his discussion about the specific contents of production in different historical periods, Marx just misses the qualitative structure ("form") of the production per se. It can be seen that Baudrillard here intends to criticize *production*, which becomes the first negative key word in his criticism. As we all know, the conception of production is all too important for Marxist historical materialism, whether it is the initial explanation of general historical

---

2 See "Preface" to this book.
3 Baudrillard, Jean. *The Mirror of Production*. Trans. Mark Poster. St. Louis: Telos Press, 1975, p. 17.

materialism founded in *The German Ideology* or the later theoretical development of historical materialism, the production and reproduction of the means of subsistence is always the fundamental paradigm of Marxist philosophy.

According to Baudrillard, the never-questioned logic of production (and the productive forces) hides deeply and grows rapidly under the cover of the cries of capitalist criticism to the extent that all the present critical discourses that seemingly transcend Marxism are haunted by this invisible evil dragon of production. In addition, Baudrillard attacks the so-called production text released from the modernity text by Barthes and Kristeva (*Tel Quel*),[4] along with the unconscious productive forces released from Deleuze's *Machines désirantes*. We seldom find so arrogant a person like Baudrillard who tramples the late *Tel Quel* and proud Deleuze! Obviously, in the eyes of Baudrillard, the post-modernist thought is tirelessly seeking a flowing true creation of life to flee the totality of the modern industry framework, but unfortunately, it always finds itself contained within the logic of production. In my opinion, Baudrillard is a theoretical prophet, who, from the standpoint *opposite* to the post-modern, perceives the secrets of the trend that madly throws out fresh eccentric ideas. Therefore, he cannot be viewed as a *positive* post-modernist.

Once the mystery is revealed, Baudrillard identifies "a productive Eros" from what he considers behind the radical Marxist critiques, which is also deemed as a man's ideal being in the industrial framework. As a result, today's social wealth or language, meaning or value, sign or phantasm—everything is 'produced' according to a labour. Good! Here appears Baudrillard's second negative key word: *labour*. (As I concluded earlier, Baudrillard was never a Marxist even from his very beginning of theoretical discoveries. Ironically, Baudrillard was engaged in the French translation of *The German Ideology*, due to which the bright elf of thoughts familiarized himself with the first original document that gives birth to historical materialism and availed himself of this advantage in his criticism of Marxism.) It is now clear that Baudrillard argues against production and labour. For Marx, production is the prerequisite of man's

---

4   See my "Barthes: Text is a Kind of Weaving" in *Tribune of Social Sciences*, 2002, 10.

entire social history and the general foundation of social existence and development. What is labour, then? According to Engels, it is the fundamental link that conveys man from the animal existence to human being; it is the dominant subjective action in the process of material production. What Baudrillard attempts to nullify is nothing but the groundwork of Marxism: the social existence and man in the vision of historical materialism. Baudrillard's logical outset is actually the *entire logical death* of Marxism. It may shed light on why he becomes so prominent in European academic circles.

He believes all the present social existence is based on the production-labour logic, which is also "the truth of capital and of political economy." Baudrillard says, Marxist critique of capitalism can be said as precise but it never generates doubt about the logic of production, which narrows the revolutionary critique and makes it lose momentum. What Marx wants is only to emancipate the productive forces from the heavy shackles of capitalism. In his opinion, even more radical critiques of capitalism since him cannot escape the same pattern. *Liberation of the productive forces* becomes a revolutionary slogan but at the same time covers a vision that would have been more grandiose and more subversive. (On second thought, Baudrillard is also falsifying the fundamental way that China is proceeding.) He says,

> the capitalist system of production is to be subverted in the name of an authentic and radical productivity. The capitalist law of value is to be abolished in the name of a de-alienated hyperproductivity, a productive hyperspace. Capital develops the productive forces but also restrains them: they must be liberated. The exchange of signifieds has always hidden the "labour" of the signifier: let us liberate the signifier and the textual production of meaning! The unconscious is surrounded in social, linguistic, and Oedipal structures: let us give it back its brute energy; let us restore it as a productive machine! Everywhere productivist discourse reigns and, whether this productivity has objective ends or is deployed for itself, it is itself the form of value. It is the leitmotif both of the system and of a radical challenge.[5]

5   Baudrillard, Jean. *The Mirror of Production.* Trans. Mark Poster. St. Louis: Telos Press, 1975, p. 18.

Baudrillard seems to spread an overwhelming net that captures Marx, who cries for the liberation of productive forces from the shackles of capitalist mode of production, seizes Barthes and Kristeva, who try to free the textual production limited to the pursuit of originality of modernity, and snares Freud and De Leon, who hope to release the unconscious Eros as man's authentic being. Behold, all this above belongs to the "discourse of productivism!" Nevertheless, it does not simply mean the modern liberalism handed down from Adam Smith and Ricardo but the very revolutionary discourse *critical of capitalism*, viz. the "leitmotif of a radical challenge." Among these radical discourses of revolution against capitalism, Marx committed the biggest crime. Baudrillard has a specific note to explain it: Marx played an essential role in the rooting of this productivist metaphor because he radicalized and rationalized the *mode of production*, giving it a "revolutionary title of nobility." Therefore, Baudrillard points the sword toward Marx to erase this sort of productivism. Hence, the third key concept is the *mode of production* that unifies the productive forces and relations of production.

Marx, in Baudrillard's criticism, has many problems. For example, he shattered the fiction of *homo economicus*, the myth which sums up the whole process of the naturalization of the system of exchange value, the market, and surplus value and its forms. (I suspect Baudrillard first learned the concept of "homo economicus" from Mauss's *Gift* before he found confirmation from Marx.) Baudrillard certainly knows that Marx transcends the capitalist economics (hypothesis of homo economicus) by mercilessly exposing and firmly negating the externalization, naturalization of the ideology of capitalist production. He does not deny this point. Nevertheless, Marx's critical method is, in his eyes, still achieved "in the name of labour power." To be specific, Marx discovers that the capitalist only pays the "value" of labour power based on the equivalent exchange relations of the market but secretly appropriates a large sum of surplus value. In this connection, Marx transcends Proudhon and other capitalist economists and establishes the scientific political economy critical of the capitalist mode of production. Baudrillard goes on to point out that, the theory of surplus value does uncover the secret of capitalist exploitation but it is the same "mythical" and "naturalized" ideology for Marx to hold the view that value is *produced* through labour. Note that here appears the fourth Marxist concept violently attacked by Baudrillard: *labour power*. Baudrillard holds that man is defined via labour power engaged in production in the philosophical discourse of Marxist historical materialism while labour power comes to be man's authentic survival mode in all social historical patterns. (This condemnation of Baudrillard's is absolutely groundless, which will be dealt with in a separate section.) Here, Baudrillard does not target against Marx's criticism or exposure of capitalism but opposes the *social ontological base* on which Marxist critique of capitalism relies. (We already know Baudrillard takes objection to Marxism due to the idea of *non-productive* existence based on symbolic relations.) He disagreeably grumbles, "Isn't this a similar fiction, a similar naturalization—another wholly arbitrary convention, a simulation model bound to code all human material and every contingency of desire and exchange in terms of value, finality, and production?"[6] It turns out that Baudrillard's anger stems from his demurral against Marx's method of using the production-value frame to universalize the entire human existence and social history, especially, the non-productive "practopian" state that he learns from Mauss. With the above words, Baudrillard seems to interrogate Marx by a sharper question: Is the entire history of human existence controlled by the logic of production?

Baudrillard already has had his answer to it: No. He believes Marx's logic of production leads to an illusion, "no longer a matter of 'being' oneself but of 'producing' oneself." According to him, the unseen humanistic logic brings about the situation that *I produce, therefore I am (je produis, donc je suis)*, or, if extended a little further, even *I produce, therefore history is*. To a certain extent, his sum-up of Marx's philosophical discourse is not completely wrong. It also explains why Baudrillard titles his book with *The Mirror of Production*. He claims, "*the mirror of production* in which all Western metaphysics is reflected, must be broken."[7] Baudrillard explains that the title borrows Lacan's theory of mirror stage, which can be found, according to him, in every aspect of political economics as

---

6   *Ibid.*, p. 19.
7   *Ibid.*, p. 47.

well. (I have to mention that Baudrillard's reference to Lacan is not legitimate here. Obviously, it shows his inadequate knowledge of Lacan's mirror theory.) Just have a look at his reasoning:

> *Through this scheme of production, this **mirror** of production, the human species comes to consciousness [**la prise de conscience**] in the imaginary. Production, labour, value, everything through which an objective world emerges and through which man recognizes himself objectively—this is the imaginary. Here man is embarked on a continual deciphering of himself through his works, finalized by his shadow (his own end), reflected by this operational mirror, this sort of ideal of a productivist ego. This process occurs not only in the materialized form of an economic obsession with efficiency determined by the **system** of exchange value, but more profoundly in this **overdetermination by the code**, by the mirror of political economy: in the identity that man dons with his own eyes when he can think of himself only as something to produce, to transform, or bring about as value.[8]*

In this short paragraph huddles a pile of Baudrillard's negative key words, *labour, value, political economy* and so on. (Later, Baudrillard adds to his blacklist other basic concepts, like, *need, labour power, use value, history, nature, law, dialectics*, etc.) As we know, Lacan's mirror theory is the negative identification of an ego's establishment that begins from a false image. Originated in the external image of an *individual*, the illusion is first mistaken by the unconsciousness as "self," and then constructed as a pseudo-self by the regulatory mirror reflection of the surrounding faces during the early period. According to Lacan, the reflection relationship (pseudo-self) that occupies the subjective self is autre (more accurately, autre I and autre* II). Therefore, the mirror stage is an ontological fraud in the initial phase of self-formation.[9] Baudrillard applies Lacan's mirror theory to the generic field of human existence. It can be counted as a logical possibility, if not a mistake. However, as the objective activity of man, production does not come from the direct objective reflection of man's subjectivity. No thinker ever mistakes production as man's real being, less to mention the absence of *unconscious*

---

8 *Ibid.*, p. 58.
9 See Chapter Three in *The Impossible Truth of Being. Mirror of Lacan's Philosophy* (2006).
*) Other.

self-reference in Lacan's logic of mirror. Ironically, Baudrillard's proud analogy is actually based on his misunderstanding of Lacan. In this way, his critical foundation will be nothingness. *Nothing is constructed from nothingness.* Baudrillard proves a good example of Lacan's satire of those crazy, self-righteous people.

According to Baudrillard, man acquires an imago from Smith-Marx mirror and then creates an illusionary objective world, a self-reference of the subject. The essence of the image is the *utilitarian logic of value*; hence, the production of mirror can be developed to *the mirror of political economy*. (He later uses such concepts as *the mirror of labour* and *the mirror of history*.) On a more profound level, Baudrillard attempts to question all the anthropocentrism centred on *utilitarian value*. It is interesting to find that Baudrillard does not dispute the supreme economization or growthism in capitalist economy but turns against Marx who stands opposite the capitalist ideology. According to him, Marx does negate the overt ahistoricality of classical economics, whilst the productive and *expressive* discourse are still two "un-analyzed" things in Marx's critical logic, furthermore, the mirror of production hides deep in Marx's inner logic.

What does it mean? The so-called productive discourse indicates Marx's theories of material production and the development of the productive forces while the expressive discourse represents Marxist production relations and the mode of production. In the eyes of Baudrillard, the capitalist schema of production is only the superficial form of representation, or "the order of representation" of the production logic. Marx does not deny the production logic per se that sustains the whole capitalist existence. Accordingly, "it is no longer worthwhile to make a radical critique of the order of representation in the name of production and of its revolutionary formula."[10]

In fact, this discovery of Baudrillard's is not that fantastic. In my opinion, it is only a sort of critical tension with pseudo-romanticism extended from the sacred thing called by Bataille. Only the elated Baudrillard regards himself as the pure child who observes the falsehood of the entire social existence and decides to tear off the "emperor's new clothes," which, to him, is nothing else but production,

---

10   Baudrillard, Jean. *The Mirror of Production.* Trans. Mark Poster. St. Louis: Telos Press, 1975, p. 20.

the mirror of production. He wants to stand out and be the first to break this magic mirror. (According to Sahlins, Gajo Petrović and Alfred Schmidt already criticized the universality of historical materialism earlier than Baudrillard.[11]) I wonder whether Baudrillard would know that his flighty conceit leads to a Don Quixotian battle and illusion. True, he is somewhat profound in some points, but he still makes the same mistake as those "cataract theorists" do. The devil that he endeavours to fight is a false image, which is nonexistent or simply gets misunderstood. (Next, we are going to deal with Baudrillard with his own means and dissect his critique about Marxism, in particular, about historical materialism.)

Baudrillard's arrangement of his text is sometimes broken and often repetitious; so I intend to choose a logical path for discussion rather than strictly abide by the original textual order, which, in my opinion, will restore the critical logic more faithful than Baudrillard's own for, regrettably, reality is really dead with him. (The subject of the death of reality is discussed in his late important text, *The Perfect Crime*, which is also the background for *The Matrix*, a movie deeply influenced by Baudrillard.)

2 REJECTION OF THE GESTALT OF HISTORICAL MATERIALISM

The avid critic Baudrillard targets the concept of labour because in his judgment it is the key of Marxist logic of production. (Indeed, this is an academic misconception and logical confusion due to mixture of different research fields.) In the beginning, Baudrillard demonstrates his intention: The real critique of political economy should not be confined to the exposition of such anthropologic concepts as need and use value that conceal themselves behind consumption but to "unmask everything hidden behind the concepts of production, mode of production, productive forces, relations of production, etc. All the fundamental concepts of Marxist analysis must be questioned, starting from its own requirement of a radical critique and transcendence of political economy."[12]

---

11   Sahlins, Marshall D. *Culture and Practical Reason*. Joint Publishing Company Limited (Beijing), 2002, p. 3.
12   Baudrillard, Jean. *The Mirror of Production*. Trans. Mark Poster. St. Louis: Telos Press, 1975, p. 20.

Baudrillard deserves to be called a genius. This is a very accurate statement in which he perceives what others cannot see and wield sword at the heart of Marxism. (I have to acknowledge that Baudrillard is sometimes terribly sober.) In his view, a profound critique of political economy should not make negations within the framework of itself but first strides beyond Marx's *transcendence* of political economy, that is, a thorough direct reflection of the methodology of historical materialism that Marx employs to transcend political economy. (Political economy should not be opposed within its own framework, which is the viewpoint of Marx when criticizing Proudhon but borrowed here by Baudrillard for his objection to Marxism.) Baudrillard realizes that Marx's secret of transcending the bourgeois classical economics is the methodology of historical materialism. This understanding is certainly right. What is left for Baudrillard to do is to transcend Marx's transcendence in turn.

Therefore, he raises two axiomatic questions:

What is axiomatic about productive forces or about the dialectical genesis of modes of production from which springs all revolutionary theory? What is axiomatic about the generic richness of man who is labour power, about the motor of history, or about history itself, which is only "the production by men of their material life?"[13]

If interpreted in a simple way, the first historical "axiom" means why the contradiction between the productive forces and the relations of production is regarded as the driving force of social historical development, while the demand to renovate the relations of production is the cause of revolution. This is an issue about social movement. The second historical "axiom" has a deeper suggestion, which can be explained as follows: Why is history only the process of producing man's material life? Then, why is production is the initiative of historical development? Moreover, why does man only acquire the "generic" richness when he is taken as the "labour power"? (We are going to have a detailed analysis about this question later. Baudrillard's simplified appropriation of the concept of "labour power" from the context of Marxist political economy is illegitimate.) Please note that it is a systematic falsification of

---

13   *Ibid.*, p. 20.

propositions. First, it belongs to the domain of philosophical questions. More specifically, it is a question directed against historical materialism. Again, I have to admit that Baudrillard precisely grasps the main issue in his critique. However, in the very beginning he chooses to ignore a theoretical blind spot, which has experienced a progressive development. Marx in the beginning first assumes that man's generic nature is labour (power) before he regards the social history of human beings as the record of the self-movement of material production; afterward, he stipulates that the contradiction between productive forces and the relations of production during the material production drive forward the entire human social history. For this, my opinion is as follows:

First, after the establishment of historical materialism in 1845, Marx did not consider labour as man's generic nature in the sense of *philosophical ontology*. Since Baudrillard must have read Althusser, he should not neglect the important historical changes in Marxist thought of Marx himself. He uses the humanistic discourse *thoroughly refuted* by Marx to fire against a disappeared logical outset, which cannot be counted as fair. Besides, Marx never universalized the historical view and anthropology with the *worker's labour power*, of which the special historical materialization only could be possible in the economic context of the capitalist mode of production. It does not belong to Marxism but results from Baudrillard's own confusion. As a matter of fact, *man's labour activity* is recognized as the fundamental position where material production creates social history. In my opinion, this is the *logical starting point* of Marx's *special historical materialism*. From the view of philosophy, Marx *starts again from the subjective dimension* which is the real and historical origin of his historical phenomenology. Baudrillard really lacks a sufficient knowledge of Marxist history. In fact, when Marx entered the final stage of building the historical materialism, he clearly opposed the stipulation of man as the wage labour. In a draft about Friedrich List's book of economics in March, 1845, Marx wrote, under the capitalist system, individual is reduced to a "productive force of wealth" because in this mode of production, as manpower, he is juxtaposed with other material forces, such as water-power, steam-power, and horse-power. Marx angrily asked, "Is it a high appreciation of man for him to figure as a "force" alongside horses, steam and water?"[14] Judging from this point, Baudrillard was a poor student of Marxism. He did not carefully read the above statement; otherwise, he would probably not smear Marx with this *anthropological labour force*.

Second, it is known that the concept of production undergoes multiple semantic and historical changes in Marx's text. However, Baudrillard's judgment on this point seems very poor, or probably, the genius is so overwhelmed by his critical impulse and ambition that he makes a silly mistake of *absolute homogeneity* of the theory of Marxism which experienced an academic progress for nearly 50 years. (I once criticized this approach of indiscriminate citation from the first volume to the last one of the *Collected Works of Marx and Engels* in a subject research. In fact, it is a Stalinist ahistorical illustration. Regrettably, this fascist-like grammar is also detectable in Baudrillard's subaltern critique under the fashion of a vanguard.) Ignorance begets impetuousness. Baudrillard is unaware that Marxist historical materialism is divided into general and special types, which possesses several concepts of production *literally similar* but substantially different in contents and meanings.

Baudrillard should know that Marx's general historical materialism discusses the common situation and common laws of human social history, while the special historical materialism mainly accounts for the historical phenomena of the capitalist society. Production, first refers to the general productive activity as a given (component) in the philosophical-historical view, which entails both the *production of man (himself) per se* as well as the material. Second, production is a *modern* concept to understand the nature of contemporary social history. In *Theses on Feuerbach, production* exists as a relational being to eliminate the binary separation of subject and object, a presence of revolutionary practice; or in *The German Ideology, production* appears in the most fundamental material creation process of modern industrial activities, being the kernel of the logic of historical materialism. The above two paradigms in *Theses* and *The German Ideology* belong to the philosophical discourse. After 1858, Marx employed multiple particular concepts of *general* and *special* production in the

---

14   Karl Marx and Frederick Engels. *Collected Works*, vol. 4. London: Lawrence & Wishart, 1975, p. 285.

context of political economy to mainly indicate the machine production in the capitalist mode of production when the commodity
production and market exchange developed to a certain level. The
complexity of Marxist theory of production above seems to confound
the clever Baudrillard, who, despite his talent, started from a flimsy
foundation to build his theory. No matter how magnificent his theoretical palace looks, it will collapse on a slight but vital push.

Then, Baudrillard makes a high-profile quotation from *The
German Ideology*—jointly translated by him–the famous statement
of general historical materialism firstly put forward by Karl Marx:

The first historical act is thus the production of the means to satisfy these needs, the production of material life itself. And indeed
this is an historical act, a fundamental condition of all history, which
today, as thousands of years ago, must daily and hourly be fulfilled
merely in order to sustain human life.[15]

Is Marx wrong? Previous thinkers only saw history as created by
hero's wills while Marx simply identified the truth of history. The
word "production" in the first sentence above is used in its *general*
sense, not referring to a special historical mode of existence. It refers
to the basic material activity that creates the entire human society,
without which man cannot survive. Accordingly, Marx and Engels
would view production as the initiative of man's social history in
The German Ideology that founds the *general historical materialism*. In addition, the word "needs" in the above paragraph is also
general. Marx is definitely aware of man's *specific* needs becoming
different in each historical phase of production. (Marx also made a
particular analysis of the different needs under different historical
conditions in *The German Ideology*. Similarly, in his later *Economic
Manuscripts of 1861-1863*, Marx wrote that "the extent of the so-
called primary requirements for life and the manner of their satisfaction depend to a large degree on the level of civilisation of the society, they are themselves the product of history, the necessary means
of subsistence in one country or epoch include things not included
in another."[16]) Although Baudrillard does not openly put down his

---

15   See "Feuerbach" in *MECW*.
16   Karl Marx and Frederick Engels. *Collected Works*, vol. 30. London: Lawrence &
Wishart, 1988, p. 44.

interpretation of the aforesaid statement, we can infer that in his eyes Marx's production and requirement here are belongings of the capitalist system. Therefore, he can make the rash conclusion that the liberation of productive forces is confused with the liberation of man and he questions: Is this a revolutionary formula or that of political economy itself?

For this question, I really think Baudrillard needs to take supplementary instructions since Marx never equated the liberation of productive forces with the liberation of man. Instead, the former is the material precondition of the latter and the real objective foundation from which the social revolutions take place. (This question will be analyzed. In details later.) Baudrillard means, it is this subject that we need to reflect upon, that is, production is deemed as the nature of history, even the unique *qualitative* aspect of man. It is for the same reason that he strongly dislikes Marx's writing in *The German Ideology*: "They [Men] themselves begin to distinguish themselves from animals as soon as they begin to produce their means of subsistence."[17] Baudrillard questions: Why should man be differentiated from other animals? In his opinion, this idea is a humanistic "obstinacy" and bigotry of political economy. This opinion would strike any normal reader: Is there anybody who does not regard people as different from other animals? Can it be that man exists in the same way as other animals do? (To Baudrillard, it is not weird at all for his spiritual teacher Bataille was always fascinated by the French pornographer writer Marquis de Sade, who claimed that man's authenticity of being was cognized through animal-like sexual impulsion and excretion.) As analysis goes on, we shall understand the true colour of Mauss-Bataille logic to which Baudrillard clings.

In Baudrillard's eyes, given that Marx regards man's existence as his own end, then Baudrillard's man will set a means (production) other than the purpose to satisfy the needs that he has, that is, he has to produce. Accordingly, man is forced to hold himself as the labour power of production, during which, the man as purpose will be separated from the man as means. It is called "alienation." Marx's critical transcendence of political economy aims to restore man with

---

17   Karl Marx and Frederick Engels. *Collected Works*, vol. 5. London: Lawrence & Wishart, 1976, p. 31.

his own end. (Of course, my paraphrase above is a rearrangement of Baudrillard's unclear, broken line of thought often interrupted by his own questions. We would be at a complete loss if following his sequence.) Baudrillard is wrong again! After 1845, Marx was no longer marked by Feuerbach's humanistic *view of alienation*. It is true that Marx still criticized the phenomenon in which the material force created by man proves to enslave himself in the capitalist social economy, as stated in the *Economic Manuscripts of 1857-1858* and *Capital* and that he also pointed out the nature of alienation in the capitalist economic relations, but he raised his disproving critiques more from the perspective of the reversed materialized social relations. Had he ever made such imprudent statement as that man ought to be restored with his own end through denial of alienation?

Baudrillard claimed that his intention was to challenge Marx, to bring down Marxism so that he could disprove the "political radicalism" pursued and contributed by "generations of revolutionaries." I am pessimistic of his wish.

3 METHODOLOGICAL ROOT CAUSE: TRANSHISTORICIZED HISTORY

Baudrillard focuses on the critique of Marxist concept of labour in his first chapter, though, his desultory thought makes a hasty leap from a hardly prepared arena of historical philosophy into the economic context, which is but an illegitimate argument. (We are going to have a detailed discussion about it in the next section.) I shall first analyze the philosophical conclusion of Chapter One because, in theory, it happens to be his methodological advance of the criticism above.

In *The Mirror of Production*, almost every chapter has a so-called summary of epistemology to show off Baudrillard's metaphysical complacency. (Except Chapter IV, all the first four chapters have summaries of epistemology.) The title of the first epistemology is "In the Shadow of Marxist Concepts," which, judging from the entire text, is intended to identify the methodological root cause of Marxist historical materialism. In Baudrillard's view, the specific, limited concepts are "universalized." (This critical logic is learned from the methodology of Marxist historical materialism.) It leads to an illegal theoretical transgression. We shall examine his critique.

Baudrillard admits that "Marxist theory has sought to shatter the abstract universality of the concepts of bourgeois thought (such as *Nature* and *Progress*, *Man* and *Reason*, formal *Logic*, *Work*, *Exchange*, etc.)."[18] Strangely, in retrospect of Marx's texts, one will fail to find him simply denying what Baudrillard judges the universality of the concepts of bourgeois thought. In my opinion, Marx does not reject nature and progress but he is against the naturalization and externalization of the capitalist mode of production; he does not oppose man and rationality but he resists the capitalist abstraction of man and hypocrisy of rationality; a fortiori, he does not reject formal logic, labour and exchange but denies the materialized social relations and fetishistic thought under the capitalist system. Ridiculously, Baudrillard states that Marx attempts to shatter the bourgeois universal thought by such concepts as "historical materialism, dialectics, mode of production, labour power" and so on, which, again, only tells his own fallacy.

First of all, historical materialism is the most universal concept, the weltanschauung called by Marx as the single "science of history" while historical dialectics is a significant logic structure of this world view. Historical materialism is in essence historical dialectics. The mode of production is the central concept of historical materialism as well as the key perspective that Marx employs to study the nature of the capitalist society. As to the last concept of "labour power," it belongs to the economic category, obviously different from the above first three concepts. In all the published texts of Marx, "labour power," is never found to be used in a broader sense of philosophy (epistemology). (Baudrillard tends to confuse thoughts of different categories. We have to adapt ourselves to the characteristic casualty of his.) More importantly, Marx is capable of transcending the classical economics of the bourgeois ideology in that he stands on the high point of historical materialism. He bases his critique and destruction of the bourgeois ideology on the profound study of economics along with the social and scientific history. After 1845, Marx abandoned his youthful declaration that the kingdom of bourgeois was dead in philosophical sense (as written in *Economic and*

---

18   Baudrillard, Jean. *The Mirror of Production*. Trans. Mark Poster. St. Louis: Telos Press, 1975, p. 47.

Philosophical Manuscripts of 1844). Unfortunately, Baudrillard is only self-righteous but wrong.

After a far-fetched criticism, Baudrillard brings forward another discovery of the epistemological root cause of Marxism: Despite Marx's correct critique of the abstract bourgeois concepts, he again "universalizes" the concepts that are used to transcend the bourgeois ideology. As a result, for him Marxist epistemology is in essence "'critical' imperialism." (This sharp criticism necessitates serious attention.) Baudrillard says the proposition that a concept is not merely an interpretive hypothesis but a translation of universal movement depends upon pure metaphysics. Marxist concepts do not escape this lapse. In his opinion, to transform a paradigm or concept into a universal formula is an old metaphysical practice, which Marx fails to avoid. He writes:

> *Instead, in Marxism history is transhistoricized: it redoubles on itself and thus is universalized. To be rigorous the dialectic must dialectically surpass and annul itself. By radicalizing the concepts of production and mode of production at a given moment, Marx made a break in the social mystery of exchange value. The concept thus takes all its strategic power from its irruption, by which it dispossesses political economy of its imaginary universality. But, from the time of Marx, it lost this advantage when taken as a principle of explication. It thus cancelled its "difference" by universalizing itself, regressing to the dominant form of the code (universality) and to the strategy of political economy. It is not tautological that the concept of history is historical, that the concept of dialectic is dialectical, and that the concept of production is itself produced (that is, it is to be judged by a kind of self-analysis). Rather, this simply indicates the explosive, mortal, present form of critical concepts. As soon as they are constituted as universal they cease to be analytical and the religion of meaning begins.*[19]

The long paragraph of Baudrillard's is only too important. It vividly displays what Baudrillard thinks as an internal criticism and insightful perspective of Marxist historical materialism. Let me explain this "classical" statement.

---

19   *Ibid.*, p. 48.

Baudrillard acknowledges Marx's effective refutation of the universality of the bourgeois political economy (the eternal existence of market economy as natural order) through critical analysis of historicality and dialectic. Marx illustrates that the bourgeois mode of production is historical (impermanent), history is *progressive* and historical dialectic denies any attempt to solidificate the present. However, when Marx extends the historical concept, it is no longer historical and in turn joins the "dominant code" of bourgeois ideology. This time, Baudrillard is not unclear in expressing his idea except the nonsense of radicalizing the concepts of production and mode of production. He tries to criticize Marx for extending a historical concept (*necessity of progress*) to the universal social history, particularly, to the primitive society where there are no such concepts as *progress* or *mode of production*. It proves Marx's theoretical violence.

In my opinion, Baudrillard plays tricks with the concepts here. *After 1845*, in dealing with the social reality of human history, especially, the capitalist society, Marx had several different historical concepts in his mind experiment. First, it is the historical paradigm which is the very nature of historical materialism—and also the methodological (and the epistemological) paradigm of *limited historicality* and *ontological subsistence timescale* in the heart of Marxism, that is, the very analytic model "under particular historical condition" specially marked by Marx and extraordinarily emphasized by me. In other words, Marx exactly rejected any transhistorical conception. (It is from this point that Heidegger's notion of sterblich dasein arises.)[20]

The second is the modern industrial production, the concept of history that forms during the capitalist development, more *fluid and revolutionary*. The dialectical nature in German classical philosophy did anticipate this historical modernity. Regrettably, Germany lacked the reality of industrial production. Marx jested in *The German Ideology* that the Germans "have no history." Obviously, history here is used in this special modern sense.

---

20   See Chapter Six in *Back to Marx: The Philosophical Discourse in the Context of Economics* (Jiangsu People's Press, 1999) and English version by Göttingen University Press in 2014.

The third one only appears after the liberation of man, which is the true development of *human history*. In the eyes of Marx, the capitalist society is still the world of "economic animals." (He abandoned the use of humanistic concepts like "inhuman.") He often calls capitalist society the "prehistorical society." The third concept is used in an ad hoc sense.

Fourth, Marx also uses the concept of history in common historical sense and researches. It is unnecessary to explain here.

Clearly, only with the second meaning can Baudrillard's criticism of historical concepts make sense. In addition, he needs to prove Marx has the attempt to impose the capitalist *modern schema of time* on the entire human history. Otherwise, however rigorous the critique is, it only ends up in falsehood.

With the above background introduction, Baudrillard's accusation turns out to be unreasonable and empty.

> *They [concepts] only evoke themselves in an indefinite metonymic process which goes as follows: man is historical; history is dialectical; the dialectic is the process of (material) production; production is the very movement of human existence; history is the history of modes of production, etc. This scientific and universalist discourse (code) immediately becomes imperialistic. All possible societies are called on to respond.*[21]

There is a significant problem in Baudrillard's reasoning. He is likely to equate Marx's thought to the old philosophical framework of Stalinist dogmatic explanation, especially, by means of simplistic inference. Smart as he is, he makes such simple errors. Where can we find in Marxist texts the aforementioned code imperialism? Although some Baudrillard's allegations are applicable to the conventional dogmatic textbooks of Marxism, the assertion that "the dialectic is the process of material production" is found nowhere. (Even in the textbooks of former Soviet Union and East European socialist countries, the dialectic refers to the study of the general laws of nature, society and human thought.) Baudrillard just makes another fabrication here.

---

21   Baudrillard, Jean. *The Mirror of Production*. Trans. Mark Poster. St. Louis: Telos Press, 1975, p. 48.

Baudrillard seems unsatisfied in this attack. Apart from his judgment of the epistemological fallacy in Marxism, he expands his target field, "What we have said about the Marxist concepts holds for the unconscious, repression, Oedipal complex, etc., as well." He thus sentences Freudian psychoanalysis to death, too.

What's more, Baudrillard is very glad about his last resort. He is confident that once he utters "check" Marx and Freud will be checkmated. The final placement is his favourite "primitive societies." (We are already familiar with the primitive societies, perceived as the ontological starting point by Baudrillard. This primitive society is certainly an imagined ideal scene of human existence refracted through Mauss-Bataille prism.) He cannot conceal his excitement in the following remark.

> There is **neither a mode of production nor production** in primitive societies. There is **no dialectic** and **no unconscious** in primitive societies. These concepts analyze only our own societies, which are ruled by political economy. Hence they have only a kind of boomerang value.[22]

Baudrillard emphasizes his conclusion with words in italics,[23] which, in my opinion, is but a little trick to amuse himself. A more accurate account should be like this: In primitive societies, there are not any modern-sense mode of production and production, and today's theories of the dialectic and unconscious are still out of sight. Marx never views today's modern production as the existential basis of the primitive societies. In the discourse of historical materialism, "when we speak of production, we always have in mind production at a definite stage of social development."[24] The mode and nature of production vary at different social stages but production always exists as the material basis of the social existence and movement. "Human life has from the beginning rested on production, and, *d'une manière ou d'une autre*, on *social* production."[25] Even in primitive societies, unless our ancestors do not eat or drink, they have to engage themselves in the survival activities of obtaining

---

22   *Ibid.*, p. 49.
23   Baudrillard attaches great importance to it.
24   Karl Marx and Frederick Engels. *Collected Works*, vol. 28. London: Lawrence & Wishart, 1986, p. 22.
25   *Ibid.*, p. 413.

food and protection against dangers. As Marx says, it is "appropriation of nature by the individual within and by means of a definite form of society."[26] *The reason why there is "the process by which he makes his living"*[27] is that man has the characteristic superior mode of survival and obtaining food, not to make an empty show to be differentiated from animals. Otherwise, not only the gift exchange and consumption enthroned by Baudrillard and his teachers would have disappeared but also the primitive peoples could have simply lost their survival opportunities.[28]

Indeed, I can say the primitive gathering activity of men cannot be called "production" by any modern language but this objective activity was the only basis for human survival. It does not belong to the utilitarian value system but it is a must. It is labelled by Marx as the *general* material production in the frame of general historical materialism. In this respect, it does not change its essence although Marx and Engels later noticed that this material production is only "a peripheral matter" in H. Morgan's rough study of the primitive societies in the late 19th century. (Marx said the primitive people do not exchange in accordance with an overturned material relation. He inferred that they "had only a CARRYING TRADE and did not themselves produce. At least production was secondary among the Phoenicians, Carthaginians, etc."[29] In other words, the material production has not become a decisive factor in primitive societies but without it man would have lost his survival foundation, which demonstrates that Marx's anthropological view is fairly comparable with Mauss's discovery later.) This is because the form of activities by the primitive people (if not called the mode of production),

---

26   *Ibid.*, p. 25.
27   Karl Marx and Frederick Engels. *Collected Works*, vol. 24. London: Lawrence & Wishart, 1989, p. 538.
28   Marx cited an example of it. He said, "It is a received opinion that in certain periods people lived from pillage alone. But, for pillage to be possible, there must be some thing to be pillaged, hence production". "And the mode of pillage is itself in turn determined by the mode of production. See *MECW* vol. 46. *If* slightly adapted, the above statement can be retailed to Baudrillard: For gift exchange (symbolic exchange) to be possible, there must be gift to be exchanged, hence production. Without "gift," there would be no large-scale consumption as in the "potlatch," without mentioning of basic survival.
29   Karl Marx and Frederick Engels. *Collected Works*, vol. 28. London: Lawrence & Wishart, 1986, p. 155.

superior to common animals in sustaining life, is an objective reality as well as a basic condition for man's survival. It needs to be clarified that Marx's theory that man's social history is generally based on the production of the material means of subsistence belongs not to the logic of political economy but to the philosophical discourse of (general) historical materialism. Baudrillard's critique confuses the discourse of political economy with the discourse of philosophy, which leaves its validity very questionable.

Moreover, Baudrillard's criticism contains a paradox of which he himself is fully unaware. He accuses Marx of projecting such contemporary concepts as production and history to primitive societies, at the same time *imposes the elementary social structure and mode of existence in primitive societies into the entire human life*. Is it not the right code imperialism? Baudrillard says he wants to break from Marxism, and from psychoanalysis. This scares no one. The boomerang he throws is certain to strike back on himself.

CHAPTER IX

ONTOLOGY OF PRODUCTION:
I PRODUCE, THEREFORE HISTORY IS

The first chapter of *The Mirror of Production* is entitled "The Concept of Labour," but Baudrillard's major critical target is the core of historical materialism: material production. In Baudrillard's view, Marx seriously objects to the capitalist mode of production and exposes the exploitative nature of capital, but he is unaware that the discourse of the philosophy of history centred on the *useful* production of labour is still the coded product of the unconscious in bourgeois system of value exchange. Baudrillard declares another battle to refute this *I-produce-therefore-history-is ontology as the ontology of Marxism* and which is even advocated by all the radical discourses of post-Marxian trend. We have to respond to this arrogant misunderstanding of and vicious attack on Marxism. First, I am going to discuss Baudrillard's view about production.

1 MIS-CRITICISM OF USE VALUE AND "EXCHANGE VALUE"

The first issue in Chapter One is the criticism of "use value and labour power," in which Baudrillard argues that Marxism is built on the specific stipulations constructed by the bourgeois system of utilitarian value and the logic of market exchange. I have mentioned such categories as use value and labour power only make sense in the capitalist system and will end up in theoretical transgression if generally applied to the entire history.

Once more, it is Baudrillard's misunderstanding of Marxism. Marx is different from the bourgeois thinkers in that he attaches *historical restriction* in theoretical application to each paradigm of particular eras. Baudrillard's accusation exactly proves Marx's unique advantage. In fact, what Baudrillard criticizes is a non-existent "pseudo-Marxism," a demonized illusion only in Baudrillard's own perverse thinking. Baudrillard says,

> *In the distinction between exchange value and use value, Marxism shows its strength but also its weakness. The presupposition of use value—the hypothesis of a concrete value beyond the abstraction of exchange value, a human purpose of the commodity in the moment of its direct relation of utility for a subject—is only the effect of the system of exchange value, a concept produced and developed by it. Far from designating a realm beyond political economy, use value is only the horizon of exchange value.*[1]

Despite this verbiage, he is not able to pick a hole in Marx. Firstly, the distinction of exchange value and use value should be counted as the early economic concept exercise of Smith and Ricardo instead of the contribution of Marx. Baudrillard is not reading carefully enough. It is true that Marx employs them in the arena of his discussion with classical economics (until the first half part of *1857-1858 Manuscripts*) but later in *Capital* he defines the duality of commodity by *use value and value*, and confirms that exchange value is merely the *superficial appearance* of value. Baudrillard ignores this point.[2] More importantly, Marx does not separate (capitalist) commodity

---

1   Baudrillard, Jean. *The Mirror of Production*. Trans. Mark Poster. St. Louis: Telos Press, 1975, p. 23.

2   Marx once said, "exchange-value is merely a '*form* of appearance,' an independent way of presenting the *value* contained in the commodity." *MECW*.

from the issues of value, exchange value and use value. Nor does he simply apply the economic concepts to the fields of philosophy and anthropology. In the first run, Baudrillard chooses a wrong target.

Secondly, Baudrillard does not accept the anthropological use value severed from the "system of exchange value," especially, the commodity's "direct relation of utility for a subject." Understandably, he longs for proceeding with Mauss-Bataille logic and radically wipes out the bourgeois utilitarian value system that does not allow the "thing (to be) thinged" (Heidegger), but where on earth does Marx make such an ahistorical abstract, eternalized concept of use value? On one hand, Baudrillard cites the specific points of Marxist economy; on the other, he arbitrarily makes ontological use of these points. What a misconception it is! Marx strictly limits the discussion of use value and value within the historical process of commodity production and exchange. He never talks about the duality of commodities in primitive and future communist societies, where commodity exchange relations are not found. Marx says, "The dissolution of all products and activities into exchange values presupposes both the dissolution of all established personal (historical) relations of dependence in production, and the dissolution of all-round dependence of the producers upon one another."[3] Here, Marx uses the concept of "fixed personal relations" in order to identify and characterize the first one among the three major social forms of humankind, which, certainly includes the primitive tribal life in Mauss-Baudrillard research. For example, the symbolic exchange during gift giving and sacrifice represents the close *kinship reliance* that is definitely personal; however, such ontological scales as value, exchange value and use value will not penetrate the entire human life and social relations until "bourgeois society" appears.[4] In addition, Marx stated, "when material production is no longer limited by exchange value, but [solely] by its relation to the overall development of the individual, all this business, with its convulsions and pains, comes to an end."[5] Marx's statement cannot be clearer

---

3 Karl Marx and Frederick Engels. *Collected Works*, vol. 28. London: Lawrence & Wishart, 1986, p. 93.
4 *Ibid.*, p. 93.
5 Karl Marx and Frederick Engels. *Collected Works*, vol. 29. London: Lawrence & Wishart, 1987, p. 12.

here! In fact, I can figure out the real intention behind Baudrillard's logical violence. He means to say that he does not agree to viewing *utility* as the scale for everything. (His utility is proposed in line with Bataille's ontological uselessness, it is not the use value in antithesis to value, which will be discussed in details later.) In the second run, Baudrillard makes a mess of an originally clear issue.

Thirdly, Baudrillard does not regard use value as the foundation of exchange value. Instead he thinks that use value is "produced and developed from the system of exchange value." I have to admit that Baudrillard is not without grounds this time. His opinion once obtained support from a classical economist, who was Adam Smith, but not Marx. In *The Wealth of Nations*, Smith first proposed that an item's usefulness determines its exchange value. Nevertheless, after man enters into the era of machine production, smart Ricardo opposed this point by saying that the direct factor that determines the item's exchange value is not its utility but rather the scarcity and amount of labour spent to acquire it.[6] Baudrillard does not understand that these men are discussing the theory of labour value *in the economic context*. In this connection, Marx discussed the relations of value and use value of the commodity from an economic perspective, as value generated from abstract labour, as the amount of value determined by the amount of labour, an as necessary labour time being the real scale of value, etc. (Pls. note that Marx later clearly left behind the term "exchange value" for value.) At the same time, Marx points out that under capitalist economic conditions the commercial development "will increasingly subordinate production to exchange value, and force immediate use value more and more into the background."[7] All in all, Marx never deals with labour value outside the economic context.

Baudrillard seems to fruitlessly thrash about against Marxism. He intends to look through Mauss-Bataille lens, goes beyond the economic field and declares: The *utility* (his appropriated "use value") of all objects, even the entire world is only the ahistorical *universal* projection of the specific mode of bourgeois existence (his "system

6   Ricardo, David. *On the Principles of Political Economy and Taxation*. London, 1821, p. 16-25.
7   Karl Marx and Frederick Engels. *Collected Works*, vol. 29. London: Lawrence & Wishart, 1987, p. 233.

of exchange value"). He thinks that Marx is the culprit for this blunder. Prima facie, it is a bizarre accusation: Is not Marx resolutely against the capitalist mode of production? And why does Baudrillard assert that it is Marx's fault? In fact, Baudrillard employs this attack to display his "insightfulness." In his view, Marx only criticizes the capitalist *mode of production*; denies the bourgeois economic and political structure, but he is unaware that the real problem lies in the capitalist *production* per se. Consequently, Marx neutralizes his concept of productive force by extending it to the foundation of the whole general social existence and progress while unable to realize it is this utility system of production that generates the entire utilitarian coordinate of values. Therefore, Baudrillard thinks Marx's criticism of the capitalist mode of production not only fails to solve the problem once for all but also obscures the deep truth of the matter to the extent that the radical revolution digresses. Baudrillard attempts to reject Marx, then his historical materialism and material production, and goes so far as criticizing any utilitarian economic view extended from the concept of production. In brief, he is critical of the *I-produce-therefore-I-am and I-produce-therefore-history-is: the ontology of utilitarian labour*. Here, Baudrillard takes it as the critique of "use value." (I shall turn to this point later.) For this reason, Baudrillard says, the final way to solve the problem is to radically rethink the needs of consumption, production, along with the labour power as the key subject of production. (The needs here are not in common sense. They refer to the utilitarian necessities created in the system of exchange value. In Mauss-Bataille logic, these needs are false; consumption is evil while non-specific and -utilitarian expenditure should be valued.)

2 THEORETICAL STICK OF SYMBOLIC EXCHANGE IN PRIMITIVE SOCIETIES

A reader will certainly entertain the question: what is the foundation of Baudrillard's attack on Marxism? Fortunately, the same chapter provides an interesting textual event, through which we may find the answer. It is Baudrillard's critique of Julia Kristeva. Here, he unequivocally demonstrates the basic logic that he relies on—Mauss-Bataille grassrootism centred on symbolic exchange. (Baudrillard is very aggressive. He is unwilling to let go of any person within his criticism.)

Despite the title "Marx and the Hieroglyph of Value," Baudrillard focuses on the rejection of Kristeva's "defense" of Marxism. He first cites a paragraph of her *Semiotica*, among which, he is particularly enraged by the following sentences, "Marx clearly outlined another possibility: work could be apprehended outside value, on the side of the commodity produced and circulating in the chain of communication. Here labour no longer represents any value, meaning, or signification. It is a question only of a body and a discharge..."[8] Kristeva is not wrong. Marx does recognize labour and production outside the system of commodity exchange. In his Notes of Anthropology, Marx stipulates several life and labour activities beyond the value of commodity. In fact, Kristeva's statement is not originally meant to defend Marx. However, the intolerant Baudrillard still vents his grudge against Marx on the innocent Kristeva because he must feel that her defense for Marx threatens the truth that only his teachers and he can understand at a time when Marx is already obviously bewildered by the bourgeois system of exchange value.

Baudrillard cleverly turns to the text of the first volume in *Capital*, which he cites before. He underscores the following sentence, "Productive activity, if we leave out of sight its special form, viz., the useful character of the labour, is nothing but the expenditure of human labour-power."[9] Baudrillard questions: Is there a conception of labour in Marx different from that of the production of useful ends (the canonical definition of labour as value in the framework of political economy and the anthropological definition of labour as human finality)? No! He is very upset.

> *Kristeva attributes to Marx a radically different vision centred on the body, discharge, play, anti-value, non-utility, non-finality, etc. She would have him read Bataille before he wrote—but also forget him when it is convenient. If there was one thing Marx did not think about, it was discharge, waste, sacrifice, prodigality, play, and symbolism.*[10]

---

8   Baudrillard, Jean. The Mirror of Production. Trans. Mark Poster. St. Louis: Telos Press, 1975, p. 42. See Note 30 of the book. Kristeva, Julia. "La sémiotique et la production," *Semiotica* 2.

9   Karl Marx, *Capital*, vol. 1. London: Lawrence & Wishart, 1977, p. 51.

10   Baudrillard, Jean. *The Mirror of Production*. Trans. Mark Poster. St. Louis: Telos Press, 1975, p. 42.

What a far-fetched interpretation! Was Marx that eager to be Bataille's student? Why should Marx read that next century stuff of discharge, anti-value, non-utility written by Bataille? It is ridiculous! Here, Baudrillard puts his teacher to the front to show his orthodox learning. Furthermore, he cites a longer paragraph of Bataille to illustrate the so-called "sacrifice economy" and the theory of symbolic exchange, which also contains Bataille's criticism of political economy and complete rejection of the concept of labour. (We have discussed Bataille's opinion in the first section.) For Bataille "the social wealth produced is *material*; it has nothing to do with symbolic wealth which, mocking natural necessity, comes conversely from destruction, the deconstruction of value, transgression, or discharge."[11] (Baudrillard's word is not often in agreement with his deeds. As an excellent photographer, he made use of his high-class camera, took many valuable pictures, held a number of personal exhibitions, and published several fine collections, from which we find no useless expenditure of "transgression and discharge.")[12] It seems reasonable for Baudrillard to accuse Kristeva of her imposition of what Marxism lacks on Marx; or, how can he prove this book of him against Marx is valuable?

According to Baudrillard, the "discharge" of human power that Marx speaks of is not a discharge with a pure waste, a symbolic discharge in Bataille's sense (pulsating, libidinal); it is still an economic, productive, finalized discharge precisely because, in its mating with the other, it begets a productive force called the earth (or matter). It is a useful discharge, an investment, not a gratuitous and festive energizing of the body's powers, a game with death, or the acting out of a desire.[13] Baudrillard says,

> What man gives of his body in labour is never **given** or **lost** or **rendered** by nature in a reciprocal way. Labour only aims to "make" nature "yield." This discharge is thus immediately an

---

11 *Ibid.*, 43.
12 Baudrillard's interest in photography began from the 1980s. A friend gave him a point-and-shoot. At first, he casually used it to take pictures. Gradually, he was fascinated by photography. He held several personal exhibitions and published a number of photo albums. I also like photography. I bought a second-hand photography collection of his from Amazon.com. Frankly, I like his unique conception of light and layout.
13 Baudrillard, Jean. *The Mirror of Production*. Trans. Mark Poster. St. Louis: Telos Press, 1975, p. 44.

274 A MARXIST READING OF YOUNG BAUDRILLARD

*investment of value, a **putting into value** opposed to all symbolic **putting into play** as in the gift or the discharge.[14]*

As we know, the gift (exchange) here is Mauss's anthropological discovery. It is a non-utilitarian structure of symbolic exchange in primitive personal relations used by Bataille as the weapon to ward off the modern kingdom of value production. Bataille obtains the useless discharge as the scene of authentic being from Sade while Marx does not understand the importance of symbolic exchange and discharge. But why should he? Baudrillard's *theoretical terrorism* (his own words) attempts to force everybody to abide by a theory, one that contains little truth. It is pure violence. As I said before, it is impossible to replace modernity with the ancient or primitive mode of human existence. It is only a beautiful dream unworthy of mentioning. Mauss-Bataille grassrootism is in essence childish. In our daily life, we are familiar with the wish "to simply maintain childhood," but, avoidance of the complexity and evils of the adult world does not justify the continual preservation of childlike simplicity and purity. A baby may feel discharge is the most pleasant sensation or may randomly destroy or waste items, which is also seen in kittens and puppies. However, the baby has to grow up and his existence will certainly be differentiated from other animals. The human history cannot be reversed or stopped; it only gets liberated through progress and revolution. There is no hope in historical reversion. For this, Marx made a wonderful comment, "An adult cannot become a child again, or he becomes childish. But does not the naiveté of the child give him pleasure, and must he not himself endeavour to reproduce the child's veracity on a higher stage?"[15] Marx's voice still echoes in our ears. He must never have expected a student of his student would attempt to transform man back into child. This act is more than childish. It is absurd.

But Kristeva has a hard time here. She is attacked without any given reason. Baudrillard proudly claims that she "would gladly be rid of value, but neither labour nor Marx." To his happiness, Baudrillard thinks he gets rid of Marx. He posits that Kristeva's problem lies in her blindness to Marx's lapse, the so-called "hieroglyph of value." In

---

14   *Ibid.*, p. 44.
15   Karl Marx and Frederick Engels. *Collected Works*, vol. 28. London: Lawrence & Wishart, 1986. pp. 47-48.

Baudrillard's eyes, it is an invisible but trapping snare; moreover, he stresses that Marx himself makes this definition. He cites the paragraph in the first volume of *Capital*:

> *Value, therefore, does not stalk about with a label describing what it is. It is value, rather, that converts every product into a social hieroglyphic. Later on, we try to decipher the hieroglyphic, to get behind the secret of our own social products; for to stamp an object of utility as a value, is just as much a social product as language.[16]*

They are indeed the exact words of Marx, but Baudrillard's citation only proves his own fault. First, Marx abandons the use of "exchange value" but chooses a precise word: The value (exchange value is merely the external manifestation of value in the process of exchange). Second, Marx indicates that stipulation of useful things as valuable only occurs in a particular historical condition, in the same way as language does. In other words, the value does not exist in the primitive societies. Does Baudrillard not understand it? Third, the hieroglyph here is meant by Marx to refer to the universal light converting everything into commodities in the *capitalist mode of production*. Marx never intends to allow this vicious light shine on all the human history or forever. He is actually against viewing the logic of capital (use value and value of every object) as an ahistorical ideological hallucination in every social form. Marx concludes that the capitalist production "based upon the basis of exchange value" is going to collapse.[17] Baudrillard has his petty tricks and sometimes his consideration seems insightful. He admits Marx is clear in meaning, even so, he proceeds:

> *this entire analysis of the mystery of value remains fundamental. But rather than being valid only for the product of labour in distribution and exchange, it is valid even for the product of labour (and for labour itself) taken as a "useful object." Utility (including labour's) is already a socially produced and determined hieroglyphic abstraction. The whole anthropology of "primitive" exchange compels us to break with the natural evidence of utility and to reconceive the social and historical genesis of use value as Marx did with exchange value. Only then will the hieroglyph be totally deciphered and the spell of value radically exorcized.[18]*

---

16   Karl Marx, *Capital*, vol. 1. London: Lawrence & Wishart, 1977, p. 79.
17   Karl Marx and Frederick Engels. *Collected Works*, vol. 28. London: Lawrence & Wishart, 1986, p. 195.
18   See Note 33 of *The Mirror of Production*. Trans. Mark Poster. St. Louis: Telos Press, 1975.

Baudrillard may deem the above analysis profound: Marx only deals with the product in distribution and exchange process; as long as people take the "utility" attitude, they fall to the hieroglyphs of value. Only through the primitive exchange relations (symbolic exchange) can they radically reject the utility of nature and break the magic of the social hieroglyphs of value. In my opinion, even a nesting bird cannot agree with the grassrootism of "useless ontology" beloved by Baudrillard and his teachers; otherwise, how can it survive without the shielding *useful* nest? In view of all the history of thought, it is a common practice to admit the utility of object because it is the basic condition for human survival. Why should Marx be picked out to blame? Could it be that Baudrillard does not know or just pretends not to understand the truth and give empty talks? If not, how can Baudrillard the photographer exist?

3 DOWN WITH THE UTILITARIAN ONTOLOGY OF PRODUCTION

The critique of "use value" leads to the falsification of the concept of labour power. Baudrillard is really good at association. He says, "the revolutionary originality of his theory comes from releasing the concept of labour power from its status as an unusual commodity whose insertion in the cycle of production *under the name of use value* carries the X element, a differential extra-value that generates surplus value and the whole process of capital. (Bourgeois economics would think instead of simple "labour" as one factor of production among others in the economic process.)"[19]

Baudrillard's text is characterized by leaping thoughts with insightful perspectives. We know that in solving the question of equal exchange between the worker and the capitalist in the market, Marx proposes the value of labour power which is his old imprecise usage, "value of labour." (According to Althusser, Marx read out the symptomatic blankness of Smith-Ricardo text.) In this way, the capitalist only pays the worker for his right to use labour. Behind the seemingly equal exchange, the added value generated in the activity of the labour power contains a part that

---

19   Baudrillard, Jean. *The Mirror of Production*. Trans. Mark Poster. St. Louis: Telos Press, 1975, p. 23.

is to be appropriated by the capitalist, which is the secret of surplus value. Here, Baudrillard seems to allude to the "revolutionary creativity" of the Marxist theory of surplus value, but his statement is opaque.

He then quotes Marx's comment on Wagner's textbook of political economy. It is a famous illustration about the relationship between the duality of labour and the duality of commodity, in which Marx underscored that his explanation of use value is achieved via analysis of particular economic formations.[20] The ad hoc clarification specifies that such economic concepts as value and use value only hold for a certain *economic social form*. Marx does not attempt to apply the theory of value into the entire social historical existence. Strangely, Baudrillard smells some philosophical sense from this pure economic discussion. He thinks that Marx still "retains something of the *apparent movement of political economy*" and "he does not radicalize the schema to the point of reversing this appearance and revealing use value as produced by the play of exchange value."[21] Once more, he is raving. But in the original discourse of Marx, under the capitalist system the use value of commodity is generated by concrete labour while value (*not exchange value*) is produced by abstract labour. Baudrillard cannot observe *duality* of labour differentiated as the abstract labour and the concrete labour in the *same* process of production. The use value emphasized by Marx is the foundation of value, that is to say, abstract labour is based on concrete labour. However, this logical sequence cannot be reversed in the economic context. The abstract is not the foundation of the concrete, except in Hegel's idealistic philosophy; value is not the basis of use value; exchange value (price) which expresses value cannot produce use value. In fact, what the pointless Baudrillard really wants to propose is that the utilitarian utility of any object is generated by the bourgeois system of commodities. I just wonder why he enters the economic context that is completely strange to him. If he goes outside the economic context, he seems capable of saying something correct:

20   Karl Marx and Frederick Engels. *Collected Works*, vol. 24. London: Lawrence & Wishart, 1989, p. 546.
21   Baudrillard, Jean. *The Mirror of Production*. Trans. Mark Poster. St. Louis: Telos Press, 1975, p. 24-25.

A MARXIST READING OF YOUNG BAUDRILLARD

> *The definition of products as useful and as responding to needs is the most accomplished, most internalized expression of abstract economic exchange: it is its subjective closure. The definition of labour power as the source of "concrete" social wealth is the complete expression of the abstract manipulation of labour power: the truth of capital culminates in this "evidence" of man as producer of value.*[22]

Look, Mauss-Bataille logic is present here, but only if we are willing to interpret it through a reversed order. First, from the perspective of the discourse of capital, man's existence is essentially for the production of value, viz. creation of useful items for the subject, which is the *ontology of production*. Second, the ontology of production is certain to posit man's existence as the labour power engaged in the activities of production, that is to say, labour power is *labour man*, which results from the "abstract manoeuvre" of man's existence by the discourse of capital. Third, only in the ontology of production can the fake needs of man (desire of the Other) emerge and the object be turned into *useful* items.

I have written a book to particularly deal with the close relations between Marxist economic research and the philosophical discourse of historical materialism. The philosophical methods of Marxism have developed with the constant achievements of economics, historiography and anthropology.[23] However, it does not mean all the specific statements of Marxist economics can be *directly converted to* the philosophical logic. Baudrillard makes a common mistake like his fellow French thinkers, who always directly apply the achievements of Marxist political economy to other disciplines. For instance, Bourdieu transplants Marx's concept of capital and puts forward such fanciful notions of "cultural capital," "symbolic capital" and "social capital"; Lacan alters Marx's surplus value into "surplus enjoyment"; Debord draws the concept of "spectacle fetishism" from Marx's economic fetishism, etc. Baudrillard follows suit and creates a "semiotic political economy" in his previous book. Here, he goes beside himself, radicalizing (in Baudrillard's own word) this simple

---

22 *Ibid.*, p. 25.
23 See my *Back to Marx: The Philosophical Discourse in the Context of Economics* (Jiangsu People's Press, 1999) and English version published by Göttingen University Press in 2014.

logical transplant for a *metaphysical* denial of Marxist economic achievement. Now the problem rises: It is actually incongruous as chalk and cheese when he smugly analyzes the specific economic concepts of labour power, value and exchange from a philosophical perspective. He does not clarify the issue but makes the problem more confounding.

Baudrillard has more to say. In his eyes, as the ontology of production, Marxist historical materialism still conceals a humanistic logic, a *potential* anthropological framework labelled by him as the double "generic" face of man, due to the fact that the existence of man has two latent dimensions, man has needs and labour power.

It should be admitted that Baudrillard grasps Marxist historical materialism per se this time. According to him, in the classic discourse of historical materialism for human activities to occur, it requires two conditions: needs and the production generated by these needs, whereas man is only the labourer engaged in production. Accordingly, the nature of Marxist humanity is the *humanism of production*. Baudrillard's comment seems correct except the inaccurate conception of labour. However, we will soon discover what on earth Baudrillard is against.

In Baudrillard's view, Marx's philosophical encoding of history is still a controlled result of the discourse of the bourgeois political economy, only he himself is unaware. This is because Marx's "needs" is in essence the "consumption of use value" of the object, which, presents the same characteristics as the concrete aspect of labour: uniqueness, differentiation, and incommensurability, in short, quality. (Again, Baudrillard is illegitimately appropriating the specific concepts of Marxist political economy.)

> *In concrete labour man gives a useful, objective end to nature; in need he gives a useful, subjective end to products. Needs and labour are man's double potentiality or double generic quality. This is the same anthropological realm in which the concept of production is sketched as the "fundamental movement of human existence," as defining a rationality and a sociality appropriate for man.*[24]

---

24 Baudrillard, Jean. *The Mirror of Production.* Trans. Mark Poster. St. Louis: Telos Press, 1975, p. 32.

Needs and labour are man's generic quality, or double generic face. As man's potentiality or nature, they both must be realized through production. Hence, production as "the fundamental movement of human existence" is the inevitable basis of Marxist philosophy. In the final analysis, the reason why we are human beings is owing to production: *I produce, therefore I am.*

I am going to deal first with Baudrillard's accusation against historical materialism. Despite several economic and philosophical misuses mentioned above, Baudrillard is not completely wrong in his understanding of Marx. His purpose is to oppose need, labour and production, reject the production of means of subsistence that is deemed by Marx as the foundation for human social existence. According to his Mauss-Bataille logic, the ideal personal relations occur in the non-utilitarian symbolic exchange framework, where there is no consideration of the object's usefulness and the gift's exchange value, even no utilitarian consumption and usage, and where the non-useful consumption reaches its culmination. Therefore, the need of utility should not appear in man's real existence, neither should the material production that aims at making useful items. As we know, it is a *backward* grassroot humanism, a western version of "self-abnegation and etiquette-restoration of Confucius," and an unrealistic practopianism. I even lose interest to refute it.

In *The German Ideology*, Marx discusses the needs as prerequisite for the historical activities of man. They stem from the *condition for life subsistence* (the most basic eating, drinking, habitation, etc.) whose development can be traced back to animals, even living organisms. Nonetheless, this condition is not generated from the living things themselves, who have to relate to their environment and make material transference (here I carefully avoid the word "exchange"), in which the necessary metabolic material is obtained from outside and their waste is discharged. (I feel uncomfortable here in writing the above words. It is embarrassing to talk about common sense biology in a serious philosophical discussion. Baudrillard often plays to the gallery, like the abnormal Sade.) Marx does not talk about man's needs from the capitalist view of utilitarian value. Otherwise, would the tribes in Australia and north Pacific coastal areas have survived without eating or habitation? Obviously, no. It is impossible to reject the basic needs of living things, unless we deny the complete existence of life. If Marx's perquisite is correct, then needs inevitably lead to man's superior activities of obtaining means of subsistence. We know that the animal kingdom abides by the law of the jungle and the survival of the fittest. Man distinguishes himself from other animals not merely by strength but, more importantly, by the adjustment of his mode of existence, which starts from change of the mode of activities that acquire survival conditions, or the mode to meet his own needs. (The young Marx already realized it before he became a Marxist. He said the animals and nature are homogeneous while man differentiates himself from nature by transcending the present existence.) When homo sapiens (or anthropoids in prehistorical period) want to satisfy their needs, they have to use tools and engage themselves in an activity to obtain the necessary means of life, which is different from other animals, viz. *production*. This is the changing and making process of nature that other animals do not have. According to Marx, it is production that causes man to be different. Marx's production here is not what Baudrillard says about the production with specific structure obtained from the bourgeois economic code but the general activities that man is engaged in to obtain the means of subsistence. It is true that the *modern industrial production* is not the foundation for the entire human history but man's survival cannot be separated from the objective action of acquiring means of subsistence, of which there is no exception, even the primitive tribes in Mauss-Bataille logic. Without this material production of changing nature, man would have died out, like other disappeared living things in the vicissitudes of history.

Baudrillard may propose that in primitive societies objects are not secured mainly through production or man's utilitarian labour. Nevertheless, direct acquisition from nature is the major mode of the survival condition for animals, to say in Marx's words, the *appropriation* of nature (not the utilitarian *possession* that Baudrillard dislikes). In Baudrillard's favourite *1857-1858 Manuscripts*, Marx analyzes the alleged "naturally formed societies" with the 19th century anthropology and historiography, which is also the primitive tribal existence to which Mauss and Bataille clung. (To be honest, Marx's discussion is not out of date even with today's standards.)

282 A MARXIST READING OF YOUNG BAUDRILLARD

Marx admits that man's initial existence starts from the appropriation of nature: "The original conditions of production appear as natural presuppositions, *natural conditions of the existence of the producer,* just as his living body, even though he reproduces and develops it, is not originally posited by himself, but appears as his own *presupposition;* his own (corporeal) being is a natural presupposition not posited by himself."[25] To survive as a race, man has to reproduce himself, which is a material presupposition. In addition, the reproduction of life (or the continuation of race) begins from the complete reliance on nature, just in the same way of animals. "Man takes possession of the ready-made fruits of the earth, to which, among others, belong the animals and especially those he can domesticate."[26] Here, "man does not originally confront nature as a worker but as a proprietor."[27] However, things change soon. Marx analyzes:

Originally the act of producing by the individual is confined to the reproduction of his own body through the appropriation of ready-made objects prepared by nature for consumption? But even where the task is only to *find* and *discover,* effort, labour—as in hunting, fishing, the care of herds—and production (i.e. development) of certain skills are soon required on the part of the subject. This means that condition in which man need merely reach for what is already available, without any tools (i.e. products of labour already destined for production), without alteration of form (which already takes place even in herding), etc., are very transitory, and can nowhere be regarded as normal; nor even as normal at the earlier stage. Of course, it has to be remembered that the original conditions of production include substances directly consumable without labour, such as some fruit, animals, etc.; thus the consumption fund is itself part of the *original production fund.*[28]

---

25 Karl Marx and Frederick Engels. *Collected Works*, vol. 28. London: Lawrence & Wishart, 1986. pp. 413-414.
26   *Ibid.*, p. 416.
27   Karl Marx and Frederick Engels. *Collected Works*, vol. 30. London: Lawrence & Wishart, 1988, p. 98.
28   Karl Marx and Frederick Engels. *Collected Works*, vol. 28. London: Lawrence & Wishart, 1986, p. 416.

In my opinion, the above analysis is accurate. Marx clearly illustrates how the initial history of humankind comes into being, how labour and production become the real objective foundation for human society, how man possesses material items only through labour and production and will get more and more reliant on them. "Real appropriation does not occur through the establishment of a notional relationship to these conditions, but takes place in the active, real relation to them, when they are really posited as the conditions of man's subjective activity."[29] Now we know that Baudrillard imagines something impossible. His brainstorm only ends up in destruction of his own logical foundation.

Here, I have to give a common lesson of Marxist history to Baudrillard. Perhaps, he is unaware that before making material production the core paradigm of historical materialism Marx posited *practice* as the logical starting point of his new world outlook in the 1845 *Theses on Feuerbach*. This concept of praxis him went through a gradual development from the *philosophical* conception of labour (generic nature) that Baudrillard disapproves (in *The 1844 Manuscripts*), the whole process of which is too complicated to have a detailed discussion here. Here we are just going to have a general introduction of the relations among them. In 1845, Marx discovered the fundamental defect of humanistic generic discourse through M. Stirner's critique, and then he eliminated the concept of labour that he had learned from Ricardian socialist economics, off his philosophical logic. He also understood that the real existent labour in history is only the "living" subjective activity of man.[30] Therefore, he restored man and his whole objectification process (in which labour is one aspect of human activity) to the foundation of his philosophy, which was the *original, revolutionary* material practice. Therefore, after 1845, labour was no longer the core of Marxism or the generic nature of man. Marx stated in *Theses on Feuerbach* that his philosophy still started from the subject, but not the Hegelian ideal initiative; instead, it is man's initiative of objective material activities. I also noted that the nature of this practice is modern, and a specific *industrial* product. (It is because the labour production in

---

29   *Ibid.*, p. 417.
30   Karl Marx and Frederick Engels. *Collected Works*, vol. 28. London: Lawrence & Wishart, 1986, p. 202.

natural economy cannot generate the totality of the revolutionary relations, the timing when "nature becomes the object" as Heidegger says.) Here, Marx observed history from the summit of historical development. When he and Engels wrote *The German Ideology*, they treated the praxis of man as a complex system of activities in the process of the social history when the labour-material production action is the *more fundamental* aspect, because it is the universal foundation of human existence and development as well as the most basic principle of the general historical materialism.

It is understandable for Baudrillard to take a Mauss-Bataille stand and hate the capitalist utilitarian system of production but he should have known that Marx also takes a critical attitude of the capitalist *production-for-production's-sake* of Ricardoism that turns man into a cap. For Marx, such economic relations determine "production not as the development of human productivity; but as the display of *material wealth,* in antithesis to the productive development of the human individual."[31]

Baudrillard wrongly imposes the label of turning man into labour power on Marx, who radically denies the transformation of man into "HANDS"-like labour power in the capitalist production process.[32] (I also notice that Sahlins is more objective than Baudrillard in this point. In *Culture and Practical Reason*, Sahlins offers a fine division of Marx and traditional Marxist interpreters. He concludes, "Marx was no crass economism of the enterprising individual."[33]) Marx aims for liberation of the productive forces and then man through his critique of the capitalist mode of production while for Baudrillard, liberation of the productive forces is itself a big mistake. His grassrootism may ask such questions: Why should history make progress? Why should an object be useful? Why should man produce? Or, is not the primitive gift swapping system premised on authentic symbolic exchange man's best existential situation? Baudrillard thinks Marx still falls a victim to the capitalist material foundation and the

---

31   Karl Marx and Frederick Engels. *Collected Works*, vol. 34. London: Lawrence & Wishart, 1994, p. 109.
32   Karl Marx and Frederick Engels. *Collected Works*, vol. 30. London: Lawrence & Wishart, 1988, p. 55.
33   Sahlins, Marshall D. *Culture and Practical Reason*. Joint Publishing Company Limited (Beijing), 2002, p. 165.

whole Western civilization that creates this foundation. In his view, besides the corrupted bourgeois economic relations and political structure, the real culprit is the *material mode of production per se*, while capitalism is only the highest level of this mode. Irritated, he says,

And productivity is not primarily a generic dimension, a human and social kernel of all wealth to be extracted from the husk of capitalist relations of production (the eternal empiricist illusion). Instead, all this must be overturned to see that the abstract and generalized development of productivity (the developed form of political economy) is what makes the **concept of production** *itself appear as man's movement and generic end (or better, as the concept of man as producer).*[34]

Baudrillard is genuinely opposed to historical materialism, to the logic of production, and to the development of productive forces as man's end. Behind this opaque expression of political economy, his strategy is clear: He denies all social existence and historical movement established on the material production, rejects the social development outlook of progressive history, and refuses to view man as the producer (labour power). Judging from the common knowledge of contemporary Western thought, Baudrillard wants to bring down *productivism*. Thus, Baudrillard's philosophy is no trivial to Marxist historical materialism. He is destined to be Marx's theoretical enemy.

In my opinion, Baudrillard's attack on Marx's theory of production is not completely original. Among the Western Marxist camp, the young György Lukács was the first to put forward this question. In *History and Class Consciousness*, when he overturned Weber's instrumental rationality based on production technology, he inadvertently came to the discovery that the controlling and exploitative character of modern capitalism is, unexpectedly, the material aspect of *production process per se,* he thought the materializing and unifying assemble line leads to the double detotalization of the existence and conception (mind) of worker. The materialization and detotalization here by Lukács are not Schiller's slavery of capital resulting from the reversed economic relations or from division of

---

34   Baudrillard, Jean. *The Mirror of Production.* Trans. Mark Poster. St. Louis: Telos Press, 1975, p. 31.

labour. It is a problem not only about the relations of production but also entails that the production itself is permeated by the venom of capitalism. This concept was first noticed by Heidegger from an ontological perspective: Dasein (being there) appears through material readiness-to-hand, which is also the onset of existential alienation and oblivion. Later this idea was inherited by late Sartre. In the same line of thought, the first one to publicize this secret in neo-Marxist history was Karol Kiosk from Czech, who put forward the concept of pseudo-practice in his *Dialectics of the Concrete.*[35] When it came to the Benjamin-Adorno's critical philosophy, this question was composed into a *general* negation, that is, criticism of the Enlightenment, the instrumental rationality, and even the entire progressive human civilization. In my view, it is the actual logic of post-Marxian thought. Now, from this outlook the concepts of practice, production and historical progression in Marxist framework are not neutral anymore; and the profound foundation of historical materialism was exposed to direct attack by Arendt's *Human Condition*, Habermas's *Toward a Rational Society*, or Leiss's *Domination of Nature*, all extending their criticism in this issue. They only fail to attain Baudrillard's depths and intensity.

4 RE-QUESTIONING THE MARXIST CRITICISM OF THE CAPITALIST MODE OF PRODUCTION

More importantly, Baudrillard's accusation of Marx also contains Marx's criticism of capitalism, which, in his view, only seizes the particular form of the capitalist material production but on a deeper level strengthens the control of this mode of production with a mere negation of the overt form. He asserts:

> *And in this Marxism assists the cunning of capital. It convinces men that they are alienated by the sale of their labour power, thus censoring the much more radical hypothesis that they might be alienated as labour power, as the "inalienable" power of creating value by their labour.*[36]

---

35 The first chapter has a specific discussion of the above conceptions. Please go there for details.
36 Baudrillard, Jean. *The Mirror of Production.* Trans. Mark Poster. St. Louis: Telos Press, 1975, p. 31.

Baudrillard italicizes his nearly four lines to stress his meaning. It shows his great concern for it. In Baudrillard's opinion, despite Marx's criticism of capitalism, his liberation still aims at the "inalienable" labour, which is also within the capitalist system of exchange value. Here, Baudrillard has two misunderstandings: First, it is true that the young Marx did advocate the theory of inalienable labour in his writing of the *1844 Manuscripts* and regard communism as the restoration of the nature of labour (aiming true labour) through sublation of alienation and private property., but after the establishment of historical materialism in 1845, this humanistic historical view of inalienable labour was abandoned by him. Second, Marx's criticism of capitalism is not that simple as Baudrillard imagines. It at least contains the following aspects: First, to analyze the systematic weakness of the capitalist mode of production from the perspective of the whole social historical development and from the prospects of productive forces; second, the exploitative nature of capitalists to occupy the surplus value in capitalist economic system; third, the materialization of personal relations in the capitalist mode of production. Obviously, Marx's criticism is radically different from the view of inalienable labour and liberation inherent in Baudrillard's humanistic logic. This time, what Baudrillard considers a fatal point is still a groundless imagination, or at most, a pseudo-target erected by the 20th century Western Marxist humanists.[37]

Of course, Baudrillard is not satisfied to stop with the criticism of the logic of the inalienable labour. His intention is to deny production and labour. In his eyes, Marx criticizes the capitalist mode of production but comes to agreement with the Western Enlightenment spirit on more fundamental concepts.

*Radical in its **logical** analysis of capital, Marxist theory none-theless maintains an **anthropological** consensus with the options of Western rationalism in its definitive form acquired in eighteenth century bourgeois thought. Science, technique, progress, history—in these ideas we have an entire civilization that comprehends itself as producing its own development and takes its*

---

37 After the 1930s, especially, after the publication of the young Marx's 1844 Manuscripts, the second generation Marxist representatives, like early Erich Fromm, Herbert Marcuse and Henri Lefebvre, tended to review Marxist philosophy with humanistic ideas, which had a great impact on the neo-Marxists of ex-communist Eastern Europe. See my *The Historical Logic of Western Marxist Philosophy*.

dialectical force toward completing humanity in terms of totality and happiness.[38]

Indeed, Baudrillard's ultimate purpose is against the rationality of Western civilization as a whole. In his opinion, Marx only opposes the corruption of the capitalist mode of production but does not negate the progression of history, which, per contra, is seen as being hindered by the capitalist relations of production. Therefore, in his comment, Marx changed nothing basic: nothing regarding the *idea* of man *producing* himself in his infinite determination, and continually surpassing himself toward his own end. He accuses:

> *Marx translated this concept into the logic of material production and the historical dialectic of modes of production. But differentiating modes of production renders unchallengeable the evidence of production as the determinant instance. It generalizes the economic mode of rationality over the entire expanse of human history, as the generic mode of human becoming. It circumscribes the entire history of man in a gigantic simulation model. It tries somehow to turn against the order of capital by using as an analytic instrument the most subtle ideological phantasm that capital has itself elaborated.*[39]

According to Baudrillard, Marx universalizes the economic framework characteristic of capitalism, generalizes production and the mode of production that are typical for the system of exchange value over the entire expanse of human history. Subsequently, Marx fails to make critical changes in the capital logic: He is against the very capitalist economic relations but only creates an "ideological phantasm that capital has itself elaborated." Universalization of production, along with "the 'dialectical' generalization of this concept, is merely the *ideological* universalization of this system's postulates."[40]

Who on earth is the real producer of the bourgeois ideology and the vicious accomplice of capital?

First, it is inappropriate, if not completely wrong, for Baudrillard to say that Marx has extended the production and the mode of production from the bourgeois rationality of political economy to the generality of history. Without the classical economics based on

38   Baudrillard, Jean. *The Mirror of Production*. Trans. Mark Poster. St. Louis: Telos Press, 1975, p. 33.
39   *Ibid.*, p. 33.
40   *Ibid.*, p. 33.

large-scale machine production, in particular, Ricardo's logic, Marx could not abstract the general conception of modern production. As I said before, it is through profound research of political economy that Marx finally developed his own philosophical discourse, historical materialism, and reached the theoretical commending height. As early as the 1850s and 1860s, Marx already initially learned the basic condition of primitive societies. At that time, he even pointed out that material production of primitive societies was *subordinate* to human reproduction. Therefore, Marx would not project the modern production and the mode of production to the entire human history. This is but Baudrillard's own fabrication.

Second, Marx never attempted a radical negation of modernity in human development and material wealth of industrial production in his criticism of capitalism. He knew material affluence is the prerequisite for human liberation and freedom. As to Baudrillard's grassrootism based on Mauss-Bataille logic, the ancient simplicity of human existence is a rejection of the advanced human civilization, I think it is at most a possibility, one for amusement. The same question: Can we really return to the original existence?

Third, Marx's historical materialism discourse builds its framework on the rationalistic recognition of social historical progression; if not, he would not raise the issue from political liberation to complete liberation of humanity. For the primitive tribal life with "limited development of productive forces," Marx firmly believed that historical development of social production is to promote disintegration of this primary form, which in turn advances the development of the productive forces. Thus he wrote: "Labour is only undertaken on a certain basis—first naturally evolved—then an historical presupposition. Later, however, this basis or presupposition is itself transcended, or posited as a transient one, which has become too narrow for the unfolding of the progressing human pack."[41] The complete social history of humankind precisely displays this progressive interaction between self-transcendence and self-sublation unmasked by Marxism. Probably, the prevailing historical trend is far beyond the narrow ideas of Baudrillard and others.

---

41   Karl Marx and Frederick Engels. *Collected Works*, vol. 28. London: Lawrence & Wishart, 1986, p. 420.

CHAPTER X

CRITIQUE OF LABOUR IDEOLOGY

Baudrillard's *Mirror of Production* reaches its first farcical climax with the onset against Marx's conception of labour. In his view, the kernel of material production is human labour. Interestingly, it is from the textual context of political economy that Baudrillard begins his interpretation of Marx's labour, but he wants to identify the illegitimate discourse of Marxist philosophy. It must be admitted that his train of thought is acute whereas his argument is regrettably invalid. I also find that Baudrillard's accusation is well prepared. He cites a number of Marxist economic remarks with irrelevant interpretations. To those who are not familiar with Marxist economics, Baudrillard is all too formidable. However, once his unsustainable logical support detected, this magnificent building of falsification is easy to collapse.

1 METAPHYSICAL EVIL OF LABOUR:
THE CONCRETE VS. THE ABSTRACT;
QUALITY VS. QUANTITY

For Baudrillard, to negate Marxist theory of material production requires further exposure of the evil nature of labour that dominates the productive activities. This time, he embarks on the issue of *reification of labour*. He discovers that the secret of Marxist theory of labour lies in the "dialectics of quality and quantity" of the so-called *theory of labour value*. It is a more micro, more specific "profound" critique. Let us read his analysis.

Baudrillard first quotes Pierre Naville's *Le nouveau léviathan*, saying that the quaintly of labour does not appear in Europe until the 18th century because previous differences of handicraft production make labour incommensurable. It is correct for the division of labour during the industrial production process gives rise to the total social labour, which leads to the abstracted labour as such, which then makes it possible for the computability of labour. Baudrillard does not deny that. He then goes to a citation from Marx, "whereas labour positing exchange-value is *abstract universal and uniform* labour, labour positing use-value is concrete and distinctive labour, comprising infinitely varying kinds of labour as regards its form and the material to which it is applied."[1] Marx's idea is very clear here: For a commodity, its value is based on the abstract labour and its use value on the concrete labour, in other words, the concrete labour and abstract labour are both at one production process of the same item, not two dual substances. Baudrillard seems to be more fascinated by use value, which, to him, is founded on the concrete, qualitative labour. (However, Baudrillard always forgets the fact that every time Marx mentions use value he refers to the use value of commodity (capitalist commodity). Marx never employs use value in its general or universal sense. It is another proof of Baudrillard's casualty in his analysis.)

Without any intermediate explanation, Baudrillard suddenly jumps to the value and use value of labour power.

---

1   Karl Marx and Frederick Engels. *Collected Works*, vol. 29. London: Lawrence & Wishart, 1987, p. 277.

In contrast to the quantitative measure of labour power, labour use value, remains nothing more or less than a qualitative potentiality. It is specified by its own end, by the material it works on, or simply because it is the expenditure of energy by a given subject at a given time. The use value of labour power is the moment of its actualization, of man's relation to his useful expenditure of effort. Basically it is an act of (productive) **consumption;** *and in the general process, this moment retains all its uniqueness. At this level labour power is incommensurable.*[2]

Baudrillard does the same thing as a smart aleck would do. His spouting about what he knows little only brings disgrace upon himself. The "value" and "use value" in Marx's writing are actually in *metaphorical* use. Marx does not make labour power into a common commodity that can be consumed by the people given that the duality of a commodity (value and use value) is generated through living labour (abstract labour and concrete labour). Does Marx say anywhere, labour power is *created and produced by labour*? Of course, no! This is a common sense! As a special commodity, labour power is used by Marx to unmask the apparent equality of capitalist exchange relations wherein the worker only receives the fees ("value") for the means of subsistence, in exchange for his wage labour. Marx metaphorically calls the sale of this *usufruct* of labour power (or "disposition over alien labour"[3]) the "use value" of labour power. Here, both the value and use value are only existent in relation to capitalism conditions. Marx says, "as a free worker, he has *no value*; only the right to dispose over his labour, acquired by exchange with him, has value."[4] The last "him" above refers to capital, the materialized (dead) labour. Here the value is a *relative* construct in antithesis to the existence of capital. Without the dominance of labour in the employment relations, the value of labour power is out of the question. Baudrillard seems to lack the slightest knowledge of it. The so-called "use value" of labour power, viz. the worker's labour per se, is not a real commodity that can be directly sold, quite apart from being *produced* by a concrete labour (domestic work). Here it needs to

---

2   Baudrillard, Jean. *The Mirror of Production.* Trans. Mark Poster. St. Louis: Telos Press, 1975, p. 26.
3   Karl Marx and Frederick Engels. Collected Works, vol. 28. London: Lawrence & Wishart, 1986, p. 211, p. 214.
4   *Ibid.,* p. 218.

be noted that in postmodern feminism, domestic work is an implicit labour to sustain and produce the labour power, although unrecognized by the prevalent patriarchal system. They think that housework creates value through labour, which is another theoretical issue and has nothing to do with Baudrillard's mess here.) Therefore, the use value of labour power, viz. the use value of living labour per se, makes sense in relation to the materialized labour (capital) that appropriates and exploits it. According to Marx:

Production based on exchange value, on the surface of which that free and equal exchange of equivalents takes place, is basically the exchange of *objectified labour* as exchange value for living labour as use value, or, as it may also to be expressed, labour relating to its objective conditions—and hence to the objectivity created by itself—as to alien property: *alienation of labour*. On the other hand, the condition of exchange value is that it is measured by labour time, and thus living labour—not its value—is the measure of values. It is a DELUSION to believe that production in all its forms and hence society rested upon the *exchange of mere labour for labour*.[5]

As everybody can see, Marx's living labour here does not indicate that man's labour (power) has certain inborn value and use value. The process when the worker sells this "specific commodity" is the *labour process itself*.[6] Poor Baudrillard! He does not understand it is within an ad hoc context that Marx discusses the "value" and "use value" of the specific commodity, the labour power. He even cuts their association with the context, abstracts them, makes a positive proposition in the logic of value theory, and in this faked context builds a compulsory misreading of Marx. All these "theoretical insights" are already embedded with the "theoretical butts" from the very beginning. *Labour power is not at all produced in the process of production since there is no abstract labour to produce it; where does the "accountability of quantity" come from?* (Allow me to have a joke here. Perhaps, Baudrillard sees many sci-fi movies, in which the intelligent robots, biotechnically replicated creatures, or cloned people, are *produced* as labour power, or more often, as

---

5   *Ibid.*, p. 438.
6   Karl Marx and Frederick Engels. *Collected Works*, vol. 30. London: Lawrence & Wishart, 1988, p. 54.

terrifying killers. Those reproduced men as real specific products are possible to possess the value and use value jointly generated by the abstract labour and the concrete labour. But it is another question of a higher context.) Baudrillard's use value of labour power is not sensible once discussed outside the stipulated context by Marx. In fact, the "concrete labour" as the foundation of production is just like a mother's childbearing and upbringing, which should have been the simple logic for Baudrillard to follow. However, Baudrillard is blind to his own blunder. Owing to his little knowledge of Marxist economics, he makes such an absurd mistake and goes on with it.

In the Don Quixote's journey against his imaginary Marx, Baudrillard claims the use value of labour power is the moment of "man's relation to his useful expenditure of effort." It is grammatically wrong in Marxist economics, as Marx never accepts the labour of worker who is the labour power under the capitalist working condition as a *general* useful consumption of human power. For Marx, not only the primitive societies are free of the issues of value about labour power and products but also the future communist society— that he deems as the substitute for capitalism—both societies are impossible to have the problems of use value and value about labour power and products. Baudrillard may not have a serious study of Marx's *Critique of the Gotha Programme*, in which Marx makes the following comment on the inaccurate expression of "undiminished proceeds of labour" in the "Programme" of the Workers' Party in Germany. It is worthwhile for Baudrillard to have a reading.

> *Within the collective society based on common ownership of the means of production, the producers do not exchange their products; just as little does the labour employed on the products appear here as **the value** of these products, as a material quality possessed by them, since now, in contrast to capitalist society, individual labour no longer exists in an indirect fashion but directly as a component part of the total labour.*[7]

Marx cannot be clearer here. Why does Baudrillard deliberately misunderstand Marx? If the formation of labour force does not involve the concrete labour in the real economic sense (not counting the mother's reproduction), there is nothing sensible in Baudrillard's

---

7   Karl Marx and Frederick Engels. *Collected Works*, vol. 24. London: Lawrence & Wishart, 1989, p. 85.

"qualitative" aspect of different concrete labours possessed by the labour power (except the different birth process of Baudrillard and Bataille). Thus, Baudrillard's next question asking how the incommensurable, qualitatively different labour forces can produce a *quantified* surplus value becomes a pseudo-proposition: Before answering it, I am really amazed by Baudrillard's poor level of political economy. Baudrillard should have come to China for a supplementary lesson of politics in a high school. To Marx, the "value" of labour power as a special commodity is the wage that the capitalist pay in the employment. This "value" is not based on what Baudrillard considers the abstract labour (the general social labour of industrial societies) developed since the 18th century. The use value of labour power is neither what Baudrillard defines as the concrete labour useful for all the people; it only holds for the very *living* labour that is *useful for the capitalist exploitation*, which is what the capitalist wants to cover. Therefore, the existence and movement of the labour force naturally become the foundation for the use value and value of common commodities for survival. Since the abstract labour is founded on value composed by the necessary labour time, how can it become incomputable? Such a simple principle is known to any profit-seeking capitalist, or even, a Chinese high school student with some basic knowledge of Marxist political economy. But the great French thinker Baudrillard turns a blind eye to it. This is very strange, indeed.

Baudrillard wants to say Marx's division of the duality of labour—the *qualitative and quantitative dialectic* of the computable abstract labour and the incomputable concrete labour—conceals a bigger philosophical fantasy: Since the 19th century, the universalization of labour (to be accurate, it is the emergence of the labour as such or abstract labour brought about by the socialized industrial production and market exchange) has initiated the universalization of work "not only as market value but as human value. Ideology always thus proceeds by a binary, structural scission, which works here to universalize the dimension of labour. By dividing (or re-dividing into the qualitative structural effect, a code effect), quantitative labour spreads throughout the field of possibility."[8] This mouthful remark of him means, in the division of the duality of the quality

8   Baudrillard, Jean. *The Mirror of Production*. Trans. Mark Poster. St. Louis: Telos Press, 1975, p. 27.

and the quantity of labour, the universality (abstraction) of labour becomes man's general nature; while labour, a special existence of man in the market economy, also extends the ideology to man's general existence and conceals this operation of codes.

I feel that Baudrillard often appears paranoid with his logic. Is there no "labour" before the emergence of capitalist industrial production and the real market economy? We should admit that in the capitalist ideology, under the universal light (with Marx's words) of the logic of capital, every conception is inevitably tainted with certain bourgeois colour. As Baudrillard learns Saussure's linguistics, he must understand it is possible to use the same concept or terminology with applying other semantic meanings. Nevertheless, at this point, Baudrillard is as ignorant as his predecessors, like Hannah Arendt or Jürgen Habermas.[9]

In my opinion, Baudrillard's analysis is an intentional distortion of Marx's duality of labour, which was proposed by him to solve the economic question of labour value and has proved much better than Smith-Ricardo's incomplete and confusing answer. Furthermore, the relation between quality and quantity drawn from the abstract labour and concrete labour is only the issue of calculating the value quantity and the way through which to expose the surplus value. Marx does not attempt at a universal value or nature from the relation of the quality and the quantity of the capitalist-characteristic *wage labour*.

Here, we have to give Baudrillard another lesson about the history of Marxism: The qualitative development of the conception of labour. The first important concept of labour of the young Marx was proposed in the *1844 Manuscripts* as an idealized human nature, when Marx himself was still influenced by Feuerbach's humanistic discourse. On one hand, he criticized the economic exploitation of the capitalist society; on the other he took this illegitimate relation as the deviation from man's authentic being—*the free, independent creation* of labour, in the words of the young Marx, the deviation as the *alienation* of labour. There are two concepts of labour: the labour idealized as man's generic (species) nature; and the alienated labour as the reversed and abnormal generic nature of man found in the reality of the capitalist society. The former is the "ought" from the

---

9   See Hannah Arendt's *The Human Condition* and Jürgen Habermas's *Legitimation Crisis*.

aspect of humanistic critique, as differentiated from the latter (the bad "is"). The paradigm of labour here in the humanistic discourse is what Baudrillard means, the abstract, universal human value. Even at that time, Marx did not universalize the alienated labour of capitalist society into a human value. Nevertheless, in his comments on Listz, March, 1845, Marx began to dissipate this humanistic logic. He abandoned the alienation of labour and used a *quotation-marked* concept of labour to illustrate the *enslaved* status of labour. Later, in Baudrillard's familiar book *The German Ideology*, Marx used the wage labour. Thus, the concept of labour was replaced by the concepts of practice and production in Marx's philosophical discourse. In his logic, on one side "labour is the universal condition for the metabolic exchange (Germ.: Stoffwechsel) between nature and man, and as such a natural condition of human life it is independent of, equally common to, all particular social forms of human life";[10] on the other side, labour is, in economic sense, the "*general possibility* of wealth as *subject* and as activity."[11] Labour cannot become the only source for wealth while the real foundation for social existence and development is the material relationship of man and the external world, which is the objective process of material production. Labour was not clearly defined in Marxist general historical materialism. Later, Marx used it more often in the economic context and seldom made metaphysical illustration of the economic concept of labour.[12] Another point is when Marx analyzed the capitalist machine production, he found "*immediate labour* as such ceasing to be the basis of production"[13] because the worker's living labour is reduced to an insignificant link in this machinery automated production system, "the value-creating power of the individual labour capacity is an infinitesimal, vanishing magnitude." Marx writes: phenomenally, "the production process has ceased to be a labour process."[14] What does

---

10   Karl Marx and Frederick Engels. *Collected Works*, vol. 30. London: Lawrence & Wishart, 1988, p. 63.

11   Karl Marx and Frederick Engels. *Collected Works*, vol. 28. London: Lawrence & Wishart, 1986, p. 222.

12   See my student Dr. Yang Jianping's *On Marx's Conception of Labour*, which has a detailed discussion about the development of Marx's conception of labour.

13   Karl Marx and Frederick Engels. *Collected Works*, vol. 29. London: Lawrence & Wishart, 1987, p. 95.

14   *Ibid.*, p. 83.

it indicate? It is quite clear that Baudrillard's complacent discovery is not new. Marx had already revealed it.

In retrospect of the above history of thoughts on labour concept, it is not difficult to find that Baudrillard cleverly avoids the concept of labour in the philosophical discourse of the *1844 Manuscripts* and tightly grabs the scientific concept of labour in Marxist economics. However, he is unaware that it is still illegitimate to posit the concept of labour with special semantic meaning in Marxist economics as the logical outset of the *ideology of labour*. I am going to further explain it in the next part.

2 GUILT OF THE PRODUCTIVE LABOUR

Baudrillard's criticism of Marx then turns from the ideology of labour of Marxism to the production-labour ideology, in which he satires Marx with a notion from Marxist historical phenomenology, namely, the *fetishism of labour and productivity*.

Baudrillard is sometimes surprisingly stubborn. With a fallacious premise, he closes himself in an assertive space without any flexibility, blindly but happily thrashing about. He does not like the concreteness of labour; nor is he disposed to the "abuse" of this concreteness and abstractness. In his eyes, Marx is playing a "game" of signification, that is, from the abstract to the concrete, from the quantity to quality, from the Labour's exchange value to use value of dialectics, the double of the game must be the result of labour productivity and fetishism. In that case, he questions, what are the reasons? Baudrillard offers his own inferences.

This time, he is quoting from the introduction of the *1857-1858 Manuscripts*. (The reason why Baudrillard daunts some people is partly due to his frequent citation of the unknown Marxist economic texts barely touched even by traditional Marxist philosophers, for which he is in striking contrast to Schmidt and Althusser.)

> *The fact that the specific kind of labour is irrelevant, presupposes a highly developed totality of actually existing kinds of labour, none of which is any more the dominating one. The most general abstractions arise on the whole only with the most profuse concrete development, when one [phenomenon] is seen to be common to many, common to all.*[15]

---

15   Karl Marx and Frederick Engels. *Collected Works*, vol. 28. London: Lawrence & Wishart, 1986, p. 41.

300 A MARXIST READING OF YOUNG BAUDRILLARD

It should be accepted that Baudrillard's reference to the Marxist text is very smart compared with traditional Marxists and Western scholars. He often shrewdly employs some of Marx's important statements ignored by scholars in the former Soviet Union and East European socialist countries, but with the majority of them put in the wrong place. (I also notice that it is the same with those keen anthropologists in the 1970s, among whom, the first was Lévi-Strauss's quote from Marx and the most distinguished one was Sahlins, who was very familiar with Marxist economic and philosophical texts, e.g. the "Anthropology and Two Marxisms: Problems of Historical Materialism" in his *Culture and Practical Reason*.[16]

Sahlins had quite a few wonderful remarks about his understanding of Marxism, far superior to Baudrillard but still wrong with some of his conclusions since he posited the logic of symbolic culture over the praxis of material production.)

With this comment, below Marx intends to illustrate that the concept of general (abstract) labour belongs to "a modern category" (capitalism). From the monetarist view of wealth as the object "capital," to the manufacturing or mercantile transference of the source of wealth from the object to the subjective activity, the commercial labour and industrial labour, and the agricultural labour of the physiocrats, all these are big steps forward . Smith makes "an immense advance" for his discovery of *labour as such* that is neither manufacturing, nor commercial, nor agricultural labour, but all types of labour. Then, Marx continues: "this abstraction of labour is the objective abstractness of modern economic activity per se considering the individuals of industrial production "which easily pass from one type of labour to another" when labour has become a means to "create wealth" in the reality of capitalism. On the other hand, the general labour emerges because during the internal division of labour in production, the old collective work is replaced by professional and specific functional work, in other words, labour is detotalized. (Schiller saw through this fact almost two hundred years ago. In his *The Aesthetic Letter*, he reflected the detotalization from the ontological perspective of man's existence.) As a result, in the

16 Sahlins, Marshall D. *Culture and Practical Reason*. Joint Publishing Company Limited (Beijing), 2002.

capitalist commodity exchange, "labour is *posited* as general only through *exchange.*"[17] This is another abstraction of objective economic activities, which makes it possible for the *conceptual abstraction.* Baudrillard, do you understand now? Marx's labour concept as such is first an objective abstraction, which springs from the detotalization of work in modern technical division of industrial production and the objective exchange of the market economy where different concrete labours form the homogeneous labour as such in the mirror of value. The labour as such in economics arises from the subjective cognition of the objective economic abstraction. (We are to understand this mystery in the next discussion by Slavoj Žižek.) Marx believes the abstraction of labour is "the point of departure of modern economics, and writes:" Even applicable in all ages, they are "a product of historical conditions and retain their full validity only for and within these conditions."[18] The above remark is very precise, even perfect.

Nevertheless, Baudrillard draws a widely separated, sensational conclusion from it. He cuts off the special context and arbitrarily upgrades it to a generalized discourse in the philosophy of history. He accuses Marx of taking the mode of labour as the essence of controlling *all* human existence because his labour dominates the rest existential spheres of humankind. Labour replaces all the forms except wealth and exchange; labour generates the use value and shapes the mode of expression of human Being. Baudrillard thinks that Marx's ideology of productive labour is a subjective violence against history and this paradigm of labour postulates the "general schema of production and needs," with the law of value universalized. He argues that the analysis of all primitive or archaic organizations contradicts it, as does the feudal symbolic order and even that of our societies. How ridiculous it is! When does Marx project the "modern" labour as such only found in the capitalist mode of production to the primitive and feudal societies?

---

17   Karl Marx and Frederick Engels. *Collected Works*, vol. 28. London: Lawrence & Wishart, 1986, p. 108.
18   *Ibid.*, p. 42.

Nay, Marx adds a particular limitation for this: In social conditions prior to capitalism, "the purpose of this labour is not the *creation of value*"; rather, "its purpose is the maintenance of the individual proprietor and his family as well as of the community as a whole."[19] In addition, in those days, Marx, equipped with limited knowledge of the contemporary anthropology and other materials, perceives that even if the primitive communal existence, (which is Baudrillard's favourite), provides possible foundation for labour production, the presuppositions of the entire social existence "are not themselves the *product* of labour, but appear as its natural or *divine* preconditions."[20] This is because at that time whether it is husbandry or agriculture, "the chief objective condition of labour does not itself appear as the *product* of labour, but is already there as *nature.* "[21] Does Baudrillard get it this time? That our world becomes the result of labour production only occurs after the late industrial civilization of capitalism. I almost lose patience when Baudrillard does not abide by general principles and often stumbles over mistakes.

He walks on an evidently wrong way but proudly deems that he grasps the weak point of Marx. He claims, "[Marx's] all perspectives opened up by the contradictions of the mode of production drive us hopelessly into political economy" because he fails "to conceive of a mode of social wealth other than that founded on labour and production, Marxism no longer furnishes in the long run a real alternative to capitalism."[22] (Baudrillard really deserves the name of a capable pioneer for he scolds the post-Marxian transcendence of radicalizing Marxism, which, unexpectedly, proves a disapproval of his own *System of Objects, The Consumer Society,* and even *For a Critique of the Political Economy of the Sign.*)

It is clear that Baudrillard is unsuccessful in his theoretical innovation. He only makes some small tricks, in which he first puts Marx's conception of labour into historical materialism (scientific philosophy) as such it was used for solving specific economic

---

19   *Ibid.,* p. 399.
20   *Ibid.,* p. 400.
21   Ibid., p. 409.
22   Baudrillard, Jean. *The Mirror of Production.* Trans. Mark Poster. St. Louis: Telos Press, 1975, p. 29.

questions[23] besides along with the rough concept of production without any careful reflection; and then he sentences this fabricated theoretical "imagery" into death.

Baudrillard insists on the radical negation of Marxist conception
of labour, of use value, but his purpose is not to promote the theory
of labour value from an economic perspective. His real attempt is to
deny labour, production and the usefulness of any object in the sense
of *philosophical ontology*. He asserts:

> *In fact the use value of labour power does not exist anymore than
> the use value of products or the autonomy of signified and refer-
> ent. The same fiction reigns in the three orders of production,
> consumption, and signification. Exchange value is what makes
> the use value of products appear as its anthropological horizon.
> The exchange value of labour power is what makes its use value,
> the concrete origin and end of the act of labour, appear as its
> "generic" alibi. This is the logic of signifiers which produces the
> "evidence" of the "reality" of the signified and the referent.[24]*

We have had enough discussion on this allegation of Baudrillard's.
He means to say, the fundamentals of our world, that is, the phenomena of taking usefulness as the present scale occurs due to the
fabrication and imposition by the system of exchange value; this
code control of the signifier makes production—into production of
useful things, makes consumption—a false satisfaction of needs,
and signification—fabrication of imageries become the dominant
order of survival. He imposes every evil onto Marx's theory of the
exchange value and the use value of labour, which, almost amounts
to Pandora's box. Baudrillard says it is the ideology of labour that
makes a false productive generic nature of man, "in this sense, need,
use value, and the referent do not exist."[25] "They are only concepts
produced and projected into a generic dimension by the development of the very system of exchange value."[26]

---

23   Marx made a particular note that his labour here refers to the wage labour under the
capitalist system. It is "in the *strict economic sense in which we use it here, and no other.*"
24   Baudrillard, Jean. *The Mirror of Production*. Trans. Mark Poster. St. Louis: Telos
Press, 1975, p. 30.
25   See Note 13 of *The Mirror of Production*. It says, "This does not mean that they
have never existed. Hence we have another paradox that we must return to later."
26   Baudrillard, Jean. *The Mirror of Production*. Trans. Mark Poster. St. Louis: Telos
Press, 1975, p. 30.

Baudrillard has been saying it over and again. Only a shallow person makes such poor repetitions

3 GOOD LABOUR AND BEAUTIFUL NON-LABOUR

Baudrillard is not satisfied with a common negation of the labour concept. He tries to go deeper and dig out the devil inside the logic of Marx. He believes that Marx's discourse of labour is first of all an existential ontology, which is established in the *1844 Manuscripts*. (In a given historical context, Baudrillard is not wrong.) To prove his opinion, Baudrillard cites Herbert Marcuse's note on the *Manuscripts*, which says labour is the ontological concept of human existence. Baudrillard must have read Althusser but he seems not to know the essential difference between the young Marx's humanistic view of the alienated labour and historical materialism.

He makes a speedy juxtaposition of the *1844 Manuscripts* and *Capital* under the same theme. First, in his quotation from the 1844 Manuscripts, labour is identified as the ideal generic nature of the subjective objectification, "coming-to-being for himself" and "self-confirmation."[27] Without warning, he then jumps over 20 years of space-time across different research fields to Marx's *Capital*, catching two early explanations about labour that are radically different from the humanistic logic. (It is a common practice of the so-called Marxist anthropologists.) In the first explanation, the useful labour as the key of the process of the material production is "a necessary condition, independent from all forms of society, for the existence of the human race; it is an eternal nature-imposed necessity."[28] The context of this statement is an example: the handcraft of cloth production that had lasted for hundreds of years used by Marx to discuss the ontological base of the eternality of labour (production). The second explanation is from *Capital*, which reads: "Labour is, in the first place, a process in which both man and Nature participate, and in which man of his own accord starts, regulates, and controls the material exchange between himself and Nature."[29] Here, it is not difficult to find that, unlike the humanistic discourse of the *1844*

27   Karl Marx and Frederick Engels. *Collected Works*, vol. 3. London: Lawrence & Wishart, 1975, p. 333, p. 338.
28   Karl Marx, *Capital*, vol. 1. London: Lawrence & Wishart, 1977, p. 50.
29   *Ibid.*, p. 173.

Manuscripts, Marx's elucidation of labour is not an abstract hypothesis of man's authentic being but an emphasis on the status of labour during the process of material production and he thus identifies material production as the eternal premise of social existence and development of humankind.

Baudrillard's strategy is actually clever. First, he carefully makes an ahistorical patchwork of the qualitatively different texts used by Marx for the same theme, then borrows early Marcuse's misreading of Marxist humanism, and finally proves the legitimacy of his accusation. Ironically, if Marcuse is proved wrong, then Baudrillard is also wrong.

Baudrillard claims Marx's ontological position of labour makes the Marxist philosophical discourse unfold in two directions: an ethic of labour and an aesthetics of non-labour.

The former exalts labour as value, as end in itself, as categorical imperative. Labour loses it negativity and is raised to an absolute value. Baudrillard believes that such a conception is existent in both capitalist and socialist ideologies. In my view, if he means to criticize the *1844 Manuscripts* by the young Marx, he has a vantage. If it is the negation of Marx's assertion in *Capital*, he is doomed to fail. The above two statements are not meant to explain the theory of labour value in the economic sense or illustrate labour as man's aim from the philosophical view, to say nothing of "categorical imperative" or "absolute value." Labour production, the fundamental of social existence, is the activity to create the basic material means for human survival, which has no rationalistic tint of *generic (species essence) philosophy* or has nothing to do with the positive value scale and coordinate of ethics. In fact, as early as in Baudrillard's familiar text *The German Ideology*, Marx rejects a concealed idealistic historical view, that is, the way of writing history according to an extraneous standard—the practice of seeking "an *ideal* to which reality [will] have to adjust itself" from outside history.[30] Baudrillard makes use of these humanistic discourses in the early *1844 Manuscripts* to assault historical materialism developed in the later written *Capital*. Without doubt, it is an unreasonable argument. If his early concepts

---

30   Karl Marx and Frederick Engels. *Collected Works*, vol. 5. London: Lawrence & Wishart, 1976, p. 49.

in *The System of Objects* are employed to crack his subsequent texts, such as *The Perfect Crime*, we would not come to sensible conclusions. Judging from the critique per se, Baudrillard is very slippery. He adroitly takes advantage of the humanistic explanation of Western Marxism. (It, of course, includes our own "humanistic" logic construct in Chinese academy. This provides the ready target for Baudrillard and others.)

Baudrillard turns to Marcuse's critique of the economic concept of labour, which is a re-interpretation of Marx's logic of labour alienation in the neo-humanistic context. Marcuse stipulates labour as man's ontological basis and puts forward the substitute relation of game and labour. Baudrillard grasps this mistake and explodes him as a stand-in of Marx. He angrily questions why Marxist dialectic leads to the "Christian ethics," to its own opposition. In Baudrillard's view, Marx's concept of labour is bound for the "aberrant sanctification of work," compared to the capitalist asceticism stipulated by Weber. In order to prove his distortion, Baudrillard adds the misconceptions of Benjamin and Lafargue, even going out of his way to invite Joseph Dietzgen's work Messiah. However, what does all this have to do with Marxism? As we all know, Marx and Engels dedicated their entire lives to the struggle against the enslaved labour and the myths of opium-like ideologies. How could they accept an almost theological ethics of labour? It is merely illusory.

The second point is the so-called "aesthetics of non-labour." Baudrillard says,

> *In the fine points of Marxist thought, confronting the work ethic is an aesthetic of non-work or play itself based on the dialectic of quantity and quality. Beyond the capitalist mode of production and the quantitative measure of labour, this is the perspective of a definitive qualitative mutation in communist society: the end of alienated labour and the free objectification of man's own powers.*[31]

Here, Baudrillard refers to the well-known paragraph about the realm of freedom in *Capital (Vol. III)*. Marx intends to express the idea that as for man's ultimate liberation, "the realm of freedom

---

31   Baudrillard, Jean. *The Mirror of Production.* Trans. Mark Poster. St. Louis: Telos Press, 1975, p. 38.

actually begins only where labour which is determined by necessity and mundane considerations ceases; thus in the very nature of
things it lies beyond the sphere of actual material production."32 (It
is almost outrageous. Does not Baudrillard know what Marx means
by "beyond the sphere of actual material production" in this citation? Why does he overlook this phrase in his criticism of Marx's
universalizing the paradigm of production?) This time, Baudrillard
is silent about the universality of production. Instead, he makes a
feint and slips to another issue, to the aesthetic meaning of the future
society expected by Marx. However, he still relies on Marcuse's account of labour to oppose Marx. He concludes that Marx's communism is still a non-labour, dis-alienated play, qualitatively the same
with capitalism. "This realm beyond political economy called play,
non-work, or dis-alienated labour, is defined as the reign of a finality without end. In this sense it is and remains an *aesthetic*, in the
extremely Kantian sense, with all the bourgeois ideological connotations which that implies."33 Baudrillard implies that Marx's communist social life only emerges from the negation of the capitalist
conception of labour, which is but the trap of the bourgeois aesthetic ideology, because Marxist criticism of the alienated labour still
"inherits the aesthetic and humanistic virus of bourgeois thought."
(Baudrillard's aesthetics here corresponds to Althusser's concept of
non-scientific ideology.)

Baudrillard speaks on volubly in self-justification.

*Here stands the defect of all notions of play, freedom, transpar-
ence, or disalienation: it is the defect of the **revolutionary imagination** since, in the ideal types of play and the free play of human
faculties, we are still in a process of repressive desublimation.
In effect, the sphere of play is defined as the fulfilment of human
rationality, the dialectical culmination of man's activity of incessant objectification of nature and control of his exchanges with it.
It presupposes the full development of productive forces; it "follows in the footsteps" of the reality principle and the transformation of nature. Marx clearly states that it can flourish only when
founded on the reign of necessity. Wishing itself beyond labour*

---

32   Karl Marx and Frederick Engels. *Collected Works*, vol. 37. London: Lawrence &
Wishart, 1998, p. 807.
33   Baudrillard, Jean. *The Mirror of Production*. Trans. Mark Poster. St. Louis: Telos
Press, 1975, p. 39.

*but **in its continuation**, the sphere of play is always merely the aesthetic sublimation of labour's constraints. With this concept we remain rooted in the problematic of necessity and freedom, a typically bourgeois problematic whose double ideological expression has always been the institution of a reality principle (repression and sublimation, the principle of labour) and its formal overcoming in an ideal transcendence.*[34]

Baudrillard imposes on Marx such misinterpretations as "repression," "desublimation" and "reality principle" advocated by the young Marcuse, a fascinated fan of Freud. He thoughtlessly makes labels or trumps up charges. But anyone who has the common knowledge of Marxism understands that Marx never uses such unscientific stipulations as play in his discussion of the future liberation of humankind. (Marx even criticized the interpretation of the liberated labour as "pure fun, pure amusement, as seen in Fourier's childishly naïve conception.")[35] In his late years, Marx never makes metaphorical examples, not to mention any psychoanalytic terminology and context. Even in the statement quoted by Baudrillard, Marx only points out that the real, liberated social life of humankind is mainly "that development of human energy which is an end in itself," simply put, it is the *overall and free development of man and mankind*. When does Marx posit the play of labour or non-labour as the communist social existence?

Baudrillard tries to refute Marxism with the mistakes done by others. It only proves he has an ulterior motive, if not ignorance. Should Marx be responsible for young Marcus's errant explanation of the Marxist discourse?

---

34   Baudrillard, Jean. *The Mirror of Production*. Trans. Mark Poster. St. Louis: Telos Press, 1975, p. 40.
35   Karl Marx and Frederick Engels. *Collected Works*, vol. 28. London: Lawrence & Wishart, 1986, p. 530.

CHAPTER XI

MARX AND THE DOMINATION OF NATURE

In the second chapter of *The Mirror of Production*, Baudrillard develops his criticism further. This time, he transforms himself into an avant-garde of ecological ethics and of anti-anthropocentric thought. In his opinion, the problem of Marxist historical materialism lies in the violent view of domination and enslavement of nature. Baudrillard thinks the ideal concept of nature is "a hidden essence" and mystical power existent in the imagery of the primitive peoples.[1] He criticizes Marx for not knowing that beneath the notion of conquering nature is nothing else but the bourgeois rationalistic logic of Enlightenment.

---

1   Mauss, Marcel. *The Gift: Forms and Functions of Exchange in Archaic Societies.* Trans. Ian Cunnison. Glencoe: Free Press, 1954, p. 61.

1 CONCEPTION OF ENSLAVING NATURE IN ENLIGHTENMENT

Baudrillard says, the conception of nature through presence of the object of labour sits at the core of the bourgeois enlightenment, while the political economy, foundation for the whole Marxism, is also founded on this conception of nature. In the eyes of the western-ers, as late as the 17th century nature signified only the totality of laws founding the world's intelligibility: the guarantee of an order where men and things could exchange their meanings *[significations]*.[2] In the end, this is God (Spinoza's "*Deus sive natura*"). The above judg-ment is basically correct. When it comes to the 18th century, the orig-inal "nature" experienced significant changes with the development of industrial production. Baudrillard regards it as "Nature's entry into the era of its technical domination." It is the first *split* between subject and Nature-object and "their simultaneous submission to an operational finality." Here, nature is no longer the totality of laws but the *object* of the subject.

> *Nature appeared truly as an essence in all its glory but under the sign of the **principle of production**. This separation also involves the **principle of signification**. Under the objective stamp of Science, Technology, and Production, Nature becomes the great Signified, the great Referent. It is ideally charged with "reality"; it becomes **the** Reality, expressible by a process that is always somehow a process of labour, at once **transformation** and **tran-scription**. Its "reality" principle is this operational principle of an industrial structuration and a significative pattern.[3]*

In my opinion, it is a general rehearsal of the views of nature by the Western technological criticism and ecological ethics preva-lent since the 1960s. Judging from the statement per se, we cannot say Baudrillard is wrong. It is actually a post-industrial resonance that frequents the technology-critical texts of late Martin Heidegger, Max Horkheimer and Theodor Adorno's *Dialectic of Enlightenment*, Leiss's *Domination of Nature*, and so on. Baudrillard adds to them his code of production principle, the concept of Signifier of semi-otics, and the idea of pseudo-reality appropriated from Lacan. In

---

2   Baudrillard, Jean. *The Mirror of Production*. Trans. Mark Poster. St. Louis: Telos Press, 1975, p. 53.
3   *Ibid.*, p. 54.

a lengthy note, Baudrillard emphasizes that during production nature is turned into commodity and codes at once, which leaves every product with both the exchange value and the "symbolic value"; the more forward a modern consumer society develops, the more important and dominant of the commodity's *manipulation of symbolic value* becomes. It is a "new discovery" by Baudrillard in his *For a Critique of the Political Economy of the Sign*.

For Baudrillard, the Enlightenment views nature as the object to be conquered and dominated, or "the very reality of its exploitation." Posited as the object, nature is dissected, utilized, made by science and technology at man's will. "Science presents itself as a project progressing toward an objective determined in advance by Nature. Science and Technology present themselves as revealing what is inscribed in Nature: not only its secrets but their deep purpose."[4]

Here Baudrillard capitalizes the initial letter of nature, similar to the derogatory generic concept presented by Stirner, Nietzsche and Lacan. It denotes the homogeneity of violence under man's rational governance. Before the brutal science and technology, Nature is forced to reveal its secrets, which are again used by the greedy man in his endless exploration of all the potentialities of nature. "*Nature is the concept of a dominated essence* and nothing else."[5] In addition, today's nature exists for the subject, if put by early Hegel's discourse, the existence for me. Therefore, nature loses its beingness facing the advance of the singing science and technology. Heidegger moans, natural thing cannot be "thinged" with its existence degenerated to human nature. Baudrillard does not suppress his anger, "everything that invokes Nature invokes the domination of Nature."[6]

According to Baudrillard, the split between the subject and nature under the capitalist production principle can be traced to an earlier period.

*The separation is rooted in the great Judeo-Christian dissociation of the soul and Nature. God created man in his **image** and created Nature for man's use. The soul is the spiritual hinge by which man is God's image and is radically distinguished from the rest of Nature (and from his own body).*[7]

---

4 *Ibid.*, p. 55.
5 *Ibid.*, p. 55.
6 *Ibid.*, p. 56.
7 *Ibid.*, p. 63.

This is the original sin. Baudrillard believes that Christianity is the most *anthropocentric* religion the world has ever known and it still constitutes the theoretical core of the *dominant* view of nature now. I feel this opinion seems to be quite justified. Nevertheless, it is not his innovative thinking but the common sense of the ecological ethics in the last century, and further.

2 "HALF-REVOLUTION" OF MARXIST VIEW OF NATURE

To Baudrillard, the concept of nature is the core of the whole Western Enlightenment thought, or moral philosophy of the Enlightenment. He says, Marx wanted to break the myth of the capitalist conception of nature, along with it the idealistic anthropology sustained by this myth but lost the name of action, Marx only partially dislocated this myth of Nature.

Marx indeed "denaturalized" private property, the mechanisms of competition and the market, and the processes of labour and capital; but he failed to question the following naturalist propositions:

> — the useful finality of products as a function of needs;
> — the useful finality of nature as a function of its transformation by labour.[8]

Baudrillard does not let go of Marx. In his view, Marxist critique of the bourgeois is not unproductive for it sees through the bourgeois ideological ruse that attempts to universalize the capitalist mode of production, but historical materialism still emphasizes the conquest and transformation of nature, and ascribes the social life as the finality of the usefulness of the object. Consequently, Marx's criticism of nature is only "half-revolution."

Here, Baudrillard goes on with his criticism of the whole historical materialism. He thinks that Marx is unable to make a critical reflection of the material production, and thus, unaware of the fact that the usefulness of labour and nature is still the core of the bourgeois enlightenment ideology. Baudrillard says,

> The functionality of Nature structured by labour, and the corresponding functionality of the subject structured around needs, belong to the anthropological sphere of use value described by

8   *Ibid.*, p. 56.

Enlightenment rationality and defined for a whole civilization (which imposed it on others) by a certain kind of abstract, linear, irreversible finality: a certain model subsequently extended to all sectors of individual and social practice.[9]

Marx criticizes the capitalist mode of production, whose logic of enslaving nature still traps him to a certain degree. In a certain sense, Baudrillard is not completely wrong. In the *1857-1858 Manuscripts*, Marx says, "for the first time, nature becomes purely an object for man, nothing more than a matter of utility; It ceases to be acknowledged as a power for itself, and even the theoretical cognition of its autonomous laws appears merely as a stratagem for its subjection to human needs."[10] Marx does admit the important role of capitalism. Unlike the romantic critique in the *1844 Manuscripts*, he fully confirms the "great civilizing influence" of capitalism by calling it "a system of universal exploitation of the natural (Ed.: nature) and human qualities, a system of universal utility, whose bearer is science itself as much as all the physical and spiritual qualities, and under these conditions nothing appears as something *higher-in-itself,* as an end in itself, outside this circle of social production and exchange."[11]

I think this understanding of Marxist view of nature is correct. Marx expects no liberation without the social historical progress and the highest level of productive forces created by the industrial civilization given that the reality of complete human liberation can only be achieved on an advanced level of material production. This is already proved by previous history: Poverty cannot directly lead to socialism and communism. Even from a historical view, Baudrillard is also right with his ecological ethics and technological criticism of the over-exploitation and the destructive use of natural resources. In fact, Marx and Engels did not entirely ignore the same problem at that time.[12] However, overdone is as bad as undone. Baudrillard makes an absoluteness out of the reasonable reflection, turns the anti-anthropocentric view in ecological criticism into an ontological

---

9   *Ibid.*, p. 56.
10   Karl Marx and Frederick Engels. *Collected Works*, vol. 28. London: Lawrence & Wishart, 1986, p. 337.
11   *Ibid.*, p. 336.
12   See my "Contemporary Ecological Horizon and the Logic of the Materialistic View" in *Philosophical Researches*, 1993, 8.

discourse, injects some Mauss-Bataille thought, then aggressively comes to negate *all the change and use* of nature by man, and finally comes to another theoretical proof of his grassrootism. In my opinion, it is a non sequitur.

Baudrillard says, "without ceasing to be ideological, the concept splits into a 'good' Nature that is dominated and rationalized (which acts as the ideal cultural reference) and a bad' Nature that is hostile, menacing, catastrophic, or polluted. All bourgeois ideology divides between these two poles."[13] For the nature that can be utilized by man, it is good; if not, man will "dominate" nature (Heidegger). Man does the same to his own kind: He that can be sublimated as a productive force is a naturally good man; if unable to enter rational regulation, he is mad. For Baudrillard, Marxism allies with this optimistic rationalization of man. He thinks even in the latest Freudo-Marxist version in which the unconscious itself is reinterpreted as "natural" wealth, a hidden positivism that will burst forth in the revolutionary struggle. (Baudrillard probably targets the aforementioned Deleuze this time.)

Clearly, in Baudrillard's eyes, nature should remain in the primordial status when it is not objectified and dominated. He follows his teacher's extreme admiration of the mystique and opaqueness of nature. In their heart, nature is absolutely not the object to be planned or made. As a result, in primitive societies, "neither Law nor Necessity exist at the level of reciprocity and symbolic exchange."[14] For this reason, Baudrillard hates the root of all evil. To him, Marx still falls a victim to the capitalist conception of nation.

The concept of production is never questioned; it will never radically overcome the influence of political economy. Even Marxism's transcending perspective will always be burdened by counter-dependence on political economy. Against Necessity it will oppose the mastery of Nature; against Scarcity it will oppose Abundance ("to each according to his needs") without ever resolving either the arbitrariness of these concepts or their idealist overdetermination by political economy.[15]

---

13   Baudrillard, Jean. *The Mirror of Production*. Trans. Mark Poster. St. Louis: Telos Press, 1975, p. 57.
14   *Ibid.*, p. 61.
15   *Ibid.*, p. 59.

Baudrillard thinks the core of the bourgeois conception of nature is still material production, which, as a basic logical start point, leads to the linear progressive conception of history wherein nature is regulated, controlled, enslaved, and endlessly produced by the always-unsatisfactory *human desire* (Scarcity). In this continual production and reproduction, miserable nature is at the mercy of man's wilful control and regulation. To Baudrillard's disappointment, Marx's communist ideal is also based on this unreflecting bourgeois conception of nature that gives rise to his vision of the material "distribution according to needs."

It is, in the eyes of Baudrillard, a revolutionary ideal is built on the bourgeois *Prometheanism of productive forces*, because Marx is fooled by "the Promethean and Faustian vision of its perpetual transcendence."[16]

> *This dialectical voluntarism, for which Necessity exists and must be conquered, is not shaken. Scarcity exists and must be abolished; the Productive Forces exist and must be liberated; the End exists and only the means need be found. All revolutionary hope is thus bound up in a Promethean myth of productive forces, but this myth is only the space time of political economy. And the desire to manipulate destiny through the development of productive forces plunges one into the space time of political economy.*[17]

Baudrillard is opposed to the development of productive forces, to the transformation and "conquest" of nature, to the historical progression, and even to any forward-looking thought of liberation. Marxism is certainly rejected with the grassrootism that is bogged down in and redirected towards the past. However, I have to repeat the same questions: Can history really go backward? Can the primitive life, favoured by Baudrillard and his dear teachers, really stop the rolling tide of history?

---

16 *Ibid.*, p. 61.
17 *Ibid.*, p. 60.

3 BIG LAW AND THE BIG NECESSITY OF NATURE

To Baudrillard, Marx does not eradicate the "moral philosophy" of the Enlightenment. He rejects its naiveté and sentimentality, its fantastic religiosity, but cannot radically break the phantasm of *Nature-imposed necessity*. He accuses:

> *By secularizing it in the economic concept of scarcity, Marxism keeps the idea of Necessity without transforming it. The idea of "natural Necessity" is only a **moral** idea dictated by political economy, the ethical and philosophical version of that bad Nature systematically connected with the arbitrary postulate of the economic. In the mirror of the economic, Nature looks at us with the eyes of necessity.[18]*

What Baudrillard wants to deny is Marx's eternal Nature-imposed necessity that men create his own social existence through their production. However, Marx insists that even in early primitive societies, man has to be engaged in material production. Baudrillard refers to a paragraph in *Capital (Vol. 3)*, in which Marx says the primitive people have to struggle against nature for survival, produce the necessary means of life, also likewise, the modern social existence and development is based on the same natural necessity. As for this material production and re-living during which man transforms nature, Marx argues: "he must do so in all social formations and under all possible modes of production. With his development this realm of physical necessity expands as a result of his wants; but, at the same time, the forces of production which satisfy these wants also increase."[19]

Baudrillard strongly resists this idea. In his opinion, just like other capitalist thinkers, Marx is unable to realize "that in his symbolic exchanges primitive man *does not gauge himself in relation to Nature*."[20] It is true that the primitive people can neither have the modern sense of self-awareness nor understand "the forces in production which satisfy these wants." However, Baudrillard misinterprets the phrase. Marx does not really mean the primitive society

---

18   *Ibid.*, p. 58.
19   Karl Marx and Frederick Engels. *Collected Works*, vol. 37. London: Lawrence & Wishart, 1998, p. 807.
20   Baudrillard, Jean. *The Mirror of Production*. Trans. Mark Poster. St. Louis: Telos Press, 1975, p. 59.

has the mode of production in modern sense. What he wants to stress is the fundamental status of common material production in social existence.

> He [Marx] is not aware of Necessity, a Law that takes effect only with the objectification of Nature. The Law takes its definitive form in capitalist political economy; moreover, it is only the philosophical expression of Scarcity. Scarcity, which itself arises in the market economy, is not a given dimension of the economy. Rather, it is what **produces and reproduces** economic exchange. In that regard it is different from primitive exchange, which knows nothing of this "Law of Nature" that pretends to be the ontological dimension of man.[21] Hence it is an extremely serious problem that Marxist thought retains these key concepts which depend on the metaphysics of the market economy in general and on modern capitalist ideology in particular.[22]

I have to admit that this paragraph is rather sensible part in Baudrillard's book. Unlike his grassrootism blindly against the material production as the foundation of social existence, he points out a problem that is reasonable from a certain point of view.

First, as for the natural laws in the sphere of science, Baudrillard's proposition is not false. From Kant, people gradually find that the essence of natural scientific laws is the historical cognitive effect by subjects in different ages, that is, man's legislating laws for nature. The presence of "natural laws" before the subject, viz, the existence of natural science, is indeed, steadily developed with the *overall objectification* of nature in the capitalist industrial practice.

Second, Baudrillard is correct if his "Law" refers to the modern social economic laws (regulations) that are first generated in the capitalist economic process, partially revealed by the classical economy, and then noticed in Marx's special historical materialism and his political economy as an effective economic law (e.g. law of value) in a *given historical condition*. He is also right if his "Scarcity" implies the false desire (e.g. the false consumption in his *Consumer Society* which echoes Debord and the Frankfurt School), which can

21 Cf. Sahlins, Marshall. "La première société d'abondance," *Les Temps Modernes* (October, 1968), pp. 641-680. (It is the original note.)
22 Baudrillard, Jean. *The Mirror of Production.* Trans. Mark Poster. St. Louis: Telos Press, 1975, p. 59

be said as the fundamental aspect of what *produces and reproduces* the economic exchange.

Third, Baudrillard says the primitive economic exchange was radically different from that of the modern society. It is a correct conclusion, too. The primitive people certainly have no idea of what we call the "natural laws," which is but the mysterious might of god in their eyes.

However, when Baudrillard draws on them to blame Marx, it becomes strange. That for him such concepts as natural law, objective necessity depend on the metaphysics of the market economy in general and on modern capitalist ideology in particular only makes sense in a special context. That is, that is true when they refer to natural scientific laws and the category of necessity in the modern era, because these concepts appear in the very early time of the Western history and have their own specific historical contents. Baudrillard is obviously arbitrary with his this assertion. In addition, if natural law and objective necessity are viewed in a correlative reliance on the bourgeois ideology, and are really necessary for people in their scientific grasp of the world (since people cannot return to Baudrillard's preferred primitive society and understand the world with something like "hau"), then it means to universalize the bourgeois ideology. What's more, Baudrillard is unaware that Marx's biggest contribution of criticizing the bourgeois ideology in his special historical materialism is the identification of the historicity of the natural order existent as social history and the *law of nature* concealed in human nature in the capitalist market economy.

Baudrillard is also ignorant of the fact that natural law has a rich variation of contexts for Marx and Marxism, too. Perhaps his flat thought cannot adapt to the multi-dimensional, complex history. As I mentioned in *The Subjective Dimension of Marxist Historical Dialectics*, besides the concept of natural law in common sense, the young Marx already had the conception of nature with different meanings and as a category of relationship in his critique of Hegelian philosophy and in his the humanistic discourse before 1845.[23] After he establishes historical materialism, in a very special metaphorical

---

23   See my *The Subjective Dimension of Marxist Historical Dialectics*, English version published by Canut Intl. Publishers, London, 2012, p. 184-185.

context of the capitalist economic process, he names the commodity-market economic law—that Baudrillard hates—as the natural law in social life, that is, the aimless movement in human social existence and development similar to that of the natural world, which I call *nature-likeness*.[24]

For example, in Marx's criticism of Thomas Malthus in the *1857-1858 Manuscripts*, he points out the latter's ignorance of the "specific historical laws of population movement" in a given situation. (This "specific" must *not be capital* in Baudrillard's logic.) Marx also tells Malthus that these laws are "indeed the history of the nature of man, his *natural* laws. But they are the natural laws of man only at a certain level of historical development, corresponding to a certain level of development of the productive forces which is determined by his own historical process."[25] Again, Baudrillard comes to his blind spot. Marxist context is very complicated. First, when Marx observes the social historical movement from the perspective of historical materialism, he always emphasizes the "lowercase" social life, the special state in a concrete historical situation. Second, Marx stipulates the "prehistorical society" (social existence before the final liberation of man), especially, the social laws of the capitalist society, as a similar status in the aimless material movement of nature. Accordingly, he identifies these lowercase, specific social laws as natural laws. Marx uses them to illustrate that this situation is going to be developed or abrogated in future social development. Ironically, Baudrillard is precisely opposed to this progress.

Baudrillard puts forward the second epistemological summary, titled "Structural Limits of the Marxist Critique," at the end of that chapter. What a big slogan! However, in my opinion, except some aforesaid points, there is nothing substantial. It is a pseudo-transcendence failure of his logic. In particular, when he concludes that the projection of the class struggle [of Marxism] onto all previous history is led to reproduce the roots of the system of political economy, he is obviously lying. In *The German Ideology* of 1845 and the *Communist Manifesto* of 1848, Marx and Engels make a theoretical

24 *Ibid.*, p. 191-204.
25 Karl Marx and Frederick Engels. *Collected Works*, vol. 28. London: Lawrence & Wishart, 1986, p. 525.

transgression due to lack of necessary materials. However, after they knew the real situation of the primitive social history through the studies of anthropology and social history, they immediately revise their text and add special attributive before their assertion, which also proves the respectable matter-of-fact spirit of Marxism. Why does Baudrillard turn a blind eye to this well known fact?

CHAPTER XII

MARX AND ETHNOCENTRISM

The third chapter in *The Mirror of Production* is titled "Historical Materialism and Primitive Societies." According to Baudrillard's own words, this chapter is going to focus on Marx's concept of history after he deals with Marxist concept of nature in the previous chapter. Its main critical target is a contemporary Marxist anthropologist Maurice Godelier and his *Anthropology, Science of Primitive Societies?* published in 1971.[1] Afterwards, Baudrillard turns against the basic methodology of Marxist historical materialism. Next, we are to analyze his criticism of historical materialism and then his discussion on the issues of primitive societies.

---

1 Godelier, Maurice. *Anthropology, Science of Primitive Societies?* Paris: Denoël, 1971.

1 THE BIG HISTORY AND THE BIG DIALECTICS

In his usual open style, Baudrillard makes a clear statement that Marxist concept of history, the same as the dominant category of nature, is a *"rewriting of History through the mode of production."*[2] In other words, the concept of history in Marxist historical materialism is not a real reflection of history but a re-coded effect by productive codes. Consequently, unlike the dominated Nature, Marxist concept of history is also a big "History."

> *Instead, the concepts of production and mode of production themselves "produce" and "reproduce" the concepts of Nature and History as their space time. The model produces this double horizon of extent and time: Nature is only its extent and History only its trajectory. They do not need somehow to have their own names because they are only emanations of the code, referential simulations that acquire the force of reality and behind which the code legislates. These are the "laws of Nature" and the "laws of History."*[3]

In a certain sense, Baudrillard is very shrewd. All the concepts in Marxist historical materialism acquire their particular historical meanings at a given (certain) level of social historical practice. The materialistic view aims to observe history through the historical movement of the production. As long as Baudrillard rejects Marx's conception of material production as the foundation of social historical existence and movement, opposes the thought of understanding the social history through the basic logic of the mode of production, he is bound to deny all the categories of historical materialism formed by this paradigm. Unsurprisingly, Baudrillard explains that Nature and History in historical materialism are but the effect of rewriting the model of material production and the mode of production: First, Nature is the extent horizon objectified by the scheme of production. Under the code of production, nature is the target of labour and the place to realize production; second, History is the continuous spreading of production, in which the time of life distorts into a trajectory of producing objects and history becomes the mere process of the changing mode of production. Therefore, Baudrillard

---

2   Baudrillard, Jean. *The Mirror of Production*. Trans. Mark Poster. St. Louis: Telos Press, 1975, p. 69.
3   *Ibid.*, p. 69.

thinks names are not necessary for nature and history that are only "referential simulations" of the code of production.

Here, we have to ask ourselves. Is Marx wrong? Is historical materialism wrong? Baudrillard's criticism of historical materialism stems from his primitive social guidelines based on Mauss-Bataille symbolic exchange. He thinks that the simple original relations between man and man, on the other hand between man and nature are completely replaced by the utilitarian productive *readiness-to-hand*. Everything of human social existence is shrouded in the shadow of exchange value; man's existence is deprived of the most authentic, non-useful happy status of survival. This is his theoretical foundation that he relies on when opposing the historical materialism.

In my opinion, Baudrillard's understanding of historical materialism is one-sided. First, Marx emphasizes that the general material production, namely, man's creative activity of transforming nature, is the common basis for the survival of the entire human social life in history, which is also called the eternal natural necessity. This cannot be denied by Baudrillard or any other one. Even in Mauss-Bataille symbolic exchange, the priceless consumption necessitates the previously *produced* objects. It cannot proceed with sheer natural objects like those used by animals. Therefore, Baudrillard's negation of production by the romantic grassrootism is not sensible. Second, Marx never legitimizes the utilitarian economic control generated in a certain given conditions of material production, and also especially, under the bourgeois ideology proliferation conditions. On the contrary, he dedicates himself to the criticism of the materialized control of the capitalist mode of production, and, of course, the distortion of nature and history by the logic of capital.

Besides nature and history, Baudrillard begins to deny the third concept in Marxist historical materialism, the concept of *Dialectic*. In his eyes, Dialectic is about the theory of Laws. The laws of Nature and the laws of History can only be "read in the Dialectic." As mentioned before, Baudrillard's initial big letters indicate man's control and dominating logic, thus the laws of the Dialectic here denote the *rule of man*. Once again, Baudrillard misses the target. Dialectic is not an invention by Marxism but a philosophical category existent since the ancient time, shining in both Eastern and Western thoughts.

When Heraclitus and Laozi, the ancient Chinese philosopher, used the dialectic as an ontological conception, the logic of production and exchange value in modern sense and Baudrillard's hatred was far from being the master of that world. Only if Baudrillard's Dialectic excludes the ancient dialectic and refers to the one that appears since the dominance of capitalist mode of production in the 18th century, I shall agree with what he says. In fact, Baudrillard's criticism of the violent logic of Dialectic mainly originates from Hegel, the modern German idealist great master, whose absolute idea system says that Nature and History are the alienation and restoration history of the absolute spirit. To say in Baudrillard's stylish words: Through the rewriting by the code of absolute idea, Thus Nature is the space for objectified ideas; History becomes the process aimed to materialize concepts; and Dialectic turns into the Logic of the conceptualized world. Perhaps some correlation is necessary here, because Hegel's logic is not his own creation either but largely a philosophical mapping of modern industrial and economical development.[4] Marxist historical materialism and historical dialectics reverse Hegel's reversed world indeed. In my understanding, Marx's transcendence is his essential removal of the concept-rapes-the reality capitalization. Specific analysis on certain historical existence is found everywhere in Marxist historical materialism texts. What is absent is exactly the abstract capitalization of the suspending hypothesis of subjective values. In his later years, Marx uses the figurative "Man" but it is a philosophical positioning for human liberation. After 1845, Marx abandons Hegelian/Feuerbachian *capitalized concepts (written with big initial letter)*. Baudrillard commits but another false accusation here.

According to Baudrillard, Marxist historical materialism makes another serious mistake of generalizing these concepts, for example, Nature, History, and the Dialectic that only belong to the framework of productive materialism. In particular, Marx subjectively extends them to the primitive societies where there are no such things as the objectified nature, history of production, and the dialectic that directly reflects the reciprocal relation between subject and object. It is illegitimate transgression. At the same time, Baudrillard appreciates

---

4   See "Section Two" in the first chapter of *Back to Marx: The Philosophical Discourse in the Context of Economics* (Jiangsu People's Press, 1999). English version published by Göttingen University Press, in 2014.

the critical deconstruction theory of Nietzsche, which, he says, aims at "deconstructing the imaginary universality of the solidest conceptual edifices (the subject, rationality, knowledge, history, dialectics) and restoring them to their relativity and symptomality."[5] He counts on Nietzsche to oppose the "logos and the pathos of production."

Again, I almost lose patience with Baudrillard, who often frames Marx by the exact things Marx opposes. When does Marx insist the universal conception? Except the premise for the existence of common society, instead the basis as the basic material production and reproduction, was the *specific, historical and actual* stipulation after historical materialism was established in 1845. He always analyzes the material production status in a given certain historical condition, a certain natural environment, certain conceptions and certain relations between people, which is the scientific "historical and transitory" methodology and historiography established in his "Letter from Marx to Pavel Vasilyevich Annenkov", in 1846"[6] Marx's methodology is meant to deconstruct any attempt to self-solidificate any conception. The zealous Nietzsche-admirer Heidegger, valued this manner of him as the most important subversion of metaphysics. Did not the profound Baudrillard know?

2 CATEGORIES OF ANALYSIS AND IDEOLOGY

Baudrillard makes every effort to continue his tenacious criticism and denial of Marxism. In the end of this chapter, he provides the usual epistemological summary, titled "Materialism and Ethnocentrism." Another carefully prepared label put on Marxism! (Baudrillard did not take part in the Chinese Cultural Revolution, but his "label factory"* does not fall behind those Chinese radicals. He is also from the so-called French Red May generation, probably inheriting this terrible and poor style of writing from that revolution.)

---

5 Baudrillard, Jean. *The Mirror of Production*. Trans. Mark Poster. St. Louis: Telos Press, 1975, p. 70.
6 See my *Back to Marx: The Philosophical Discourse in the Context of Economics*. Marx uses 7 givens and 2 certains to illustrate this specific historical analysis, which manifests the direct opposition to the universalization of conceptions.
*) Label factory: Ultra radical left leaders of the Chinese Cultural Revolution period, randomly labeled everyone they disagreed, in a sense they ran a label factory, Mao used this term to criticize them.

As said by Baudrillard, Marx "outlined the formula for" epistemology in his labour theory, or in relation with labour. He likes quoting from the *1857-1858 Manuscripts*. I discover that he uses the same text source here. To be specific, it is Marx's statement about the "method of political economy" in the introduction, where Marx says that labour simply seems an economic category but actually, it is a modern category and it is the modern relations which create this simple abstraction. Therefore, Marx points out:

> *Even the most abstract categories, despite their validity in all epochs— precisely because they are abstractions—, are equally a product of historical conditions even in the specific form of abstractions, and they retain their full validity only for and within the framework of these conditions.*[7]

Marx's description just rebuts the above criticism by Baudrillard, who does not even understand the dialectical thought due to lack of the spirit of dialectics. Baudrillard wonders why labour belongs to all the times on one side, and only applies for some certain eras (time) on the other side. He calls it "mystery." However, it is Baudrillard who invents the big modern mysteries if judged by his own logic. (He later uses such concepts as "implosion," "simulacrum," etc., which, obviously, is mystification.)

Indeed, Marx is very clear here: Labour, as the most important dominating aspect of human production, runs through the entire history; wherever man exists, there is labour and production; labour belongs to all the times from this perspective. Nevertheless, the particular circumstances and preconditions of labour in a given period are not the same, e.g. the simple labour in primitive societies observably differs from today's labour engaged in information-based automated production, which rightly proves that the conceptual abstraction of labour only fully applies for and within these conditions. Marx's explanation is rather plain for those who have the common knowledge of the dialectics. How can it be a mystery? Here, Baudrillard may confuse ignorance with sharpness.

---

7 Karl Marx and Frederick Engels. *Collected Works*, vol. 28. London: Lawrence & Wishart, 1986, p. 42.

Baudrillard is intentionally misleading in that he soon fabricates another logical conversion in his following text. After his criticism of Marx's mystification of labour, he instantly concocts a new logical link by saying that "this is the same mystery as the simultaneous subordination of infra- and superstructure, and the dialectical coexistence of a dominance and a determination in the last instance."[8] This is an obvious trap.

His terms infra- and super-structure, respectively refer first to the economic foundation and then political/legal superstructure in the social formation, and his terming "a dominance and a determination" means enslaving dominance and control, and finally the decisive role which the economic power (rule) plays in an economic social form (Germ.: Ökonomische Gesellschaftsformation).

They are obviously three important *special* conceptions of historical materialism. And obviously, these concepts are not universal for all the historical periods. In Marx's late years, he often abstracts some philosophical concepts with common features when analyzing the capitalist economic issues. These understandings and critical points only suit certain economic social forms. Marx is left with little time for some ad hoc limitations. For example, in the description of the general principles of his special historical materialism in the *Critique of Political Economy*, Marx does not notice that the modern economic structure and superstructure, including the decisive role of the economic power, constitutes unlimited universality. Such lapses of him are seriously misread by the Second International and the Stalinist textbook dogmatism, which generated many unscientific explanations of historical materialism. Baudrillard grasps these misguided expressions and maliciously extends them to the whole historical materialism. It is his real purpose.

Therefore, he does observe a fault of Marxist expression and instantly makes a detour to the previous concept of labour by Marx. It is also true that Marx explicitly says, "the positing of the individual as a *worker* is itself a product of *history*". (A good proof of rebutting his falsification of Marx's universality of the concept of labour in the previous part.) However, Marx does not say labour *activity* (but the

8   Baudrillard, Jean. *The Mirror of Production*. Trans. Mark Poster. St. Louis: Telos Press, 1975, p. 84.

concept of labour) is a historical product. Instead Marx points out that in the process of production, labour activity (labour) becomes the social labour *as such*, the modern-sense indistinguishable *abstraction* of labour, which is, without doubt, the effect of the modern capitalist social development, with its abstraction as the *objective* abstractness in the economic exchanges.[9] Without specific analysis, Baudrillard continues his attack against Marx's concept of labour. He cites what Sahlins says "labour is not a real category of tribal economy"[10] and canonizes it in his criticism of Marx. When he accuses the abstraction of the concept of labour by Marx, he does not expect it. He continues his aim:

> *At the same time that it produces the abstract universality of labour (of labour power), our epoch produces the universal abstraction of the **concept** of labour and the retrospective illusion of the validity of this concept for all societies. Concrete, actual, limited validity is that of an **analytic** concept; its abstract and unlimited validity is that of an **ideological** concept. This distinction concerns not only labour but the whole conceptual edifice of historical materialism: production, productive forces, mode of production, infrastructure (not to mention the dialectic and history itself). All these concepts are in fact historical products. Beyond the field that produced them (especially, if they want to be "scientific"), they are only the metalanguage of a Western culture (Marxist, to be sure) that speaks from the height of its abstraction.[11]*

Baudrillard offers a series of assertions, among which is the heterogeneous relation between an analytic category and ideology. A careful reader may find it is still the appropriation of the categories of Althusser's "science" and "ideology." This analytic category concerns the "concrete, actual, limited validity" of the concept, while the ideological concept is featured with the "abstract and unlimited validity." In my opinion, there is nothing fresh here. Those

9   See my *Back to Marx: The Philosophical Discourse in the Context of Economics*. Published by Göttingen University Press in 2014, In particular, pages from 566-572. Also, see the first chapter in *The Sublime Object of Ideology* by Slavoj Žižek.

10   Quoted from Baudrillard's note about Sahlins's *Original Affluent Society*. To be more strict, is there a real category of "economy" in primitive societies? Or, the alleged "symbolic exchange"? Judging from Baudrillard's own logic, it is all illegitimate for Mauss-Bataille and Sahlins's modern discourse to describe the primitive societies.

11   Baudrillard, Jean. *The Mirror of Production*. Trans. Mark Poster. St. Louis: Telos Press, 1975, p. 85.

methods of concrete, actual, limited (temporary) historical analysis are the kernel of the methodology of Marxist historical material- ism. Ironically, Baudrillard borrows them to act against Marxism in turn. In addition, his definition of ideological categories is too lim- ited. Universality is only an insignificant character in modern ideol- ogy research efforts and it is difficult to be clarified once separated from the hegemonic discourse of the ruling class. More importantly, Marx should be the last one to be blame. What we see here is that Baudrillard packs labour, production, mode of production, infra- structure, history and dialectic as within the ideological categories, as the rape of the whole social history by the Western metacultural language (the hegemonic ideological discourse of West-centralism).

We cannot accept this opinion. Amid Baudrillard's list of histori- cal materialist categories, except infrastructure (the economic foun- dation) in fact which indeed belong to the special historical mate- rialism, the majority are the concepts of Marxist general historical materialism that have the common feature of the abstraction, through examination of common features in entire social history. According to Baudrillard, these concepts are the product of history. It is not wrong. Marx would not oppose this view.

(During the establishment of historical materialism, what Marx emphasizes most is that any concept belongs to a given age.) However, it does not mean we can totally ignore the actual labour activities as the basis of human social survival, the whole life expe- rience, the certain modes of production, the historical progress of human social history, and the dialectic relations ranging from the simple to the endless always being existent in societies. They are not the same as the representation of these social existence(s) or the dynamic, conceptual expressions of history. Baudrillard is easy to be proud of his argument. It proves but another non sequitur.

3 IS THE ANATOMY OF MAN A KEY TO THE ANATOMY OF APE?

Baudrillard seems to expect the probable counter-argument. He explains that his criticism is not arbitrary but sustained by evidenc- es. He cites Marx's view that *the anatomy of man is a key to the anatomy of the ape*, which is an important metaphor of historical epistemology. (Baudrillard usually seizes the most important part in Marxist logic. I have to pay my respect for his sharpness.) His quotation is in the introduction of the *1857-1858 Manuscripts*, following Baudrillard's previous citation about labour. The statement is very important. Let us read the whole paragraph:

> *Bourgeois society is the most advanced and complex historical organisation of production. The categories which express its relations, and an understanding of its structure, therefore, provide an insight into the structure and the relations of production of all formerly existing social formations the ruins and component elements of which were used in the creation of bourgeois society. Some of these unassimilated remains are still carried on within bourgeois society, others, however, which previously existed. only in rudimentary form, have been further developed and have attained their full significance, etc. The anatomy of man is a key to the anatomy of the ape. On the other hand, rudiments of more advanced forms in the lower species of animals can only be understood when the more advanced forms are already known.*[12]

Marx has two implications here. First, it means the capitalist society is by far the most advanced and miscellaneous society that we have ever seen, and from the understanding of whose modern productive organization and social structure, we can more easily perceive the under-developed social and productive organization that disappear in the past. It is a theoretical commending height. For the same reason, Baudrillard cites another remark from Marx, "It requires a fully developed production of commodities before, from accumulated experience alone, the scientific conviction springs up."[13] Marx believes that modern capitalist mode of production is built on the ruins of the old social existence, thus inevitably bearing the relics of the past and also the signs of the future social development. It reflects the view of social history as a diachronic, correlative, and progressive course, as well as demonstrates the historical epistemology confirmed by Marx. That is, to research the advanced, the varied social structure of modern time is of help for us to understand the lower social structure that is abrogated or absorbed by itself. This view certainly belongs to the scientific systematic epistemology and historical epistemology.

---

12   Karl Marx and Frederick Engels. *Collected Works*, vol. 28. London: Lawrence & Wishart, 1986, p. 42.
13   Karl Marx, *Capital*, vol. 1. London: Lawrence & Wishart, 1977, p. 79.

In fact, Baudrillard's quotation corresponds to two other statements in which Marx has a discussion about the continuous historical development of social structure. Marx immediately follows the above words with the statement that "what is called historical development rests, in general, on the fact that the latest form regards earlier ones as stages leading towards itself."[14] (Baudrillard refers to the same words in his later discussion.) In the chapter "on capital" of the same script, Marx puts forward a more specific view that the mode of production in any social existence does not develop from nothing. The historical development of society is a continual process of totalization, in which the new structure develops on the ground of the previous social condition and primary structures. In this respect, Marx offers an opinion about the organic movement of society.

> *This organic system itself has its premises as a totality, and its development into a totality consists precisely in subordinating all elements of society to itself, or in creating out of it the organs it still lacks. This is historically how it becomes a totality. Its becoming this totality constitutes a moment of its process, of its development.*[15]

This is a comprehensive view of the diachronic and organic development of social structure. For Marx, knowledge and perception of the advanced types of social organism undoubtedly facilitate the understanding of the earlier primary social forms.

The second implication of the famous statement is its figurative sense, that is, the anatomy of man who exists as the highest life form, will help us to understand the physiology of the lower animals. (Of course, here Marx presupposes Darwinian biological evolution that man evolves from "ape.") Marx intends to explain that it is the same with the understanding of human social history: The modern capitalist mode of production is like man whose anatomy is a key to observe the "ape," the early existent social structures. It is a very accurate metaphor. In my opinion, we cannot deny this major Marxist epistemological assertion even though Darwinian evolution theory seems not that scientific today.

---

14   Karl Marx and Frederick Engels. *Collected Works*, vol. 28. London: Lawrence & Wishart, 1986, p. 42.
15   *Ibid.*, p. 208.

But, Baudrillard does not think so. He does not accept Marx's degrading comparison of his beloved primitive social existence to the life of "ape." (Baudrillard says, "Althusser also notices this metaphor, but he replaces it with the structuralist ideology after eliminating the residue of Marxist natural evolution".) For Baudrillard, it is an incorrect association: Biological anatomy is radically different from the social life; thus schemata of two different fields do not match; this linkage amounts to saying that "the adult can comprehend the child only in terms of the adult."[16] Can an adult really understand the world of the child? Baudrillard's answer is no. He says, in any case, in the presupposition of this continuity [Marx's metaphor] there is a (positivist) alignment of numerous analytic approaches together with those of the so-called exact sciences, which does not fit for his symbolic existence and special meanings of man. Baudrillard believes that Marx is totally blind to the important "ruptures" between different social forms. His remark is alarming: This rupture concept of him is "far more profound than the one Althusser detects."[17] Oh, yes, we are already familiar with Baudrillard's profoundness.

It is known that under the influence of Gaston Bachelard's "epistemological break", Althusser introduces it (coupure) to his research on Marxism's thought history. Then, Baudrillard can stealthily appropriate this very result of the broken history of thought, the "ideological" and "scientific" paradigms from the Marxism of Althusser. (Baudrillard only makes a simple conversion as "ideology" and "analysis.")

In fact, what Baudrillard wants to say is that in the common sense of social progress, not all different social forms and lives are classified by higher or lower, simple or complex relations, especially, the social existence of primitive symbolic exchange and gift circulation, which is not a lower social life at all but the right objective for human existence worthy of man's rethinking and effort to realize. In this regard, how can it be referred to as "ape"? Baudrillard cannot bear it. "Let us say in passing that the metaphor of the ape is worthless—certainly the ape's anatomical structure cannot be illuminated

---

16   Baudrillard, Jean. *The Mirror of Production*. Trans. Mark Poster. St. Louis: Telos Press, 1975, p. 86.
17   *Ibid.*, p. 86.

starting from the "contradictions" of human anatomy." It explains why the rupture of him is "more profound" than that of Althusser.[18]

Baudrillard then questions whether the capitalist economy ret-rospectively illuminates medieval, ancient, and primitive societies. Obviously, his reply is negative because in the primitive life, "the magical, the religious, and the symbolic are relegated to the margins of the economy. And even when the symbolic formations expressly aim, as in primitive exchange, to prevent the emergence with the rise of economic structures of a transcendent social power that would escape the group's control, things are arranged nonetheless so as to see a determination by the economic in the last instance."[19]

Baudrillard's explanation here seems to criticize Marx's simpli-fied careless extension of the capitalist economic materialization to all the previous social existence, which is but a misunderstanding of historical materialism. What Marx insists through this historical epis-temology is the common principle of the general historical material-ism, that is, the production and reproduction of the material means of life is the foundation for the entire social existence and develop-ment; besides that, man's social existence defines man's conception. In no way does Marx attempt to inflict the specific social mode and special thinking within a certain period on other social historical pe-riods and forms. Baudrillard's problem is made by himself. He first equates the labour and material production of all human societies to the capitalist production and economic mode, and then demonizes Marxist historical materialism into a simple historical formula. In his writing, Marx becomes a crazy man labelling everything with the capitalist ideology. But who is on earth the ridiculous one?

On the other side, Marx does not neglect the fact that the ancient social life is not that utilitarian or so "alienated" when compared with the contemporary capitalist social life. Thus Marx argues: "In this way, the old view according to which the man always appears in however narrowly national, religious or political a determination as the end of production, seems very exalted when set against the mod-ern world, in which production is the end of man, and wealth the end

---

18 *Ibid.*, p. 86.
19 *Ibid.*, p. 87.

of production."[20] However, the wonderful past has inevitably gone; history cannot go back; and we cannot return to the ancient "exaltation." In the eyes of Marx, the beautiful social historical life of man is not a return to the distant past but the actual forwardness and emancipation. He says, "The absolute unfolding of man's creative abilities, without any precondition other than the preceding historical development, which makes this totality of this development— i.e. the development of all human powers as such, not measured by any *previously given yardstick—an end-in-itself,* through which he does not reproduce in any specific character, but produces his totality, and does not seek to remain something he has already become, but is in the absolute movement of becoming?"[21] In addition, shall we return to the primitive living condition?

4 HISTORICAL MATERIALISM AND WEST-CENTRISM

In Baudrillard's view, Marxist historical materialism is deeply trapped in the framework of the capitalist political economy. In the kingdom of capital, the productive force is a crucial element. As a result, Marx makes the hypothesis that the productive forces exist in any societies. This time, Baudrillard assaults another key concept of historical materialism.

The productive force in the philosophical discourse of Marxist general historical materialism is a concept used to gauge the development level of material production in a certain social historical period. Marx says in *The Communist Manifesto* that capitalism creates a huge productive force like invoking a daemon, the speed of which even far surpasses that of the previous centuries put together. However, it does not mean the productive forces only exist in capitalist society. In fact, if there is social material production, there is men's collective power to transform nature. Even in primitive societies where material production does not dominate, it still sustains the life as actual material basis; otherwise, the "hau" much admired by Baudrillard with his teachers would not happen without those gifts to be exchanged or consumed. No matter how the primitive people degrade utility, they would not survive on symbolic exchanges or

20   Karl Marx and Frederick Engels. *Collected Works*, vol. 28. London: Lawrence & Wishart, 1986, p. 411.
21   *Ibid.*, pp. 411-412.

witchcrafts. Baudrillard's paranoid negation of the role of material production and productive forces in social existence has even deviated from the common knowledge.

Here, Baudrillard is mainly dissatisfied with what he believes the Marxist forceful extension of the bourgeois social economic categories to other societies. He cites the paragraph next to the metaphor of man and ape in the *1857-1857 Manuscripts*, in which Marx says it is understandable in certain sense to utilize the capitalist economic categories for the comprehension of other social forms. It is obviously an ad hoc stipulation of him. The "certain sense" means, as the most advanced social form so far, the contemporary capitalist social structure can carry out self-examination to observe the social forms sublated by itself. This self-critical analysis will begin a scientific perception of history. Marx says,

> *The Christian religion was able to contribute to an objective understanding of earlier mythologies. Similarly, it was not until the self-criticism of bourgeois society had begun that bourgeois [political] economy came to understand the feudal, ancient and oriental economies.*[22]

This last sentence undoubtedly irritates Baudrillard, who could not tolerate the "Western Centrism" in this statement. To Baudrillard, it is true that Western culture firstly begins a self-critical approach but the premise is exactly based on the interpretation of itself as a universal culture while all Other cultures are arrogantly put into museum for the exhibition of relics imagined by Western culture. It should be admitted that Baudrillard's analysis represents a correct self-reflection, which also goes in line with later post-colonialism and Orientalism's logic. Baudrillard says,

> *It [Western culture] "aestheticized" them [other cultures], reinterpreted them on its own model, and thus precluded the radical interrogation these "different" cultures implied for it. The limits of this culture "critique" are clear: its reflection on itself leads only to the universalization of its own principles. Its own contradictions lead it, as in the previous case, to the world-wide economic and political imperialism of all modern capitalist and socialist Western societies.*[23]

---

22   *Ibid.*, p. 43.
23   Baudrillard, Jean. *The Mirror of Production*. Trans. Mark Poster. St. Louis: Telos Press, 1975, p. 89.

The self-criticism is very perceptive. In fact, after a serious reading of the Russian commune and the ancient oriental societies in the final stage of his theoretical researches, Marx is aware that his own *special historical materialism* only applies for the Western Europe; in addition, he admits the unique form "Asian mode of production," from which we can know that Marx never has the idea of imposing the interpretative mode of Western culture on other cultures. Otherwise, Marx would not hold the view that Russia is possible to by-pass the Caudine Forks in its choice of revolutionary ways.

Baudrillard's background theory is completely correct in this issue, but his censure of Marxist historical materialism is still an improper parallel. To him, Marx illegitimately applies the schema of political economy to the primitive societies where there is no material production or economic structure at all. In my opinion, Baudrillard always confuses issues with radical differences. Marx never intends to treat the modern production schema as the basic structure of primitive societies. He only says *in a certain sense* our perception and knowledge of the capitalist social structure helps clarify the existential conditions of the ancient society from which today's society originates. For us, this knowledge can also be the reference for the Oriental societies different from the West. Is all this worth the labelling of "Western Centrism"?

Baudrillard is arbitrary when he says, "The impossibility for historical materialism of going beyond political economy toward the past as evidenced by its incapacity to decipher primitive societies, applies as well for the future by the same logic. It appears more and more impotent, thus incapable of outlining a revolutionary perspective truly beyond political economy. It flounders "dialectically" in the impasses of capital, just as it flounders in the miscomprehension of the symbolic."[24] Baudrillard's worry is unwarranted. Historical materialism will not flounder because this scientific methodology never has the ambition to anchor any specific scientific mode, to directly decipher the code of primitive societies, or to replace anthropology, let alone a straight, concrete description of the future society. It is no more than a research "guide" for us to know the world and the history of ourselves. Baudrillard thinks that he knows Marxism, he understands historical materialism but in fact, he is always a layman with his messy understanding of historical materialism.

---

24   See Note 74 of *The Mirror of Production*.

CHAPTER XIII

RIDDLE OF MONKEY ANATOMY AND
APE ANALYSIS

Baudrillard makes an extensive criticism of the basic concepts of Marxist historical materialism, in particular, the negation of the famous metaphor that the anatomy of man is a key to the anatomy of ape. In order to verify the judgment, Baudrillard abruptly shifts to the analysis of the "archaic and feudal mode" prior to the capitalist mode of production, from which he chooses two typical issues for discussion: the slave-master relationship and the labour of the artisan. Following Baudrillard's opposition against the study of the past from a modern standpoint, we see a fantastic scene: Baudrillard is interpreting the archaic and feudal life with the symbolic relation in primitive life! If in line with Marx's metaphor, the experience of monkey anatomy further mystifies the riddle of ape survival.

1 NEW DIALECTICAL INTERPRETATION OF THE MASTER AND THE SLAVE

The previous section discusses Baudrillard's teaching that we should get rid of West-centralism, the Western complex of enslaving Other cultures because another post-colonialist trend of thought arises when we illuminate the past with the contemporary capitalist ideology, which, of course, is a conceptual colonization for the Westerners to reflect on their past, not for the culture of Other. This opinion seems persuasive. Baudrillard adds, although its most "scientific" inclinations toward earlier societies,[1] post-colonialist trend "naturalizes" them under the sign of the mode of production. Here again their anthropological relegation to a museum, a process originated in bourgeois society, continues under the sign of its critique.[2] Then, how can we avoid such a silly mistake of cultural imperialism? Baudrillard goes out of his way to offer Marxists a satisfactory model. He first analyzes Marx's archaic society and selects the popular example of the dialectic of master and slave after Hegel's *Phenomenology of Mind.*

---

1   The most advanced bourgeois thought also exports its models (its viruses) under the cover of the most "objective" critical epistemology. For if the final aim of anthropology is to contribute to a better knowledge of objectified thought and its mechanisms, it is in the last resort immaterial whether in this book the thought processes of the South American Indians take place through the medium of theirs. What matters is that the human mind, regardless of the identity of those who happen to be giving it expression, should display an increasingly intelligible structure as a result of the double reflexive forward movement of two thought processes acting one upon the other, either of which can in turn provide the spark or tinder whose conjunction will shed light on both. And should this light happen to reveal a treasure, there will be no need of an arbitrator to parcel it out, since, as I declared at the outset, the heritage is untransferable and cannot be split up" (Lévi-Strauss, *The Raw and the Cooked*, trans. J. and D. Weightman [New York: Harper and Row, 1969], pp. 13-14). This is the extreme of liberal thought and the most beautiful way of preserving the initiative and priority of Western thought within "dialogue" and under the sign of the universality of the human mind (as always for Enlightenment anthropology). Here is the beautiful soul! Is it possible to be more impartial in the sensitive and intellectual knowledge of the other? This harmonious vision of two thought processes renders their *confrontation* perfectly inoffensive, by denying the difference of the primitives as an element of rupture with and subversion of (our) "objectified" thought and its mechanisms. Quoted from the note by Baudrillard.
2   Baudrillard, Jean. *The Mirror of Production.* Trans. Mark Poster. St. Louis: Telos Press, 1975, p. 91.

Baudrillard believes that Marx's analysis of slavery stems from the status of wage labour in political economy, especially, the analysis of labour. For Baudrillard, Marx's worker does not sell but remise his labour or product. (To be more precise, what the worker sells is the right to use the labour force.) In comparison, the slave sells neither labour nor product nor the labour force. Therefore, the issue of slavery lies in the master's ownership of the slave's labour power. In Baudrillard's eyes, Marx is wrong because there is no separated labour and labour power for the slave. That the nature of slavery is alienation-exploitation just derives from Marx's the very economic assumption:

> We are faced again with a presumption of the economic through the grid labour-labour power. The symbolic relation master-slave is conceived as a kind of husk whose "real" kernel will be extracted in the thread of history (in fact, in the thread of the theoretical model that will impose this principle of reality). What is lost in this process is everything that is exchanged in the master-slave relation and everything not reducible to the alienation-exploitation of a labour power.[3]

Baudrillard seems very pleased because he teaches Marx a lesson who does not understand *the symbolic relation is the nature of all societies*. However, his rejoice comes too early.

First, Marx never employs the concept of labour that only exists in the capitalist mode of production to investigate slavery or other social forms prior to capitalism. What Marx does is to study certain social existence and movement preconditioned by given modes of production, in particular, the production relation under specific historical conditions. Marx says, "In real history, wage labour arises from the disintegration of slavery and serfdom—or from the decay of communal property as seen among the Oriental and Slav peoples."[4] We can see that he does not take the free labourer who detaches from the means of production and possesses his independent labour power as the pre-capitalist schema of labour relations, instead the labour forms are always branded with their peculiar features. Furthermore, Marx clearly states that in slavery production

---

3   *Ibid.*, p. 94.
4   Karl Marx and Frederick Engels. *Collected Works*, vol. 28. London: Lawrence & Wishart, 1986, p. 13.

"the slave does not come into consideration at all as *an exchanger*"5 because everything of him, including his own existence, is kept by the master. The slave is impossible to freely exchange or sell his labour power. In this attachment relationship, there is no separated labour power. "The slave stands in no relation whatsoever to the objective conditions of his labour; rather, *labour* itself." His labour is juxtaposed with the live-stock tools or "as an appendage of the soil."6 How can Baudrillard think that Marx trades off the economic presumption of labour power against the kernel of slavery? Or is Baudrillard talking too freely?

However, he still feels his accusation is not enough. So, he puts on a long face and teaches us: There is not "a relation of reciprocity" between the master and the slave, that is, the value relationship defined in the individualistic and altruistic context does not exist; the slave and the master attachment is "in the sense of an *obligation*." What obligation, then? Baudrillard does not offer a clear explanation but stresses that "in the original relation, the slave, or rather the relation master-slave, is unalienable in the sense that neither the master nor the slave are alienated from each other, nor is the slave alienated from himself as is the free worker in the private disposition of his labour power."7 For that reason, Baudrillard again loses his temper. He thinks that Marx indiscriminately "projects" the "the illusion of Western humanist rationality" only found in capitalist society (the abstract and alienated social relations) "on earlier forms of domination, explaining the differences as some historical underdevelopment, is to miscomprehend all that the earlier formations can teach us about the symbolic operation of social relations."8

We are tired of this groundless allegation. Baudrillard repeats the same mistake in the same text, which forces me do the same worthless repetition. I already mentioned that Marx abandons the humanistic discourse after 1845. Nor does he use the value-hypothetic *logic of alienation* to measure any historical reality, even the capitalist economic relations, not to say the social relations in slavery.

---

5   *Ibid.*, p. 345.
6   *Ibid.*, p. 413.
7   Baudrillard, Jean. *The Mirror of Production*. Trans. Mark Poster. St. Louis: Telos Press, 1975, p. 95.
8   *Ibid.*, p. 96.

Besides, when Marx talks about the slavery and serfdom in past Western societies, he marks with a particular note that "this does *not* apply e.g. to the general slavery of the Orient, [or dose] *only* from the European POINT OF VIEW."[9] Unexpectedly, Baudrillard even stipulates the brutal slavery control as some symbolic operation of the relations of responsibility. If this opinion is confirmed in Mauss-Bataille discourse and the slavery turns out to be the symbolic exchange relation favoured by Baudrillard, then he is to blame for all this. (Interestingly, I doubt whether Mauss would agree with this theoretical transgression.)

2 DIFFERENCE BETWEEN THE ARTISAN'S WORK AND THE USEFUL LABOUR

Baudrillard tries to be unconventional with such a grand narration as "the Archaic and Feudal Mode," but he only discusses a far-off slave and master relation and deals with the alleged "feudal mode" embodying the artisan's work. Is it Baudrillard's abstraction? Or, if we do him a favour, can it be interpreted as having two different modes of production? According to Baudrillard's own logic, any conception of production and labour in pre-capitalist times is illegitimate, and then what is the thing that the slave does but which cannot be called as labour? Baudrillard does not offer a new paradigm and we are not able to find the answer. However, he strains after novelty by telling that the artisan's *work* differs from labour. Moreover, he profoundly points out that work has the meaning of "demiurge" according to its etymology.

Baudrillard says it is not correct to regard the artisan as the owner of his labour or product because it is still coding the artisan with the logic of production. (Obviously, he indicates productivist Marxism.) The artisan's work differs from labour, because there is no such separation as labour power and product or subject and object; artisan only views his own work as the symbolic relationship. To me, the symbolic relation seems to be Baudrillard's magic bullet. It is not only the secret of slavery but also the true meaning for the artisan to live.

---

9   Karl Marx and Frederick Engels. *Collected Works*, vol. 28. London: Lawrence & Wishart, 1986, p. 419.

342   A MARXIST READING OF YOUNG BAUDRILLARD

Something in the material that he works is a continuous response to that which he does, escaping all productive finality (which purely and simply transforms materials into use value or exchange value). There is something that eludes the law of value and bears witness to a kind of reciprocal prodigality. In his work, what he bestows is lost and given and rendered, expended and resolved and abolished, but not "invested." [10]

Baudrillard explains that it is in the same way as we use language where there is no utilitarian purpose but an immediate reciprocity of exchange *through language* where there are both no producers and consumers. "In the primitive exchange gift, the status of goods that circulate is close to language. The goods are neither produced nor consumed as values. Their function is the continuous articulation of the exchange." [11] The primitive exchange of gifts retains "the personal quality of the exchange." [12] (It is completely nonsense. In the potlatch and the "kula," woman is given as the gift. She is clearly not an equal exchanger, not even a human being. Baudrillard's equality only refers to the chiefs or the clan rulers. It is the social nature beyond the knowledge of Mauss, Bataille, Baudrillard and other idealist thinkers.) Although the artisan's quid pro quos has clear purpose and value, he and his product are not separated.

Baudrillard takes the work of art as an illustration of this unique artisan/work relationship. In his eyes, the work of artisan resembles the creation of artists instead of labour.

Artisanal work (according to etymology, "demiurge"), which draws a radical difference between work and labour. **Work is a process of destruction as well as of "production,"** *and in this way work is symbolic. Death, loss and absence are inscribed in it through this dispossession of the subject, this loss of the subject and the object in the scansion of the exchange.* [13]

For Baudrillard, if we examine the artisan from the perspective of historical materialism or define the work with the paradigm of production and labour, we shall see no truth. He cries: "The work of art and to a certain extent the artisanal work bear in them the inscription

10   Baudrillard, Jean. *The Mirror of Production.* Trans. Mark Poster. St. Louis: Telos Press, 1975, p. 99.
11   *Ibid.*, p. 98.
12   *Ibid.*, p. 98.
13   *Ibid.*, p. 99.

of the loss of the finality of the subject and the object, the radical compatibility of life and death, the play of an ambivalence that the product of labour as such does not bear since it has inscribed in it only the finality of value."[14]

It is true that Marx says the artisan's labour is "half-artistic" but he mainly refers to the "particular skill" in the artisan's labour.[15] But, Baudrillard really confuses us, when he says: The artisan's work is neither labour nor production and this work is without the finality of purpose after binary separation."Like the functional consumption and destruction of artworks, it symbolizes the ambivalence of life and death play".

Judging from any aspect, this statement is almost incomprehensible. I think Baudrillard should make a concrete description of the artisan's work, e.g. a shoemaker, in what sense is his shoe making process a kind of destruction? What specific destruction is it? Why do not the pair of shoes have the function of utility? Why do the shoes sign the mystical life and death? Most of all, how does a shoemaker survive if his "work" only produces a useless, defective pair of shoes?

I just wonder why Baudrillard writes such incredibly ridiculous things in a serious academic work. Two radically different matters are bound together. It is common knowledge that the nature of artistic creation is of no utilitarian value. For the artist, the work of art materializes his will of life; for the audience, it is to experience another existential being. Personally, I like Itzhak Perlman very much. When listening to his violin, I do not notice his physical existence but feel a surging passion of life in that beautiful melody. In contrast, the shoe artisan works not for creation but survival. Marx takes the patriarchal production of agricultural artisanship as an example, in which "the great majority of the population satisfies most of its needs directly by its labour, the sphere of circulation and exchange is very narrow."[16] Production is not primarily for exchange. "Here labour itself is still half the expression of artistic creation, and half

14   *Ibid.*, p. 99.
15   Karl Marx and Frederick Engels. *Collected Works*, vol. 28. London: Lawrence & Wishart, 1986, p. 507.
16   *Ibid.*, p. 345.

an end-in-itself, etc."[17] The example of craftsmanship does not have this above separation when we later enter in the capitalist mode of production, but only in the artisan's work, "labour still belongs to the labourer; with a certain self-sufficient development of limited specialised capacities, etc."[18] Although the artisan is possible to present his own creation in the product, it does not mean he can shake off the existential purpose for survival. In addition, most of the artisans cannot reach up to a decent artistic level. "Clay Figurer Zhang" and "Scissor Zhang Xiaoquan" (two renowned ancient Chinese artisans) are only the very few who rise to fame with their high artisanal skills.

In my opinion, Baudrillard's pseudo-romanticism teems with grand, magnificent but empty talks, without much serious academic research. Here is another example form him: "Praxis, a noble activity, is always one of use, as distinct from poesis which designates fabrication. Only the former, which plays and acts, but does not produce, is noble."[19] Whereas someone as Baudrillard considers only the praxis that "does not produce" as "noble," they cannot ignore the fact that it is the common people who are engaged in those mediocre but useful productive activities, for instance, the production of Baudrillard's high-class camera or operational computer, that provide the opportunity for him to do such noble activities like photography or academic researches.

3 THE LOGICAL ANATOMIES OF MAN, MONKEY AND APE

Baudrillard says, "All these facts converge toward one point: the inadequacy of the concepts of labour, production, productive force, and relations of production in accounting for, let us say, pre-industrial organization (the same holds also for feudal or traditional organization)."[20] Yes, even though Baudrillard does not mention Marx's name and quote from the Marxist texts as before, we are still able to understand what Baudrillard wants to object behind the lines. The concluding section titled "Marxism and Miscomprehension" of this chapter reveals his intention to escalate the criticism of Marxism.

17   *Ibid.*, p. 421.
18   *Ibid.*, p. 421.
19   Baudrillard, Jean. *The Mirror of Production*. Trans. Mark Poster. St. Louis: Telos Press, 1975, p. 101.
20   *Ibid.*, p. 101.

He first makes a critical summary of Marxism, in particular, historical materialism.

The idea that in all societies the relations of production, and consequently, politics, law, religion, etc., presuppose that in all societies the same articulation of human activities exists, that technology, law, politics, and religion are always necessarily separated and separable; it is to extrapolate to the totality of history the structuration of our own society, which is inevitably meaningless outside of it.[21]

In my understanding, this summary has a very specific purpose. It targets the introduction of *Critique of Political Economy* written by Marx in 1858, which is seen as a classic representation of historical materialism. In that famous explanation of his research methodology, Marx does not add any historical limitation to the property relation and the corresponding economic base, legal superstructure, etc., all of which cannot be found in primitive societies. For Baudrillard, there are at least two logical transgressions here: One is the diachronic imposition of what do not exist in pre-capitalist Western societies, on their social lives; the other is the synchronical imposition of what the West has on those non-Western societies (Baudrillard's "ethno-centralism"). For a clear explanation, let us first read the complete paragraph from Marx.

In the social production of their existence, men inevitably enter into definite relations, which are independent of their will, namely relations of production appropriate to a given stage in the development of their material forces of production. The totality of these relations of production constitutes the economic structure of society, the real foundation, on which arises a legal and political superstructure and to which correspond definite forms of social consciousness. The mode of production of material life conditions the general process of social, political and intellectual life. It is not the consciousness of men that determines their existence, but their social existence that determines their consciousness. At a certain stage of development, the material productive forces of society come into conflict with the existing relations of production or—this merely expresses the same thing in legal terms—with the property relations within the framework of which they have operated hitherto. From forms of development of the productive forces these relations turn into their

---

21   *Ibid.*, p. 106.

fetters. Then begins an era of social revolution. The changes in
the economic foundation lead sooner or later to the transforma-
tion of the whole immense superstructure.[22]

Marx's description here is not the general historical materialism
that is applicable to all the history. He is explaining the method to
study the capitalist mode of expression, which mainly belongs to
the special historical materialism, namely the concrete exemplification of *economic social forms* of general historical materialism. For
instance, social existence determines ideology; certain productive
forces inevitably generate corresponding relations of production; it
is a general law for all the human history that the development of
productive forces are the fundamental drive for social revolution;
the material mode of production conditions all the social and spiritual life; the economic base (infrastructure) and political/legal superstructure are closely related. None of these are found in primitive
societies. They are only applicable for later development of social
history. Secondly, when Marx studied the oriental societies in his
late years, he made it clear that his special historical materialism
only applies in the social development road of Western Europe.[23]
In traditional explanations of the Marxist textbooks, Marx's above
statement is wrongly interpreted as the common view of historical
materialism without any necessary ad hoc limitations. In this sense,
Baudrillard's criticism is not totally incorrect. However, Marx should
not to be responsible for this mistake. Differed from Baudrillard's
simplicity and harshness, Sahlins observes and criticizes the problem of understanding of this statement in a general context, and even
detects that the conventional "Marxism has ignored Marx," which
also means the negligence of the specific research of oriental societies done by Marx himself.[24]

Baudrillard is quite tenacious in chasing Marx. He states that
when dealing with the primitive societies, Marxism "works *in the
imaginary* like the man who, having lost his key in a dark alley,

---

22   Karl Marx and Frederick Engels. *Collected Works*, vol. 29. London: Lawrence &
Wishart, 1987, p. 263.
23   Karl Marx and Frederick Engels. *Collected Works*, vol. 24. London: Lawrence &
Wishart, 1989, p. 346.
24   Sahlins, Marshall D. *Culture and Practical Reason*. Joint Publishing Company
Limited (Beijing), 2002.

looks for it in a lighted area because, he says, that it is the only place where he could find it. Thus, historical materialism does not know how to grasp earlier societies in their symbolic articulation. It only finds in them what it could find under its own light, that is, its artificial mode of production."[25] Then, what is the key in the "dark alley"? Baudrillard's answer is the relation of exchange set up by the symbolic order. Baudrillard tells us:

> *The symbolic sets up a relation of exchange in which the respective positions cannot be autonomized:*
> *– neither the producer and his product;*
> *– nor the producer and the user;*
> *– nor the producer and his "concrete" essence, his labour power;*
> *– nor the user and his "concrete" essence, his needs;*
> *– nor the product and its "concrete" finality, its utility.*[26]

As we know, it is a negative delineation of Mauss-Bataille logic, in striking contrast against the capitalist structure of value exchange. According to Baudrillard, Marxist historical materialism cannot make a correct explanation of them because "the repression of the symbolic nourishes all the rationalist political illusions, all the *dreams of political voluntarism*, that are born in the terrain of historical materialism,"[27] and because Marxism is ignorant of that symbolic exchange. It cannot account for the primitive societies at all. Historical materialism has the critique of the capitalist economy and its relations of production as its object and primitive societies, kinship, language and the symbolic, are not its province. In other words, historical materialism only applies to the capitalist society but fails to explain the primitive society, in particular, the dominant kinship and symbolic exchange in it. When Marx extends the mode of historical materialism to the pre-capitalist social existence, he does the same thing which he is against, thus, becomes an accomplice to eternalize the capitalism. In this regard, historical materialism can explain neither the nature of primitive societies nor the radicality of separation in our societies, and therefore the radicality of subversion.

25 Baudrillard, Jean. *The Mirror of Production.* Trans. Mark Poster. St. Louis: Telos Press, 1975, p. 107.
26 *Ibid.*, p. 103.
27 *Ibid.*, p. 108.

Baudrillard must have a happy catharsis through the criticism. In his eyes, Marxist historical materialism is simply stupid while his symbolic exchange mode—a conclusion from primitive social existence—is universal. A common reader may feel strange. First, as I have mentioned several times, Baudrillard's distortion of Marxist historical materialism leads to errant conclusions. What Marx underscores is always the concrete, historical, actual analysis of any historical phenomenon. He would never make such a simple mistake of using a concrete social mode to explicate other societies. When Marx says it is helpful to perceive the social life in previous primary social forms by the anatomy of the Western capitalist society that is the most advanced social development so far we have seen, he just means what he says, nothing more. Marx does not have the ambition to promote the capitalist mode of existence to previous historical periods of Western society or other non-Western social existence. In dealing with the pre-capitalist social history, he uses no capitalist mode of production to simply schematize it. Instead, Marx insists on the historical, concrete and realistic investigation by the help of the general historical materialism, getting support from its such important common principal as that material production is the foundation for any social existence in history, but he never seeks the logic of capital in a non-capitalist social existence. Obvious as the point is, Baudrillard chooses to turn a blind eye once again, which is hard to explain.

Baudrillard is against the metaphor of ape anatomy, but his own thought in turn reveals a deeper logical intention: in his textual context of opposing Marx's idea to use anatomy of man in the analysis of the ape, his own analytic logic is nothing else but *the secret use of monkey anatomy to schematize the ape*. Why should the logic of primitive symbolic exchange (monkey) be the secret of archaic and feudal social existence (ape)? Isn't it an attempt to eternalize the logic of primitive social existence? Baudrillard's boomerang strikes himself this time.

CHAPTER XIV

HISTORICAL MATERIALISM AND EUCLIDEAN GEOMETRY OF HISTORY

Titled "Marxist and the System of Political Economy," the last chapter is a conclusive summary of Baudrillard's critique of Marxism. He questions historical materialism as a whole, criticizes Marxist theories of class and revolution, and most of all, denies the political economy on which historical materialism is built. Let us first analyze his ironical statement, "Euclidean geometry in history" that is targeted on historical materialism. After it, we shall deal with other charges of Marxism one by one.

1 LEGITIMACY OF ARTICULATING THE ARCHAIC HISTORY WITH A CONTEMPORARY DISCOURSE

According to Baudrillard, historical materialism is generated from capitalism. Its generation process is filled with class struggles of the modern mode of production. Therefore, theory and praxis, the dialectic of the productive forces and the relation of production, the law of contradiction, the homogeneity of space—all the kernel concepts of historical materialism are organized with the ideal capitalist mode of production. For Marx, the capitalist mode of production is regarded as the highest point of historical development, which of course possesses the "absolute advantage" (man for anatomy) can perceive all the previous historical social forms. (Baudrillard bears particular dislike towards Marx's metaphor that "the anatomy of man is a key to the anatomy of ape.") No wonder Baudrillard says, "In earlier formations, men blindly produced their social relations at the same time as their material wealth. The capitalist mode is the moment when they become conscious of this double and simultaneous production, when they aim to take it under rational control. This concept would appear only in the final stages of capitalism and in its critique, illuminating in one stroke the entire earlier process."[1] In my opinion, Baudrillard is generally correct in saying so. Most of the scientific concepts of historical materialism only fit under the historical condition of modern production, which is defined by the contemporary capitalist mode of production in Europe.

Behind these Marxist concepts, Baudrillard continues, there are two theoretical presumptions:

> – *A process of historical development is already there in all earlier societies (a mode of production, contradictions, a dialectic) but they do not produce a concept of it and hence do not transcend it.*

> – *The moment of becoming conscious of the process (the production of the critical concept connected to the conditions of the capitalist formation) is also the decisive stage of its revolution.*[2]

---

1   *Ibid.*, p. 112.
2   *Ibid.*, p. 112.

First, the contradiction movement and dialectic law of the mode of production already exist in early human societies, only people do not have these concepts then; second, the criticism of capitalism by Marxist historical materialism is also the crucial phase for the real, self-conscious emancipation of man. In this regard, Baudrillard's above statement is generally acceptable. However, something is wrong with his following words.

Baudrillard says historical materialism describes the general laws of society, which is indeed "perfectly Hegelian." Like the risk of absolute idea, human social history happens in a finalistic way, develops and reaches the summit in the realm of freedom, as in communism. But Baudrillard believes the early period humans know not what the purpose of history is and "they lived neither historically nor within the mode of production."[3] Only we consider ourselves standing at the historical high point and looking down at previous ones, hence retrospectively, treating the present society "as the principle of explication of earlier formations."[4] Consequently, we schematize the primitive life with the conceptions and thoughts they do not understand, which is no doubt a theoretical violence. Baudrillard jauntily declares from his standpoint of the modern discourse, "As if by chance, the *reality* of the mode of production enters the scene at the moment when someone is discovered who invents the *theory* of it."[5] He means only through the conception of the mode of production can people construct the actual existence of the mode of production. It is not simplistic idealism; it is a conceptual imperialism in which concepts rapes reality.

Baudrillard is really considerate for the primitive peoples, but his opinion is a fallacy. For example, the existence of animals and plants is different from man and they do not have the consciousness of their own existence, least to mention the conception of knowledge, and then, if we borrow Baudrillard's logic, is it impossible for human beings to understand their existence via science and technology? Does Baudrillard mean only through the languages or information code of the animals, bird, bugs, flowers, grass, trees themselves can people

---

3   *Ibid.*, p. 112.
4   *Ibid.*, p. 114.
5   *Ibid.*, p. 113.

non-violently understand them? As a matter of fact, it is like an adult who can know more about the childhood significance than a kid can. Similarly, people in the advanced level of social development, equipped with the experience, knowledge, and wisdom accumulated through generations for thousands of years, are sure to better observe the nature of social history and movement than their predecessors do. For this reason, Marx says standing at the high point of the capitalist industrial development, with our scientific knowledge of the outer nature, with the being-for-itself of the humanized material system brought by the industrial praxis, with the unprecedented complexity and full expansion of the economic social structure, we can better understand the present, know our past, and vision the future. Marx has nothing wrong.

It would be sensible if Baudrillard expressed in this way: First, the primitive peoples are not self-conscious of the historical development since time is always visualized in the circle of sunrise and sunset, four seasons in the husbandry and agriculture of the natural economy. However, it does not mean history stops in progress. Or else, Baudrillard was still a primitive man who could not have had philosophical thoughts or have taken up his beloved photography. It cannot be a change of abracadabra. Second, the primitive people do live with a mode of production but not with a modern mode of production like capitalism. So long as man exists, he must product and live in a certain mode even if material production has not been dominant in their life; he cannot do without production and reproduction. The conception of the mode of production does not mean capitalism although it is abstracted from the perception of the capitalist social structure. Meanwhile, it can be used to describe the previous social existence. Here, I have a question. Does the primitive society have what Mauss and Baudrillard call the symbolic conception? Or more precisely, Baudrillard's anthropological symbolic concept is proposed by the French structural linguist Lévi-Strauss in the middle 20th century. We can see, it is not only a product of capitalism, but also the product of an advanced capitalism. Then, what about Baudrillard's "symbolic exchange"? Is not it a rape of primitive society by such a modern concept? Where does the symbolic relation come from in the primitive life? If we still remember Baudrillard's accusation, it amounts to saying "only when people create the *theory* of symbolic exchange can the *reality* of symbolic exchange enter their vision," is that right?

Another point to note is, unlike Hegel's absolute-idea conception of history, Marx finds his teleological and theodicial absolute-idea is only a reversed reflection of the history of human social praxis. When Marx denies Hegelian's idealism, he does not negate the self-purposeful movement of human social history but reveals that in capitalism and its preceding social history there exist the contradiction between the individual will and the collective blindness, as well as a regular resultant purpose of the finality of history. Historical materialism is a methodological self-consciousness of the knowledge of historical laws. It offers a methodological explanation for what Baudrillard cannot see though.

2 DOES HISTORICAL MATERIALISM HAVE THE UNIVERSALITY OF SCIENCE?

Baudrillard makes the firm conclusion: "The materialist theory of history cannot escape from ideology." According to the classic negative ideological theory, the conclusion means historical materialism replaces the actual things with imaginary relations as it always attempts to move through the entire process of history, very similar to "the Euclidean geometry of this history."[6] (Baudrillard is really eloquent with his vivacious analogy.) In this respect, he asks three questions in a row.

> *But what authorizes science in its scorn of magic or alchemy, for example, in this disjunction of a truth to come, of a destiny of objective knowledge, hidden from the infantile miscomprehension of earlier societies? And what authorizes the "science of history" to claim this disjunction of a history to come, of an objective finality that robs earlier societies of the determinations in which they live, of their magic, of their difference, of the meaning that they attribute to themselves, in order to clarify them in the infrastructural truth of the mode of production to which we alone have the key?*[7]

6   *Ibid.*, p. 114.
7   *Ibid.*, p. 114.

Like Mauss-Bataille, Baudrillard regards the witchcraft and magic in the primitive societies as the authentic being of man that has not been poisoned by the system of utilitarian value. He is dissatisfied with the negation and transcendence of ignorance and darkness by modern science. In his eyes, the primitive culture and modern science are not in the same timeline. Should science acquire the absolute authority? Should historical materialism declare itself the only "science of history" after the non-scientific conception of historical rupture, and think of itself the key to solve the mystery of history? No! No! No! Baudrillard says,

> *It is only in the mirror of production and history, under the double principle of indefinite accumulation (production) and dialectical continuity (history), only by the arbitrariness of the **code**, that our Western culture can reflect itself in the universal as the privileged moment of truth (science) or of revolution (historical materialism). Without this simulation, without this gigantic reflexivity of the concave (or convex) concept of history or production, our era loses all privileges. It would not be any closer to any term of knowledge or any social truth than any other.*[8]

The reactionary logic of the mirror of production and the mirror of history! Baudrillard dots the i's and crosses the t's here. He means, we are in this huge reflection mirror of production and history. Through endless material production that accumulates a utilitarian system of exchange value; through historical dialectic that constructs a progressive, teleological human history—a double concave-convex mirror of logic; through the scientific truths that reflect the cognition and historical process as well as historical materialism about social reforms (they are mutually supplementary to each other), the Western culture turns itself into a universal authoritative discourse and basic code. According to Baudrillard, this history is simulated by the mirror of production and the mirror of history. Once we have this huge mirror broken and the source light of science and dialectic put out, the staged imaginary play of history would instantly disappear and the whole Western hegemony of culture would get lost for good. Baudrillard thus say, "This is why it is important to begin with this *ethnological reduction* and to strip our culture."[9]

---

8   *Ibid.*, p. 115.
9   *Ibid.*, p. 115.

In essence, Baudrillard's accusation of historical materialism aims at opposing the schematization of all the history with one discourse of historical philosophy since there is not a universal truth. In this connection, Baudrillard's anti-West-centralism and denial of the absolute discourser of universal philosophy are right. His view represents the important epistemological achievement of natural science and social practice in the 1930s and 1940s. On the other hand, he goes too far in his denial of science, historical materialism and Marxism, which, ironically, just oppose the very universality that he is against. Indeed, Baudrillard's cherished anthropology is itself a scientific discipline. The reason why Mauss and other anthropologists can jump out of the contemporary philosophical discourse and actually reflect the heterogeneous social relations in the primitive tribes is that they have a historical view and the materialist scientific spirit based on reality.

First, since Einstein, modern science has abandoned the metaphysical trace of universality, absoluteness and eternality in classic scientific view while *historicality, relativity and temporality* become the basic attribute of theoretical logic. We gradually come to the discovery that the objective truths treated as universal in the past without exception contain the subjective cognizance of the limited conditions in a certain historical period. At the same time, science more and more has a restricted meaning within a given framework of reference. This is a modern anatomy of Kant's proposition that man legislates universal laws for nature. The metaphysical science framework targeted by Baudrillard has already become a historical vestige left by the modern scientific view that has the same goal to fulfill as he does. Therefore, Baudrillard's sensational nihilistic denial of science makes no sense.

Second, Marxist historical materialism is not that stupidly ridiculous in Baudrillard's description. Excluding the overshadow of conventional interpretation, in particular, Stalinist doctrines since the Second International, the real Marxist historical materialism provides no universal formula or mirror reflection but a methodological guide for people to research and face the historical reality. (Engels gave a special discussion of it in his lifetime.) Marxist historical materialism, in its general sense, only discovers that material production (not limited to the modern capitalist production and economic mode) is the foundation of human social life, including primitive societies where material production does not dominate. As for this point, we Chinese have had too many tragedies, which is the experience not known to Baudrillard who lives in an advanced capitalistic country. When a nation rejects the fundamental material production and substitutes it with some *symbolic relations*, it is to end up in actual crisis of survival. (For example, the huge political symbolic structure during the Chinese Cultural Revolution, when the farmlands were removed of the "capitalist" sprouts; when the social life was fully symbolized, codified by the "proletariat revolution," the whole society was just on the verge of collapse! It is a terrible memory that lingers in many Chinese minds. The same tragedy happened in the Khmer Rouge of Cambodia.) The methodology of historical materialism does not only stress a temporal, linear historical progress; more importantly, it underscores the given context for observation and research, concluded by Lenin as the specific analysis for the specific problem. What it refuses is the abstract universality. In this point, Baudrillard is wrong for what he denies is his own method in disguise.

I have to point out that the mirror of production and the mirror of history targeted by Baudrillard are not only turned against Marxism but the complete modern human culture. It is decided by Mauss-Bataille logic of grassrootism. This ridiculous view is itself a compulsive extension of primitive life, of certain social relations into the whole human history. It denies modern culture. It is a huge *symbolic mirror*. Since Baudrillard is opposed to the restoration of historical materialism, how can he prove the legitimacy of their *restoration of anthropology*? When he schematizes the entire human history with the abstraction of symbolic exchange, why does not he take into consideration the illusory privileged ideology?

3 OUTDATED ECONOMIC ROOT OF HISTORICAL MATERIALISM

Baudrillard then criticizes Althusser's interpretation of Marxism. However, due to his shallow understanding of Althusser, his miscomprehension of Althusser's *quasi-structuralist* hermeneutic context, I do not think it is worthwhile to be entangled in this question.

We should pay attention to a new issue raised in this discussion: Is the *economic root* of Marxist historical materialism outdated? The bourgeois attack on Marxism usually focuses on the foundation of natural science on which the philosophical discourse is generated. Rarely has one noticed the more important basis, the economics, not to mention the declaration of a dead Marxism by proving the historicality of this economic logic. It is completely new subject, a virulent topic.

Baudrillard's criticism is often insidious. He makes the following reasoning: Marx thinks himself stand at the highest point of the capitalist economic development brought by the industrial mass production described in Ricardo's economics; he thinks he has got the key to analyze all the history, but, today's economic development has far surpassed what Ricardo's economics can deal with, and can the contemporary social history still be studied by the Marxist key that is already *not the highest point of social economical development*? He gladly says:

> But with the addition that, strictly speaking, in Marx's time, the commodity form had not at all attained its generalized form, and has had a long history **since Marx**. Thus Marx was not in a historical position to speak scientifically, to speak the truth. In that case, another break imposes itself, one that would risk making Marxism appear as a theory of a surpassed stage of commodity production, hence, as an ideology. At least, if one wanted to be scientific![10]

Regrettably, Baudrillard wastes his wisdom. In his eyes, since Marx, political economy has spread into wider fields, e.g. consumption as the production of signs, needs, knowledge, sexuality. Many things have erupted in the "infrastructure." Therefore, the distinction between Marxist superstructure and economic basis is outdated. "Something in the capitalist sphere has changed radically, something Marxist analysis can no longer respond to."[11] The most important reason is that political economy is based on material production in Marx's time but is unable to find its reliable foundation in today's life. In Baudrillard's eyes, current social existence is definitely not founded on the decisive theory of material production. "Thus, when

10   *Ibid.*, p. 117.
11   *Ibid.*, p. 118.

the system becomes monopolistic, labour time and production costs cease to be the decisive criteria (and become surplus value?)."[12] As a result, the present social reality decides that Marxist political economy critique cannot be extended into a universal theory. Baudrillard seems logical in his reasoning.

He further cites three phases of the mode of exchange value system, or the development of commodity economy, in Marx's *Poverty of Philosophy*: First, in ancient and feudal societies, exchange is limited to surplus products while the majority of objects are beyond the scope of commodities and exchange; second, since the capitalist development, the whole "industry" is within exchange; third, the universalization of commodity exchange, in which everything becomes exchangeable, including those beyond the sphere of commodity exchange in the past, for example, "virtue, love, conviction, knowledge, conscience, etc."[13] Baudrillard agrees to this division but discovers a problem in Marx's third phase, in which, it is not some penetration into other spheres by the relation of commodity exchange but a phase during which the "new social relation" takes effect. For him, Marx does not see through the nature of this new social existence:

> *In Marx's projection this new phase of political economy, which in his time had not yet fully developed, is immediately neutralized, drawn into the wake of phase 2, in terms of the market and "mercantile venality." Even today the only "Marxist" critique of culture, of consumption, of information, of ideology, of sexuality, etc. is made in terms of "capitalist prostitution," that is, in terms of commodities, exploitation, profit, money and surplus value.[14]*

According to Baudrillard, it is to employ the second-phase terms—the logic of the capitalist economic phase based on material production—to refer to today's life. Baudrillard thinks it is even the same with the French situationalist thought that he once supported, although their theory of spectacle society has a radical transcendence of Marxist political economy; the material commodity pileup

12   *Ibid.*, p. 125.
13   Karl Marx and Frederick Engels. *Collected Works*, vol. 6. London: Lawrence & Wishart, 1976, p. 113.
14   Baudrillard, Jean. *The Mirror of Production*. Trans. Mark Poster. St. Louis: Telos Press, 1975, p. 120.

has turned out to be a splendid control of spectacles. In essence, it is still "the 'infrastructural' logic of the commodity."[15]

In my opinion, Baudrillard's falsification of Marxist historical materialism is all nonsense. However, it at least opens a profound issue, that is, historical materialism must adapt itself to the continual change of social economic structure and life. First, Baudrillard is unaware that Marxist historical materialism is not a metaphysical assertion or closed conclusion. A key to the mystery of history, it comes from social historical practice and develops into a functional mode of thought. The nature of historical materialism is to break any traditional metaphysics through its own historicality of time, which is already identified by Heidegger.

Second, when Marx says historical materialism is established on the highest level of production mode brought by what Ricardo calls the practice of the industrial mass production, he has no intention to anchor this scientific method in the 19th century capitalist economic and political structure. On the contrary, it is the nature of the ever-lasting revolution in the capitalist mode of production that enables Marx to perceive the historical nature of all philosophical method-ologies. Historical materialism is the science of history; it claims no invariable historical nature; it will continual to guide us in our understanding of the new social historical life as the development of actual historical praxis changes its own structure.

Third, whether it is Baudrillard's appropriated control of code or various subversive social phenomena in "consumer society," the latest changes in capitalist society have not shaken the foundation of material production on which the social existence and move-ments are built. (We are to have particular discussion on it later.) Contemporary development and changes of capitalist economic and political reality will not lead to an outdated historical materialism, on the contrary, will provide fresh amenable environment for it to grow, like China's rising social economy that will certainly promote the new development of Marxism in China.

---

15 *Ibid.*, p. 120. As for situationalism, see my "Introduction" to the Chinese version of Debord's *Spectacle of Society*.

4 ORIGIN AND NEW REVOLUTION OF *THE POLITICAL ECONOMY OF THE SIGN*

Baudrillard then begins to sell his theory of "the political economy of the sign." (It is the major point in his near early *For a Critique of the Political Economy of the Sign*.) In his opinion, it is a new era now, more specifically, the capitalism in Marx's age has turned into a social existence controlled by another structure. "This mutation concerns the passage from the form-commodity to the form-sign, from the abstraction of the exchange of material products under the law of general equivalence to the operationalization of all exchanges under the law of the code. With this passage to *the political economy of the sign*, it is not a matter of a simple 'commercial prostitution' of all values ."16

Here, all values are made into the "exchange-sign value under the hegemony of the code." According to Baudrillard, it is "a structure of control and of power much more subtle and more totalitarian than that of exploitation" observed by Marx. It should be noted that unlike those postmodernist philosophers who positively reflect this post-industrial social existence, Baudrillard holds a critical attitude of it. Nevertheless, he does not mean to negate capitalism but moans the complete loss of his cherished relation of symbolic exchange. "The important question is not this one but rather that of the symbolic destruction of all social relations not so much by the ownership of the means of production but by *the control of the code*."17 It is a very important coordinate of logic that tells us with what criteria of value Baudrillard judges a true or false reality.

Another important question is, Baudrillard disagrees with the hypothesis that his political economy of the sign is a derivative of Marxist political economy. (He is always to escape Marxism.) In his eyes, today's capitalist social life has a revolution equally important to the early industrial one. For all that, Marxist logic has lost the flexibility of the "theoretical curvature" that makes it sensible in the new social existence that is not monopolistic capitalism at all. He opposes the dialectical continuity between the political economy of the commodity and the political economy of the sign. Here comes

16   *Ibid.*, p. 121.
17   *Ibid.*, p. 122.

the rupture. This is a completely new hegemony of social structure that is not in the schema of the mode of production. "The monopolistic system transfers its strategy to a level where the dialectic no longer operates. In the monopolistic system, there is no longer any dialectic of supply and demand; this dialectic is short-circuited by a calculation of foreseeable equilibrium."[18] In contrast with the traditional structure of competition in capitalism, the monopolistic system constructs consumption into a control, a prohibition of the occasionality of needs, and a socialized process of code planning. It is a logic framework not dominated by labour time; it is only a construct of code play.

> *It means that one goes from a system of productive forces, exploitation, and profit, as in the competitive system dominated in its logic by social labour time, to a gigantic operational game of question and answer, to a gigantic combinatory where all values commutate and are exchanged according to their operational sign. The monopolistic stage signifies less the monopoly of the means of production (which is never total) than* ***the monopoly of the code.***[19]

Ontological dimension of social reality disappears in its formula of signification. In traditional political economy, all the Marxist concepts and theoretical meanings can be connected with economic or political reality; today, "the code no longer refers back to any subjective or objective 'reality,' but to its own logic."[20] As for this issue, Baudrillard later expresses in his *Symbolic Exchange and Death* that it is a change from the old vertical relation of signification with actual reference object to the horizontal relation of signification among codes without any reference object. (Even a common reader of Saussure can tell it is appropriation of the basic structuralist linguistics, in which generation of meanings by the linguistic signs first escapes the old reflective mode. The casual relation between the signifier and the signified changes the relation of the object (actual existence) and its representative image in the reflection theory to the one between concept (existence = nature) and the sign that identifies this conception—the sound-image. In other words, language

---

18   *Ibid.*, p. 125.
19   *Ibid.*, p. 127.
20   *Ibid.*, p. 127.

is essentially among relations; a system of linguistical relations instead of one-to-one direct references of the objects.[21] No wonder Baudrillard says,

The signifier becomes its own referent and the use value of the sign disappears to the benefit of its commutation and exchange value alone. The sign no longer designates anything at all. It approaches its true structural limit which is to refer back only to other signs. All reality then becomes the place of a demiurgically manipulation, of a structural simulation. And, whereas the traditional sign (also in linguistic exchanges) is the object of a conscious investment, of a rational calculation of signifieds, here it is the code that becomes the instance of absolute reference, and, at the same time, the object of a perverse desire.[22]

Baudrillard believes Marx encounters an embarrassment here. In this code control, "the final reference of the products, their use value, completely disappears. Needs lose all their autonomy; they are coded. Consumption no longer has a value of enjoyment per se; it is placed under the constraint of an absolute finality which is that of production."[23]

If put in a simple way, Baudrillard means to say, in today's monopolistic system, the production under the code control is no longer for the object's use value that is fabricated by the code; need and desire are not man's real appeal, but "the desire of the Other's desire"; it is the same with consumption, which is a controlled, made up event. Therefore, Baudrillard asks, when production loses its own fundamentality, the dialectic of productive forces and relations of production is still legitimate in its existence?

It should be admitted that Baudrillard is very astute in his analysis of present capitalist economy and society. He perceives the dominant control structure of the logic of capital—the code control. However, he makes an error by regarding the *dominant* power of society as the ontological base. He then goes further to deny the only real foundation for social existence: material production. This mistake will unavoidably lead to a bigger one about the issue of actual revolution.

---

21   See Chapter Four in *The Impossible Truth of Being. Mirror of Lacan's Philosophy* (The Commercial Press, 2006).
22   Baudrillard, Jean. *The Mirror of Production*. Trans. Mark Poster. St. Louis: Telos Press, 1975, p. 128.
23   *Ibid.*, p. 128.

After Baudrillard denies Marxist critique of the capitalist mode of production and negates political economy and historical materialism, he refuses the scientific socialism that aims at revolving the bourgeois social reality. In the second half of the last chapter in *The Mirror of Production*, Baudrillard proposes his own substitute plan: the revolution of *symbolic subversion*.

For Baudrillard, the key of today's social control is not what Marx calls the "profit and exploitation," which is only "the inaugural modality" of capitalism, "the infantile phase" of political economy. At present, "the truly capitalist phase of forced socialization through labour and the intensive mobilization of productive forces has been overturned."[24] Under the code control, the nature of social life becomes "a desublimation of productive forces; there emerges the "immense social domestication"; the general public are more and more integrated by production tools; welfares and humanistic material life put out the revolution fire with demobilization. The capitalist system utilizes "the economic reference (well-being, consumption, but also working conditions, salaries, productivity, growth)"[25] and successfully eradicate the actual possibility of subversive revolution. (According to Baudrillard, through self-regulation, capitalism can offer Marx what his revolution wants. For this reason, Marxism is the "ideology of labour" that is utilized by capitalism.) During the process of integrated domestication, Marx's proletariat revolution does not show up in time mainly because the worker is degraded to the most substantial confirmer of capitalism in the ideology of productivism. Does not socialism want to "change life"? Agreed! When the bourgeois satisfy the general affluence of society, the "actual revolt" against economic exploitation "has placidly become the victory of the proletariat."[26] The revolutionary proletariat disappears below the horizon of welfare countries and finally returns to history. At the same time, those revolutionary powers that once beyond Marxist attention have emerged, in particular, those marginalized people who do not directly oppose exploitation and profit, for example, young students, women, collared people and so on. In Baudrillard's opinion, they are the *resistance against the code control*.

---

24 *Ibid.*, p. 131.
25 *Ibid.*, p. 139.
26 *Ibid.*, p. 159.

> *The Black revolt aims at race as a code, at a level much more*
> *radical than economic exploitation. The revolt of women aims at*
> *the code that makes the feminine a non-marked term. The youth*
> *revolt aims at the extremity of a process of racist discrimination*
> *in which it has no right to speak. The same holds for all those*
> *social groups that fall under the structural bar of repression, of*
> *relegation to a place where they lose their meaning. This position*
> *of revolt is no longer that of the economically exploited; it aims*
> *less at the extortion of surplus value than at the imposition of the*
> *code, which inscribes the present strategy of social domination.*[27]

Baudrillard says, their resistance involves no class struggle though, it reveals the weakness of current capitalism; they are the hope of new revolution in this fight without apparent clear target. Why? Because this Cultural Revolution is taking effect in antithesis to the function of Marxist historical materialism; "this whole critique *is turned back against materialism in an integral way.*"[28] The reality is, "the *production* of social relations determines the mode of material *reproduction.*"[29] The matter is reversed. He says, "It is directly at the level of the production of social relations that capitalism is vulnerable and en route to perdition. Its fatal malady is not its incapacity to reproduce itself economically and politically, but its incapacity to reproduce itself *symbolically.*"[30] Baudrillard tells us that in primitive societies, the symbolic exchange relation is a continual "circle of giving and taking." Indeed, it is from the destruction of the ontological *mutual relations* that power comes up. Therefore, the only way out to beat down current code capitalism is to rely on symbolic subversion; it is this fatality of symbolic disintegration under the sign of economic rationality that capitalism cannot escape. Baudrillard believes that subversion by the symbolic, to some degree, arises under the label "cultural revolution." Its kernel is the symbolic; it is a symbolic logic, the abolition of the imaginary of political economy; it makes the revolution of culture object any Marxist economic-political revolt. His ideal is like the French Red May storm.

---

27   *Ibid.*, p. 135.
28   *Ibid.*, p. 150.
29   *Ibid.*, p. 142.
30   *Ibid.*, p. 143.

Those of May, 1968—in every case the revolution does not speak indirectly; they are the revolution, not concepts in transit. Their speech is symbolic and it does not aim at an essence. In these instances, there is speech before history, before politics, before truth, speech before the separation and the future totality. He is truly a revolutionary who speaks of the world as non-separated.[31]

This is Baudrillard's substitute plan for Marx's scientific socialist revolution. As expected, it is a revolution of the symbolic, whose pursuit is but the conceptual disalienation and separation, the imaginative usurpation, the fantastic rose in the dream. The worker's slogan is "Never Work."[32] "Something in all men profoundly rejoices in seeing a car burn."[33] Now it is not difficult to understand why Baudrillard's symbolic revolution is easy to be objectified in sci-fi movies. For him, the future revolution is like Neo's magic in the blockbuster *Matrix*, where the subjective idea can bend and twist the iron spoon; the imagination can shield the barrage; guerrillas can even *symbolically* escape Matrix's control through the phone line. Like all postmodern anti-Marxist thoughts, this seemingly radical revolution of conception is but the moon in the water, the flower in the dream. When the resistance against the actual political-economic framework disintegrates, people have no choice but to be hopelessly and endlessly enslaved by capital. No wonder Marx says in his late period, the postmodern is the best accomplice of the bourgeois at present.

We can finally make a conclusion about this aggressive *Mirror of Production*: Baudrillard is determined to deny Marxist historical materialism and replaces it with a nasty "mirror of symbol," which is just an idealistic cliché despite his gaudy, postmodernist ornament. In essence, he just imagines reality from voidness. This is the final and proper judgment of Baudrillard.

---

31   *Ibid.*, p. 166.
32   In May, 1968, the workers of FIAT in Italy shouted the slogan "Never Work" in their strike. Baudrillard says they do not want bread and butter but strike for strike's sake.
33   Baudrillard, Jean. *The Mirror of Production*. Trans. Mark Poster. St. Louis: Telos Press, 1975, p. 141.

PART THREE

FROM THE SIGN TO THE MORTAL SIMULATION— A CRITICAL READING OF *SYMBOLIC EXCHANGE AND DEATH*

CHAPTER XV

Structural Value—A Replacement for Qualitative Value

CHAPTER XVI

Non-productive Labour and Suffocation of Social Revolts

CHAPTER XVII

Simulation and Resistance against the Contemporary Symbolic Dominance of Capital

CHAPTER XVIII

Simulacra and Simulation: Vista of the Bourgeois Kingdom

With the completion of his *For a Critique of the Political Economy of the Sign and The Mirror of Production*, Baudrillard has already stepped away from the elimination of shaping objects and towards the empty pseudo-symbolic sign system; towards a deconstruction and dislocation of the whole material production system from classical economics. Thus he exposes and criticizes all the concepts in traditional Western philosophy of history and political economy. Three years later, when he finished writing *Symbolic Exchange and Death* in 1976, Baudrillard seemed to have experienced a greater transition in his thoughts. As I understand it, this should be the second important transition in his theoretical modelling. The first transition should be from the theoretical space of the other in *The System of Objects and The Consumer Society* to the self theoretical situating in *Pour une Critique de L'économie Politique du Signe*. In this transformation of his whole thinking space, he finally establishes the new start for his original theoretical situating. If, in *For a Critique of the Political Economy of the Sign and Symbolic Exchange and Death*, he has, on the ground of the logic of the symbolic exchange grassroots romanticism, mainly criticized Marx for his concept of historical materialism on the basis of the argument that the mode of material production is actually the unconscious conspiracy of the bourgeois ideology, he now criticizes Marx's concept of labour and production from the angle of the new development of contemporary capitalism in this text, *Symbolic Exchange and Death*. At this moment, the simulation, which is used by Baudrillard as a key concept to paint the social being of contemporary capitalism, enters the stage. Meanwhile, reality, which serves as a fundamental domain without the thing-in-itself, starts to act as the point of support for his logical criticism. I think that Baudrillard at this time has started to be deeply influenced by Lacan's thoughts, even though this kind of influence nevertheless was generated by misinterpretation. In this step of his *Murder Trilogy*, Baudrillard goes directly towards real death, thus falling into a mental situation that is completely pessimistic.[1] (In his later *The Perfect Crime*, he logically recalls this real process of death once again.) Therefore, Baudrillard puts an end to his career of serious academic study, and steps into his later status of logical paranoia.

It seems to me that the introduction and the first chapter of this book perfectly resemble an academic work. However, starting with the fourth section of Chapter 2, the logical ordering of his writing changes into something akin to scholarly essays. Belles-lettres gradually takes the place of the rigorous theoretical thinking. From here on his thoughts change weirdly into a kind of metaphysical thinking. Our discussions here, therefore, mainly focus on the first two parts of this book, especially the contents related to Marx's theories in Baudrillard's original and theoretical logic situating.

---

1   Poster has also noticed this, saying that *Symbolic Exchange and Death* marked a transition of Baudrillard's political position, to which was added a bit of pessimism.

INTRODUCTION: DEATH AGAINST DEATH: UNDERSTANDING BAUDRILLARD AS A THEORETICAL TERRORIST

In the very beginning of *Symbolic Exchange and Death*, Baudrillard writes a rather puzzling preface. With a brief textual illustration, he states that the symbolic exchange, which has been regarded as in real existence in human society, has been hidden mysteriously in the construction of modern society's living conditions. Life in capitalist society today is established on the basis of *real* death. (Clearly this theme is related to Lacan's thoughts in his later years. However, unlike the previous two books, Baudrillard does not directly identify the existence of this recessive theoretical logic background, because at this moment he has already gained clout and thus needed no other disproving logical Other.) Nonetheless, the reversed meaning would be: the symbolic exchange means death to the composition of the real social being today. This should be the main logical order of this book, a hidden theme (Keller believes that this preface is Baudrillard's summarization of his new way of study. This belief makes some sense. Additionally, Kellner also judges correctly that at the time "building on Bataille's principle of excess and expenditure, Mauss' concept of the gift, and Jarry's pataphysical desire to exterminate meaning, Baudrillard champions 'symbolic exchange' and attacks Marx, Freud, and academic semiology and sociology."[2] Gane is also sure about the two stages in Baudrillard's conception of history, which are pre-simulacrum age (modeled by symbolic exchange) and the post-symbolic exchange simulacrum age. Although this kind of summarization is not accurate enough, it at least refers to an important theoretical situating event.)

The symbolic relation, which managed society and constructed life in primitive society, has already been completely eroded and destroyed by value system of economic utility in today's bourgeois social life. Although Marx tried to provide us with a realistic concept of revolution by criticizing political economy, this revolution, based on the essentialism of production, "long since became a revolution in accordance with the Law."[3] (According to Baudrillard's logic in *The Mirror of Production*, Marx's expectation of revolution, which takes development of productivity forces as historical noumenon, shares the same essence and the same structure with capitalist productivism. The conceptualization of socialism is no more than another development process of industrial capitalism, an enlarged, more indulgent process. Having had the previous discussions, we should be very familiar with this viewpoint.) Also, after Marx, the most significant radical concept should be the psychoanalytic discourse founded by Sigmund Freud, which faces the revolution deep in men's souls. This is an ideological movement aimed at releasing the self-unconsciously depressive desire production. However, as Baudrillard see it, as long as liberation is present as a law of *production and value*, it can never eliminate the structural net of capitalist domination. (Here Baudrillard mentions ambiguously that a kind of method of social relations established on the basis of value devastation has appeared recently, which is also a rebellion that was never related to revolutions and historical rules. Nevertheless, he does not directly mention the specific referent which "recently appeared." I guess the referent may be the "post-modern" streams, represented by Francois Lyotard and Derrida.)

---

2   Kellner, Douglas, "Introduction: Jean Baudrillard in the Fin-de-millennium", in *Baudrillard: A Critical Reader*, Jiangsu People's Press, 2005, p. 8.
3   Baudrillard, Jean, *Symbolic Exchange and Death*, translated by Lain Hamilton Grant, London: Sage, 1993, Preface p. 1.

According to his viewpoint, Baudrillard seems to believe that only two things are able to eliminate the spell of production-value system—namely, Mauss' symbol/gifting and Saussure's trans-situation graphic—for only with these two things it is possible to see the other side of a value and a law, which is repressive and unconscious. That is to say, Mauss and Saussure are the real saviors. We acknowledged that symbolic exchange and code control are also two important images of the other in the early days of Baudrillard's ideological construction. However, this time Baudrillard is to build up his own independent thinking space. It will no longer simply divert their theories to his own, but flatly takes up a method that he refers to as "theoretical violence." He combines these two theories, with the "reasonable core" of Freud, the "death drive," directed into a logical contradiction like a suicide. Baudrillard wants to use Mauss against Mauss, Saussure against Saussure, and Freud against Freud in order to "radicalize" his theory with this death paradox, so that a unprecedented revolutionary explosion will burst forth. (Baudrillard is always fond of making astonishing remarks. But this is the first time that I find him oppose to Mauss in his texts. Possibly he wants to use this opposition to flaunt his determination that all his theories should be original. I have noticed that he wrote in *Cool Memories IV*, "what is the point of writing? Since the 'accursed share' became a magic potion, the most radical analysis serves merely as a vaccine and a laxative. By reactivating criticism, you render the objective fury of the facts bloodless."[4] He really does so. After the abnormal Marquis de Sade and Georges Bataille, he wants no more of aperients.)

Specifically, this logic is a kind of reversibility based on the principle of involution:

> *Everywhere, in every domain, a single form predominates: reversibility, cyclical reversal and annulment put an end to the linearity of time, language economic exchange, accumulation and power. Hence the reversibility of the gift in the counter-gift, the reversibility of exchange in the sacrifice, the reversibility of time in the cycle, the reversibility of production in destruct ion, the reversibility of life in death, and the reversibility of every term and value of the langue in the anagram. In every domain it assumes the form of extermination and death, for it is the form of the symbolic itself.*[5]

4   Baudrillard, Jean, *Cool Memories IV*, translated by Zhang Xinmu, etc., Nanjing University Press, 2009, p. 57.
5   Baudrillard, Jean, *Symbolic Exchange and Death*, translated by Lain Hamilton Grant, London: Sage, 1993, Preface p. 2.

Yet what, then, is "reversibility?" As I understand it, here Baudrillard's reversibility should be the reversed negation that is subversive and the ordered abolishment—"de-order" or "out of order" in my understanding. In a word, he is no longer re-coding in the same rule, but thoroughly deconstructing and de-ordering. Here not only Marx's logic of production has been destroyed, but Mauss and Saussure have also been blacklisted. To be more specific, the logic of production development, the logic of life's linear evolution, and the logic of time's withering away all have to be transformed by destruction. Meanwhile, the relation of giving gifts and the language relation of the trans-situation graphic have to be transformed by death itself. Baudrillard may have realized that only if he completely eradicates the image of the Other that lies deep in his heart can he really stand up independently with his original ideological construction. If in the previous texts Baudrillard mainly wants to prove that he is smarter than his teachers and forefathers, at this moment, what he wants is an epoch-making rupture of thought. Just as Lacan kills his theoretical father while shouting, "Go back to Freud," Baudrillard also feels it necessary for him to commit a logical patricide that can serves him as an important logical channel. Of course, I do not think that every theoretical detail in his expression is worth carefully deliberating. On the theoretical logic platform Baudrillard provides we really cannot find any logical clues that can be orderly linked, because only expressions like "abolishment" and "death"— words full of theoretical violence—can be heard in his discourses. In *Cool Memories*, he wrote: "The only seductive theory: the one in which concepts recede to infinity, lose themselves in features ever more extreme, lending themselves to indefinite paradox..."[6] What on earth happened that put him into such a frenzy?

We find that the "grown up" Baudrillard now has a brand-new theoretical situation. After eliminating the last resources of his teachers, Baudrillard stands on the remains of Marx's concept of liberation of productive forces and on the critical dimension of Saussure's symbolic constitutive image construction, and finally gets his own unique achievement in theory: he suddenly believes that the foundation of

---

6   Baudrillard, Jean, *Cool Memories I*, translated by Zhang Xinmu, etc., Nanjing University Press, 2009, p. 18.

our world today is no longer a realistic being, but an illusion based on the fake images of multiple simulacra.[7] (This was the "truth" that Neo, when he was unconsciously in an illusion, had been told in *The Matrix*.) The generating element of this new pseudo-situating world is called *simulation*,[8] and the pseudo-situating world which has been constructed by the self-simulating *hyper real*[9] of this kind of code is called *hyper reality*. (Hyper reality, which is different from the hyper real, is my interpretation of this notion. As I understand it, the hyper real, according to Baudrillard, does not refer to the adulteration of reality, and rather identifies the ontological support behind real life. It is the hyper real that supports the pseudo-realistic word that is misinterpreted by men. I think that just as with Lacan's impossible real existence, the hyper realistic world of Baudrillard is also the anti-constructivism noumenon thinking that grew up within the logical clues of surrealism (Surréalisme).[10] Next, we will explain the basic meaning of these four terms specifically.) This jump is a very big one in terms of theoretical logic, and it also establishes that Baudrillard has creatively constructed his own logic after critical contemplating the academic resources of Other. Baudrillard becomes completely

---

7   The word "simulacre" has the meaning of "idol" in ancient French, and could also mean phantom, illusion or simulation. Baudrillard used this word to focus on the interaction between human beings and the world, and a way of approaching an object so as to dispel it. The word could be translated as "仿佛", but I think "拟像 (ni xiang)" is the best translation here. According to studies conducted by Martin Jay, the concept of simulacre was used by Bataille and Klossowski to refer to the aspects that cannot be communicated with symbols. In Cool Memories I, Baudrillard confirmed that the word "simulacre" was used by the French writer Pierre Klossowski. See Baudrillard, *Cool Memories I*, translated by Zhang Xinmu, etc., Nanjing University Press, 2009, p. 11.

8   The word "simulation" has the meaning of "fake" in French, and more or less the same meaning in English. The word has the meaning of emulation in Chinese, and was used by Baudrillard to create a new sense, without the meaning of imitating the real object. Therefore, I believe that "拟真 (ni zhen)" fits the context better.

9   The original French word of "hyper real" was "Surreal." The translation here could be generated under the background of Surrealism, but judging from the context here, the translation of "超真实" is suitable. See Baudrillard, Seduction, in *The Mirror of Production*, translated by Yang Haifeng, Central Compilation and Translation Press, 2005, p. 168. While in *Cool Memories IV*, Baudrillard created the concept of "hyper savoir." See Baudrillard, *Cool Memories IV*, translated by Zhang Xinmu, Nanjing University Press, 2009, p. 92.

10   Baudrillard has also pointed to this historical clue, saying that in Surrealism, objects with a higher certainty than everyday objects can only be constructed in "special moments when arts and imagination play their role," but all social life today are excessively contaminated by the hyper reality in another sense.

independent in his theoretical thoughts, which is the basic factor of the second important logical détournement in his thoughts as I have already mentioned.

Baudrillard becomes ordinary in this revolutionary situating and starts to announce that the previous philosophical theories of knowledge that face objective reality and the modeling of relation are merely fitted to a certain stage of the capitalist utilitarian "law of value." Today, material existence and relations with definite functions in the commodity economy that Marx once faced have all fallen into a sort of new status that is indeterminate and out-of-order. "Every reality is absorbed by the hyper reality of the code and simulation. The principle of simulation governs us now, rather than the outdated reality principle. We feed on those forms whose finalities have disappeared. No more ideology, only simulacra."[11] (According to Freud, what takes the place of "the reality principle" should be "the pleasure principle;" in surrealism it should be the artistic imagination; in Lacan's theory, however, it should be the impossibility of being.) This identification is significant identification and has some metaphysical sense. What Baudrillard means is that today all beings have the disorder indeterminacy in contrast with the reality of the definite order based on the utilitarian function in the exchange value of economy. That is to say, indeterminacy, which in the past only existed in the symbolic exchange and *mana* relations of society, now is realistically possessed by hyper reality. From "consumer society" to "sign society," we then come to this hyper realistic "simulation society." Baudrillard's concepts are actually incidents of ontological terrorism.

I have found a very complicated gestalt logical shift:

To specify the shift in the surface convex context, we will find two shifts here: the first level of shift begins with *The System of Objects*, throughout which Baudrillard shifts the entities into objective "me" function and symbolism function, and thus material existence has been replaced by the brand-new simulation; as for the second level of shift, we still remember that relative to the concreteness of material existence, disorder indeterminacy in the past was precisely

---

11   Baudrillard, Jean, *Symbolic Exchange and Death*, translated by Lain Hamilton Grant, London: Sage, 1993, Preface p. 2.

Baudrillard's ideal rule set for symbolic exchange. However, inde-terminacy now crazily occupies the ontological empty space of the original symbol (reality) in the way of a simulacrum. Obviously, this empty space is of a Lacanian style.

We will find, if we meditate further, that in Baudrillard's reces-sive logic pit the previous authentic "I symbolize, therefore I am" of the capitalist age, in which the law of value works, has firstly been alienated into the illusory "I exchange, therefore I am (exchange value)" and then been overshadowed by Marx's "I produce (work), therefore I am (use value)," which is less scolding and more help-ful. In *The Consumer Society* (1970), Baudrillard uses "I differen-tiate, therefore I am" to substitute for Marx's "I produce (work), therefore I am (use value)", while in *For a Critique of the Political Economy of the Sign* he wants to illustrate the shift from the logic of exchange value in economy to the logic of the exchange value of the sign. "I symbolize, therefore I am," as the quadratic of alien-ation, appears on the stage. (It is certain that apart from "I" in the "I symbolize, therefore I am" can be the real human being, other "I"s should all refer to *ordinary people*.) Based on Lacan's logic of negation of ontology, all of these statements can be interpreted as "I exchange, therefore I am not," "I produce, therefore I am not," and "I symbolize, therefore I am not." The new term Baudrillard now presents is: *I simulate, therefore I am*. This is horrible alienation. (Can it be regarded as the cube of human being's alienation? We can make nothing of it. The multiple involution of alienation of human being, together with the renaturation death, both form the axis of the key theoretical situating in Lacan's philosophy.) Simulation is more real than reality, therefore it makes reality die in a more thorough way. (It is just in this sense that Baudrillard later claims that reality now is becoming a "mother dog" abandoned by men.)[12] But sadly the presentation of simulation is very much like that of real exis-tence. Baudrillard identifies it as *hyper actuality*. Hyper actuality is indeed situating! Of course, this kind of situating is a new illusion used to cover the "perfect crime," which has murdered actuality.[13] In Baudrillard's opinion, this illusion with pseudo-situating is the form

12 Baudrillard, Jean, *The Perfect Crime*, translated by Wang Weimin, Commercial Press, 2000, p.8.
13 *Ibid*, p.4.

produced from the reality combined with mass media and digital reasoning, which is to say that the relation between actuality and phantoms becomes more complicated.[14] Reason being, hyper actuality is present as pseudo-phenomenon—that pseudo-essence behind hyper reality. Best states that in this pseudo-world of Baudrillard, the original critiques on phenomenology by Marx and Guy Debord have been deconstructed for the economic material and landscape. There is no reality can be found behind phantasy. Therefore, the phantoms no longer exist.[15] In fact, it is not the phantoms that no longer exist, but the phantom opposed to the present truth in traditional critical theories has been deconstructed, for it is replaced by the situating simulation without actuality. The simulation is the foundation of existence in ontological sense for men and objects. "The reality principle has disappeared, but it has left us with reality, which keeps on running like a headless chicken."[16] (In *The Intelligence of Evil or the Lucidity of Pact*, Baudrillard wrote: "There was a reality principle. Then the principle disappeared and reality, freed from its principle, continues to run on out of sheer inertia. It develops exponentially, it becomes Integral Reality, which no longer has either principle or end, but is content merely to realize all possibilities integrally. It has devoured its own utopia. It operates beyond its own end."[17] The actuality has already died; however, the hyper actuality is still running forward, being the "headless chicken.") In this pseudo-reality, headless but running, the essence and phenomenon in traditional ontology (epistemology) have died together in the simulation of the original essence of objects. Compared to the Nature Being and Social History Being of the past, this pseudo-reality is more perfect. This pseudo-reality is also a "perfect crime" which tries to murder history without traces. The murderer in this crime, however, has exactly the alibi to testify it. "The perfect criminal is the one who lays claim to

14   Horrocks, Christopher, *Baudrillard and Millennium*, translated by Wang Wenhua, Peking University Press, 2005, p.55.
15   Kellner, Douglas, "Introduction: Jean Baudrillard in the Fin-de-millennium", in Baudrillard: *A Critical Reader*, translated by Chen Weizhen, etc., Jiangsu People's Press, 2005, p.74.
16   Baudrillard, Jean, *Cool Memories V*, translated by Zhang Xinmu, etc., Nanjing University Press, 2009, p.39.
17   Baudrillard, Jean, "The Intelligence of Evil or the Lucidity of Pact," Chinese translation by Qiu Deliang, Cultural Studies Monthly, October 2004.

the crime he has not committed, who conceals his innocence behind the mask of crime. *He* is much harder to unmask."[18] (Baudrillard in his later years argues that the perfect crime conducted by simulation is usually contaminated by "bacteria, viruses and disasters," which clearly shows the truth of events. They should be our traumatic "signature" in this simulated world.[19] This idea is very close to Lacan's real concept in his later years.)[20] Obviously, Baudrillard's original logical situating here cannot enter the hetero-type mind.

Baudrillard argues that in the post-industrial age that is currently arriving, reality has been absorbed by hyper actuality's contents of codes and simulations. The new *principle of simulation* will take over the ruling place and administrate this new world, replacing the *reality principle* of the previous era—an era of the law of value. Right here, apart from the real world of symbolic exchange, which presents as death, four different pseudo-reality scenes appear and enhance each other: The first one is the pseudo-objective world of the use value, which was confirmed by Marx and yet has just been criticized by Baudrillard; the second is the economic pseudo-relation of exchange value Marx repudiated; the third is the code-situating pseudo-world of the exchange value of the sign, identified earlier by Baudrillard; and the fourth, Baudrillard's new creation, is the simulated hyper realistic pseudo-world standing above the code. Moreover, in these four new pseudo-worlds we have completely lost our purpose for living, as life is in itself generated by various kinds of simulated models. Therefore, the ideology of the false social relation is eliminated as well. Also, since the latest simulacrum now does not contain the *original actuality*, there are only simulacrums, no ideologies. However, *the simulacrums are crazier than ideologies*. Right here, Baudrillard finishes the shift from the capitalist "society of the sign" to the unique "society of simulation" he has discovered. He declares that this is the new world. In this new pseudo-situating world he, for the first time, really succeeds in rising above all of his teachers. All those masters, Marx, Freud, Saussure, Heidegger, Lefebvre,

18 Baudrillard, Jean, *Cool Memories IV*, translated by Zhang Xinmu, etc., Nanjing University Press, 2009, p.81.
19 Baudrillard, Jean, *The Perfect Crime*, translated by Wang Weimin, Commercial Press, 2000, p.43.
20 Zhang Yibing, *Impossible Real of Being*, Commercial Press, 2006, Chapter X.

Barthes, and Debord, become nothing. In front of this new image of simulacrum stands only our great Baudrillard, alone. Only he can illustrate this new logic game. (In this sense, Kellner states that this book "marks Baudrillard's departure from the problematic of modern social theory.")[21] In Baudrillard's own words: "I have dreamt of a force-five conceptual storm blowing over the devastated real."[22]

For sure it is this crazy for Baudrillard to make such a logical fracture. However, he is still conscious enough to provide people with a theoretical link in his reasoning, or else he could prove the validity of his academic work. Hence, he states it is necessary to restore the whole pedigree of the laws of value and images for the cognition of the systematic hegemony and fairyland at present. Baudrillard wants to illustrate a kind of historical relation, which is the relation between political economy (law of value), accompanied by simulacrum as the second level, and the "structural revolution of value"—the third level simulacrum which is the by-product of simulation theory. Herein lies the most important illustration of theoretical situating in this book. According to the definition given by Baudrillard later in this book, simulacrum, being the basic relation between men and the world ever since the Renaissance, has approximately experienced three historical orders, one after the other.

The three orders of simulacra, running parallel to the successive mutations of the law of value since the Renaissance, are:

> - *The counterfeit is the dominant schema in the "classical" period, from the Renaissance to the Industrial Revolution.*
>
> - *Production is the dominant schema in the industrial era.*
>
> - *Simulation is the dominant schema in the current code-governed phase.*
>
> *The first-order simulacrum operates on the natural law of value, the second-order simulacrum on the market law of value, and the third-order simulacrum on the structural law of value.*[23]

21   Kellner, Douglas, "Introduction: Jean Baudrillard in the *Fin-de-millennium*", in *Baudrillard: A Critical Reader*, translated by Chen Weizhen, etc., Jiangsu People's Press, 2005, p.11.
22   Baudrillard, Jean, *Cool Memories III*, translated by Zhang Xinmu, etc., Nanjing University Press, 2009, p.61.
23   Baudrillard, Jean, *Symbolic Exchange and Death*, translated by Lain Hamilton Grant, London: Sage, 1993, P 50. 1. The concepts of "simulacre" and "simulation" are

In fact, this process is also a social and historical process in which the capitalist value system, noted by Baudrillard, plays a part. Of course, in this book he emphasizes the relation between the second stage and the third stage. Hereon, we will briefly illustrate these concepts conceived by Baudrillard.

As previously mentioned, in Baudrillard's concept of ontology in face of the world, existence of man is not the concrete material existence, but the relevant associated existence, which is clearly based on the ontological concepts of Heidegger (Marx). In the horizon of this ontology of relations, the symbolic exchange relation of authenticity, which he has adopted from Mauss-Bataille, is the fundamental concept. (In the first chapter of this book I have identified that this kind of authenticity is not the values suspended of abstract humanism, but the ever-existing historical fact in all kind of primitive societies around the world.) On the contrary, in the process of the development of human society, the idealized (real) relation of symbolic exchange of man gradually moves towards death. The previous indeterminate symbolic world, which does not adhere to material function. (This direction and essence is the same as Lacan's negative ontology of relations.) In his books *The System of Objects, The Consumer Society, For a Critique of the Political Economy of the Sign, and The Mirror of Production*, Baudrillard gradually falsifies the process of the change of disorder symbolic exchange from the orderly functional utility, then the exchange value system, to the structure of code value system. However, here he mainly explains the essence of the pseudo-relation world ever since the establishment of the capitalist world. In a new original situating frame, he no longer complies with Saussure, who simply identifies the current pseudo-reality nature of capitalism by using the relation of code. Instead, he identifies the way of existence of this pseudo-relation world as a *simulacrum* (this word has already been seen in *The Consumer Society* and *For a Critique of the Political Economy of the Sign*, yet at those times did not become the key paradigm of Baudrillard's academic structure) because in a capitalist society with

easily mixed up. In his Chinese translation, the Taiwanese scholar Hong Ling correctly illustrated the "three-tier order" of simulacre expressed in Simulacre and Science Fiction. However, just in his foreword, he mistakenly wrote the same expression in Symbolic Exchange and Death as the three-tier order of "simulation." See *Simulacre and Simulation*, Chinese translation by Hong Ling, Taiwan Times Publishing, 1998, p.233; p.5.

industry and modernity, relationships between men and the outside world are mainly based on *imitating* and *simulating* the external referents and is aiming at objectively control nature so as to make it used by men. However, in the development of modern capitalism, the simulacrum has been carried forward to a simulation stage that is *against the simulacrum.*

This relation of simulacra, in the so-called capitalist situation of social existence, has been specifically divided into three different phases or "three-orders" by Baudrillard: the first-order is "the 'classical' period, from the Renaissance to the Industrial Revolution." In this period, the relation between man and the world appeared to be the orderly relation between man and the natural world with a "counterfeit" essence. (Baudrillard later further explains in his book *Simulacres and Simulation* that the simulacra in this period have a nature of naturalism, and are "founded on the image, on imitation and counterfeit, that are harmonious, optimistic, and that aim for the restitution or the ideal institution of nature made in God's image."[24] This idea is of exactly the same structure as the objective framework of dualistic cognition.) That is to say, the relations mainly present in a form that men learn from nature, comply with the natural law, imitate the way of existence of nature, and make and shape objects according to nature. (Personally I believe that we should never take this distinction seriously, for it is completely without historical support. In the realistic process of social history, the "counterfeit" definitely did not begin with capitalist industry.) Moreover, Baudrillard chooses to call the law effective in that period the "natural law of value," which means the process to involve the natural materials in the utilitarian system "for me." (It is a domineering behavior not to speak based on common sense when one becomes more comprehensive in his studies.)

The second phase is the "industrial era," in which the mode of simulacra is "production." It is "the law of value of commodity" that is at work in this stage. Obviously, "production" refers to modern material production in the narrow sense set by Baudrillard. (In *Simulacres and Simulation* he identifies this stage with the nature

---

24   Baudrillard, Jean, *Simulacre and Simulation*, Chinese translation by Hong Ling, Times Publishing, 1998, p.233.

of productivism, and argues that it exists on "force, its material-ization by the machine and in the whole system of production—a Promethean aim of a continuous globalization and expansion, of an indefinite liberation of energy (desire belongs to the utopias related to this order of simulacra).")[25] Here, instead of shaping the natural materials by processing, men mainly have to produce products that do not exist in the natural world. Production is no longer merely an imitation of nature, but a means to destroy the original order of natu-ral materials and *create* a man-made ordering world of usefulness in material existence. In fact, this stage serves as a social-historical situation that has been constructed by commodity-market economic relations. Men have created a kingdom of economic value; however, they have lost themselves in this material production. According to Baudrillard, Marx's thoughts obviously belong amongst concepts relevant to this stage.

The third phase is the "code-governed phase" that Baudrillard has just identified. He clearly states in *Simulacres and Simulation*: simulacra in this phase are "founded on information, the model, the cybernetic game—total operationality, hyper reality, aim of total control."[26] In this new era, men no longer relate with the outside world directly; however, they build up the world by simulating. Therefore, in a rigid sense, simulation has already become *anti-sim-ulacrum*, as the relations of simulacra in the first two phases both have the objective world and the referent, while the third world is itself *without object and referent*. It is a kind of code-relation world with *no external relation of reference*, and it can reproduce on its own. We can alternately call it *a world of structural value generated by its own*. Of course, we can also see the traces of Saussure, who came up with the symbolic structuralism that abolishes the objective relation of reference. (Actually the relationship between simulacra and simulation can be considered as Baudrillard's most ambiguous concept in his later years. Fred Rush, for example, has always mis-taken simulation for simulacrum and inaccurately identified simula-tion as "copy without the origin."[27] However, simulation is not *copy-*

---

25 *Ibid.*
26 *Ibid*, Pp.233-234.
27 Lash, Scott &John Urry, *Economics of Signs and Space*, translated by Wang Guangzhi, Commercial Press, 2006, p.21.

ing at all. Some argue that Baudrillard's viewpoint here has been affected by relevant arguments in Plato's *The Republic*. In my opinion, it may make sense on the surface level of his discourse, but the theoretical situating is actually completely different.[28] I have also noticed that some masters like Bauman and Harvey make mistakes on this issue as well, for they usually wrongly identify simulacrum as simulation.)[29]

Baudrillard says that in the second phase, political economy is premised by the exchange value of economy (including Marx's criticism based on "the real liberation of production") and the exchange value of the sign (including his completed criticism based on "the real liberation of meaning"). Yet in the new simulacrum in the third phase, capital no longer belongs to the category of political economy, and it starts to manipulate the pseudo-situating reality within a dominant structure of "mode of simulation"—hyper reality. (Baudrillard finally gets rid of the phantom of Marx's "political economy" in the depth of his logical situating.) The commodity economy, without any doubt, is not absent, but "the entire apparatus of the commodity law of value is absorbed and recycled in the larger apparatus of the structural law of value, thus becoming part of the third order of simulacra."[30] *The structural law of value* is now his new creation. The "becoming" definitely refers not to the fact that the commodity economy has become the sub-system of the frenzied world of simulation today. The law of value of commodity economy is just a kind of imagined reference (like the phantom-like use value that exists in the exchange value), which exists in the situating of the structural law of value of simulation. Similarly, the natural law of value of the first-order simulacra also exists puppet-like in the imaginary reference of the construction of the relation of the second-order exchange value of commodity.

Baudrillard claims that the third-order simulacrum—the simulating hyper actuality—is the (pseudo) essence of this post industrial world today. Additionally, the construction of hyper reality

28   Dai Abao, *The Strength of Termination*, China Social Sciences Press, 2006, p.159.
29   See: Bauman, Zygmunt, *Life in Fragments*, Cambridge University Press, 1995, p.151; Harvey, David, *The Condition of Postmodernity*, Blackwell, 1990, p. 300.
30   Baudrillard, Jean, *Symbolic Exchange and Death*, translated by Lain Hamilton Grant, London: Sage, 1993, Preface p. 2.

even presents a certain kind of disorder *indeterminacy* relative to the determinacy of the exchange value of economy. Of course, this indeterminacy is pseudo-indeterminacy. Baudrillard complacently continues to say that in order to deal with such an indeterminate hyper actuality, only his theory and practice of symbolic exchange, which is also indeterminate, will work. Why is that? It is because all existing revolutionary critical theories belong to the inner logical situation of the second-order simulacra. In his words in *The Mirror of Production*, they ascribe to the logic of productivism.

> *Contemporary revolutions are indexed on the immediately prior state of the system. They are all buttressed by a nostalgia for the resurrection of the real in all its forms, that is as second-order simulacra: dialectics, use value, the transparency and finality of production the 'liberation' of the unconscious, of repressed meaning (the signifier, or the signified named 'desire'), and so on.[31]*

"A nostalgia for the resurrection of the real" is used by Baudrillard in a comic way to describe a variety of possibilities for liberation which appear in the whole process of industrial modernization: dialectics, the use value and the transparency of production belong to Marx and his critical theories on society; unconsciousness and the liberation of the repressed sense organs belong to Freud and the following derivation of those radical discourses. Baudrillard wants to illustrate that the revolutionary referents, which appear throughout the second phase of simulacra, are merely the pseudo-"actuality" permitted inwardly or unconsciously by the second-order code of simulacra, because the realization of "actuality" conspires with the industrial simulacra and is a program under manipulation. Marx and Freud, therefore, would never have been able to conceive of this fact. (This point of view, in *The Mirror of Production*, has already been illustrated adequately by Baudrillard. The difference with the critical logic in his original theoretical situating is that he can no longer use Marx's methods and discourses to fight against Marx.)

Baudrillard believes that the world today has stepped into the third-order simulacra, and thus become the pseudo-world constructed by the reflection of hyper actuality. Therefore, the simulacra world of industrial production is converting into a new kingdom of

---

31   *Ibid*, p.3.

simulation. If it is the rational, referential, functional, historic machine of consciousness that corresponds with the industrial machinery, something that matches the mechanism of codes must be the
irrational irreferential, uncertain and floating system of unconsciousness. (These statements obviously echo the logic of post-modern
discourses.) Here, "cybernetic operativity, the genetic code, the aleatory order of mutation, the uncertainty principle, etc., succeed determinate, objectivist science, and the dialectical view of history and
consciousness."[32] I really have no idea when Baudrillard began to
care about the modern development of natural science. The theories
of cybernetics and mutationism put forward between 1930 and 1940,
and the earlier "Uncertainty Principle" by Heisenberg, all come into
Baudrillard's theoretical vision. Some of the recent achievements
in the field of biological genetics also come to the fore. We are well
aware of the fact that the concept and background of cybernetics
could never exist without the system concept and information theory
that is put in opposition to substantialism. It serves as the foundation
of the complex view of science, so as to eliminate the simple linear
conception of nature. However, mutationism, which has a core of
random prominence, explains the existence of the *situating essence
of contingency* on a deeper level. (Althusser's thoughts in his old age
were also influenced by this concept—the so-called *"meet by ac-
cident" materialism.*) The Uncertainty Principle is unquestionably
the uncertain limit of subjective cognition identified on the basis of
practical ontology, while the genetic code has opened up the horrible
new prospect of human beings in creating new lives—full of inde-
terminacies unexpected in the scientific development. Men have encountered the self-elimination of the ordering purpose in their own
scientific teleology ("questioning" and dominating nature).

Baudrillard characterizes the new development of natural science
with the purpose of claiming that his view of simulation towards the
world has changed substantially. More importantly, he wants to declare the end of those radical liberation discourses in the new hyper
reality. Therefore, he believes that men can never use the dream-
boat of teleonomy to fight against the disorder of historicity when
we take the tension of the traditional liberation of the second-order
simulacra into consideration. Also, they are unable to compete with

---

32 *Ibid.*

dislocation and the sequencing scatter of molecular by using political consciousness; it is impossible to apply political economy in order to fight against the non-material code; it is unlikely one could deal with DNA in the microcosm via class struggle. Baudrillard wants to claim that all traditional liberation discourses are out of date. In 2004, he wrote in *The Intelligence of Evil or the Lucidity Pact* that, "it is not that way at all now, with the rise of a world order exclusive of all ideology and exclusively concerned with the circulation of flows and networks. In that generalized circulation, all the objectives and values of the Enlightenment are lost, even though they were at its origin. For there was once an idea, an ideal, an imaginary of modernity, but these have all disappeared in the exacerbation of growth."[33] Baudrillard obviously intends to be the Savior of this pseudo-world, which is in the process of sinking. The last hope he gives us is only that symbolic chaos can burst into codes. However, symbolic chaos is in fact death. Obviously, this is a rather pessimistic conclusion. (Interestingly, according to some scholars, Baudrillard in his *The Perfect Crime* also raises a fourth form of simulacra—the strange attractors. The generating of this new form of simulacra is always "viruses," or the development of cancerous cells, splitting infinitely without foreseeable results.[34] I think this may not be the real theoretical reference of Baudrillard. In the mean time, he was keen on the issues that might be the referent of his self-mockery, "to play with computer viruses from 60ies.")

When Baudrillard says that we are left only with theoretical violence and have to use death to against death, I believe that his traditional logic formula has already cleared up. The deaths here represent the *plural form* of death. If symbolic exchange is actuality, then the process of changing the material existence into the utilitarian existence of men will be the first death of actuality, which appears as Marx's ontology of productive labor and in effect is the nature of the whole of the Enlightenment's modernity. Yet, as Marx discovered, the actuality of direct relations between men in productive labor has died in the exchange value of economy—this death is the second

33 Baudrillard, Jean, "The Intelligence of Evil or the Lucidity of Pact," the Chinese translation by Qiu Deliang, Cultural Studies Monthly, October 2004.
34 Horrocks, Christopher, *Baudrillard and Millennium*, translated by Wang Wenhua, Peking University Press, 2005, p. 33; Ritzer, George, Postmodern Social Theory, Huaxia Press, 2003, p. 139.

death of "actuality." For the third time, the exchange value of economy has converted into the exchange value of the sign, so "actuality" has no other choice but to die again. However, when the code and the existence of simulation appear without any referents and objectified references, actuality is revived in hyper actuality. However, in essence this death is its last but its most perfect death. (Many years later Baudrillard describes this process of murdering actuality in detail in his *The Perfect Crime*. Researcher and translator Dai Abao correctly illustrates the historical clue (Lefebvre and Barthes) to Baudrillard's hyper actuality concept, and understands profoundly that hyper actuality is the death of actuality. However, he has not interpreted the referent of the actuality any more.)[35] Therefore, as for the actuality that has died quite a number of times, symbolic exchange means death in pseudo-actuality. Thus, Baudrillard tells us that to use death against death is our final way out. (Mark Poster argues, "When Baudrillard argues that escape from the code is found only in death ... he gradually moved to one of bleak fatalism,"[36] which is a profound theoretical perspective.) At this moment, Mauss-Bataille's symbolic relation, ever present in primitive tribes, has become the catalyst which "radicalizes" all hypotheses of liberation, because only the bi-direction association of symbolic exchange can deconstruct the control of the single dimension of the sign. Baudrillard states: "The symbolic demands meticulous reversibility, ex-terminate every term."[37] (Cook notices and discusses the character of deconstruction that is given to symbolic exchange by Baudrillard, because his symbolic exchange at this time presents as death—this "disastrous form.")[38] Using Mauss to fight against Mauss means making Mauss present in the way of death. Afterwards, Baudrillard even claims that philosophy leads us to death![39]

---

35 Dai Abao, *The Strength of Termination*, China Social Sciences Press, 2006, p. 167; p. 161.
36 Kellner, Douglas, "Introduction: Jean Baudrillard in the *Fin-de-millennium*", in Baudrillard: A Critical Reader, translated by Chen Weizhen, etc., Jiangsu People's Press, 2005, p. 111.
37 Baudrillard, Jean, *Symbolic Exchange and Death*, translated by Lain Hamilton Grant, London: Sage, 1993, Preface p. 5.
38 Kellner, Douglas, "Introduction: Jean Baudrillard in the *Fin-de-millennium*", in *Baudrillard: A Critical Reader*, translated by Chen Weizhen, etc., Jiangsu People's Press, 2005, p. 205; p. 208.
39 Baudrillard, Jean, *Cool Memories V*, translated by Zhang Xinmu, etc., Nanjing University Press, p. 105.

Obviously, metaphysically playing with the concept of death does not give Baudrillard the ultimate capacity to subvert the logic of capital, which has existed and already swallowed the whole world. Directly speaking, without the realistic resistance governed by capitalism, this semantic terrorism, no matter how scary it is, is still in conspiracy with the dominance of capital. Therefore, we can conclude that this "simulation-simulacra" original theoretical situating, which Baudrillard puts forward in a very special way, seems to be extremely ill-grounded in face of the realistic globalization of capitalism's powerful logic of dominance.

CHAPTER XV

STRUCTURAL VALUE—A REPLACEMENT FOR QUALITATIVE VALUE

In the first section of "The End of Production," the first chapter in his *Symbolic Exchange and Death*, Baudrillard seems to want to proceed with the subjects he discussed in *The Mirror of Production*. The logic loop in his theoretical situating, however, has now changed greatly. His focus of thinking has transformed from criticism of the political economy of the sign into constructing the simulating revolution in value theories. As he sees it, the law of value in traditional political economy has separated itself from its original track seen in the process of operation in modern capitalism and surpasses the traditional mode of commodity economy. Value no longer directs the specific utility of real existence, but turns to its own uncertain structure of code. Structural value, which Baudrillard conjures from nothing, takes the place of the qualitative value of referents in Smith-Marx's labour production. This academic event has been labeled by Baudrillard as a revolution. With this revolution, he once again announces the death of labour and production.

1 WHAT IS THE STRUCTURAL REVOLUTION OF VALUE?

This discussion arises from Baudrillard's rethinking of Saussure's linguistics. (Previously, during the discussion about *For a Critique of the Political Economy of the Sign*, we have already mentioned that one of Saussure's analogies between language semiotics and political economy has become the convex logical Baudrillard's outset. Baudrillard then obtains the logic equalities—the signified equals the signifier while the use value equals the "exchange value.") Baudrillard points out that Saussure compares the relation between the lexical items in linguistics to the money relation in economics: money on the one hand can be cashed into assets, while on the other hand can play the role of finance in its own monetary system. Additionally, Saussure attaches greater importance to the latter, which is *structural value* in the same sense, when he emphasizes on the structural dimension of language in his language semiotics. Not wrong. (In the first section of Chapter II in *Course in General Linguistics*, he indeed mentions in analogies the two "systems of equivalence among different objects" in the value theories of political economy. Moreover, when discussing the binary dimension between synchronic axis and diachronic axis, he emphasizes the structurally decisive role of the synchronic axis.[1] In his introduction, Baudrillard blatantly announces that he will use Saussure to fight against Saussure and to commit a radical patricide. However, when Baudrillard enters the specific logic situating, Saussure sneaks back in through the back door. Obviously, Saussure is still a phantom of the other that Baudrillard cannot rid himself of.) But there is apparently a deliberate misinterpretation of Saussure here, namely, secretly changing the original axes (synchronic and diachronic) into *functionality* and structure. This deliberate misinterpretation is an extremely important trick in the logical order, because in the following logic construction Baudrillard will equate these axes with the functional use value and structural "exchange value" in Marx's theories.

---

1   Saussure, *Course in General Linguistics*, translated by Pei Wen, Jiangsu Education Publishing House, p. 90; Saussure, *Course in General Linguistics*, translated by Tu Youxiang, Shanghai People's Publishing House, 2002, p. 121.

As in Marx's analysis: use-value plays the role of the horizon and finality of the system of exchange-values. The first qualifies the concrete operation of the commodity in consumption (a moment parallel to designation in the sign), the second relates to the exchangeability of any commodity for any other under the law of equivalence (a moment parallel to the structural organization of the sign). Both are dialectically linked throughout Marx's analyses and define a rational configuration of production, governed by political economy.[2]

Baudrillard means to say that in Marx's logic order of dualistic value, the existing real of the shaped object is the use value; and by referring to this real, the commodity economy has built up an image system of exchange value. Baudrillard asserts that a new revolution has completely put an end to the "classical economics" of value theory. The form of value that directly refers to the material form of commodity has been sublated. The constructive form of value that is present today is a more radical one, newly discovered by Baudrillard himself. According to him, the nature of this new value revolution is to break up the traditional theoretical situating of value, and even switches off the *referenced* connection between the dual attributes in traditional metaphysics of the whole Western world. For instance, "exchange value" is based on use value; phenomenon refers to the essence; attribute depends on substances. (The reference here is basically essentialist, internal, and fundamental in our previous discussion. As for Derrida, this reference should be called level-centralism. Obviously, Baudrillard also wants to eliminate essentialism here; however, his way of de-ordering: to deny the *real*—is unique.) Baudrillard says that the referential value is thus destroyed for the interest of the structural game of the only value. The reference system in the relation has been disordered, and the "real" no longer equals a certain reality, but becomes autonomous. To say it in a more amplified way, he writes:

The structural dimension becomes autonomous by excluding the referential dimension, and is instituted upon the death of reference. The systems of reference for production, signification, the affect, substance and history, all this equivalence to a 'real' content, loading the sign with the burden of 'utility', with gravity— its form of representative equivalence—all this is over.[3]

---

2   Baudrillard, Jean, *Symbolic Exchange and Death*, translated by I. Hamilton Grant, London: Sage, 1993, p. 6.

3   *Ibid.*, p. 6-7.

392   A MARXIST READING OF YOUNG BAUDRILLARD

Please pay attention to the "real" as used by Baudrillard here. This usage is the aforementioned referential relation that occupies the ontological vacancy as pseudo-real after the death of symbolic exchange. As he illustrates in *For a Critique of the Political Economy of the Sign*, the real forcefully imposes utility (use value), which serves for men's interests, onto objects in a form of shaped labour production. The basis of "exchange value," then, refers to the use value that presents as real. However, in the existing structure of modern capitalist society, newly illustrated by Baudrillard, the industrial age, as a referential structure (usefulness) that the "real" refers to, has been destroyed. The critical dimension (phenomenology) which reproduces nature has been replaced and obstructed by the auto-synthesis of code. The presence of the code-made simulation is preconditioned by the *reviving* of the real. The convex appearance of simulation is precisely the re-construction of the symbolic relation, but it must be a pseudo-situating! At this moment, the real no longer *refers to* any other pseudo-things. It is the real, the hyper real, because it is *even more realistic than the real*. The simulation seems like Jesus, who steps out of his tomb, more realistic and closer to the godhood than anyone else does. (Of course, we have identified that the hyper real should be the portrayal to illustrate the embarrassing situation of the real after numerous instances of death. The god of simulation, who died and was revived, is the unclear evilness of the code.)

> Now the other stage of value has the upper hand, a total relativity, general commutation, combination and simulation—that is simulation, in the sense that, from now on, signs are exchanged against each other rather than against the real (it is not that they just happen to be exchanged against each other, they do so on condition that they are no longer exchanged against the real).[4]

The essence of simulation is to "never to exchange with reality!" It has nothing to do with the real, however, and is more realistic than the real. The simulation is not the imitation of a real objectiveness that came before it, but the self-situating of the pseudo symbolic relation without any foundation; it will be an endless process of self-reproduction. (This reminds us of Lacan's pseudo subjective world and pseudo existence of desire, which are built up

---

4   *Ibid.*, p. 7.

by nothingness (symbolic code) on the basis of ontological nothingness.) This meaning is the original revolution of structural value
that Baudrillard flaunts. He believes that the world today is a symbolic game in which a code exchanges with itself—the structural
synchronic relation about "relativity of the whole"—identified by
Saussure. Saussure argues that the sign no longer refers to a real
object, and Baudrillard extends Saussure's meaning by saying that
the social code does not refer to the *second real*, which has served as
the real, essence, purpose, and foundation in social existence; now
the rule is to get rid of all self-exchanges and repeated re-construc-
tions among codes decided by the foundation. ("The second real" is
a notion that Baudrillard invented by imitating Hegel's "the second
nature." As I interpret it, this idea should refer to the real social relation in social existence.) Therefore, "the emancipation of the sign:
remove this 'archaic' obligation to designate something and it finally
becomes free, indifferent and totally indeterminate, in the structural
or combinatory play which succeeds the previous rule of determinate
equivalence."[5] In Baudrillard's eyes, production today has already
lost its certain purpose and runs wild as code because traditional production is likely to be operated in accordance with the needs of consumption. Yet the desire that constitutes need is constructed by the
symbolic pseudo-situating of code. Thus, this fake consumption has
determined a timid production like a copycat which loses its original
definite purpose and begins to run purposelessly in the wake of commodities—commodities that are continuously becoming outmoded
and dying. If in the past capitalist production was "to produce for
the sake of production" (Ricardo), production today produces for the
sake of the symbolic inner chaos of code. In addition, money today is
separated from the reference of the gold standard; labour is divorced
from the reference of productive needs—all are floating like the
sign and replacing one another, throwing themselves into boundless
speculation and inflation. Just like those electronic display boards
for finance and stock markets, in this era that is being electronically
informationized, speculation and inflation are changing as if at the
speed of 300,000 km/sec. This age is completely different from the
age of classical capitalism—the "dialectics of the sign and the real"
era that has already died. Everything in the capitalist world today

---

5   *Ibid.*

informs us the death of the "real" which dialectics intends to promulgate. Regardless of whether the real refers to production or signification, the objective determinacy in original industrial manufacturing has died; the determinacy of the law of value in the commodity economy has been lost; the determinacy of the objective reference of the sign has been erased; and the disorder "indeterminacy becomes dominant". (Please pay attention to this "indeterminacy." Previously in Baudrillard's thoughts, it has been mainly used to identify the indefinite relation of the symbol, which adheres to the instrumental existence of material definiteness. However, the dominant indeterminacy today is the false indefiniteness made up by "structural value revolution," so that it has to be interpreted as *pseudo-indeterminancy*. This interpretation is the nature of simulation.)

Baudrillard says that the view of revolution towards this structural value was first characterized in his *For a Critique of the Political Economy of the Sign* with the notion of "the political economy of the sign." However, there it seemed at most an "expedient." Although it was still concerned with value and the law of value, the content was totally different. Accurately speaking, this value theory with the structural exchange of the symbolic sign acting as its core no longer belongs to traditional economics. Therefore, it is the important mental revolution to end the political economy supported by material production and the traditional sign system sustained by way of referential reappearance. Everything in our life today has been swallowed and reconstructed by simulation. As a result, we have reached a new era after the fracture of history.

> *The end of labour. The end of production. The end of political economy. The end of the signifier/signified dialectic which facilitates the accumulation of knowledge and meaning, the linear syntagma of cumulative discourse. And at the same time, the end of the exchange-value/use-value dialectic which is the only thing that makes accumulation and social production possible. The end of the linear dimension of discourse. The end of the linear dimension of the commodity. The end of the classical era of the sign. The end of the era of production.*[6]

---

6   *Ibid.*, p. 8.

The above is an extremely famous assertion that Baudrillard makes in this book, and it is the most critical announcement following his creation of his original theory. Nine "ends" have been used to declare the end and death of many modern things. (In fact, we can now understand why we must sequentially study his thoughts. From *The System of Objects* and *The Consumer Society* to *For a Critique of the Political Economy of the Sign* and *The Mirror of Production*, we have followed his logic thinking and ceaseless theoretical reconstruction, walking all the way from "the consumer society" to "the society of the sign," onwards to the "society of simulation" today, at which point we are able to understand the meaning of his "revolution." Otherwise we would never know the real referents of his "ends" here. This constitutes the essence of my non-vertical mode in the research of history of ideas. In 1971, Henri Lefebvre, one of Baudrillard's teachers, pointed out the issue of the "ends" in his book *Space and Politics*. He identified the various "ends" encountered by Marxism, such as the end of the state capitalism, the end of deprivation, the end of philosophy, the end of history, the end of family, and so on. Of course the "end of labour" should be the core "end." He wrote that today the automation of production allows us to consider the end of production and labour.[7] However, Baudrillard's theory of ends is much more systematic and explosive.)

Firstly, "linear dimension" is actually the historical dimension in Marxist historical materialism and the diachronic dimension in traditional semiotics. The historical order of the development of the commodity economy and the evolution of language and discourse is a reference of today and the past. However, when all capitalist existences have lost their references, the linear dimension will no longer exist. There will be no *history*. (Fukuyama's *The End of History* shares the same logic as Baudrillard's on this issue. Of course, the contents of the former also include the judgment of ideology the blocking on one's way to communism.) Secondly, proclaiming the end of labour, production, and political economy is not completely new. In *The Mirror of Production*, Baudrillard already made excessive metaphysical assertions on the "end." Thirdly, Baudrillard

---

7 Lefebvre, Henri, *Space and Politics*, translated by Li Chun, Shanghai People's Publishing House, 2008, Pp. 86-87.

A MARXIST READING OF YOUNG BAUDRILLARD

creatively announces the end of "the classical era of the sign."
According to his illustrations in his *Espace et Politique: le Droit a la
Ville II*, this announcement refers to the "be denied" of the theories
of the sign with referents.

As Baudrillard observes, the coming of the simulation era of
capitalism could be the cause of the mutation of a certain existing
situating on multiple levels in social life. The nature of this mutation, however, is a kind of "interchangeability" between opposites in
traditional dialectical contradiction.

> *Everywhere we see the same 'genesis of simulacra" the commut-
> ability of the beautiful and the ugly in fashion, of the left and the
> right in politics, of the true and the false in every media message,
> the useful and the useless at the level of objects, nature and cul-
> ture at every level of signification. All the great humanist criteria
> of value, the whole civilization of moral, aesthetic and practical
> judgment are effaced in our system of images and signs.*[8]

The beautiful things fashion magazines display today will be out
of date tomorrow; the left wing party that comes into power by hold-
ing to socialist guiding principles today may turn into an accomplice
of the imperialist right wing and invade other countries; the hot-
test topic today in the mess media could turn out to be a lie; useful
things may prove to be useless waste. That every single thing is "unpredictable" is precisely the effect of code's simulating dominance.
(Obviously, this pseudo-indeterminacy is just the thing that is highly
welcomed by the postmodern streams. Yet it is also the thing that
Baudrillard criticizes and rejects here. Therefore, it is reasonable for
him to deny his own "post-modernism." Baudrillard is indeed not a
post-modernist.)

Baudrillard says that just as with the objective changes in realistic existence, academic ideology becomes unpredictable as well.
"Theoretical production, like material production, loses its determinacy and begins to turn around itself, slipping abysally [en abyme]
towards a reality that cannot be found."[9] (I think this statement reflects his feeling towards the postmodern streams present at that

---

8   Baudrillard, Jean, *Symbolic Exchange and Death*, translated by I. Hamilton Grant,
London: Sage, 1993, p. 9.
9   *Ibid.*, p. 44, note 3.

time in French educational circles. The "abysally [en abyme]," "turn around itself" is precisely the "anything would do" by Feyerabend. Clearly Baudrillard occupies a critical position of opposition to Lyotard and Derrida, so it is really a ridiculous logical irony that Baudrillard has been misinterpreted as a master of post-modernism in both the US and China.) Baudrillard regards theoretical production today as a "floating theory," which floats as currency.

> No matter what perspective they come from (the psychoanalytic included), no matter with what violence they struggle and claim to rediscover an immanence, or a movement without systems of reference (Deleuze, Lyotard, etc.), all contemporary theories are floating and have no meaning other than to serve as signs for one another. It is pointless to insist on their coherence with some 'reality' whatever that might be.[10]

Those masters of postmodernism, including Deleuze and Lyotard, as you can see, have been pushed onto the seat of judgment by Baudrillard. In Baudrillard's point of view, academic thinking now has already lost the specific "use value," just like production. Academic research is in itself meaningless, while "greeting each other" serves as a new and original way. (Jameson defines the present as an era without depth in thought.) Actually, the above is a vivid and profound portraiture of the "post-modern" stream. (This theoretical issue reaches a level of depth that was neglected by Kellner and Best when they wrote *Postmodern Theory* and *The Postmodern Turn*.)[11]

More importantly, Baudrillard has sensed accurately and profoundly that this is not merely a change in value theory and ideology. All the changes come from the sudden transformation of the real master of the world—capital. "It is not the revolution which puts an end to all this, it is capital itself which abolishes the determination of the social according to the means of production, substitutes the structural form for the commodity form of value, and currently controls every aspect of the system's strategy."[12] Baudrillard is absolutely right. Therefore, the interchangeable world presented by postmodern streams is just the brothel of capital's universalityness.

---

10   *Ibid.*
11   I raised this question to Kellner in person during his visit to Nanjing University in October 2007, but he did not give me an answer.
12   Baudrillard, Jean, *Symbolic Exchange and Death*, translated by I. Hamilton Grant, London: Sage, 1993, p. 8.

However, it is no longer the brothel for prostitution but for replacements and exchanges. (This point is similar to Jameson's judgment that the post-modern stream is the cultural logic of late capitalism.) I think that the theoretical intention of Baudrillard's analysis in estimating the quality of the contemporary cultural stream is crucial and profound. However, his further conclusion later on is, unfortunately, totally absurd.

2 HOW DOES THE AGE OF PRODUCTION END?

After declaring the revolution of structural value theory, Baudrillard has to prove the assertion with theoretical logic. He is consistent in this practice. His first testimony was "the death of production," which he touched upon in *The Mirror of Production*. But here he wants to testify more specifically on how the era of production ends.

Baudrillard believes that we are at the end of the production age. Obviously, as we have already identified, production here is capitalist industrial production in a narrow sense, instead of the material production that serves as the foundation of human society. Marx defines material production as the first "historical event" that was used by human beings to separate ourselves from nature. Therefore, Baudrillard says that production and the law of value of commodity can show up simultaneously. Additionally, before the emergence of this kind of production, "everything is deduced, from the grace (God) or beneficence (nature) of an agency which releases or withholds its riches."[13] (This expression is an imitation of Marx's.) In fact, "production," in Baudrillard's words, can only be legal when mixed with meaning of the capitalist industrial production. Yet Baudrillard, who does not think normally, never sees the common sense mistakes in his own logic. Therefore, he insists on not regarding hunting and tool making in the primitive clans as production. The farm production and animal husbandry, the basis of the entire existence of agricultural civilization, are not production as well. As a matter of fact, when we step out of his extraordinary language, Baudrillard means that agricultural production is not industrial production. This idea is absolutely nonsense.

---

13   *Ibid.*, p. 9.

In his further analysis, Baudrillard starts commenting on economics. (In the previous discussion of *The Mirror of Production*, we were much obliged to his poor knowledge foundation in economics.) Baudrillard argues that in traditional economics we are able to acquire value by referring to labour just because of the emergence of productive labour, and that the law of value is the common equivalence relation of labour. Labour becomes quantifiable, which gives Marx a chance to find out the surplus value that has been sheltered by capitalists. In this way, Marx's critique on political economy can be set up firmly. Apparently, the fundamental references of this critique should be the social production and mode of production and just in the conceptual logical order of production had Marx discovered labour force: the "surplus" created by special commodities. This discovery in fact constitutes the rational motivation for criticizing the capitalist system. It is his logical summary of the theory of Marxist political economy. We really cannot be too cautious when wrestling with Baudrillard. It is ridiculous for a person who does not really understand the political economy to pretend to be seriously analyzing Marx's economics.

As a matter of fact, according to Marx, the reason for the presence of the law of value is not the appearance of common labour production. Its presence becomes historically legal due to the historical presence of the capitalist mode of production. It was after the 14th century that industrial production, a mode that completely differed with the agricultural production (to live at the mercy of the elements), the foundation of realistic society throughout the middle ages, gradually appeared in Europe during the process of material production. Nascent industrial material production was established on the basis of the objectification of the whole natural world (Heidegger). The nature of industrial production should be the creative material reconstruction of industrial labour. Moreover, the new social wealth that has orderly industrial products as its main body appears as the brand-new result of industrial production. Differing from the "natural wealth" of agricultural civilization, it was first identified as "social wealth" by William Petty and was a new kind of wealth for humans. Additionally, the operating ways of social economy in some developed European countries (Italy, the Netherlands, and Britain) changed into capitalist commodity-market economy only in a certain phase in history. The elaborate division of labour that continuously occurs in industrialized production (which was developed from the workshop handicraft industry) necessitates general social labour and exchange in production. This necessity, however, gives rise to the division between the abstract labour (which forms value) and concrete labour (which creates use value) and can be regarded as the economic premise of capitalist commodity production. The free labourers who have nothing at all merely become special commodities relative to capital in a capitalist market economy. The fragmental concrete labour cannot directly cash itself in the division of labour, and thus, in order to realize itself, has to enter into market exchange as the result of the aggregate social labour. In addition, by this medium the surplus value is able to be possessed without any compensation in the production process, but is shielded in the equal form of the exchange process. Baudrillard cannot form a scientific understanding that all political economies started from the classic economy; however, he presumptuously changes Marx's scientific theory of social criticism, which is based on the study of economics.

Dissimilar to his theoretical objectives in *The Mirror of Production*, Baudrillard no longer directly attacks and distorts Marxism's historical materialism and labour theory of value; instead, he mainly wants to tell us that time has changed and that the social formation (described by Marx with concepts like production, form of commodity, labour force, equivalence relation, and surplus value) with definite, realistic support of economy, has already become a thing of the past. Revolutions today merely stand on the ground of "abolishing the law of commodity value." (I have found that this assertion is exactly the logical expansion found in the last part of the discussion in *The Mirror of Production*.) He believes that the original "social formation of production" identified by Marx is disappearing. Therefore, if we still pin our hopes for revolutions on production and the commodity law of value, real revolution will never take place. He thinks that capital has acquired a completely new way of ruling mode—a "purest and illegible form of social governance."

It no longer has any references within a dominant class or a re-lation of forces, it works without violence, entirely reabsorbed without any trace of bloodshed into the signs which surround us, operative everywhere in the code in which capital finally holds its purest discourses, beyond the dialects of industry, trade and finance, beyond the dialects of class which it held in its 'produc-tive' phase—a symbolic violence inscribed everywhere in signs, even in the signs of the revolution.[14]

This field of research is brand new. According to my understand-ing, Baudrillard probably means that we consider past political rule and economic process as the objective processes that are really visible—the same as we find references in the class structure and dominant power (workers would know exactly whom to shoot at, as Fromm said.) and regard the governance now as the invisible control of the symbolic codes which have lost all their realistic references and are merely the disorder codes in self-references. Different from early capitalist governance, which was covered in bloodstains, the dominance and enslavement of the sign is not bloody at all, for its control starts from one's own mind. Now the proletarians and the oppressed class have no idea whom to shoot at. In this way, extrinsic painfulness is definitely transformed into intrinsic ego-anxiety.

Therefore, if in Marxist historical materialism production serves as the foundation of all historical constructions, it is history, creates history labour, becomes the historical rationality and the finishing mode of generality through unimaginable fabrication. Marx's criti-cism of capitalism at that time was mainly based on the problems that appeared (relative to material production and the labour pro-cess) in the capitalist production mode. Baudrillard claims that the contemporary capitalist reality has completely changed everything, since production has become the production of the code. Therefore, remaining stuck at the historical dimension of traditional material production and the realistic reference point to criticize capitalism will be a terrible illusion. Hence, once we see production as code, we have to pass through many material evidences like machines, factories, working hours, products, wages and money; also, it is important for us to encounter more formalized but equally "objec-tive" evidences, such as surplus value, market, and capital in order

---

14 *Ibid.*, p. 10.

to discover the rules of the game. This search requires destroying various logic relations of the capitalist mechanism and all kinds of critical relations in the scope of Marxism (although they are analyzing the capital, they belong to the second degree phenomenon—the critical phenomenon of capital) for the purpose of finding the basic signifier of production and the social relation which has been established by production and been hidden under the historical illusion of the producers (and theoreticians).[15]

Obviously Baudrillard still intends to criticize capitalism here, but he holds the opinion that Marx's critical concept and the traditional capitalist material production it faces have become things of the past. In present capitalism, which is produced by codes, this kind of criticism can only be a "superficial" criticism in the second degree. Therefore, the age of production ends, and all the traditional critical theories offered by Marxism are out of date. This idea is Baudrillard's conclusion and his most important and famous argument amongst his theories.

Baudrillard argues that for this reason the commodity law of value in classical economics transitions into a brand new structural law of value. He still wants to identify the dominance of capital, just to be "smarter" than Marx to find the new changes in the operating law of capital for the fact that in the structural law of value, the loss of all references makes it impossible for the revolution to have a substantive reference. How can you condemn it guilty when no bloody proof has been found? How can we make a punitive expedition against the irresponsible subject and the indefinite sign that does not even appear at the crime scene?

Does material production, however, really come to an end? Definitely not. I believe that this claim is merely Baudrillard's illusory historical idealism. Firstly, in the economic growth of the developed capitalist society that Baudrillard lived in, a mode of production that is dominated by electronics and information technology has surely become the most significant *leading* factor of the complete social existence, but it has not changed the foundational status of the process of material production. (Things related to the

---

15   *Ibid.*, p. 11.

relationship between leading factors and the basic determinants in the development of social history have been specifically discussed in my book *The Subjective Dimension of Historical Dialectics of Marx*.)[16] For example, in foundational industrial production (such as steel, large machinofacture, and the making of ships and automobiles), the industrial design conducted by using computers becomes the premise of production. However, this is just a means of changing the original complex labour that was conducted on graph paper by the brains of engineers into an operation using computer interfaces. The objectification of the design still has to be realized via the concrete *process of material production*. Although we have to admit that the design and production of Microsoft software is no longer the traditional industrial production that is based on the re-construction of material, does it really open up a new mode of modern production based on information without any need of material production? No matter how advanced the Windows system becomes, it cannot directly produce food, clothes, or other necessary material commodities. As for those industries producing codes, such as mass media, which seem to possess a position of great dominance in social life, they can never be rid of the huge sum of advertising costs paid for by productive capital. Precisely in the intrinsic relationship between manufacturing the desire to consume and material production, those industries constitute the deceptive conspirators of industrial capital (material production). Secondly, in those developing countries that are out of Baudrillard's field of vision, modern material production of industry is just the thing that is being pursued. The material production of industry has developed at a horrible speed and directly effects the life of the developed capitalist society. The so-called "made in China" panic can be regarded as a powerful exemplification, no?

In my opinion, Baudrillard misinterprets the sign-like leading factors that appear in the social life today as being the all-foundational conditions of society, for he cannot correctly handle the relation between these two things in social existence. He has forgotten the fact that human society can never survive with just codes. It is true that codes control our minds; however, they cannot change the

---

16   Zhang Yibing, *The Subjective Dimension of Historical Dialectics of Marx*, 2nd Edition, Nanjing University Press, 2002, Foreword. English version by Canut Intl. Publishers London 2012.

society into a spiritual illusion. This truism should be the foundation of reality. I think that Baudrillard's error can be considered as a basic idealistic mistake on par with that made by Bishop George Berkeley.

3 THE LABOUR THAT HAS BEEN EMPTIED BY CODES

In order to illustrate the legitimacy of his declaration of the division of history, Baudrillard further expounds the death of labor (laboor theory), which serves as the most significant element in Marx's and all other classical political economy. Also, differently from in *The Mirror of Production*, instead of direct attacking the logical generalization of Marxist concept of labour, he starts to demask the fact that shaping labour has changed in the new social reality. This time Baudrillard tells us that the key element of unfairness in Marx's criticism towards capitalism, the labour force creating surplus value, is "not a *force* anymore" now It is no longer a creative shaping force which really exists, but has become "the sign out of signs" in *structural code*. It is being produced and consumed like other symbolic things, and being exchanged with other "non-labour," even "leisure" things. Labour force has been alienated in the structural order of code. I think that all of the above is a bald-faced lie. When we escape from this dense metaphysical fog, we easily find that even in the IT industries, such as software design and Internet communication sectors all over the world, the fact that coder workers working in different levels are serving as the labour commodities that create the surplus value, they objectively exists, yet not exist in the form of common labourers as in the age of Marx. These coding labourers, whose job is the so-called "profession for young people only," are being pressed and exploited in a degree no less harsh than that faced by physical labours in the process of traditional process. I have seen for myself that these coders forgo eating and sleeping for days for the sake of a bidding project.

Baudrillard believes that, more importantly, labour is no longer the "special historical practice" which contains a certain kind of special order social relation. It becomes merely "a series of operations describing characteristics"—another set of self-repeated operations about symbolic signs in constructive codes. This fact also means that labour, which operates as sign, is no longer an unbearable suffering (dissimilation) in the historical reality, and may even no longer be an object which is able to wait for freedom. Again Baudrillard is wrong. In the international labour division system of contemporary giant monopoly capitalists, the blue-collar workers, who are invisible according to Baudrillard, are just reproduced in the processing industries in Asia and Latin America. The degree of the labourers' suffering might have already surpassed that seen in the times of Marx and Engels. Additionally, a similar situation has appeared in some underground plants in America and Europe employing illegal immigrants. This reality may well explain the reason why Baudrillard cannot understand the phenomena that "Marxism, Christianity and psychoanalysis have found refuge in Latin America?"[17] God, inconscience and the proletariat are moving to the subtropical zone, for the oppressed labour still exists there.

However, Baudrillard is too clever to see the fact that:

Sign-form seizes labour and rids it of any historical or libidinal significance, and absorbs it in the process of its own reproduction: the operation of the sign, behind the empty allusion to what it designates, is to replicate itself.[18]

Baudrillard believes that labour today has been emptied of all its meanings, including deep-seated desire and real purpose. Now, labour is the self-reference of the sign. (Here Baudrillard specially takes Lyotard in postmodern streams as an example, for Lyotard argues that workers' entertainment space, which is also the burning desire, can be met in the corruption of value and the capital rules.) If in Marx's time the shaping labour which handles material objects could refer to the social reality, it is at present no longer productive, and has become a reproduction assigned to labour. It has become a habit, for the present production has no specific content but the meaningless growth of statistics figure, an inflation of the accounting sign. Obviously this thinking is an exaggeration. Baudrillard believes that capitalist labour has become "a huge ceremony of the sign of labour."

---

17 Baudrillard, Jean, *Cool Memories V*, translated by Zhang Xinmu, etc., Nanjing University Press, 2009, p. 49.
18 Baudrillard, Jean, *Symbolic Exchange and Death*, translated by I. Hamilton Grant, London: Sage, 1993, pp. 10-11.

You are asked only to consider value, according to the structural definition which here takes on its full social significance, as one term in relation to others, to function as a sign in the general scenario of production, just as labour and production now function only as signs, as terms commutable with non-labour, consumption, communication, etc.—a multiple, incessant, twisting relation across the entire network of other signs. Labour, once voided of its energy and substance (and generally disinvested), is given a new role as the model of social simulation, bringing all the other categories along with it into the aleatory sphere of the code.[19]

Baudrillard claims that today's code world is the "second being" that we have never before encountered, and if the past social life, materialized shaping labour, and even the capitalist exploitation of workers have the direct "familiarity" and "intimacy," then the world today is constituted by the practice of abstract symbolic sign. Everything becomes a floating variable, and the pseudo-situating code-world as the "second being" takes "all the imagination" away from the previous life. Here "all the imagination" refers to the symbolic relationship as an important support of life situating, while the pseudo-symbolism of sign exchange just replaces the real situating imagination. (This "second being," as the "second reality" mentioned above by Baudrillard as the essence of the false, is also a theoretical rewriting of Hegel's "second nature.")

In my opinion, Baudrillard's description of the code world in today's developed capitalist countries is indeed quite reasonable and profound, but the problem is, if people are getting away from the past artisan/work relationship, and if capitalists in today's developed capitalist countries can hardly exploit the workers through the method of squeezing absolute surplus value, then do these two aspects prove that this kind of injustice no longer exists? Will the injustice in the enormous profits of transnational corporations involved in information networks, e-commerce, and globalization come to naught because of the random code? We can admit that the relationship between capital and labour and their interdependent mode has changed, and labour itself in the so-called "knowledge economy" era is changed; however, the secret of generation and appropriation

---

19   *Ibid.*, p. 11.

of surplus value unmasked by Marx will still exist. We just need to consider how to deal with this new fact with Marx's theories, rather than using dazzling and confusing discourse to mask it like Baudrillard does.

Baudrillard also identifies that today's labour is not "a force," but "a definition, an axiom;" besides which, the essence of labour is not only the subjugating violence occurring in concrete shaping at the level of energy, but also the *con-symbolic violence*. This identification certainly surprises most of the readers, because it is *a reflexive intention* at a deeper sense, it is a logical backtracking, to where the stance and starting point of the theoretical logic originates from Mauss-Bataille's grassroots romanticism in Baudrillard's mind. Baudrillard believes that we must distinguish between what belongs to the production *mode* production and what belongs to production code and before entering the law of commodity value, first of all the labour force, is a status, "a structure submitting to the code." What does the above mean? Baudrillard intends to illustrate the *production* culture of humans as a practice of code transforms natural existence through shaping to the utilitarian value of humans, and it transforms the world at the property level to the symbolic sign code of humans, which is much deeper than the change of the quality of material. What is more frightening that truly occurs in labour "is to remove indeterminacy from nature (and man) in order to submit it to the determinacy of value."[20] (It should be noted that he questions all the human civilization based on material production instead of describing what happens nowadays, and criticizes the passing production era.) Here the first "uncertainty" refers to natural existence outside the utilitarian production system and the symbolic exchange of humans living in primitive tribes, while in the second "certainty" the human-oriented utility is violently inscribed by production on objects and human beings through shaping labour. (Indeed, we have noticed in the fact explained above by Baudrillard, the *certainty* (reference) of production once again becomes the *pseudo-indeterminancy* (non-reference) in the practice of sign code. This logical conversion is very complex.) Baudrillard says that we can certainly experience it from "the crazy manufacturing of bulldozers, highways, and 'economic

20   *Ibid.*, p. 13.

bases' in our lives." It is obvious that Baudrillard still bears a grudge against Marx, because in his opinions, Marx does not realize the problems underlying production itself, and "instead leads us astray with the *dialectic* of productive forces, reaching the *disastrous* end of this process."

If in the above analysis Baudrillard mainly undertakes the abstract illustration of theoretical logic in terms of the death of the concept of traditional labour, then he will again concentrate on the "labour conversion" in today's life. Baudrillard says that in current society, the differences between traditional special labour and general labour are becoming indistinct, and with the disappearing of the differences of labour property (concrete labour) in "the scientific idealism of production," the new labour system constructs an interchangeable network, he writes:

> *The labour process itself has become interchangeable: mobile, polyvalent and intermittent structures of absorption, indifferent to every object and even to labour itself, when understood according to its classical operation and applied to localise each individual within a social nexus where nothing converges except perhaps within the immanence of this operational matrix, an indifferent paradigm which identifies every individual according to a shared radical, or a syntagma which links them into an indefinite combinatory mode.*[21]

Baudrillard is very fashionable in that he transplants a lot of new concepts and terms into the traditional economy, thereby decorating his theoretical revolution. But what on earth is he driving at here? According to my understanding, Baudrillard intends to point that when the traditional shaping labour is emptied by the structural code, a new *flexible labour*, with the practice of sign at its core, emerges.

In Baudrillard's eyes, today's labour (including casual labour), is as "an omnipresent code," is "as the fundamental oppression, as a control, and as a permanent occupation of some adjusted time and place, invades the whole life." This kind of labour is no longer the original productive shaping labour, but a social imagination, a construction of the social situation, and furthermore all people are involved in the "permanent mobilization" of this new type of labour:

---

21   *Ibid.*, pp. 13.

This is the tendency of every current strategy that turns around labour: 'job enrichment,'6 flexitime, mobility, retraining, continuing education , autonomy worker-management, decentralisation of the labour process, even the Californian utopia of domestic cybernetics... "Labour power is no longer brutally bought and sold, it is designed marketed and turned into a commodity— production re-enters the sign system of consumption".[22]

I think the above is Baudrillard's discussion of the new circumstances appearing in developed capitalist societies today. According to his understanding, there is no longer the direct exploitation so detested by Marx, that is, that exploitation which pulls people out from life and hands them over to the sinister man-eating machine system. On the contrary, today's system finds for everyone a proper position, an "individualized job." If in the path an individual must adapt to the work, now "labour will adapt to each person." If you are unemployed, you will receive an "unemployment benefit calculated in accordance with your personal data," and thus everyone becomes a terminal in the entire network.

In fact, on the basis of Baudrillard's discussion of the new circumstances appearing in contemporary capitalist production modes, a new understanding of and revolutionary conclusion about Marxism can certainly be reached. Flexible labour, the so-called "people-oriented" way of working, flexible international division of labour, and globalization of capital operations, are no more than the most "humanized" means of existence of today's capitalism's logic. When Toshiba from Japan says, "Toshiba advances together with China's 'four modernizations'" or when McDonald's and KFC from the United States succeed in producing local fast food of the Chinese-style, these phenomena are connected with the issue of maximizing the exploitation of surplus value's flow into the pockets of capitalists on a global scale. In this regard, the French Regulation School, Harvey from the United States, contemporary and late Marxism School scholars like Derek, Wallerstein, Frank, Amin, Arrighi, and other important leftist scholars have carried out a lot of useful research. Nowadays, they are still actively and unyieldingly fighting against the capital logic, and finding new possibilities for the struggle against flexible production and flexible labour

---

22   *Ibid.*, p. 14.

appearing in the network of contemporary international monopoly capitalism. Contrarily, Baudrillard comes up with pessimistic metaphysical ideas negating the real struggle. Baudrillard never considers the point that Marx's historical materialism and the entirety of political economy are not only a conceptual revolution, but a guide to the proletarian revolution; he will never consider what people in today's bourgeois world obtain within the structural value he creates. When all is emptied by the sign code, can people do no more than mere submission to the capitalist logic that is claiming a worldwide victory? Baudrillard's analysis of contemporary capitalism is very profound at many levels, but it also bears the features of fallacy and one-sided profundity, because he does not provide real critical weapons and a path to liberation after he rejected the Marxist critique.

CHAPTER XVI

NON-PRODUCTIVE LABOUR AND SUFFOCATION OF SOCIAL REVOLTS

In Baudrillard's book *Symbolic Exchange and Death*, the first chapter, as well as its second section, both fall under exactly under the same heading, namely, "the end of production."[1] In Section Two, Baudrillard proposes a striking view. As the basis of contemporary capitalist society has shifted from productive labour to non-productive labour, in particular to the working pattern led by service industries, an unprecedented shock has been delivered to the realistic ground of traditional revolutionary theories. With the disappearance of the "illusion of production,"[2] or more precisely, the disappearance of class forces that rely upon industrial workers as the main body of revolutions, production has transferred to non-production, and traditional labourers and their working space has vanished as well. Therefore, from Baudrillard's perspective, new social changes in the capitalist world will paralyze traditional social revolt and revolution. This chapter turns to his related theories first, and makes corresponding explanations.

---

1 Baudrillard, Jean. *Symbolic Exchange and Death*, Trans. I. Hamilton Grant. London: Sage Publication Ltd, 1993, p. 6.
2 *Ibid.*, p. 30.

1 PRODUCTION TRANSFERS TO NON-PRODUCTION

Baudrillard first pretends to give a retrospective about "the 'pre-scientific' phase of the industrial system."[3] (As a matter of fact, this phase is what Marx detailed in *Capital* and his manuscript—the phase of machinery of capitalist industrial production.) Soon after that, he quotes from Marx's *Economic Manuscripts of 1857-1858*, trying to re-describe new qualitative contents which have already emerged in this phase of capitalist domination; that is, during the process of capital's maximum exploitation of labour power, capital is "multiplied to infinity by the accumulation of knowledge;"[4] the accumulation of knowledge and of skill is absorbed into capital, and hence it appears as "an attribute of fixed capital"[5] and an accomplice of capitalists. Therefore, Baudrillard attempts to introduce his own ideas.

Baudrillard asks us to notice that Marx himself also saw a new trend, namely, that in the phase of machinery, the end of primitive accumulation marks "the decisive turning point of political economy: the transition to the preponderance of dead labour, to crystallized social relations incarnated in dead labour, weighing down on society in its entirety as the code of domination itself."[6] This sentence itself is not completely false, but Baudrillard here regards "the hegemony of dead labour over living labour"[7] as *science and technology* with knowledge as its essence, instead of *industrial capital* in Marx's original sense. Hence, he pays particular attention to the remarks that Marx made during his middle and late period, such as "the production process has ceased to be a labour process,[8]" "man steps to the side of the production process, instead of being its chief actor,[9]" etc. (As is well known, in the *Economic Manuscripts of 1857-1858* and the following *Economic Manuscripts of 1862-1863*, Marx did talk about the role of science and technology played in the process

---

3   *Ibid.*, p. 15.
4   *Ibid.*
5   *Ibid.*
6   *Ibid.*
7   *Ibid.*
8   *Ibid.*
9   *Ibid.*, p. 16.

of capitalist production, and even mentioned the gradual change of production process into the application process of science and technology. He also noticed that workers' labour under the capitalist mode of production became auxiliary to the operation of machines; and that the machine system became capital's accomplice, throwing workers hungry into the streets. However, Marx never held that science and technology would directly turn into capital.) Baudrillard means that Marx sensed a certain new phenomenon in the development of capitalism as well, but he is unable to identify its new nature. Baudrillard believes that what he highlights are things Marx did not notice. He intends to put forth that science and technology itself is also *guilty*: "Marx have retained a belief in the innocence of machines, the technical process and science—all of which were supposedly capable of becoming living social labour once the system of capital was liquidated, despite the fact that this is precisely what the system is based on."[10] (This idea is certainly not new.)

As mentioned above, (in the traditional western Marxism logic, it is the young Georg Lukacs who first talked about this subject— that productive forces are guilty—he wrote about this unconsciously in his book *History and Class Consciousness*. After him Martin Heidegger and Jean P. Sartre both made ontological extensions on this issue. Walter Benjamin and Theodor Adorno first clearly designated the guilt of such productive forces and scientific technologies ("technological ideology"), while Jürgen Habermas's earlier work— *Technology and Science as Ideology* (1968) was a systematic interpretation of this concept.)

As far as I am concerned, Baudrillard's misunderstanding of Marx's previous standpoints is mainly because he ahistorically solidifies the concepts of labour and production in the traditional political economy. To him, it seems that either labour or the value-creating living labour is *equal* to manual labour ad infinitum, while production is always equal to material production concretely shaped under the capitalist condition. Therefore, when new changes take place in the process of capitalist production today, he fussily forms arbitrary theoretical assertions:

---

10   *Ibid.*, p. 15.

With the hegemony of dead labour over living labour, the whole dialectic of production collapses. Following the same basic schema as the central oppositions of rationalist thought (truth and falsity, appearance and reality, nature and culture), all the oppositions according to which Marxism operates (use-value/exchange-value, forces of production/relations of production) are also neutralised.[11]

Baudrillard's error here is his inability to understand that the hegemony of dead labour over living labour that Marx mentioned does not refer to the direct oppression of the actual machine system (including the knowledge system) against workers. Here "dead labour"[12] is only an inverted metonymy, meaning that surplus value created by labour in turn becomes the master—capital, which reabsorbs living labour—enslaving and exploiting workers. Capital here is not *material*, but has the presence of a sort of dominant and ordered *social relation*. (As Marx designated in *Wage-labour and Capital*, blacks are not born slaves yet become slaves under slavery.) Both the machine system and the knowledge system can only become ad hoc "fixed capital"[13] in the dominant and ordered framework of capital logic. (In this regard, Pierre Bourdieu's elaborations are to some extent valid. He puts forward concepts such as *social capital* on the basis of prestige and status and *academic capital* on the basis of academic accumulation, as these new capitals today have become changeable capitals, capable of acquiring surplus values.) I realize that Baudrillard here is really acting far from intelligently, for he exaggeratedly integrates passages from Marx into his logical situating of mandatory understanding as long as Marx's sentences resemble his own ideas. From my perspective, *the dialectic of production* in today's capitalist society does not break down in any way, and only takes on a new form of expression.

The key to the problem is still staked on the understanding of *living labour* itself. I must admit that on this point that the concept of productive labour that Marx referred to as value creating requires updating, but let us first turn to Baudrillard's related account.

---

11   *Ibid.*, p. 16.
12   *Ibid.*, p. 15.
13   *Ibid.*

Baudrillard focuses on Marx's historical clarification about service labour, believing that Marx's original distinction between productive and non-productive labour is problematic. He says, according to Marx, *"labour becomes productive only by producing its own opposite (that is, capital)."*[14] However, the reality of capitalism today proves that every Marxist definition of labour is split. Because

This definition did not even consider that capital might take root in something other than the "productive" precisely, perhaps, in labour voided of its productivity, in "unproductive" labour... By misunderstanding "unproductive labour," Marx concedes the real undefined character of labour on which the strategy of capital is based.[15]

Baudrillard is so naïve that he simply solidifies producibility factors into production in the shaped *material operation* in order to show Marx's narrowness of mind. Nevertheless, if Marx's definition is to say that labour becomes productive as long as it produces its own opposite (that is, capital), then what about the thousands of mental workers all over the world nowadays who are designing software under the charge of Bill Gates? Are they not producing their own opposites (that is, capital) every day? Their labour is of course *productive*! Another example is that international capital invested into consulting and services industries in modern China are also absorbing new living labours, whereas such labours do not adopt the style of work in Marx's time. However, Baudrillard does not think this way. He persists in adherence to the historical boundary of Marx, and feels proud that he is beating the productive labour of the nineteenth century to death. In reality, Baudrillard's self-righteous style is no doubt a sort of ridiculous and stupid metaphysics.

It should be admitted that Marx, who lived in the development stage of industrial capitalism in the nineteenth century, dealt with the social realities around him objectively and put forward historical and concrete opinions in accordance with his era. This reality should not be the aspect where Marx is to blame. Any person living in today's world should not become overly proud simply for noticing new social realities Marx never saw. The point is to see whether the methodological essence of Marx's thought is wrong or not! From my

14   *Ibid.*, p. 17.
15   *Ibid.*

perspective, the methodology of historical materialism Marx used to observe social existence and historical development is still correct, only we should apply it to new observations and understandings in accordance with the changes of history and reality. Clearly, Baudrillard does not make a direct defense in bourgeois ideology. He would like to criticize contemporary capitalism, but he merely is making a high exaltation of his own uniqueness by simply denying Marx. This logical relation is extremely complex. Here the practical issue is that Baudrillard solidifies the historical defining boundaries of Marx's concepts concerning production and labour, etc. He does not expand the boundaries according to new circumstances today; on the contrary, he simply uses today's realistic changes to prove Marx's "misunderstandings"[16] in order to make his own criticism of contemporary capitalism seem more brilliant and more radical than Marx's.

2 LOWERING LABOUR TO SERVICES AND LIBERATION OF FREE TIME

Also in this sense, Baudrillard claims that changes in social reality today have shaken the traditional "non-productive"[17] edifice.

A concrete example he cites here regards service industries, which become more and more important in today's capitalist society. From his perspective, service labour in Marx's context is also a marginalized non-productive labour. However, Baudrillard believes,

Today all labour falls under a single definition, which is the definition of service-labour, that bastard, archaic and unanalyzed category of service-labour, and not the supposedly universal classical definition of 'proletarian' wage-labour.[18]

Obviously, this service is a magnified concept. To Baudrillard, "every labour is reduced to a service, labour as pure and simple presence/occupation, and consumption is the 'prestation' of time."[19] He has a simple logical deduction: whatever labour that is not manual labour in Marx's sense can be regarded as a service, including work at the computer, at the cash register, at the telephone, or anywhere

16   *Ibid.*
17   *Ibid.*
18   *Ibid.*
19   *Ibid.*

where there is no expenditure of sweat in manual labour. "The service rendered conjoins the body, time, space and grey matter,"[20] whose essence is actually the "presence of time."[21] As a matter of fact, such a judgment is extremely superficial, because although both sit at the computer, the attendants at the front desk of a Hilton Hotel and designers at the Volkswagen research institute do not provide homogeneous "services."[22] The mental labour they expend and the social value they actually create can never be compared on the same level. Most of all, Baudrillard believes that in such services with "time presence,"[23] production disappears, the surplus value vanishes, and the meaning of labour and wages changes as well. In short, the logic tool Marx used to criticize capitalism is invalid. For Baudrillard, it does not mean capitalist domination is no longer in force, but rather the arrival of "the dawn of its real domination, solicitation and total conscription of the 'person.'"[24] Once again appears the seemingly deep superficiality.

Actually, what Baudrillard cannot see is right behind non-manual "service"[25] on the convex side, that is, the important transition of contemporary advanced capitalist society from material, industrial production to post-industrial production such as the information and electronic industries. The proportion of the blue-collar workers amongst industrial workers has been decreasing since the late 1950s, and the labourers in contemporary capitalist countries are no longer Marx's manual workers. This social reality is a new one regarding which Western Marxists and leftist academics have already reached certain consensus. Among the academic achievements we can find, starting from Paul Baran and Paul Sweezy's *The Monopoly Capital* in the 1960s and Harry Braverman's *Labour and Monopoly Capital* in the 1970s, to the French Regulation School today, research on both economic transformations and changes in complex social relations in contemporary capitalism have made significant progress, and play a fundamental role in late Marxist studies such scholars

20 *Ibid.*
21 *Ibid.*
22 *Ibid.*
23 *Ibid.*
24 *Ibid.*
25 *Ibid.*

as Fredric Jameson, Arif Dirlik, David Harvey, Antonio Negri, and Michael Hardt, et al. (In the fall of 2006, we, jointly with British scholars, held the first Seminar on Contemporary Capitalism, in which Professor Sean Sayers's topic of discussion was labour under the contemporary capital system. In 2007, the theme I discussed with Slavoj Žižek, a visiting scholar at Nanjing University, was also about labour and production under the contemporary capitalist mode of production.) Sadly, Baudrillard completely neglects serious scientific research as such, and instead is interested in flowery and unreal metaphysical assertions, because only they allow him to think randomly.

No wonder he makes the bold statement,

> *In this sense labour can no longer be distinguished from other activities, particularly from its opposing term of free time, which, because it implies the same mobilization and the same investment (or the same productive disinvestment),... In short, it is not only the imaginary distinction between productive and unproductive labour which is shaken up, but also the distinction between work and rest itself.*[26]

Baudrillard's assertion as such seems to aim at Marx's distinction between work time engaged in slavery production and free time for subjects' creative use of talents. In other words, since all labour today is done in front of computers, it then *homogenizes with* other practical activities, even to the extent of there being no difference between creative and non-labouring free time. (Here, as Baudrillard is an *unconscious West-centrist*, we should first point out one of his blind spots, which is that since the 1970s, developed countries in Europe and America began to transfer industrial production with serious environmental issues and labour intensive industries to Latin America and Asia, now mostly along the coastal areas in east China. Indeed, Baudrillard can hardly find manual labour and traditional productive labour in France today; however, labour and production still exist in this *unequal* world, as does labour time, which is obviously different from "free time."[27])

---

26   *Ibid.*, p. 18.
27   *Ibid.*

Baudrillard always intends to show his profundity through the denial of Marx.

First of all, Baudrillard talks about the relationship between Marx's "complex labour"[28] and today's free time from a microscopic perspective. He says people can defend for Marx by connecting complex labour with services, and make further extensions on the possibility of the space presence of liberation of free time like Herbert Marcuse did, but Baudrillard is dead set against it. For Baudrillard, "the system, throughout the technical progress and automation, produces free time as the extreme reification of labour power as the accomplished form of abstract social labour time, simply by being the inverted simulation of non-labour."[29] Actually, Baudrillard entirely fails to understand the ad hoc theoretical context concerning the problem of simple labour and complex labour that Marx proposed *in the economic research*. If the simplicity and complexity of labour that Marx mentioned in the nineteenth century can correspond with hand labour and skilled labour within physical labour, the abstract *necessary labour* time then becomes the basic scale of value in variant labour relations; hence, the relation and value of complexity and simplicity still exists with today's software design and the objectified (i.e. communication engineering cable-laying and the industrial assembly line) labours of general hardware. More importantly, Marx's free time does not refer to non-labour (production) time (like leisure time), which is beyond the control of capital, but to the free existence out of man's ultimate liberation after the *complete smashing of capitalist mode of production*. Even in the most advanced capitalist society today, there has never existed free time in Marx's sense. (Since Guy Debord, attention has been paid to the problem concerning capital-controlled, non-productive free time, which is a condition for the reproduction of labour power, or leisure time, controlled by capital logic.)

Secondly, Baudrillard is also opposed to regarding education, training, and schooling as "complex labour."[30] Here he suddenly turns on Adam Smith, because the latter already regarded the

---

28 *Ibid.*, p. 44.
29 *Ibid.*, pp. 44-45, note 8.
30 *Ibid.*, p. 44.

training of workers as capital invested in machine manufacturing. "This is an error instruction; education, training and school are not long-term investments. They are rather the direct social relation of domestication and control. Capital doesn't look for any complex labour in this, but indulges in absolute waste, sacrificing an enormous part of its 'surplus-value' in the reproduction of its hegemony."[31] Obviously, Baudrillard is still discussing the economics beyond the political economy; thus, he is unable to grasp the relation amongst education, training, and capital investment from the standpoint of *the whole process* of social production of capital, as this relation can never be well explained only in terms of the direct process of production and simple social relations. (Furthermore, thanks to his overly-simplistic thinking, Baudrillard hardly begins to understand the ideological features of the capitalist education system itself and secrets in the complex production process of academic capital in schools and research centres, discovered by Althusser (*Ideology and Ideological State Apparatus*), and Bourdieu (*Reproduction* and *The State Nobility*) et al.)

3 DISAPPEARANCE OF WORKERS AND WORKPLACE

Baudrillard believes that in today's capitalist society not only labour but also workers in Marx's sense disappear; because the skilled worker Marx preferred to call is "no longer a labourer, but merely a worker facing the total in-differentiation of labour."[32] Of course, this opinion is related to Baudrillard's above mentioned concept of service. As everything becomes service, the labourer then loses "the content of labour and specific wages"[33] in the traditional sense. In today's capitalist society, "we no longer work, but merely perform 'acts of production.' This is the end of production-culture; hence the contrary appearance of the term 'productive.'"[34] Today there is no labourer as subject, for the worker is only a "productive agent."[35]

31 *Ibid.*, p. 45.
32 *Ibid.*, p. 18.
33 *Ibid.*
34 *Ibid.*
35 *Ibid.*

This "productive agent" is no longer characterized by its exploitation, nor by its being raw material in a labour process, it is characterized by its mobility and interchangeability, by being an insignificant inflection of fixed capital. The "agent of production" designates the ultimate status of Marx's worker who, as he said, "steps to the side of the production process."[36]

Here the discourse of Baudrillard is overly metaphysical. He conceals an opinion Marx proposed in his mid to late studies of political economy, precisely, in the phase of the machine ("fixed capital"[37]) production, skills which were originally included in the material shaped labours and have already been separated independently. The process of production has already become *application* of science and technology, and workers are playing a more and more adjunct and inferior role in the production process, which Baudrillard refers to as uselessness. On the other hand, as manual labour is only adjunct and secondary in mechanized production process, manual labour then is no longer the labour Marx referred to as productive labour which creates value and surplus-value, but instead a productive agent in the industrial mass production. Also in this sense, Baudrillard declares the disappearance of labourers.

Due to his careless reading, Baudrillard has no idea that since the 1960s the problem of the new working class in advanced capitalist countries has become a subject of research for many Western leftist scholars. In the automated and electronic age, the problem that the function and status of traditional physical workers in the production process are declining is getting general attention. Most importantly, Western Marxists and many leftist scholars have begun to study the new questions arising in the capitalist production process and in the whole process of social production, i.e. the important role of white collar workers in the automated production process, functions of pink collar workers in the service industries, the status of steel collar workers as represented by robots, as well as the supervisory function of computer programming workers in the information and electronic industries. Great theoretical concern has been given to these questions, from which some new important theoretical achievements have entered the general knowledge foundational for contemplating

36 *Ibid.*
37 *Ibid.*

the issue of working class in contemporary capitalist study. No one else has made philosophical and political conclusions as cavalierly as Baudrillard has done without first undertaking serious scientific research on these new economic and social phenomena.

In the eyes of Baudrillard, along with the disappearance of labourers disappears the factory as the work site and the determinate work time, as "society as a whole takes on the appearance of a factory."[38] He believes,

> *The factory must disappear as such, and labour must lose its specificity in order that capital can ensure the extensive metamorphosis of its form throughout society as a whole. We must therefore formally recognize the disappearance of the determinate sites of labour, a determinate subject of labour, a determinate time of social labour, we must formally recognize the disappearance of the factory, labour and the proletariat if we want to analyze capital's current and real dominance.*[39]

Baudrillard adamantly uses a total of four "musts"[40] here, as if he is the creator of this new world. One may easily get lost if one reads Baudrillard only for his literal meaning. Actually, what he means to say is that today's capital logic has displaced itself from simple economic domination to an extensive process of omnipresent social existence. Capital steps out of the economic process, becoming the master of all modes of human existence. His is a very grand assertion.

Baudrillard illustrates this point with an ad hoc example in the notes. Specifically, he discusses the development of workers' housing conditions in capitalist society. He says, in Marx's time, workers' housing was simply a 'dorm' directly attached to the factories of capitalists. At that time, workers' housing was "a functional site for the reproduction of labour power, a strategic site for both manufacture and business. Housing was not invested with the form of capital."[41]

---

38 *Ibid.*
39 *Ibid.*
40 *Ibid.*
41 *Ibid.*, p. 45.

However, in the process of capitalist development,

*Gradually, housing is invested as a space-time marked by a direct and generalized process of the control of social space. It becomes a site of reproduction, not of labour but of the **habitat itself as a specific function**, as a direct form of social relation; no longer the reproduction of the worker, but of the inhabitant herself, the user After the proletariat, the 'user' has become the ideal type of the industrial slave. The user of goods, of words, the user of sex, the user of labour herself (the worker or the "agent of production" becomes the user of the factory and of her labour as individual and collective equipment, as a **social service**), the user of transport, but also the user of her life and death.*[42]

(I find that, like the evaluation Marx made on Hegel, the idealistic Baudrillard also provides something interesting and positivistic in the footnotes every now and then.) Here Baudrillard means that housing used to be a reproductive site for labour power, but now has gradually become a site for the reproduction of "users"[43] who are no longer workers. As with the disappearance of labourers, it is the "users" who are controlled by capital logic. Housing is no longer a reproductive site of workers, but of users. It should be recognized that Baudrillard's analysis here is valid in spite of its roughness. Although in Western developed countries, ordinary wage earners can have separate housing (house), there is still no comparison with the mansion of the rich in the real world. From the very start, the so-called "users" in the capitalist society are not absolutely homogeneous.

Baudrillard continues his metaphysical assertions. He believes, in today's capitalist society, factories and principles of labour have exploded and scattered over every aspect of society. Labour is everywhere because there is no real labour. This is the "capital's trap."[44] The model of the factory spreads throughout the social space, thereby, "the asylum form, carceral form, and discrimination have begun to invest the whole social space, every moment of real life."[45] Thereupon, he cites an example of home-based digital work in the United States.

---

42 *Ibid.*, p. 45, note 10.
43 *Ibid.*
44 *Ibid.*, p. 18.
45 *Ibid.*, p. 19.

Thus the Californian utopia of the cybernetic disintegration of the "tertiary metropolis:" home-based computer labour. Labour is pulverized into every pore of society and everyday life. As well as labour power, the space-time of labour also ceases to exist: society constitutes nothing but a single continuum of the processes of value. Labour has become a way of life. Nothing can reinstate the factory walls, the golden age of the factory and class struggle against the ubiquity of capital, surplus-value and labour against their inevitable disappearance as such.[46]

Baudrillard's way of thinking is always different from others. Generally speaking, Marxists would find the *flexible production logic* through changes of modern labour forms, because people are still under capital's domination and exploitation of labours in the traditional non-labour workplace, even though they may not go to factories or companies. The place where Baudrillard asserts lies the obliteration of labour is the consolidation and regeneration of labour in the logical structure of contemporary capital.

Baudrillard cannot see the real *flexible changes* of capital logic, as well as the essence of its new manipulation form. He keeps on writing poems: "there have always been churches to hide the death of God, or to hide the fact that God was everywhere; there will always be animal reserves and Indian reservations to hide the fact that they are dead; there will always be factories and labour to hide the death of labour, the death of production, or the fact that they are everywhere and nowhere."[47] He believes that it would be wrong for us to want to oppose ubiquitous capital in any discreet form. Revolt has lost the determinate target; therefore, today's capital seems to move ever farther away from Marx's exhaustion. This point reflects Baudrillard's political pessimism.

Baudrillard indeed has never stopped his critique of capitalism, but he cannot adhere to the position of Marxism and the methodology of historical materialism. After his denial of Marx, he loses a powerful weapon to fight against the capitalism. Even though he discovers the new nature of capitalism—for example, in simulation and in the simulacrum—most of his conclusions are pessimistic. I am afraid that this pessimism is probably an important reason for Baudrillard's later move toward metaphysics.

---

46   *Ibid.*, p. 45, note 11.
47   *Ibid.*, p. 19.

4 HOLLOWIZATION OF CURRENCY AND STRUGGLES IN THE ILLUSION

Here, Baudrillard makes another important "discovery,"[48] namely the hollowization of capital-oriented money itself as the social realization form of value. He states that the homology Saussure established between labour and the signified on the one hand, and wages and the signifier on the other, is a sort of new base from which to construct political economy. (We do not know where this conclusion comes from. We have already quoted Saussure's statement in the previous section, but Baudrillard does not specify the relationship between labour and the signified on the one hand, and wages and the signifier on the other.) Nonetheless, today the situating basis of social relations no longer exists, because signifiers are severed from the signified, wages are severed from labour, and the traditional theoretical structure with its comparable referents is annihilated completely as well. This statement can be manifested in two aspects:

First of all, production itself is severed from every social reference or finality, so that it enters "a growth phase"[49] without objectification. Here Baudrillard means that production in capitalist society today does not exist to meet people's real needs. If David Ricardo's production is akin to Marx's "production for the sake of production,"[50] then today's production is *for the sake of growth*. In this regard, Baudrillard holds that it is the end of traditional production:

> We enter a phase where neither production nor consumption retains any proper determinations or respective ends. Both become caught in a cycle or spiral, they are overcome by a confusion propagated by growth which leaves the traditional social objectives of production and consumption well behind. This process has only itself as an end. It no longer targets needs or profits. It is not an acceleration of productivity, but a structural inflation of the signs of production… production for production's sake.[51]

Baudrillard says production as such is shown through space programs, industrial park projects, as well as social and individual training programs. Society must have progress and a growing GDP; thus, production is a must. In other words, society has to produce for the sake of growth.

48 *Ibid.*, p. 21.
49 *Ibid.*
50 *Ibid.*
51 *Ibid.*

Secondly, Baudrillard believes that in the system of capitalist society today, the monetary sign is severed from every aspect of social
production and then enters a phase of "speculation and a limitless
inflation."[52] This belief is still the continuity of the situating logic
without a system of reference. Production is severed from needs, becoming a hollow growth; wage is severed from the "right"[53] price of
labour power; currency is severed from "real production"[54] as well.
Ipso facto, currency itself is emptied once again.

> *Purged of finalities and the **affects** of production, money becomes
> speculative. From the gold-standard, which had already ceased
> to be the representative equivalent of a real production but still
> retains traces of this in a certain equilibrium (little inflation , the
> convertibility of money into gold, etc.), to hot money and gener-
> alized flotation, money is transformed from a referential sign into
> its structural form.*[55]

Baudrillard is quite funny. He mentions the end of production
above, only to designate a "real production"[56] here. Perhaps the
problem is the narrowness of his logic. According to his logic in *The
Mirror of Production*, the concept of production is a certain rape of
modernity; if it is true, how can he put forward a real production here?
Furthermore, he has just declared the hollowization (loss of aim) of
production in today's capitalist society; hence, currency here should
be severed from the hollowing-out production as such. It should be
nothing on nothing in Lacanian sense. However, Baudrillard ignores
the overall logical identity for the sake of remarks on the logical
convexity. Luckily, this choice does not affect the theoretical viewpoints he intends to express. He believes that "money can thus be
reproduced according to a simple play of transfers and writings,
according to an incessant splitting and increase of its own abstract
substance."[57] If money in the past was "the first '*commodity*' to assume the status of a sign and to *escape use-value*,"[58] then,

---

52   *Ibid.*
53   *Ibid.*
54   *Ibid.*
55   *Ibid.*
56   *Ibid.*
57   *Ibid.*, p. 22.
58   *Ibid.*

*Today however, money sanctions a further step: it also **escapes exchange-value**. Freed from the market itself, it becomes an autonomous simulacrum, relieved of every message and every signification of exchange, becoming a message itself and exchanging amongst itself. Money is then no longer a commodity since it no longer contains any use-value or exchange-value, nor is it any longer a general equivalent, that is, it is no longer a mediating abstraction of the market.[59]*

Today's money is a free-floating signifier freed from any reference (the signified, i.e. "the mental equivalent of the gold-standard"[60]), whose simple play of flotation can annihilate a nation's economy. If the conscious subject in the past was the mental equivalent of the gold-standard currency system, then the hollowed-out money of today is just like Freud's unconscious. *"The unconscious is the mental equivalent of speculative currency and hot money!"*[61](Please note, the unconscious here is not the thing that grows out of the repression of man's original desire in Freud's sense, but the unconscious in Lacan's intellectual situating, namely the placeholder of the Other discourse after the absence of the subject. Therefore, saying "the unconscious is the mental equivalent of speculative currency and hot money"[62] designates that the essence of today's capitalist economic process is a sort of karate in creation ex nihilo. This opinion is profound, because both the recent Southeast Asian financial crisis and the current capitalist financial crisis sweeping all over the world result from such karate.)

Baudrillard has raised a question: can subjects still exist in this emptied world? "Today, individuals, disinvested as subjects and robbed of their fixed relations, are drifting, in relation to one another, into an incessant mode of transferential fluctuations."[63] In such a state, what else could a social revolution be?

In Baudrillard's eyes, today's proletariat is corrupted, because when proletarians live in "the illusion of production,"[64] that is, under the policy of high welfare, they often think their use value is

---

59 *Ibid.*
60 *Ibid.*, p. 23.
61 *Ibid.*
62 *Ibid.*
63 *Ibid.*
64 *Ibid.*, p. 29.

rewarded. Therefore, "they have looked likely to be the last to re-act, since it is they who can entertain the illusion of 'productive' labour for longest."[65] (According to Herbert Marcuse's old saying, the working class has been already integrated into the capitalist system.) Labour unions and political parties are dead as well, for "all that remains for them to do is die."[66] Today, those labour unions and socialist labour parties in advanced capitalist countries have already become capital's accomplices and the most powerful political traders. The strike is dead as well, since "strikes change nothing fundamental at last."[67] "At best, strikes merely snatch only what, in the end, capital would have conceded anyway."[68] People strike for the sake of striking; therefore, strikes have ceased to be a sort of relation of forces influencing politics, but become an end in and of themselves.

So, with the death of all of the forces of resistance, what else can people do in the face of the terrible capitalism? Baudrillard once again mentions "the May Storm" of 1968 in France, which surpassed "the illusion of production,"[69] but we never know whether it really was the path to man's ultimate salvation. Therefore, when Baudrillard denies the realistic possibilities of every revolution with the application of a poststudy method, his final conclusion is certain to be pessimistic. Obviously, Baudrillard's political idea here takes a big step backwards compared with that in his book *The Mirror of Production*. Aesthetic redemption of traditional Western Marxism almost becomes a science fiction war of special effects when it comes to Baudrillard. It is only a matter of course that the director of *The Matrix* would draw inspiration from his book.[70]

---

65   *Ibid.*, p. 30.
66   *Ibid.*, p. 26.
67   *Ibid.*, p. 24.
68   *Ibid.*
69   *Ibid.*, p. 29.
70   In 1999, American directors Wachowski brothers (Andy Wachowski and Larry Wachowski) were influenced by Baudrillard's book *Simulacres et Simulation* before shooting the film *The Matrix*. It was said that the Wachowski brothers invited Baudrillard to play a role but were rejected. In the movie there is nevertheless a scene where the protagonist Neo symbolically holds the book *Simulacres et Simulation*. *The Matrix* was produced by Warner Bros., USA in 1999. Length: 136 min. Leading actors: Keanu Reeves, Laurence Fishburne and Carrie Anne Moss.

CHAPTER XVII

SIMULATION AND RESISTANCE AGAINST THE CONTEMPORARY SYMBOLIC DOMINANCE OF CAPITAL

In Baudrillard's book *Symbolic Exchange and Death*, the early sections of Chapter One mainly focus on discussing the death and end of traditional social theory model so as to further declare the death of Marx, while in the final section of this chapter he finally arrives at the invention in his original logical situating: simulation. This time, he still takes political economics as the playful object, but the stress has transitioned to a totally new critical perspective concerning the development of contemporary capitalism. I think that this section, despite its self-righteous critique of Marx, might be the best part of this book, and includes some things that really deserve our serious attention. However, the possibility for liberation Baudrillard provides us with at last—the resistance of original symbolic exchange against the symbolic dominance of capital—is still quite disappointing.

1 THE OBSCENE PRESENCE OF CAPITAL LOGIC IN SIMULATION

Baudrillard says that for people who have entered an entirely new bourgeois world of signs in modern times, there is a "real"[1] for reference: political economics. (Of course, according to the analysis Baudrillard makes, the real as such has already experienced a death, namely with the absence of symbolic exchange. Hence, the real is always present *in quotation marks*.) The "real"[2] happens to be a simulation in symbolic signs, because political economics "acts as the horizon of a defunct order whose simulation preserves it in a 'dialectical' equilibrium."[3] Defunct means dead, but the dead is *reconstructed* in the way of a revival via simulation, acting as a dialectical equilibrium in a kind of mirror image of otherness contained in the totality of the sign-situating world. This argument is quite odd. From the Baudrillard's perspective, as with the symbolic society, the "real"[4] in the simulation is the subjective situating in the relation *imaginaire*, "the code (the structural law of value) uses the systematic reactivation of political economy (the restricted market law of value) as our society's imaginary-real. Furthermore, the appearance of the restricted form of value is an attempt to obscure its radical form."[5] (If I am not mistaken, this logical form in which imagination (the defunct "real"[6] in the simulation) supports the social reality is apparently influenced by Lacan. However, Baudrillard never plans to succumb to Lacan in a fundamentalist style, as seen in his statements, Lacan's ideas are often presented in an overly-misinterpreted way.)

What exactly do these puzzling remarks mean? According to my understanding, Baudrillard here means that in contemporary capitalist societies, although the philosophical discourses and thinking paradigms of traditional societies are dead, they often reoccur in the way of imagination, supporting capital's dominance of today with ideological logic (Baudrillard's simulation). For example, "profit,

---

1   *Ibid.*, p. 31.
2   *Ibid.*
3   *Ibid.*
4   *Ibid.*
5   *Ibid.*
6   *Ibid.*

surplus-value, the mechanics of capital and the class struggle: the entire critical discourse on political economy is staged as a referential discourse."[7] These things in the past only happened in the law of commodity value Marx had identified, whereas they may now return to the stage of social criticism *in the way of imagination* even though they are dead in today's symbolic capitalism.

Perhaps for Baudrillard this view still requires a concrete clarification; hence, he uses value as an example. He says that value in traditional social existence has a kind of vague mystique (i.e. Marx's inverted table-turning, when analyzing commodity); however, the mystification of value in today's social life has transferred to the *mystification of structural value.* According to Baudrillard, in today's capitalist society, the economic slavery system, compared with that in the past, has become more "obscene,"[8] or shameless. (In Žižek's words, "they know very well what they are doing, but still, they are doing it."[9] Žižek regards this ideology as the "ideology of cynicism."[10]) Por eso, he cites a wonderful example of an advert for the Banque Nationale de Paris (BNP), which reads: "I am interested in your money—fair's fair—lend me your money and you may profit from my bank."[11] (Once again, he clarifies this example in the footnotes.) To illustrate himself, Baudrillard makes a meticulous discursive analysis.

To begin with, it is the *public prostitution of contemporary capital.* "This is the first time that capital (in its front line institution, namely international finance capital) has so clearly and openly stated the law of equivalence, and, surprisingly, in the form of an advertising slogan."[12] In the past, the nature of such "immoral"[13] transactions was something shameful; capitalists usually would maintain a tacit silence. Hence, similar advertisements in the past time all covered it up, but symbolically dominated people's unconsciousness.

---

7 *Ibid.*
8 *Ibid.*
9 See my essay "Ideology of Cynicism" in *Marxism and Reality*, 2004, 4.
10 *Ibid.*
11 Baudrillard, Jean. *Symbolic Exchange and Death*, Trans. I. Hamilton Grant. London: Sage Publication Ltd, 1993, p. 46, note 21.
12 *Ibid.*
13 *Ibid.*, p. 47, note 21.

(Nowadays, the same phenomena quite often happen around us as well.) Capital is candid with us, nakedly, and convexly. Baudrillard says, "this candor is a second-degree mask."[14] (Baudrillard really likes the "second"[15] situating, whose historical context is Hegel's "second nature,"[16] but he often applies it to illustrate complex reflexive relations, or original restoration which has already changed.)

Second is the deep desire, produced by *direct obscenity* of contemporary capitalist economy. Baudrillard says the seeming aim (the first-degree mask) is to convince people to take their money to BNP for a deal, whereas the real strategy is this "man to man"[17] ideological logic of bourgeois cynicism:

> *Saying 'let's not be sentimental about this' 'no more of the ideology of dependence' 'cards on the table' etc., and so to seduce people by means of the obscenity of revealing the hidden immoral law of equivalence... Hence, the smell of lechery about this advert, the salaciousness and smuttiness of the eyes glued to your money as if it were your genitals. The technique used by the advert is a perverse provocation which is much more subtle than the simplistic seduction of the smile.[18]*

Baudrillard goes on to affirm that, under the influence of today's capital, "people are seduced by the obscenity of the economic, taken to the level of the perverse fascination that the very atrocity of capital exercises on them."[19] It is similar to a bugger saying to another man, "I am interested in your arse—fair's fair—lend me your buttocks and I'll bugger you."[20] Put in this way, capitalists in the past would feel shameful to occupy belongings of others, so they persisted in hiding the exploitative relation as such, whereas today's capitalists solicit in the way of public prostitution. Impudence has its own infinite charm.

Third is the law of *capital's control of signs* at a deeper level. Baudrillard says, it is not enough, the mystification of structural value is often embodied in the concave underside beyond people's

---

14   *Ibid.*
15   *Ibid.*
16   *Ibid.*
17   *Ibid.*
18   *Ibid.*
19   *Ibid.*
20   *Ibid.*

awareness, because the advertising executives are clearly aware that "this advert, with its vampiric image, scared the middle classes, so as to provoke negative reactions. Why did they take this risk?"[21]

> *Here we have the strangest trap: the advert was made to con-*
> *solidate the resistance to the law of profit and equivalence so as*
> *to be better able to impose the equivalence of capital, profit, and*
> *the economic in general (the 'fair's fair') at a time when this is*
> *no longer true, when capital has displaced its strategy and so is*
> *able to state its 'law' since it is no longer its truth. Announcing*
> *this law is nothing more than a supplementary mystification.*[22]

What is the new law of capital today? Or, what is the object covered up by a convex mask at the surface? Baudrillard says that "capital no longer thrives on the rule of any economic law, which is why the law can be made into an advertising slogan, falling into the sphere of the sign and its manipulation."[23] That is to say, the real winner is *capital's manipulation of signs at a deep level.* Here capital slips in and out of shadows, almost unmasking itself and exposing the law of equivalence covered up in the traditional concave underside, precisely the equivalent exchange of commodity value; nonetheless, the law of equivalence emerges only to "secure *credibility*,"[24] a kind of credibility that comes from the *defunct* economic order. This credibility is a sort of imaginary support in the reconstructed *simulation.* Such a situating of economic relation in imagination supports and constitutes the reality, but it disguises that "the credence sums up in itself the identity of the capitalist order and comes from the symbolic order."[25] Here, "unmasking itself"[26] is precisely the second-degree mask! To let you see is, as it were, a deeper disguise. (This is a typical Lacanian logic; however, as far as I am concerned, it is overly arbitrary for Baudrillard to quote Lacan's remarks, dragging Lacan's Imaginary, Symbol, and Real *concerning the individual subject* into the social field. It is always problematic to be too simple. At this point, Žižek's approach seems to be much better and

---

21 *Ibid.*
22 *Ibid.*
23 *Ibid.*
24 *Ibid.*, p. 48, note 21.
25 *Ibid.*
26 *Ibid.*, p. 47, note 21.

a lot more professional.[27]) Anyway, this idea should be counted as the most brilliant and profound statement I have ever seen among Baudrillard's critique of contemporary capitalist ideology.

In Baudrillard's eyes, "capital no longer looks to nature, God or morality for its alibis."[28] Nature here refers to natural law as it has been conceived since the age of enlightenment and the natural order that starts with economic physiocratism. In the natural ideology as such, the capitalist mode of production is designated as the natural lifestyle of human beings, while looking to God for its "alibis,"[29] or the proof of innocence, undoubtedly refers to the "Mission"[30] theory of Max Weber, which integrates worldly profit-seeking activities with divine attributes; not to mention morality, which is always the last fig-leaf in the recognition of bourgeois existential legitimacy, from Adam Smith to John Rawls. Here Baudrillard means that to-day's capital directly goes for its existential place in the critiques and revelations of itself made by the political economics of spectralized Marx. I am shameless, but if you want the money, you are welcome to take it. Please note, shamelessness is not a self-reference of capital itself, but the critical designation *resimulated* by logical ordering of political economy. People can feel an unprecedented candor from such simulations; thereby, it is in the simulated situation of the dead critique of the political economy that people are willing to fall into the unhidden trap of capital. The above is a new domination strategy of capital's manipulation of signs. Let me tell you that *this is a trap*. The capital simulation really caters to the greed of man. (In the American movie *The Devil's Advocate*, the devil is the embodiment of man's desire and greed.[31])

27   Žižek, Slavoj. *The Sublime Object of Ideology*. London: Verso Books, 1997.
28   Baudrillard, Jean. *Symbolic Exchange and Death,* Trans. I. Hamilton Grant. London: Sage Publication Ltd, 1993, p. 31.
29   *Ibid.*
30   *Ibid.*, p. 52.
31   *Devil's Advocate*, distributed by Warner Bros. in 1997.

2 SIMULATION AT THE SECOND LEVEL

Here it seems that Baudrillard quite appreciates Pierre Bourdieu's theory of reproduction.[32] He believes that in contemporary capitalist society, all products and labour exist beyond simple usefulness and uselessness; hence, there is no productive labour, but *non-productive* reproduction and reproductive consumption. What is non-productive reproduction then? It refers to *contentless* reproduction replacing qualitative production in a system of reproduction, whose nature is "revolving around itself in a gigantic tautology of the labour process."[33] (Non-productive reproduction is the simulated manifestation in the real world of tautological ideology Baudrillard once discussed.) In this respect, Baudrillard feels that his idea approximates with Bourdieu's, because the research Pierre Bourdieu and Jean-Claude Passeron made on the academic system under the control of contemporary capital relates "whose alleged autonomy enables it to reproduce the class structure of society very efficiently."[34] (Actually, I think this approximation with Bourdieu reflects Baudrillard's self-righteous thinking. Bourdieu's reproduction does not have Baudrillard's specialized meaning for non-productive, but proves the inner production mechanism and process of how universities reproduce the bourgeois "elites"[35] from the perspective of sociology.)

Baudrillard says that in the past, reproduction of production relations in capitalist societies took place alongside commodity production, which is a result of shaped labour. "A commodity must have a use-value in order to sustain the system of exchange-value."[36] This process is the first-level scenario. However, "simulation is today at the second level: a commodity must function as an exchange-value in order better to hide the fact that it circulates like a sign and reproduces the code."[37] (Once again, we encounter this lovely "second."[38])

32   Bourdieu, Pierre and Passeron, Jan-Claude. *Reproduction in Education, Society and Culture*. London: Sage Publication Ltd, 1990.
33   Baudrillard, Jean. *Symbolic Exchange and Death*, Trans. I. Hamilton Grant. London: Sage Publication Ltd, 1993, p. 27.
34   *Ibid.*, p. 31.
35   *Ibid.*, p. 52.
36   *Ibid.*, p. 31.
37   *Ibid.*
38   *Ibid.*

Baudrillard means that in a Marxist context "a naturalist phantasy,"[39] referring to use-value, already exists—that is , use-value is the foundation of "exchange-value."[40] Nonetheless, he does not know that use-value appearing as the reference frame is constructed by exchange-value. (We have already been made familiar with this point of view.) Nevertheless, in the law of structural value of signs today, the reference frame of *imaginary situating* is the dead "exchange-value."[41] According to Baudrillard, it is a new sort of "economistic phantasy."[42] "In the structural play of the code, exchange-value plays the same role as use-value used to play in the market law of value, the role of the simulacrum of reference."[43] Hence, today's society functions at the Marxian-critical level in order to mask the real domination of capital logic in the *Symbolic field*. Baudrillard provides quite a profound designation. He would like to tell us that the real domination of contemporary capitalism has transferred to the control of pseudo-symbolic code, whereas society still examines itself within the critical dimensions provided by Marx. The critical-ness may exactly prove capitalist social progress in the political and economical spheres after Keynes's revolution and war so as to *ignore and forget* the emergence of new symbolic domination.

> *The social relations of symbolic domination utterly submit to the mode of production (both the forces of production and the relations of production), where we find, in the apparent movement of political economy and the revolution, a new legitimacy and the most perfect alibi.*
>
> *Hence the necessity of resurrecting and dramatizing political economy in the form of a movie script, to screen out the threat of symbolic destruction. Hence, the kind of crisis, the perpetual simulacrum of a crisis, we are dealing with today.*[44]

In this respect, Baudrillard is extremely profound. His perspective indeed transcends all existing social critical theories. Nevertheless, it is unnecessary for Baudrillard to desperately depreciate every existing social theory in order to earn legitimacy for his theoretical

39 *Ibid.*, p. 48.
40 *Ibid.*
41 *Ibid.*
42 *Ibid.*
43 *Ibid.*
44 *Ibid.*, pp. 31-32.

invention. He brings such critique against ecology as well. In his view, capital may "burst from these liquefied values"[45] because of its loss of "the ethical, ascetic myth of labour;"[46] thus, "in order to reestablish finalities and to reactivate the principle of economics, we must generate shortages once again."[47]

> *Hence ecology, where the danger of absolute scarcity reinstates an ethic of energy conservation. Hence the crisis of energy and raw materials, a real blessing for a system which, in the mirror of production, only reflects a fluctuating, empty form. The crisis will enable the return of a lost referentiality to the economic code, and will give the principle of production a gravity that evaded it. We will rediscover a taste for ascesis, that pathetic investment born of lack and deprivation.*[48]

Baudrillard believes that the ecological crisis is a crisis no longer of production, but of reproduction. It is another secondary crisis! In this sort of artificial crisis, "production haunted by shortages uses itself as a resource, once more discovers a natural necessity where the law of value is tried out again."[49] He seems to say that the critical tension of ecology is precisely the new survival strategy of the simulated logic of capital. (Despite his theoretical artificiality, Baudrillard indeed blazes a new path with his thinking. His is an explanation different from Marxist critical dimension of capitalism in the ecology.) From the perspective of Baudrillard, "it is comforting to think that it was 'great capital' that provoked the crisis, because it restores a *real* political-economic agency and the presence of a (hidden) subject of the crisis, and therefore a historical truth."[50] The statement amounts to the simulation at the second level in the sense of Baudrillard. Simulation is not the *simulated production of an existing object*, but *in the sense of a spectre*, a *reconstruction* of the never-existed real (i.e. production, labour, and use-value). Simulation is an *open conspiracy* of code: a code plays at the symbolic level in order to confirm its existential legitimacy. Simulation means *an ideological support of imaginary remnants for symbolic*

---

45 *Ibid.*, p. 32.
46 *Ibid.*
47 *Ibid.*
48 *Ibid.*
49 *Ibid.*
50 *Ibid.*, p. 33.

existence. The above is an extremely deep critical reflection. It is in this sense that Baudrillard begins to regard "economic simulation,"[51] such as ecological crises, as something "at the fringe of a process of reproduction, into which it is entirely absorbed."[52] He inquires, have there ever been "*real* shortages"[53] today? Have "shortages ever had a use-value?"[54] The answers are negative, because everything belongs to the simulation produced by "the code's hegemonic control"[55] of capital, and "the mythical operation of the economy."[56] What a terrifying reflection!

I think Baudrillard's analysis of simulations in the domination logic of contemporary capitalism has its significance; nonetheless, his imprudence both in deprecating all other social theories and in stereotyping new social phenomena, especially his attack on Marxism by way of caricature, reflects his lack of theoretical confidence.

3 SYMBOLIC EXCHANGE: THE ONLY WAY OUT FOR THE RESISTANCE AGAINST CONTEMPORARY CAPITAL LOGIC

So, do we still have the ability to fight against capital's domination in such a simulated society, whose essence is the situating of pseudo-symbolic code? Is Marxism still the appropriate theoretical direction for us to take to destroy today's capitalist domination? These questions are the theoretical entrance where Baudrillard intends to show his brilliance. He is discontented with the fact that intellectuals left aside Marxism after the "May Storm"[57] of 1968 in Europe. (I find that most of Baudrillard's judgments differ from normal people's. In reality, in Europe directly following May '68, the entire intelligentsia turned sharply right and started to get rid of the direct use of the resources of Marxist theory. The so-called postmodern perspective is the direct consequence of this turn. Marx's spiritual legacy merely functions at a deeper level of Derrida's "spectral." Probably, Baudrillard's signified is precisely the "simulated" aspect

---

51   *Ibid.*
52   *Ibid.*
53   *Ibid.*
54   *Ibid.*
55   *Ibid.*
56   *Ibid.*
57   *Ibid.*, p. 34.

at the second level—that is, Marx is referred to *in the criticized and negative sense*. His is a thinking level that can hardly be understood by normal people.)

According to Baudrillard, scholars today believe that "everything can be expressed in terms of political economy and production. Sociologists, human scientists, etc. turn to Marxism as the discourse to which they refer."[58] (Note that, as might have been expected, Marx is present as the defunct referential discourse.) As far as Baudrillard was concerned, May '68 "marked the decisive step in the *naturalisation of political economy*."[59] (According to my understanding, here Baudrillard may be referring to Gilles Deleuze, Pierre Bourdieu et al., because both Deleuzian machines désirantes and Bourdieu's critique of academic capital and social capital are new logical variations of Marx's critique of political economy.) Baudrillard thinks otherwise, saying that the simulated existence of political economy merely secretly coincides with the second level illusion provided by capital logic. We should throw off the mask, as the governance of contemporary capitalism is "based on things voided of their substance, and simulacra immediately anticipate every determination of our lives."[60] Here no longer exist such historical farces as the Napoleon III-type slapstick Marx once confronted, which can be "effortlessly overcome by real history."[61] Simulacrum has the nature of *otherness*, and simulacrum constitutes phantoms. In the past, Marx thought that "living labour power was the objective historical and necessary foundation of capital, he could only think that it was digging its own grave,"[62] whereas Baudrillard believes that it would be simulated illusions created by capital to talk about labour power and revolution. As capital has buried labour power, the regeneration and presence of labour power are no doubt simulated, that is, *referenced after death*. More subtly, he states,

> *It turns labour power into the second term of a stable opposition with capital. It makes this rupturing **energy** which should shatter the relations of production into a term homogeneous with the*

---

58 *Ibid.*, pp. 33-34.
59 *Ibid.*, p. 34.
60 *Ibid.*, p. 35.
61 *Ibid.*
62 *Ibid.*

relation of production , in a simulation of opposition under the
sign of dead labour From now on a single hegemonic agency
(dead labour) divides into capital and living labour The antago-
nism is resolved by a binary apparatus of coded operativity.[63]

This opinion is still *an opposition in the simulation* because according to the clarification Baudrillard mentioned above, the binary
configuration of critical logic as such will immediately lose its critical significance in contemporary capitalist society as soon as labour
is dead in the generalization of nonproductive service-labour.

On the other hand, Baudrillard says, contemporary capital seems
to have a "Marxist's intuition,"[64] because if capital sticks to the terrain of production, it is heading for its real death. "Everything happened as if it had clearly understood Marx on this point and had,
in consequence, 'chosen' to liquidate production so as to go onto
another kind of strategy."[65] He does not mean that capital always
had this "productivist view;"[66] it is more likely that capital "only
ever played at production, even if this meant that production had
to be abandoned at a later stage, were it to draw capital into fatal
contradictions."[67] From Baudrillard's perspective, today's capitalist
system does not exist on the plane of the "real,"[68] as economic infrastructure and superstructure do; hence, it is impossible for people to
destroy the new capitalist system of code via political and economic
revolution in the real world, as "everything produced by contradiction, by the relation of forces, or by energy in general, will only feed
back into the mechanism and give it impetus, following a circular
distortion similar to a Möbius strip."[69] (Once again, we see the weird
appropriation of Lacan's theories.) Thereby,

*We will never defeat the system on the plane of the **real**: the worst*
error of all our revolutionary strategies is to believe that we will
*put an end to the system on the plane of the **real**: this is their*
imaginary, imposed on them by the system itself, living or surviv-
ing only by always leading those who attack the system to fight

---

63   *Ibid.*, p. 35.
64   *Ibid.*
65   *Ibid.*
66   *Ibid.*, p. 36.
67   *Ibid.*
68   *Ibid.*
69   *Ibid.*

*amongst each other on the terrain of reality, which is **always the reality of the system.**[70]*

The reason why this system (later, in the film *The Matrix*, the system is symbolically reinforced to be the all-powerful "Matrix") can never be defeated on the plane of the real is that "it thrives on symbolic violence."[71] Baudrillard believes that it does not refer to "a violence 'of signs,' from which the system draws strength, or with which it 'masks' its material violence,"[72] but the thing deduced "from a logic of the symbolic."[73] The essence of this violence of signs is "the seizing of power by the unilateral exercise of the gift."[74] This logical situating is quite complex.

The first level of logical situating here, specifically, the *"logic of the symbolic,"*[75] is the symbolic exchange relation Baudrillard used as the authentic foundation for his theories. On the basis of the abovementioned discussions, we know that the essence of symbolic exchange is a sort of disordered practice of the gift without the measurement of values. Actually, the nature of the gift exchange should be *bilateral*. Nonetheless, "when this reversibility is broken, precisely by the unilateral possibility of giving (which presupposes the possibility of stockpiling value and transferring it in one direction only), then the properly symbolic relation is dead and power makes an appearance: it will merely be deployed thereafter throughout the economic apparatus of the contract."[76] This statement is the transformation at the first level of situating, that is, the transformation of symbolic exchange relation into utilitarian value relation; whereas the symbolic violence in the contemporary capitalist system mentioned here by Baudrillard is a simulacrum of the code at the second level of situating. If in the value exchange relation at the first level is the "unilateral gift"[77] of economy, at the second level is the "unilateral gift"[78] of omnipresent pseudo-symbolic code. The symbolic

---

70 *Ibid.*
71 *Ibid.*
72 *Ibid.*
73 *Ibid.*
74 *Ibid.*
75 *Ibid.*
76 *Ibid.*, p. 48.
77 *Ibid.*, p. 36.
78 *Ibid.*

exchange of authenticity is bilateral and disordered, whereas the pseudo-symbolic relation of code simulation is *unilateral and ordered*. The unilateral symbolic relation as such is the domination of desire! The violence of signs, which is everywhere and at every instant in today's advertising and mass media, is the most powerful violence, and "nothing is any longer permitted to escape."[79] Baudrillard believes that the economic violence inflicted on him in the economic relations is "nothing next to the symbolic violence inflicted on him by his definition as a productive force."[80] This belief might be a little bit exaggerative.

Baudrillard supposes that the only solution for resisting symbolic violence is to "turn the principle of its power back against the system itself: the impossibility of responding or retorting. *To defy the system with a gift to which it cannot respond save by its own collapse and death*."[81] (The above is perhaps the real meaning of "turn Mauss against Mauss"[82] discussed in the preface of this book.) Generally speaking, this death is symbolic death. Admittedly, the symbol here is pseudo-symbol. The only time symbolic violence cannot exert is its own death. After all, the weapon of resistance used to confront contemporary capital logic is still Baudrillard's symbolic exchange, owing to the fact that only the counter-gift, the reversibility of the symbolic exchange, abolishes power. Symbolic exchange turns out to be "a radical otherness" in Baudrillard's rejection of the kingdom of signs in modern times. (Douglas Kellner correctly holds that Baudrillard has "both technophobia and nostalgia for face-to-face communication."[83]) It is just this time that Other threatens with its life.

---

79   *Ibid.*
80   *Ibid.*, p. 39.
81   *Ibid.*, p. 36-37.
82   *Ibid.*, p. 1.
83   Kellner, Douglas. *Baudrillard: A Critical Reader*. Cambridge: Basil Blackwell Ltd, 1994, p. 160.

CHAPTER XVIII

SIMULACRA AND SIMULATION: VISTA OF THE BOURGEOIS KINGDOM

Simulacra and simulation (simulacres et simulations) is the title of another book, written by Baudrillard in 1981. It not only includes the main content of his original situating, but also a brand new theoretical modelling that he applies to re-paint the entire picture of capitalism. In Baudrillard's eyes, starting from the counterfeit, which is the primary form of simulacra, via production, and on to the model formation of simulation, the bourgeoisie finally completes the recreation of world. This process is a "trompe L'oeil"[1] genesis. As for the discussion of this issue, Baudrillard starts from Chapter Two of *Symbolic Exchange and Death*, whose very core is the discussion of the three orders in the simulacra world of capitalism. However, it is after he touches on this new problem that his core theoretical logic begins to fall apart. The clarity of his thinking in the previous chapter is almost gone, leaving only discursive prose lade more with fragments of empirical phenomena than with universal principles, and with more belles-lettres signs than real ideas. What a picture

---

1   Baudrillard, Jean. *The Perfect Crime*, Trans. Chris Turner. London: Verso, 1996, p. 21.

of code simulation! However, we also find that when Baudrillard stops intentionally opposing Marx, the deep thinking presented in the theoretical logic of his social critique is indeed remarkable.

1 THE COUNTERFEIT: HIERARCHICAL TRANSGRESSION OF SIGNS AND SIMULACRA OF NATURE

As quoted in the Introduction of this book, Baudrillard has already divided the simulacra world peculiar to the capitalism into three orders, precisely *counterfeit, production*, and *simulation*. Additionally, the three orders are historically related to three periods of capitalist development and three laws (three orders), that is, the natural law of value from the Renaissance to the Industrial Revolution, the market law of value in the industrial era, and the structural law of value in the current code-governed phase.

Baudrillard begins by talking about the form of simulacra at the first stage of capitalist development, namely the counterfeit from the Renaissance to the Industrial Revolution and the counterfeit operating on the natural law of value. (His title for this section, *The Stucco Angel* shines too aesthetic. Obviously, this "counterfeit"[2] is ad hoc, since during the historical process of man's social production before feudal society, labour tools were produced on the basis of the imitation of natural materials or living creatures. Even so, Baudrillard here specializes counterfeit as the signified with bourgeois characteristics.) He says that the counterfeit is born with the Renaissance. One important demarcation is that the presence of counterfeit and the destructuration of feudal order occur at the same moment. This is a unique point.

Firstly, the counterfeit appears in the hierarchical transgression of signs. As in the rank-based feudal society and caste society, "signs are protected by a prohibition which confers an unequivocal status on each."[3] (Similarly, monarch, minister, and subject in ancient China possessed their own fixed symbols and signs. At that time, everyone knew that the imperial robe and the mandarin jacket could not be casually worn by the masses.)

---

2 Baudrillard, Jean. *Symbolic Exchange and Death*, Trans. I. Hamilton Grant. London: Sage Publication Ltd, 1993, p. 50.
3 *Ibid.*

*In feudal or archaic caste societies, in cruel societies, signs are
limited in number and their circulation is restricted. Each retains
its full value as a prohibition, and each carries with it a reciprocal obligation between castes, clans or persons, so signs are not
arbitrary.*[4]

"Counterfeit"[5] of signs is not possible in ceremony, as the mixing
of signs is punishable. (Therefore, we can find that the counterfeit
of Baudrillard here particularly refers to a sort of symbolic *sign relation*.) The problem Baudrillard does not pursue seriously is the
specific order of symbolic relations in the feudal structure.

When the bourgeoisie first appeared on the stage of history, one
of the first occurrences was the *emancipation* of the signs. "The end
of the obligatory signs is succeeded by the reign of the emancipated sign, in which any and every class will be able to participate."[6]
Along with the change in their status, the rising capitalists cause
the signs to present emancipated flotation, which is the original historical appearance of the counterfeit. (Efrat Tseelon also elaborated
on the symbolic order of clothing prohibitions within the feudal hierarchy in European medieval times, and on the imitation of these
clothes coinciding with the appearance of the capitalist class in the
late fourteenth century.[7])

For from a limited order of signs, (the 'free' production of which
is prevented by a prohibition), we pass into a proliferation of signs
according to demand. These multiple signs, however, no longer
have anything to do with the restricted circulation of the obligatory
sign, but counterfeit the latter Counterfeiting does not take place
by means of changing the nature of an 'original', but, by extension,
through completely altering a material whose clarity is completely
dependent upon a restriction.[8]

---

4   *Ibid.*
5   *Ibid.*
6   *Ibid.*, pp. 50-51.
7   Tseelon, Efrat. "Fashion and Signification in Baudrillard". *Baudrillard: A Critical
Reader*, edited by Douglas Kellner. Cambridge: Basil Blackwell Ltd, 1994. pp. 119-134.
8   Baudrillard, Jean. *Symbolic Exchange and Death*, Trans. I. Hamilton Grant.
London: Sage Publication Ltd, 1993, p. 51.

I think the logic of this paragraph is fairly clear. Here Baudrillard clarifies the historical occurrence of counterfeit, namely the first-order simulacrum, in the sign relations. The counterfeit of free signs is the destructuration of the obligatory, fixed, and ordered signs of feudal society, and especially refers to sign transgression caused by the status changes experienced capitalists in early capitalist social life. Sign transgression as such often presents itself as a transcendence of the original, obligatory sign prohibitions; escaping the prohibitions; and "counterfeiting"[9] new signs according to needs for status. This process is an emancipation of signs, an emancipation of the signifier from the oppression of the solid signified, and a transformation from feudalistic, objectified reference of signs to free arbitrariness. (I do not know whether Baudrillard has the intention of seeking a historical and realistic basis for the logic of Saussure's theory of the arbitrariness of signs, but if he does, his remarks here should be really considered profound and of great historical significance.) Baudrillard says, "non-discriminatory (the sign is nothing any longer if not competitive), relieved of every constraint, universally available, the modern sign nevertheless still simulates necessity by giving the appearance that it is bound to the world."[10] (This "giving the appearance"[11] coincides with the succeeding simulation.) This remark is dense with meaning.

Secondly, the counterfeit is the *simulacra of nature* in the early process of capitalist production. Baudrillard believes, "this problematic of the 'natural' and the metaphysics of reality was, for the bourgeoisie since the Renaissance, the mirror of both the bourgeois and the classical sign."[12] In my view, this statement is quite perceptive. Obviously, in both Western experimental science and the dualistic logic of philosophy in modern times, even the historical occurrence of the *natural ideology* of the entire bourgeoisie relates to the "mirror of the classical sign."[13] (I find that although Baudrillard keeps on criticizing Marx, his analysis here more or less embodies the methodology of historical materialism. I'm afraid there is a sort of

---

9   *Ibid.*, p. 50.
10   *Ibid.*, p. 51.
11   *Ibid.*
12   *Ibid.*
13   *Ibid.*

deep, theoretical unconsciousness, or theoretical simulation, in his unconsciousness.)

Baudrillard says it is in the Renaissance that the "forgery was born along with the natural."[14] (The *appeared* nature is no doubt the Nature Heidegger mentioned, which as a whole becomes the object of industrial production, rather than the natural material existence in general.) Examples he cites here are "the deceptive finery on people's backs, the stucco interiors, Baroque theatrical scenery."[15] It seems that Baudrillard sings highly of stucco and Baroque art, the former in particular, because

> From these incredible achievements with stucco and Baroque art we can unravel the metaphysics of the counterfeit, as well as the new ambitions of Renaissance man. These latter consist in an earthly demiurgy, the transubstantiation of all nature into a single substance, a theatrical sociality unified under the sign of bourgeois values, beyond differences of blood, rank or caste.[16]

Baudrillard's judgment is basically correct. In his view, "the Promethean designs of the bourgeoisie are first engrossed in the *imitation of nature*, before it throws itself into production."[17] As for stucco, Baudrillard offers the following concrete description: "In the churches and palaces, stucco embraces all forms, imitates all materials: velvet curtains, wooden cornices, and fleshy curves of the body."[18] This sort of artificial, new compound substance transfigures into "a sort of general equivalent for all the others,"[19] and "a mirror of all the others."[20] (I think the metaphysical uplift as such has gone a little far.)

According to the definition he offers above, right now it is the so-called law of value of nature that takes a leading role. I mentioned in the previous section that the law of value of nature specifically refers to the existence of natural objects forced to integrate into the utilitarian value system of man following the shaping of labour. However,

14 *Ibid.*
15 *Ibid.*
16 *Ibid.*
17 *Ibid.*, p. 52.
18 *Ibid.*
19 *Ibid.*
20 *Ibid.*

one of Baudrillard's judgments is of validity. He believes the later bourgeoisie already bears witness in the counterfeit "to the same project of universal control and hegemony, to a social schema in whose foundations the internal coherence of a system already operates."[21] (The "the internal coherence"[22] here is identity in Adorno's sense. The control of nature will inevitably turn into the control of social life; the liberating force of enlightenment will definitely move towards a deeper self-enslavement.)

2 PRODUCTION WITH NO PROTOTYPE AND REPRODUCTION OF SERIES

In Baudrillard's view, in taking a metaphysical perspective of the counterfeit—the first order in the bourgeois world of simulacra—we can find an important qualitative clue: the counterfeit, the simulacra, and the objectified nature under imitation still exist in a heterogeneous relation; *the real is still in existence*; the simulacra exist as convex *representations*, all of which means there is coexistence of representations and objects. (Please pay attention to Baudrillard's real here. It is not the symbolic exchange as the real being of man and society, which Baudrillard verified repeatedly in the previous section, but a general reference to the objective being of common things and phenomena. Nonetheless, later, in *The Perfect Crime*, the meaning situating of the real is greatly generalized.) The counterfeit does not abolish qualitative difference, "it presupposes the dispute always in evidence between the simulacrum and the real."[23] Baudrillard says, "all art thrives on this difference"[24]. In actuality, there are "disputes"[25] in epistemology.

However, the second order in the bourgeois world of simulacra is completely different. It is the simulacrum that operates on the market law of value and that found in the industrial era.

The second-order simulacrum simplifies the problem by the absorption of appearances, or by the liquidation of the real, whichever you prefer In any case it erects a reality without images,

---

21 *Ibid.*
22 *Ibid.*
23 *Ibid.*, p. 54.
24 *Ibid.*
25 *Ibid.*

without echo, without mirrors, without appearances: such indeed
is labour, such is the machine, such is the entire industrial system
of production in that it is radically opposed to the principle of
theatrical illusion.[26]

The second-order simulacrum presents itself with "four with-outs," which are "without images, without echo, without mirrors, without appearances."[27] It is with these metaphysical descriptions that Baudrillard defines the system of *industrial production*, whose essence is labour and machine. (Obviously, the labour here is ad hoc; it is the industrial labour which creates value in the capitalist mode of production, instead of general human labour. I once emphasized that the most important qualitative character of industrial production is to create something that has never existed in nature before. Industrial production, for the first time, changes man's dependence on nature characteristic of agricultural production. Baudrillard here also abstractly expresses the same idea.) From Baudrillard's perspective of Baudrillard, human beings do not eliminate simple counterfeits with imitative objects and enter into (re)production until they realize the machine system of industrial production. Meanwhile, "we are leaving natural law and its play of forms in order to enter the market law of value and its calculations of forces."[28] In the sense of economics, this idea represents the entering into commodity-market economic mode of production peculiar to capitalism. Henceforth, the law of value of nature gives way to the law of value of commodity production. Of course, what occurs at the same moment is the objectification process of science and technology, which is isomorphic with industrial production. Hence, Baudrillard holds a negative attitude towards science. No wonder later he directly says, "forgetting of the original murder is part of the logic and triumphant unfolding of science."[29] (Here "murder"[30] means that the object is deprived of its naturalness, converting it into shaped utility cantered on man's needs; while forgetting is not an ontological loss as in Heidegger's

---

26   *Ibid.*
27   *Ibid.*
28   *Ibid.*, pp. 54-55.
29   Baudrillard, Jean. *Seduction*, Trans. Brian Singer. Montreal: New World Perspectives, 1990, p. 56.
30   *Ibid.*

theoretical situating. I think that Baudrillard's "forgetting"[31] here is misrecognition and logical strabismus in the Kantian sense of mistakenly taking man's legislation against nature to be objective laws of external nature. It is a deep malaise of dialectical materialism in Stalin's dogmatic system.)

The second-order simulacrum is identified as "the industrial simulacrum,"[32] in which production is everything. Please note that the production Baudrillard mentions here is not ordinary material production, but an ad hoc setting of metaphysics, that is, *production with no original origin*. If in pre-industrial times there was the objectified nature-ordered image of the simulated stereotype in the labour-shaped counterfeit, then the starting point of industrial production would be non-prototyped manufacture and ordering. It is in this regard that Mark Poster makes the following analysis. In the simulacra,

> *The distinctions between object and representation, thing and idea are no longer valid. In their place Baudrillard fathoms a strange new world constructed out of models or simulacra which have no referent or ground in any "reality" except their own. A simulation is different from a fiction or lie in that it not only presents an absence as a presence, the imaginary as the real, it also undermines any contrast to the real, absorbing the real within itself. Instead of a "real" economy of commodities that is somehow bypassed by an "unreal" myriad of advertising images, Baudrillard now discerns only a hyperreality, a world of self-referential signs.*[33]

If Poster's clarification aims at the second order simulacra of Baudrillard, it is valid to point out that the "distinctions between object and representation"[34] disappear, and simulacra no longer refer to any "reality,"[35] whereas Poster ignores Baudrillard's qualitative division of three orders of simulacra. As in the counterfeit—the first-order simulacrum—the boundary of object and representation is still

31   *Ibid.*
32   Baudrillard, Jean. *Symbolic Exchange and Death*, Trans. I. Hamilton Grant. London: Sage Publication Ltd, 1993, p. 55.
33   Poster, Mark. *Jean Baudrillard: Selected Writings*. Stanford: Stanford University Press, 2001, p. 6.
34   *Ibid.*
35   *Ibid.*

in existence; simulacra only annihilate the objectified originality in the modern situation of capitalist industrial production. (Out of the same logical confusion Baudrillard stirs in the third-order simulacrum—hyperreality—which is constructed by simulation, without specific explanations. What a pity!)

It is in this sense that we can say the industrial bourgeoisie is the genuine *demiurge* of mankind. Compared with the world history of capital, the Genesis of God appears to be so primitive and weak. Here,

> *A new generation of signs and objects arises with the Industrial Revolution- signs with no caste tradition that will never have known restrictions on their status, and which will never have to be counterfeits, since from the outset they will be products on a gigantic scale. The problem of their specificity and their origin is no longer posed: technics is their origin, they have meaning only within the dimension of the industrial simulacrum.*[36]

Different from the signs in the counterfeits, the simulacrum of code in the production has lost its original model. (This loss is the realistic social basis for Saussure's linguistic revolution.) Now it is series that are the existing form of objects, which are the results of production. (We have encountered this series before in Baudrillard's books *The System of Object* and *For a Critique of the Political Economy of the Sign*, but the signifieds there are different.) The nature of series is the appearance of two or more identical objects. Baudrillard believes that the relations between seriesly produced objects are entirely new.

> *The relation between them is no longer one of an original and its counterfeit, analogy or reflection, but is instead one of equivalence and indifference. In the series, objects become indistinct simulacra of one another and, along with objects, of the men that produce them. The extinction of the original reference alone facilitates the general law of equivalences, that is to say, **the very possibility of production.***[37]

36 Baudrillard, Jean. *Symbolic Exchange and Death*, Trans. I. Hamilton Grant. London: Sage Publication Ltd, 1993, p. 55.
37 *Ibid.*

Different from the counterfeit in the first order, the simulacrum of industrial production has already lost its archetype. The nature of artificial manufacture is not an imitation, but a recombination and an ordering of new material. The existing forms of products are *simulacra of one another* with infinite possibilities. Industrial production, heterogeneous with the counterfeit in the face of natural objects, is in essence a non-counterfeiting serial *manufacture*. Therefore, it is only possible for industrial products to replicate in large numbers in *the process of reproduction*. Additionally, reproduction here is neither a repeated simple reproduction nor a creative expanded reproduction, which serve as the production process in the general study of economics, but a ruptured *ontological paradigm*, whose nature is precisely *serial production*. The reproductive series is the form and discipline of a new era. Grasping this point is rather crucial to understanding Baudrillard's logical ordering in this section. Fredric Jameson provides a fairly proper explanation for this point. He first describes the difference between simulacrum and "copy." To him, generally speaking, copies are imitations of original works, and will be marked as copies forever". The original work, though being imitated, has the real value; whereas the copy is just imitated from the original work for us to appreciate. Hence, the value of copy is *secondary*. Copy helps you to acquire the feeling of reality, and know your position, while simulacrum does not.

Jameson has restricted Baudrillard's simulacrum to industrial production, deeply corresponding with Baudrillard's context regarding the second-order simulacrum. (Nonetheless, the problem here is that he does not also notice the three different orders of simulacrum.) Given five million identical T-type cars, ten million identical Apple computers, in this case, there is no production of shaped objects but a *reproduction* of simulacrum. The interesting point is that Baudrillard here abruptly mentions a western Marxist, Walter Benjamin. As a member of the Frankfurt School, Benjamin is the "first to draw out the essential implications of the principle of reproduction."[38] (I have said that Baudrillard's reproduction here is not a historic continuity of production in Marx's sense, but a sort of *non-productive*

---

38   Baudrillard, Jean. *Symbolic Exchange and Death*, Trans. I. Hamilton Grant. London: Sage Publication Ltd, 1993, p. 55.

reproduction.) Baudrillard says that Benjamin discovered this reproduction process in the fields of art, cinema, and photography. "Reproduction absorbs the process of production, changes its goals, and alters the status of the product and the producer."[39] (He obviously refers to Benjamin's book *The Work of Art in the Age of Mechanical Reproduction*.) What is more, Baudrillard believes that Benjamin is also the "first (with McLuhan after him) to grasp technology as a medium rather than a 'productive force,'"[40] as from his perspective, the essence of reproduction is serial repetition, and in reproduction, "any given thing can simply be reproduced."[41] Such thinking is no doubt revolutionary. (Baudrillard says that the Black boys would be rather amazed when seeing two identical books for the first time.) Additionally, Baudrillard points out that reproductive repetition is the only real foundation for the new *equivalence relation* of the bourgeois. (I find that Baudrillard seldom shows respect to Western Marxist thinkers. No doubt, the credit he gives Benjamin is exceptional.)

It is from here that Baudrillard starts to criticize Marx again, because he believes that it is wrong for Marx to regard science and technology as productive forces. In spite of that belief, Marx did not pay attention to the sort of serial reproduction in Benjamin's research . Therefore, Baudrillard feels that Walter Benjamin and Eric McLuhan are wiser than Marx, because they noticed something new, namely that, "the real ultimatum, lay in reproduction itself."[42] As "the social finality of production is lost in the series"[43], "simulacra prevail over history"[44]. However, what does not occur to Baudrillard is that Benjamin and McLuhan may never find new things in the following century as well if they lived in Marx's time.

According to Baudrillard's clarification, the stage of serial reproduction is ephemeral, which refers to 'the industrial mechanism, the production line, and the growth of reproduction'[45]. (Interestingly, it

---

39   *Ibid.*
40   *Ibid.*, p. 56.
41   *Ibid.*
42   *Ibid.*
43   *Ibid.*
44   *Ibid.*
45   *Ibid.*

seems to be ironic every time when positivistic terms are employed in Baudrillard's text. De facto, it is not a transitory period for the development of capitalist industry from machinery industries to production lines, which almost covers the development of several centuries from the seeds of capitalism (machines and steam engines in the machinery industries) to the first half of the 20th century.)

Baudrillard keeps on saying that the second-order simulacra—reproduction or serial production terminates in the end of primitive accumulation. This is asymmetrical to his ideas mentioned above. Obviously, it is an inaccurate relation of history and logics. He believes, "as soon as dead labour gains the upper hand over living labour (that is to say, since the end of primitive accumulation), serial production gives way to generation through models"[46]. Pattern formation—modelling marks a new start in the bourgeois world of simulacra.

3 SIMULATIONS: PATTERN FORMATION AND DIFFERENTIAL CODE MODULATION

According to the previous illustration, we know that the third order in the bourgeois world of simulacra is *simulation*. However, the nature of historical structure of the so-called simulation is not the serial production or reproduction any more, but the model in the code-dominated era and structural law of value in today's capitalist society.[47] (Obviously, Baudrillard reforms his definition of the model in *The System of Objects*, as the model here is heterogeneous from the series. It is indeed a theoretical invention of Baudrillard's.) In Baudrillard's eyes, the model is a brand new form of the existing mode of men and objects during the development process of capitalism. (Therefore, James Der Derian once raised a very interesting question, "are we entering an era in which the Marxist, concrete and steel Lenin is to be replaced by the hyperrealist, laser and integrated circuit: Baudrillard?"[48]) In this modelling mode, traditional mode of material production of simulacra has been completely changed:

46   *Ibid.*
47   The word "model" Baudrillard uses here is often used as a verb. As mentioned above, I think it is more accurate to use the word "modelling" proposed by a contemporary sociologist Andrew Pickering to express the meaning of situating here.
48   Kellner, Douglas. *Baudrillard: A Critical Reader*. Cambridge: Basil Blackwell Ltd, 1994, p. 179.

In this case it is a matter of a reversal of origin and end, since
all forms change from the moment that they are no longer me-
chanically reproduced, but conceived according to their very re-
producibility, their diffraction from a generative core called a
'model' We are dealing with third-order simulacra here. There
is no more counterfeiting of an original, as there was in the first
order, and no more pure series as there were in the second; there
are models from which all forms proceed according to modulated
differences.[49]

There are some key words in these so-called third-order simulacra. One is model/mold, referring to the existence and presentation
form of objects and humans in the third-order simulacra; the second
is modulation/*differential modulation*, referring to the fundamental
property of generated objects based on specific models. According
to my understanding, modulation/*differential modulation* is the nature of simulations as well. Baudrillard holds that, compared with
simulations, the period of capitalist industrialization is only the bud-
ding stage of simulacra. It is only today that we have just entered the
third order—simulation. Hence, "only affiliation to the model has
any meaning, since nothing proceeds in accordance with its end any
more, but issues instead from the model, the 'signifier of reference',
functioning as a foregone, and the only credible, conclusion."[50] In
this sense, simulations are actually *anti-simulacra*. In Baudrillard's
own words, it is called anti-representation or anti-reference. For
him, the mechanism of representation is no longer in existence today, only existing the mechanism of simulation." (Therefore, one
of Tseelon's explanations is not valid, describing three "orders" of
simulacra respectively with relations between presentation and reality: in the first order, simulacrum of imitation, "appearances disguise reality;" in the second order, production, "appearances create
an illusion of reality;" in the third order, simulation, "appearances
invent reality."[51] In fact, in Baudrillard's situating logic here, production and simulation have already lost presentations for reference.
There is no reality behind simulation. Simulation is the hyperreal,

49   Baudrillard, Jean. *Symbolic Exchange and Death*, Trans. I. Hamilton Grant.
London: Sage Publication Ltd, 1993, p. 56.
50   *Ibid.*
51   Kellner, Douglas. *Baudrillard: A Critical Reader*. Cambridge: Basil Blackwell
Ltd, 1994, p. 120.

more real than the real; whereas the surreal is its manifestation of the pseudo-world. As a result, it is of no validity to translate simulation into "imitate reality."

All the self-invented things are usually not easy to understand for the reason that it is difficult for people to access this over-narrowed situating path of logic. Based on Baudrillard's earlier explanations, reference is *the fundamental corresponding relation* ontologically. Obviously, his response is negative. Therefore, he only calls it the "signifier of reference";[52] the signifier, which is severed from signified, here stands for the nothingness. In this way, the signifier of reference precisely refers to the rupture of referential correlation. Without the reference of ontology, the whole existence will lose its own end, as, for instance, with the advancement of human society originally inspiring the bourgeoisie, or the linear evolution of biological species. Now everything can be generated via modelling, because the living creature modulated and configured by cloning miraculously creates biological changes which would have required thousands of years' evolution in the past. The world history of today's capital modulated by the calculation method of global finance is no longer an objective process beyond human beings. In those different forms of simulations, both biological evolution and social advancement are dead. Compared with the second-order simulacra, "modulation is ultimately more fundamental than serial reproducibility, distinct oppositions more than quantitative equivalences, and the commutation of terms more than the law of equivalences; the structural, not the market, law of value."[53] This statement is Baudrillard's clarification of today's era, a simulated era. (Baudrillard believes, in this regard, Benjamin and McLuhan's analyses stay at the borders of reproduction and simulation, and anyway, they have moved a step forward in comparison with Thorstein Veblen, et al.)

What on earth, then, constitutes the simulations modulated from the forms of modelling? Baudrillard answers that there is no code of entity. (Different from his previous book *For a Critique of the Political Economy of the Sign*, Baudrillard consciously refuses to

52   Baudrillard, Jean. *Symbolic Exchange and Death*, Trans. I. Hamilton Grant. London: Sage Publication Ltd, 1993, p. 56.
53   *Ibid.*

use the discourse of political economy; instead, he applies his inde-pendently-constructed-logical-space to express his original ideas.) Today's philosophy is "the metaphysics of indeterminacy and the code."[54] He says,

> The great man-made simulacra pass from a universe of natu-ral laws into a universe of forces and tensions, and today pass into a universe of structures and binary oppositions, after the metaphysics of being and appearance, after the metaphysics of energy and determinacy, the metaphysics of indeterminacy and the code.[55]

The statement corresponds to three metaphysical appearances in three stages of the capitalist world of simulacra: first is counter-feit, related to "metaphysics of being and appearance"[56] in accord-ance with the natural law; second is "metaphysics of energy and determinacy"[57] relevant to the production of forces and tensions; third is "metaphysics of in the determinacy and the code"[58] related to structures and binary oppositions. (Just a reminder, the binary op-positions here do not refer to the contradictory relationship of tradi-tional binary oppositions in Newtonian mechanics.) Simulation is the metaphysics of code.

From Baudrillard's perspective, simulation is the code of no en-tity. That is to say, the nature of simulation is that of no territory, nor of a referential being or a substance. "It is the generation by models (la generation par les modeles) of 'a real without origin or reality.'"[59] If the common sense is that territory precedes the map, it is now map survives territory. Simply put, code generates existence. (Baudrillard's assertion here reminds us of the obligatory *pseudo-precession* in Lacan's ontology.[60] Martin Jay also believes "what Jean Baudrillard has dubbed the 'hyperreal' world of simulations means we have become seduced by images that are signs of nothing

54   *Ibid.*, p. 57.
55   *Ibid.*
56   *Ibid.*
57   *Ibid.*
58   *Ibid.*
59   Baudrillard, Jean. *Simulacra and Simulation*, Trans. Sheila Faria Glaser. University of Michigan Press, 1994, p. 1.
60   Zhang Yibing. *The Impossible Truth of Being: Mirror of Lacan's Philosophy*, The Commercial Press, 2006. pp. 22-24.

but themselves. Because such images now precede their referents, Baudrillard calls "the precession of simulacra."[61])

According to Baudrillard's explanation, there are two crucial things in today's capitalist world of simulacra: one is binary digitality, the other is DNA. In his own words, "digitality is its metaphysical principle (Leibniz's God), and DNA is its prophet."[62] The simulation does not become possible until the appearance of both of these things. Please note, the "binary oppositions" here are not the contradictory oppositions of action and reaction known since Newton, but the digital analogue composed of "zero" and "one" in computer storage. Thereby, Sara Schoonmaker has a description for this, a "simulation is based upon the reproducibility of objects according to a binary model. The epitome of such a model is the digital code read by computers, that translates all questions and answers, all of reality, into a binary opposition between zero and one."[63] The creator today is the binary code in information-programming. Because of that, Baudrillard seems to bitterly hate the computer, saying "the computer will take over everywhere from the operation of thinking, leaving the brain to lie fallow, as the mechanistic technologies of the nineteenth century have already done with the body. People are becoming increasingly zombie-like."[64] Along with the emergence of computers, mobile phones, and other electronic media equipment, there comes a further phase of the "electronic colonization" of people's sense organs: "tactility and the digitality (of screens) substituting for touch; film substituting for the skin; the visual substituting for looking; voice command substituting for the voice, and all the virtual sensors (including erotic ones) substituting for the body and sensuality."[65] Instead of facing existence with their true feelings, people try to stimulate the original empirical phenomena in Lacanian sense via virtual media. This is a terrible initialization.

61   Jay, Martin. *Downcast Eyes: The Denigration of Vision in Twentieth-Century of French Thought*. Berkeley and Los Angeles: University of California Press, 1994, p. 554.
62   Baudrillard, Jean. *Symbolic Exchange and Death*, Trans. I. Hamilton Grant. London: Sage Publication Ltd, 1993, p. 57.
63   Kellner, Douglas. *Baudrillard: A Critical Reader*. Cambridge: Basil Blackwell Ltd, 1994, p. 170.
64   Baudrillard, Jean. *Cool Memories I*, Trans. Chris Turner. New York: Verso, 1990, p. 213.
65   Baudrillard, Jean. *Cool Memories IV:1995-2000*, Trans. Chris Turner. New York: Verso, 2003, p. 103.

Baudrillard even believes,

With that science, we are entering an era of exhaustivity, which is also an era of exhaustion. Of generalized interactivity abolishing particularized action, of the interface which abolishes challenge, passion, and rivalry between peoples, ideas and individuals which was always the source of the finest energies.[66]

Baudrillard also says that the introduction of the computer no doubt marks the end of the consumer society. That is to say, the capitalist consumer society transforms into a more dreadful, digital-coded simulation society. (Kim Sawchuk holds that it means the important transformation of Baudrillard from the theory of linguistic signs to information coding theory. "A code in this model is a pre-programmed sequence of instructions biogenetically replicated."[67])

I believe that Baudrillard is truly a pioneer. Digitalization and molecular biology have become the foundation for his theoretical logic construction. Nonetheless, this theoretical description is almost desperate. (Later in his book *The Perfect Crime*, he describes the digitalized world by saying, "the key concept of this Virtuality is High Definition. That of the image, but also of time (Real Time), of music (High Fidelity), of sex (pornography), of thought (Artificial Intelligence), of language (digital language), of the body (the genetic code and the genome)."[68] The world becomes ready-made; whereas in fact it is a realm of shadows. What happens here is that bodies no longer to project their shadows under the light, but *shadows to project their bodies in the simulation*, which might be mere "shadows of shadows."[69] The world is just a *technical artifact*. Presumably, this idea might be the real logical framework from the story in *The Matrix*. On this point, Jonathon S. Epstein and Margarete J. Epstein once used a metaphor of shadowplay, saying that "sociology becomes a shadowplay in which the players remain unaware that the shadows are mere representations and proceed as if they were 'real.'"[70] This metaphor is vivid but inaccurate, because in the

66　Baudrillard, Jean. *Cool Memories I*, Trans. Chris Turner. New York: Verso, 1990, p. 150.
67　Kellner, Douglas. *Baudrillard: A Critical Reader*. Cambridge: Basil Blackwell Ltd, 1994, p. 93.
68　Baudrillard, Jean. *The Perfect Crime*, Trans. Chris Turner. London: Verso, 1996, p. 29.
69　*Ibid.*, p. 33.
70　Kellner, Douglas. *Baudrillard: A Critical Reader*. Cambridge: Basil Blackwell Ltd, 1994, p. 143.

Baudrillardian sense, today's simulation is not the shadow projected from the light (the real), but the shadow projects the real.)

Baudrillard supposes that traditional reality collapses completely in today's world of simulation. He says, simulation is

> *the meticulous reduplication of the real, preferably through another reproductive medium such as advertising or photography. Through reproduction from one medium into another, the real becomes volatile, it becomes the allegory of death, but it also draws strength from its own destruction, becoming the real for its own sake, a fetishism of the lost object which is no longer the object of representation, but the ecstasy of denegation and its own ritual extermination: the hyperreal.[71]*

In the simulation, the real is re-modulated from the unreal, which is more real than the real. Now, "the real is produced from matrices, memory banks and command modules and with these it can produced an indefinite number of times."[72] This more real does not mean that simulacra will be more real than the real, but means that simulations take the vacancy of the dead real and exert the *ontological pull* of existence more successfully than the real which has never been present. Therefore, Baudrillard defines the real as hyperreal. (As for this definition, Christopher Horrocks has a rather popular explanation. Kellner's explanation, however, places more weight on cultural life. In his view, Baudrillard's surreal mainly refers to "entertainment, information, and communication technologies provide experiences more intense and involving than the scenes of banal everyday life. The realm of the hyperreal (i.e., media simulations of reality, Disneyland and amusement parks, malls and consumer fantasylands, TV sports, and other excursions into ideal words) is more real than real, whereby the models, images, and codes of the hyperreal come to control thought and behaviour."[73]) Actually, this hyperreal is the false nature of the surreal pseudo-world. The hyperreal is identified in the ironic sense; therefore, it is "the real desert"[74] simulated by digital code. In this way, Baudrillard puts forward that

---

71   Baudrillard, Jean. *Symbolic Exchange and Death*, Trans. I. Hamilton Grant. London: Sage Publication Ltd, 1993. pp. 71-72.

72   Kellner, Douglas. *Baudrillard: A Critical Reader*. Cambridge: Basil Blackwell Ltd, 1994, p. 103.

73   *Ibid.*, p. 8.

74   Baudrillard, Jean. *Cool Memories I*, Trans. Chris Turner. New York: Verso, 1990, p. 86.

"under the subtle torture of science, all the real ever confesses is its nonexistence."[75]

In Baudrillard's view,

The hyperreal represents a much more advanced phase inso-far as it effaces the contradiction of the real and the imaginary. Irreality no longer belongs to the dream or the phantasm, to a beyond or a hidden interiority, but to the hallucinatory resemblance of the real to itself.[76]

Baudrillard says that from the traditional perspective, "the very definition of the real is that of which it is possible to provide an equivalent reproduction. It is a contemporary of science, which postulates that a process can be reproduced exactly within given conditions, with an industrial rationality which postulates a universal system of equivalences."[77] (Here, there is a minor problem in Baudrillard's argument. As according to his theoretical logic manifested above, representation is connected with the simulacra of counterfeiting, but heterogeneous to the productions of serial replications. Moreover, representation here is in harmony with the principles of science and industry. This is as paradox of the logic in the unconsciousness.) Nevertheless, in the simulation today, the prototype is murdered; every referent is "in liquidation" (une liquidation). As a result, there is no representation in the traditional ontology; hence, in the simulation, there is "no more mirror of being and appearances, of the real and its concept; no more imaginary coextensiveity."[78] Baudrillard thinks that from the representation to the simulation, the general phases of the image are:

1. it is the reflection of a basic reality. 2. it masks and perverts a basic reality. 3. it masks the absence of a basic reality.4. it bears no relation to any reality whatever: it is its own pure simulacrum.[79]

---

75   *Ibid.*, p. 86.
76   Baudrillard, Jean. *Symbolic Exchange and Death*, Trans. Iain Hamilton Grant. London: Sage Publication Ltd, 1993. pp. 72.
77   *Ibid.*, p. 73.
78   Baudrillard, Jean. *Simulacra and Simulation*, Trans. Sheila Faria Glaser. USA: University of Michigan Press, 1994, p. 2.
79   *Ibid.*, p. 6.

The first procedure is the presentation in traditional epistemology. From the being of the objectified real, we can gain the representational cognition, serving as the projection of the real. The second procedure has become the false image in misconception, the third is the ideological sorcery, and the fourth is today's simulation. In order to explain the nature of simulation, Baudrillard cites a vivid example about the simulacrum of God. He says iconoclasts* in theology are extraordinarily rational because they know a fact:

> *The omnipotence of simulacra, this facility they have of erasing God from the consciousnesses of people, and the overwhelming, destructive truth which they suggest: that ultimately there has never been any God; that only simulacra exist; indeed that God himself has only ever been his own simulacrum.*[80]

Baudrillard uses this argument to account for the existence of simulation. In the simulation, actuality, which seems to be in real existence, has never existed before; it turns out to be the avatar of its own simulacrum. However, under the compulsive repetition of code, the hyperreal generates from the radiating compound of a self-set-mode. It is more real than the real. (The example he cites most is of theme parks like Disneyland in Los Angeles, USA. In several books, he discusses in depth the effects of counter-construction of simulated imaginary objects have on people's lives. In *Cool Memories*, he even identifies Disneyland as "the only place in the world where the simulacrum is a home-grown product."[81] Kim Sawchuk once cited an example about hyperreal chickens, in which he said that the genes of most chickens on the farm have been preset, so that they become bigger, more tasty and better looking. However, the chickens are not real or natural, but *simulated* birds. Compared with them, the naturally-grown chickens appear to be ugly and unreal.[82] Indeed, one of the similar issues we encounter in China's social life today circles the differences between wild and culturally manipulated plants and animals.)

---

80   *Ibid.*, p. 4.
81   Baudrillard, Jean. *Cool Memories IV: 1995-2000*. Trans. Chris Turner. New York: Verso, 2003, p. 96.
82   Kellner, Douglas. *Baudrillard: A Critical Reader*. Cambridge: Basil Blackwell Ltd, 1994, p. 104.
*) People who engage in or support iconoclasm are called "iconoclasts", a term that has come to be applied figuratively to any individual who challenges established dogma or conventions.

In the Chapter Three of *Symbolic Exchange and Death*, Baudrillard uses today's fashion crazes to illustrate the nature of simulated being. I think that fashion here should especially refer to the fashion which has run wild in the contemporary society. It is the third instance of such a concentrated discussion of fashion following *The Consumer Society* and *For A Critique of the Political Economy of the Sign*. Baudrillard believes that "the astonishing privilege accorded to fashion is due to a unanimous and definitive resolve."[83] As in the fashion of capitalist society today, all the references for the referent and nature have gone, except for the differential games among pseudo-symbolic signifier chains without the signified. In fashion life, people constantly change clothes, watches, and cars, not for the enjoyment of the *real use* of these commodities (the use-value generated by shaped labour production), but because they are latest fashion symbols. "There is no longer any determinacy internal to the signs of fashion, hence they become free to commute and permutate without limit. At the term of this unprecedented enfranchisement, they obey, as if logically, a mad and meticulous recurrence."[84] This rule applies to fashion as clothes, the body and objects, even to the sphere of politics, morals, economics, science, culture, and sexuality. Every sphere tends, in the style of fashion, to "merge with models of simulation, of differential and indifferent play, the structural play of value."[85] Reading backwards, fashion no longer follows the law of commodity value with the exchange value against use value, but follows the structural law of the value of symbolic code with no reference, whose foundation is a self-referring differential chain that has lost the signified but kept the signifying codes while the model molded by the chain of signifiers forms a simulated world which is more real than the real. From Baudrillard's standpoint, everything nowadays exists under the influence of fashion, precisely because of its potential to "revert all forms to non-origin and recurrence."[86] (This "non-origin" is precisely the nature of simulation.) He believes, fundamentally, that "fashion imposes upon us

---

83 Baudrillard, Jean. *Symbolic Exchange and Death*, Trans. I. Hamilton Grant. London: Sage Publication Ltd, 1993. pp. 87.
84 *Ibid.*
85 *Ibid.*
86 *Ibid.*, p. 88.

the rupture of an imaginary order: that of referential Reason."[87] The secret of fashion is *ontological rootlessness*. (Again, this logic is Lacanian: hollow man, hollow objects, and hollow pseudo-events.) Therefore, Baudrillard makes a comparison between the reference-free logic of fashion and the referential logic of commodity.

> *Under the sign of the commodity, all labour is exchanged and loses its specificity—under the sign of fashion, the signs of leisure and labour are exchanged. Under the sign of the commodity, culture is bought and sold—under the sign of fashion, all cultures play like simulacra in total promiscuity Under the sign of the commodity, love becomes prostitution—under the sign of fashion it is the object-relation itself that disappears, blown to pieces by a cool and unconstrained sexuality. Under the sign of the commodity, time is accumulated like money under the sign of fashion it is exhausted and discontinued in entangled cycles.*[88]

He means here that in the capitalistic logic of commodity we still sell and buy useful and functionalized objects, while the logic of fashion is to always sell and deceive people into buying symbolic signs which are simulated objects of desire. This exchange is indeed symbolic, yet it is a simulated, pseudo-symbolic exchange. True, the logic of fashion is paradoxical non-reality. Fashion is always retro, and yet always exists on the basis of the abolition of the past. This trend is "the spectral death and resurrection of forms."[89] As fashion without a system of reference and quality,

> *This is the despair that nothing lasts, and the complementary enjoyment of knowing that, beyond this death, every form has always the chance of a second existence, which is never innocent since fashion consumes the world and the real in advance: it is the weight of all the dead labour of signs bearing on living signification—within a magnificent forgetting, a fantastic ignorance.*[90]

Within fashion, the acquired objects of desires (seductive pseudo-symbolic signs) keep on dying, and yet, keep on being revivified. "The desire for death is itself recycled within fashion, emptying it of every subversive phantasm and involving it, along with everything

---

87   *Ibid.*, p. 87.
88   *Ibid.*, p. 88.
89   *Ibid.*
90   *Ibid.*

else, in fashion's innocuous revolutions."[91] Any fashion product will immediately lose its charm along with the disappearance of the illusion of advertising. The fashion product you buy today will die as soon as a new fashion trend appears, but desire, falsely fulfilled, lights up again with the new product, which is the revival of the dead fashion. Thereupon, you fall into the chain of fashionable desires, which is an unstoppable Ferris wheel of doom. (Raoul Vaneigem says that the unstoppable changes of fashion precisely coincide with consumer society's need for the domination. It is through such partial and fragmental changes that the bourgeoisie try to stop the fundamental revolution. He points out that, unfortunately, in the escape towards death, in the ceaseless running, there is no true future but a past that is hastily decorated and thrown back.)

Baudrillard holds that the logic of fashion belongs to the framework of modernity, whose nature is the unstoppable *"myth of change."*[92] "Modernity is a code, and fashion is its emblem";[93] likewise, although fashion and political economy generate in the same era, fashion is now situated in an "even more formal abstraction than political economy."[94] Supposing the agent of exchange value in the commodity-market economy is the general equivalent (currency), then in the differential exchange of fashion, the agent is only a model.

*Models are this kind of general equivalent diffracted throughout the matrices which govern the differentiated fields of fashion. They are shifters, effectors, dispatchers, the media of fashion, and through them fashion is indefinitely reproduced. There is fashion from the moment that a form is no longer produced according to its own determinations, but **from the model itself**— that is to say, that it is never produced, but always and immediately **reproduced**. The model itself has become the only system of reference.*[95]

Therefore, fashion is one of the most urgent performances of the model simulation, acting as a mirror to reflect this new world of simulation.

91   *Ibid.*
92   *Ibid.*, p. 90.
93   *Ibid.*
94   *Ibid.*, p. 92.
95   *Ibid.*

A MARXIST READING OF YOUNG BAUDRILLARD

4 THE VIOLENCE OF CODE DOMINATION AND PALE SPECULATION TO DEATH

Be aware, there is a major ontological transition here: the appearance of *simulation time*. Baudrillard believes that compared with historical linear time, the three-dimensional framework of past, present, and future in reality today is completely eliminated, because everything can be pre-simulated—in other words, the past, present, and future can be simulated in precession. (I find that William Bogard also noticed this point and made further discussions of it.[96] Later, Baudrillard applies the cyclical time of fashion we discussed above to illustrate this point. The endless upgrade and transcendence also applies for the economic development and fashion. Fashion, in particular, provides the best sphere to integrate the forceful changes and impulses. The entire fashion industry introduces a differentiated culture and end the continuity of all history. Thus, events do not proceed along a historical axis but push forward in vacuum. In this context, Baudrillard also says that in this manufactured hyperreal, "by the cloning of reality and the extermination of the real by its double,"[97] "not only have the traces of our past become virtual, but our present itself is given over to simulation."[98] The key to this problem is that the form of simulation has fundamentally changed all social existence today. In this regard, Kellner makes an important summary:

> In the society of simulation, identities are constructed by the appropriation of images, and codes and models determine how individuals perceive themselves and relate to other people. Economics, politics, social life, and culture are all governed by the logic of simulation, whereby codes and models determine how goods are consumed and used, politics unfold, culture is produced and consumed, and everyday life is lived.[99]

---

96   Kellner, Douglas. *Baudrillard: A Critical Reader*. Cambridge: Basil Blackwell Ltd, 1994, p. 313.
97   Baudrillard, Jean. *The Perfect Crime*, Trans. Chris Turner. London: Verso, 1996, p. 25.
98   *Ibid.*, p. 23.
99   Kellner, Douglas. *Baudrillard: A Critical Reader*. Cambridge: Basil Blackwell Ltd, 1994, p. 8.

Moreover, Baudrillard also believes that in today's social life, social control managed by ends (goal setting) in the past has given place to social control "by means of prediction, simulation, programmed anticipation and indeterminate mutation, all governed, however, by the code,"[100] which is "a neo-capitalist cybernetic order"[101] with modelling as its extant foundation. Therefore, Baudrillard thinks that traditional power is dead. There is no power any more, which means that "the whole of society has gone over into voluntary servitude."[102] Therefore, obligatory power from outside is meaningless, because the new capitalist order today has no more need of power to maintain mysterious and voluntary servitude as such. Power has to go bankrupt, becoming a useless function. Hence, power can only go bankruptcy by itself and become a useless function. (That is why he tells us to forget the anti-power-distribution of Foucault.[103])

> *This mutation is the outcome of an entire history where God, Man, Progress and even History have successively passed away to the advantage of the code, where the death of transcendence benefits immanence, which corresponds to a far more advanced phase of the vertiginous manipulation of social relations.*[104]

Indeterminate code governance turns out to be the "real violence,"[105] as the capitalist society today has *unbreakable* control. In this simulated control, future ends people expected in the past are dead; the other side of the City of God, the emancipation of Man, and the progressive historical course are all entirely abolished as well. (Later, in *The Perfect Crime*, Baudrillard says that today people think that they have gotten rid of external enforcement, but the fact is that the free manifestation of code is just the new form of control, "by comparison with which the horrors of alienation were very small beer."[106]) It is under the violence of the sign that come the silent majorities. The silence and submission of the masses exists

100 Baudrillard, Jean. *Symbolic Exchange and Death*, Trans. I. Hamilton Grant. London: Sage Publication Ltd, 1993. pp. 60.
101 *Ibid.*
102 Baudrillard, Jean. *Cool Memories II, 1987-1990*, Trans. Chris Turner. Duke University Press, 1996. pp. 27.
103 In 1997, Baudrillard wrote down *Oublier Foucault*.
104 Baudrillard, Jean. *Symbolic Exchange and Death*, Trans. I. Hamilton Grant. London: Sage Publication Ltd, 1993. pp. 60.
105 *Ibid.*
106 Baudrillard, Jean. *The Perfect Crime*, Trans. Chris Turner. London: Verso, 1996, p. 27.

exactly because various kinds of "opinion polls, information, publicity and statistics" under the control of code plunge us into a state of "stupor."[107] Supposing people can still feel oppression and humiliation directly under the tyranny of traditional absolutism, then in today's democratic society under the control of code, we are addicted to being happily dominated.

Baudrillard has another important view: if the alienated relation of subject and object still exists in the capitalist mode of industrial production, and at the same time people know there has been a fundamental existential rupture, then they can resist and fight accordingly. Conversely, things are quite different in the era of simulation, which completely abolishes the "difference" between true and false, between real and imaginary. Even if this society looks ill, that illness is simulated; even if difference and alienation are still in existence, they are specifically modulated as "production" to *display your agony*.[108] (Like his above malicious attack on the ecology, ecological disease is a pretend illness in the modulation of modelling, used to create artificial economic shortages and energy crises; it is a simulated product used for people to "rediscover a taste for ascesis, that pathetic investment born of lack and deprivation."[109]) In this sense, Baudrillard says that "when the real is no longer what it used to be, nostalgia assumes its full meaning."[110] This saying is profound, but the problem Baudrillard does not understand is that if the above is true, will people still rise to revolt against the social oppression and domination?

We must ask, moreover, what are the masses in Baudrillard's eyes? Baudrillard says that the masses are also generated by simulations. It seems that the masses are the general representations of public opinions; in fact, on the contrary, *"they are the site of the implosion of the social. The masses are the increasingly dense sphere*

107   Baudrillard, Jean. *Selected Writings,* Edited. Mark Poster. Standford University Press, 2001. pp. 212-214.

108   Baudrillard, Jean. *Simulacra and Simulation,* Trans. Sheila Faria Glaser. USA: University of Michigan Press, 1994, p. 3.

109   Baudrillard, Jean. *Symbolic Exchange and Death,* Trans. I. Hamilton Grant. London: Sage Publication Ltd, 1993. pp. 32.

110   Baudrillard, Jean. *Simulacra and Simulation,* Trans. Sheila Faria Glaser. USA: University of Michigan Press, 1994, p. 26.

in which the whole social comes to be imploded, and to be devoured in an uninterrupted process of simulation."[111] (Implosion is a term Baudrillard appropriates from McLuhan, specifically referring to a process of the self-replication and unlimited proliferation of information.) The masses, as the final product of the implosion of all sociality, are a sort of "dense sphere"[112] fabricated by simulation, and public opinion and social tides are simulated by bourgeois democracy. Horrible! From Baudrillard's perspective, when facing the implosive domination of the simulated world, we cannot revolt. Why not? Baudrillard's explanation is that implosion is a sort of "other violence,"[113]

> *...because it escapes the traditional schema of explosive violence: implosive violence that no longer results from the extension of a system, but from its saturation and its retraction, as is the case for physical stellar systems. A violence that follows an inordinate densification of the social, the state of an overregulated system, a network (of knowledge, information, power) that is over-encumbered, and of a hypertrophic control investing all the interstitial pathways.*[114]

Baudrillard says that we cannot resist the implosive domination as such for the reason that it is disordered, undecided, and randomized. The only solution to deal with such violence is symbolic death, and our only way out is "the refusal of meaning and the refusal of speech."[115] Be aware, symbolic death here does not refer to the death of symbolic exchange as the authentic social relation, but to the death of code and signed pseudo-symbols that stand for the presence of simulation today. Hence, symbolic death here can be read as *the re-death of the dead symbol.* This symbolic re-death directly blasts the codic simulation.

---

111   *Ibid.*, p. 68.
112   *Ibid.*
113   *Ibid.*, p. 71.
114   *Ibid.*
115   *Ibid.*, p. 85.

CONCLUSION

SEDUCTION, DEATH AND DISAPPEARANCE

Baudrillard's final weapon requires him to transfer from Adorno's negative dialectics to ironic dialectics, which *faces the nothingness*. Probably this is the reason why in 1979 he deepened the simulation, this radical and negative otherness in such aesthetic, hollow, and ironic paradigms like seduction (De la seduction). Baudrillard says that "the simulation hypothesis is merely a maximalist position. The seduction hypothesis is merely a formal abstraction."[1] Seduction is *a trap strategy taking advantage of the weak points of subject*. The simulation generates seduction, which makes people lose their virginity in the ontology; or, to put it more broadly, Lacanian seduction is the real secret of the reign of capitalism in postmodern times. In actuality, researchers have not reached a consensus on the status of seduction in Baudrillard's development of thought. Many of them are inclined to regard seduction as a new thought shift for Baudrillard after simulacra-simulation. (For example, Kellner regards seduction as a major shift in Baudrillard's thought, valorizing seduction

---

1   Baudrillard, Jean. *Cool Memories I*, Trans. Chris Turner. New York: Verso, 1990, p. 27.

as "his alternative to production and communicative interaction."[2] This point is vague. Poster seems to have a similar idea, saying, "seduction might be a model to replace the model of production, which prefigures Baudrillard's later term, the hyperreal, with all of its post-modernist implications."[3] I think Poster merely provides the opposite explanation, as seduction here, in Baudrillard's sense, is his ironic illustration of postmodern phenomena. Baudrillard is a real critic of postmodernism.) As for myself, I hold that seduction is not a new thought shift of Baudrillard's, and rather reflects his improved understanding of the form of simulation (post-modernism).

According to Baudrillard's own definition, "seduction takes from discourse its sense and turns it from its truth."[4] This idea is intriguing. I think that seduction here is obviously not vulgar temptation in the common sense, but something again metaphysicalized. As for Baudrillard, it is because of this *seduction demonstrated on the basis of symbolic meaning* that the simulation of signs and fashion in today's capitalist society is able to capture people. We can take a look at Baudrillard's clarification of seduction. He thinks that the excellence of seduction in the post-modernism lies in its double negativity:

One is conscious rejection of psychoanalytic distinction and opposition concerning manifest and latent discourses. Baudrillard identifies—as with Freud's antagonistic play between conscious and unconscious, between identity and self, in which the unconsciousness and identity in the concave underside of latent discourses always force the consciousness and self—these manifest discourses that "say what it does not want to say."[5] It is a violent *determination* to reveal the nature of the concave underside. However, Baudrillard says, today's seduction finds "determinations and profound indeterminations," for the reason that "depth always peeks though from behind the break, and meaning peeks from behind the line."[6] The

---

2   Kellner, Douglas. *Baudrillard: A Critical Reader*. Cambridge: Basil Blackwell Ltd, 1994, p. 14.
3   *Ibid.*, p. 81.
4   Baudrillard, Jean. *Seduction*, Trans. Brian Singer. Montreal: New World Perspectives, 1990, p. 53.
5   *Ibid.*
6   *Ibid.*

line is a demarcation, and also a break. In Baudrillard's book—*For A Critique of the Political Economy of the Sign*, the line is always between exchange value and use value, the signifier and the signified. In other words, the line is a sort of *logical determination of critical revelation from phenomena to essence*. As mentioned above, in *Symbolic Exchange and Death*, Baudrillard has already criticized the referential logic of traditional capitalism, and in the structural value revolution, he has completely eradicated the illusions of the referential referents, and explained the modelling of self-referring differential code based on the convex simulacra and simulations in contemporary capitalism.(Probably, the above is the metaphysical determination found throughout the Western world since the Eleatic School. There are appearance/being (The Eleatic School), sharer/Idea (Plato), worldliness/City of God (Christianity), this world of experience/Thing-in-itself (Hume/Kant), and phenomenon/ essence of ideology (Hegel), amongst which only the line of Hume and Kant is really a blocked relation; all of the rest are "determinations" of the main logic which reveal the concave nature from the convex surface. Additionally, Baudrillard thinks that such logical determination to reveal nature is the Western metaphysical discourse of "the violence and terrorism of interpretation."[7]

Interpretation is the second thing that postmodern seduction consciously opposes. "Interpretation is what breaks the appearance and play of the manifest discourse and, by taking up with the latent discourse, delivers the real meaning."[8] Interpretation is precisely the enlightenment discourse, via lumen rationale, turning something beyond comprehension into something understandable, turning something hidden in the concave place into something *lightened* and catchable, thereby liberating concealed secrets. Hence, under the enlightenment interpretation of capitalism, there are "all the characteristics of objectivity and coherence,"[9] which are the logical paths to the capitalist totality. (This is also the guilty witness in Adorno's logic of identity deconstruction.) However, interpretation always "neglects and forgets the meaning of appearance"[10] in the

---

7   *Ibid.*, p. 55.
8   *Ibid.*, p. 53.
9   *Ibid.*, p. 57.
10 *Ibid.*, p. 53.

demasking. After the demasking and liberation of nature and truth, appearance and phenomenon are always abandoned in the wilds of thought. *"All meaningful discourse seeks to end appearances*: this is its attraction, and its imposture."[11] Baudrillard says, so far, that it has become a nuisance to pursue the interpretive discourse of identity. "Not only does it subject the domain of appearances to incalculable damage, but this privileged search for hidden meanings may well be profoundly in error."[12] It is because of the logical clarity that the seductive discourse of contemporary (postmodern) capitalist class will delete "/," which differentiates manifest discourse from latent discourse so as to "invalidate"[13] latent discourse, "substituting the charm and illusion of appearance."[14] (Namely, Derrida intends to eliminate all ranks (sense/sensibility, male/female, etc.) constructed by the "line," which is also the postmodern depthlessness and pla-narity in Jameson's sense.) In today's seduction, appearance is not superficial at all, because "which truly renders discourse seductive is its very appearance, its inflections, its nuances, the circulation (whether aleatory and senseless, or ritualized and meticulous) of signs at its surface."[15] When the underlying significance is deleted, when the logical structure of grand narrative is deconstructed, just take a leap of faith and do whatever works.

> *All appearances conspire to combat and root out meaning (whether intentional or otherwise), and turn it into a game, into another of the game's rules, a more arbitrary rule—or into another elusive ritual, one that is more adventurous and seductive than the directive line of meaning.[16]*

The above is the latest seductive logic of the bourgeoisie in postmodern times, which eliminates meaning and stays focused on meaningless appearances.

What is more, from Baudrillard's perspective, even as pioneering as Freud and Saussure were, they eventually fell into the interpretive discourse of identity, for the reason that neither of them gave up the

---

11   *Ibid.*, p. 54.
12   *Ibid.*
13   *Ibid.*, p. 53.
14   *Ibid.*
15   *Ibid.*, p. 54.
16   *Ibid.*

pursuit of meaning (the real), and therefore missed the real seduction of ideas. Baudrillard thinks that only Lacan fully realized the nature of seduction. He almost yells, "it is not an inconsiderable source of entertainment to see seduction sweep across psychoanalysis with Lacan."[17] This statement is an important logical identification. In Lacanian discourse, what is related to seduction? As I understand it, seduction always targets at the pathetic pseudo-agent of desire, and seduction is precisely the discovery of the cause of desire, that is, the famous Lacanian object a (objet-petit-a)[18]). Object a (objet-petit-a) is not a direct attractiveness, but the remnant of the impossibly existing real in the realistic failure. This is a vestige which has not been completely symbolized. As an unrealistic object of desire, it occurs in the depths of human existence in the form of the symbolized remnant object a (objet-petit-a). Man looks forward to something impossible that is always on the other side to reality. Here, something is the logical variation in Lacan's ontology of negative relation of the *thing*-in-itself in Kant's epistemology. Moreover, Lacan, in his later years, directly specified it as the *capitalized Thing (la Chose/ the Thing)*.[19] Lacan thinks that the object a is the reason causing not only the concealment of the desire of subject, but it is also the power linking the subject between truth and knowledge. With the above analysis we know that object a brings us hopes for existence based ontologically on that irrecoverable *loss*. Obviously, different from the obligatory violence of the *precession* of mirror image and Other, objet-petit-a (object a) is *sent away in advance* and preset in another world, with no real realization in realistic society. However, as the metonymic object of desire ((objet métonymique du désir)), it becomes *the real cause for the formation of desire* and that forever-missing and eliminated *nostalgia* of self-construal and the ontological existence of subject.[20]

---

17   *Ibid.*, p. 57.
18   In French, the direct meaning of *objet-petit-a* is the little a which is the cause of the object of desires, which does not directly equal to that a which is the other in the mirror stage.
19   Zhang Yibing. *The Impossible Truth of Being: Mirror of Lacan's Philosophy*, The Commercial Press, 2006, pp. 346.
20   *Ibid.*, p. 351.

In my view, if Lacan identifies that desire-generated, impossible-in-presence latent object in the post-psychoanalytic context, Baudrillard then illustrates from his perspective how the object a constructs people's pseudo-desires in the postmodern reality of capitalism. This is a step forward from the nature of concave underside to the seduction of the convex surface. There is no more nature in a hurry to become convexity behind the postmodern seduction; there is no more real currently absent (i.e., absence of God, absence of truth and absence of the revolution) waiting to be beckoned in the concave underside. Today the biggest seduction is the seemingly superficial images and appearances; the most tempting object is precisely the impossibility of nature and truth. Therefore, Baudrillard says that the best way to preserve the seduction of revolution today is to announce the impossibility of revolution. (This statement instantly reminds us that Ernesto Laclau and Chantal Mouffe define their socialism strategy as a new revolutionary strategy of impossibilities.) It is here that stands the mystery of seduction Baudrillard identifies.

What, then, is the relationship between seduction and simulation? Baudrillard now divides simulation into two parts: the *disenchanted* simulation and the *enchanted* simulation. The former is the hyperreal, more real than the real, the height of simulation; while the latter is "more false than the false."[21] This statement is fresh and new. Baudrillard believes, *falser than false* is exactly "the secret of appearances"[22] that postmodernity relies so heavily upon today, that is, it is *nature without nature*. Here, Baudrillard's introduction of the "trompe-l'oeil (realistic illusion)"[23] is for the illustration of the enchanted simulation. There are no narratives (the grand narratives are deconstructed), no compositions (compositions and authors are dead together), nor even any objects; thereby descriptive discourses are gone! (Is it not the postmodern atmosphere Lyotard preaches?) However, what remains to seduce people? It is still the

---

21   Baudrillard, Jean. *Seduction*, Trans. Brian Singer. Montreal: New World Perspectives, 1990, p. 60.
22   *Ibid.*
23   The *trompe-l'oeil* refers to a certain simulacrum which almost can be regarded as the genuine, like the thrilling images in three-dimensional movies such as heavy sea and flying train.

simulation, but the present simulation only reacts to the "scraps of social life" and will "parody their theatricality."[24] "They are the anti-representation of the social, religious and artistic, blank and empty signs which are the expression of anti-formality."[25] The enchanted simulation of the seductive type and the typical space of traditional Renaissance patterns are merely inverted, becoming, namely, the object's simulation that is *specter-like and impossible to exist*. In these simulations as such, it is for the lack of "depth that a real source of light provides"[26] that the entity does not have shadows and concave points. (The real source of light is the metaphor to enlighten rationality. In Derrida's words, postmodernity just interrupted the day dream of the rational logos.) Thereby, under the shine of "this mysterious light without origin,"[27] existence falls into the black hole and becomes the *hyperpresence*. Here, people encounter a mirror which does not reflect, with nothing behind it, therefore with "*no horizon, no horizontality*."[28] Everything since the Renaissance has decayed. In the very excess of appearances, insignificant resemblance and irony become everything. *Meaninglessness is the secret of postmodern capital's tremendous seductive charm*. (In this sense, Jameson says that postmodernism did not present its profoundness until in the cultural logic of late capitalism.) Lacan thinks that the nothingness of our ontological being is a scandal, whereas today,

> In that place where meaning should be, where sex should occur, where words point to it, and where others think it to be-there is nothing. And this nothing/secret, this, the seduction's un-signified moves beneath the words and their meaning, and moves faster than their meaning.[29]

Baudrillard says that "seduction is immediately reversible, and its reversibility is constituted by the challenge it implies and the secret in which it is absorbed."[30] The reversible logic here is critique,

---

24 *Ibid.*
25 *Ibid.*
26 Baudrillard, Jean. *Selected Writings*, Edited. Mark Poster. Standford University Press, 2001, p. 155.
27 *Ibid.*
28 *Ibid.*, p. 157.
29 Baudrillard, Jean. *Seduction*, Trans. Brian Singer. Montreal: New World Perspectives, 1990, p. 80.
30 *Ibid.*, p. 81.

negation, and deconstruction, overthrowing all—whatever works. Today's post-modern discourses often absorb certain nihilistic secrets when negating everything; nonetheless, no one has ever noticed that such nihilistic secrets are the charm of successful seduction (a fact well-proven by the history of global development in post-modern discourses in the 1970s). It is "for the void—the hole that, at any point, is burned out by the return of the flame of any sign, the meaninglessness that makes for seduction's unexpected charm."[31]

> *Seduction's enchantment puts an end to all libidinal economies, and every sexual or psychological contract, replacing them with a dizzying spiral of responses and counter-responses. It is never an investment but a risk; never a contract but a pact; never individual but duel; never psychological but ritual; never natural but artificial. It is no one's strategy, but a destiny.[32]*

"We seduce with our death, our vulnerability, and with the void that haunts us. The secret is to know how to play with death in the absence of a gaze or gesture, in the absence of knowledge or meaning."[33] (In this sense, Efrat Tseelon says that Baudrillard's seduction is "based on the attraction of the void-presence which hides absence"; moreover, das Nichtige and the meaninglessness are exactly the features of postmodern fashion.[34]) This judgment is valid. Baudrillard says, anyway, that we live in the meaninglessness. "If simulation is its disenchanted form, seduction is its enchanted form."[35] Seduction is our fate in the postmodern era.

I really do not know whether it is for the same reason that Baudrillard's following critiques of simulated reality become more and more irrational, their structure more and more disordered, their clear and rational situating logic almost being completely taken over by divergent, poetic, and formless situating. After the 1980s, most texts Baudrillard wrote were maxims, travel notes, metaphorical lines, and Pascalian-Nietschean fragments, not all of which contained innovations and new qualitative theories; they are "often

---

31   *Ibid.*, p. 84.
32   *Ibid.*, pp. 82-83.
33   *Ibid.*, p. 83.
34   Kellner, Douglas. *Baudrillard: A Critical Reader*. Cambridge: Basil Blackwell Ltd, 1994, p. 126.
35   Baudrillard, Jean. *Seduction*, Trans. Brian Singer. Montreal: New World Perspectives, 1990, p. 180.

entertaining" instead.[36] He is inclined to refuse rational logic. He even declares, "well-ordered resentment always begins at home."[37] According to him, the rational critique of reality begins at home; on the contrary, his poetic chaos starts from facts. What an inverted logic!

In his later years, Baudrillard is pained because he finds that "we are no longer fighting the specter of alienation, but that of ultra-reality. We are no longer fighting our shadows, but transparency."[38] Obviously, traditional negative criticism does not work any longer. Therefore, "to think extreme phenomena, thought must itself become an extreme phenomenon; it must abandon any critical pretensions, any dialectical illusions, like the world, into a paradoxical phase, an ironic and paroxystic phase. It has to be more hyperreal than the real, more virtual than virtual reality."[39] (In this sense, Kellner thinks that Baudrillard turns to metaphysical cynicism.[40] Moreover, Kellner points out that the late Baudrillard's metaphysics are under direct influence of Alfred Jarry's pataphysics.[41])

In the critical thinking space Baudrillard has constructed for us, "there is no one to turn to, nowhere to go, and nothing to be done!"[42] As a result, Baudrillard has to say that "dying is nothing, you have to know how to disappear… To disappear is to pass into an enigmatic state which is neither life nor death."[43] Thereafter, he begins to play with "disappearance," creating various kinds of mysterious virii for the disordering. His thinking is more and more inclined to becoming a disintegrative toxin destroying the social orders of reality and logical orders of thinking, and to become a speculation on death. (After

36 Kellner, Douglas. *Baudrillard: A Critical Reader*. Cambridge: Basil Blackwell Ltd, 1994, p. 17.
37 Baudrillard, Jean. *Selected Writings*, Edited. Mark Poster. Standford University Press, 2001, p. 267.
38 Baudrillard, Jean. *The Perfect Crime*, Trans. Chris Turner. London: Verso, 1996, p. 66.
39 *Ibid*.
40 Kellner, Douglas and Steven Best. *The Postmodern Turn*. New York: The Guilford Press, 1997. Later, Baudrillard also admitted this turn. Please refer to Baudrillard, Jean. *Fragments: Cool memories III, 1990-1995*, Trans. Emily Agar. Verso, 1997.
41 Kellner, Douglas and Steven Best. *The Postmodern Turn*. New York: The Guilford Press, 1997.
42 Kellner, Douglas. *Baudrillard: A Critical Reader*. Cambridge: Basil Blackwell Ltd, 1994, p. 66.
43 Baudrillard, Jean. *Cool Memories I*, Trans. Chris Turner. New York: Verso, 1990, p. 24.

the 9-11 attack on America in 2001, he ironically named the war on terrorism launched by the USA as war "against wolves" when he explained the original cause of terrorist attacks, whereas he believes that the real cause for the attacks was the virus of Western culture itself. It is called the war against the wolves. However, he realizes that it is not effective to use war against the virus because the virus has been with us for a long time: without the frontline and the rear, the enemy is inside our heart, that is, we have to wage war against our cultural heart. It would be the fourth world war, which is not between the nations, people, systems and ideologies but between humanity and its own self. We are the virus; and this so-called "World War IV" is precisely the death and disappearance of human beings.) Baudrillard even says that such mysterious things can only be "rediscovered beneath these notes like a watermark" after his death.[44] I think it is an inevitable result for Baudrillard to shift from the symbolic exchange of grass-roots romanticism to pessimistic death, and again from death to the seductive game of taking advantage of vulnerability, and then to mysterious "disappearance." As Baudrillard covers the real existence of capitalist modes of production by simulations and code, he has no other choices but suicide in the sign language and making weird remarks to kill time.

Baudrillard once intimately expressed his agony frankly in *Cool Memories I*. In actuality, the various paradigms of convex theories he has arduously made all alone are nothing more than consciously ordered masks (or disguises) of logic; moreover, these masks are often manifested as contradictory and strategic cynicism. Actually, he is fully aware that these theories are nothing more than a convex mask for people's attention. Hence, the mask you make is also the other who keeps eyes on you; and the relationship between you and the other is a comprehensive monarch-subject relationship. Before the invention of new masks, what he did was maintain his old mask. (For instance, before the invention of "simulacra-simulation," he had to carefully keep up the mask of the "political economy of the sign;" before the invention of "seduction", the mask of "exchange-sign value" had to be confirmed.) He says meticulous precautions should be taken towards the mask, with no activation of functions

---

44   *Ibid.*, p. 63.

the mask has at the time you find it. Even so, this is unceasing and "haunts us like a slow-burning, indirectly fuelled flame."[45] His late period is as tense as walking on eggs at night. He constantly fears that the other may one day have "switched allegiances," and that the other's judgment of what is good and bad may have altered, because this were to happen, the seductive power of mask might disappear.[46] Therefore, Baudrillard is always the first to say "quit" when his mask is about to lose its seductive power. In a lecture promoting his new book, *The Conspiracy of Art*, Baudrillard was asked who he is. He answered, "who am I? I don't know. I am a substitute for myself." Later, he raised this question again and answered it in *Fragments: Cool Memories III, 1990-1995*.

Who are you then, J.B., you who speak of simulacra, but a simulacrum yourself?

Answer: it is because I exist that I can advance the hypothesis of the universal simulacrum and simulation. You who are already unreal cannot envisage the unreality of things. You who are merely the shadows of yourselves cannot advance the hypothesis of transparency.[47]

This is not a joke.

In his later years, Baudrillard wrote down a few melancholy lines:

Disappearance of the object into its system

Disappearance of production into its mirror

Disappearance of the real into the simulacrum

Disappearance of the Other into its double

Disappearance of the majorities into their silence

Disappearance of Evil into its transparency

Disappearance of seduction into the orgy

Disappearance of crime into its perfection

Disappearance of memory into commemoration

Disappearance of illusion into its end and, finally,

---

45   *Ibid.*, p. 39.
46   *Ibid.*
47   Baudrillard, Jean. *Fragments: Cool Memories III, 1990-1995*, Trans. Emily Agar. Verso, 1997, p. 22.

Disappearance of the illusionist himself, on stage, in the full glare of the lights.

The illusionist, having displayed all his art, cannot but make himself disappear (without knowing how)48

This is the conclusion of all his thoughts: the shaped object disappears in the functional system; material production breaks in the false mirror, the real is absent in the hyperreal of simulation; transparency and orgy delete evil and seduction, and the crime of every murder reaches its perfection because of the alibi. Baudrillard himself is an illusionist who displays illusions in the full glare of the lights on stage. When the play is over, even though he does not want to play, he has lost his way to disappear.

Baudrillard passed away in Paris on March 6th, 2007, and on March 13th, his funeral was held at the Montparnasse cemetery inside Paris city. Philosopher René Schérer quoted Baudrillard's words, "it should look like this, as if Baudrillard's funeral has never happened. Even better, from now on he will live forever."(Tout ça est parfaitement normal, l'enterrement de Baudrillard n'a pas eu lieu et c'est tant mieux, à présent il va vivre.) Of course, he is more real than himself only when he is in the hyperreal of simulation.

Pathetic Baudrillard. Amen!

---

48   Baudrillard, Jean. *Cool Memories IV: 1995-2000*. Trans. Chris Turner. New York: Verso, 2003, p. 12. Actually, at the end of *Fragments: Cool Memories III*, Baudrillard also wrote down the conclusion of his thoughts. At that time he did not use the word "disappearance," but used the word "keep".

Keep objects as a system

Keep production as a mirror

Keep death as an exchange

Keep the world as a simulacrum

Keep the evil transparent

Keep the majorities silent

Keep your seduction alive

Keep your memory cool

Keep yourself as an other

Keep perfection as a crime

Keep illusion for the end

Keep online for the while.

Please refer to Baudrillard, Jean. *Fragments: Cool Memories III, 1990-1995*, Trans. Emily Agar. Verso, 1997, p. 152.

BIBLIOGRAPHY

Bataille, Georges. *Eroticism, Expenditure and General Economy*. Changchun: Jilin People's Publishing House, 2003.

–, *Visions of Excess: Selected Writings, 1927-1939*. Theory and History of Literature, V. 14. Minneapolis: University of Minnesota Press, 1985.

-, *History of Eroticism*. The Commercial Press, 2003.

Baudrillard, Jean. *Cool Memories (5 Volumes)*. Verso, 1990-2004.

–, *For a Critique of the Political Economy of the Sign*. St. Louis: Telos Press, 1981.

–, *The Consumer Society: Myths and Structures*. Theory, Culture & Society. London: Sage Publications Ltd, 1998.

–, *The Mirror of Production*, Trans. Mark Poster. St. Louis: Telos Press, 1975.

–, *The Perfect Crime*, Trans. Chris Turner. London: Verso, 1996.

–, *The System of Objects*. Radical Thinkers. London [u.a.]: Verso, 2005.

–, *Seduction*, Trans. Brian Singer. Montreal: New World Perspectives, 1990.

–, *Selected Writings*, Edit. Mark Poster. Standford University Press, 2001.

–, *Simulacra and Simulation*, Trans. Sheila Faria Glaser. University of Michigan Press, 1994.

–, *Symbolic Exchange and Death*, Trans. I. Hamilton Grant, London: Sage, 1993.

Benjamin, Walter. *Works of Walter Benjamin*. Beijing: Chinese Social Science Press, 1999.

Benveniste, Emile. *Problems of General Linguistics*, Miami, 1971.

Best, Steven and Douglas Kellner. *Postmodern Theory: Critical Interrogations*. Macmillan, 1991.

–, *The Postmodern Turn*. New York: Guilford Press, 1997.

Bourdieu, Pierre and Passeron, Jan-Claude. *Reproduction in Education, Society and Culture*. London: Sage Publication Ltd, 1990.

Chaptal, Jean-Antoine. *De l'industrie française*, Ant. Aug. Renouard. 1819.

Clark, Eric. *The Want Makers: The World of Advertising: How They Make You Buy*. Viking, 1989.

Debord, Guy. *The Society of the Spectacle*, Trans. Donald Nickleson-Smith, New York: Zone Books

Godelier, Maurice. *Anthropology, Science of Primitive Societies?* Paris: Denoël, 1971.

Heidegger, Martin, and David Farrell Krell. *Nietzsche*. San Francisco: Harper & Row, 1979.

Hess, Moses. *The Essence of Money*. Trans. Adam Buick. Rheinische Jarhrbücher zur gesellschaftlichen Reform, Darmstadt, 1845.

Hillier, Bill. *Space is the Machine: A Configurational Theory of Architecture*. Cambridge, UK. Cambridge University Press, 1996.

Jay, Martin. *Downcast Eyes: The Denigration of Vision in Twentieth-Century of French Thought*. Berkeley and Los Angeles: University of California Press, 1994.

Horkheimer, Max and Theodor W. Adorno, Gunzelin Schmid Noerr. *Dialectic of Enlightenment: Philosophical Fragments*. Stanford University Press, 2002.

Kellner, Douglas. *Baudrillard: A Critical Reader*. Cambridge: Basil Blackwell Ltd, 1994.

Kristeva, Julia. "La sémiotique et la production," *Semiotica* 2.

Lash, Scott and John Urry, *Economics of Signs and Space*. London: Sage, 1994.

Lefebvre, Henri. *Everyday Life in the Modern World*. Continuum International Publishing Group, 2002.

Lévi-Strauss, Claude. "Introduction to Sociology and Anthropology", in: *Sociology and Anthropology*. Shanghai Translation Publishing House, 2003.

–, *The Savage Mind*, University of Chicago Press, 1966.

List, Friedrich. *The National System of Political Economy.* Cosimo, Inc., 2006.

Marx, Karl and Frederick Engels. *Collected Works*, London: Lawrence & Wishart.

Mauss, Marcel. *A General Theory of Magic,* Trans. Robert Brain. London: Routledge & Kegan Paul, 1972.

–, *The Gift: Forms and Functions of Exchange in Archaic Societies*. Glencoe: Free Press, 1954.

Pickering, Andrew. *The Mangle of Practice: Time, Agency, and Science*. Trans. Xing Dongmei, University of Chicago Press, 1995.

Poster, Mark. *Jean Baudrillard, Selected Writings, An Introduction*. Stanford University Press, 1988

–, *The Second Media Age*. Cambridge: Polity Press, 1995.

Ricardo, David. *On the Principles of Political Economy and Taxation*. London, 1821.

Sahlins, Marshall D. *Culture and Practical Reason*. Joint Publishing Company Limited (Beijing), 2002.

-, "La première société d'abondance", in: *Les Temps Modernes* (October, 1968).

Saussure, Ferdinand de. *Course in General Linguistics*. Trans. Wade Baskin. New York: McGraw-Hill Book Company, 1965.

Sturrock, John. *Structuralism and Since: From Lévi-Strauss to Derrida*, Liaoning Education Press, 1998

Vaneigem, Raoul. *The Revolution of Everyday Life*. Trans. Donald Nicholson-Smith. Rebel Press, 2001.

Veblen, Thorstein. *The Theory of the Leisure Class*. Forgotten Books, 1965.

Yang Haifeng. *Towards Post-Marx: From Mirror of Production to Mirror of Symbols*. Central Compilation & Translation Press, 2004.

Yuasa, Hiroo. *Georges Bataille: Consumption*. Trans. Zhao Hanying: Hebei Educational Publishing House, 2001. 155.

Zhang Yibing. Barthes: "Text is a Kind of Weaving", in: *Tribune of Social Sciences*, 2002, 10.

–, "Contemporary Ecological Horizon and the Logic of the Materialistic View", in: *Philosophical Researches*, 1993, 8.

–, "Historical Materialism and Historical Situating", in: *Journal Historical Research*, 2008, 1.

–, "Ideology of Cynicism", in: *Marxism and Reality*, 2004, 4.
–, "In and Out of Men's Egocentrism", in: *Philosophical Trends*, 1996, 6.
–, "On Social Practice", in: *Jianghai Academic Journal*, 1988, 5.
–, "Post-Marxism is not Marxism", in: *Journal of Nanjing University*, 2003, 2.
–, "Practical Construction", in: *Fujian Tribune*. 1991, 1.
–, "Practical Scheme", in: *Journal Seeking Truth*, 1989, 5.
–, "Problems, Ways, Methods: Reflections on New Academic Heights in Marxist Philosophical Studies", in: *Academic Monthly*, 2007, 5.
–, "Western Marxism, Post-Marxism and Late Marxism", in *Journal of Fujian Tribune*, 2000, 4.
–, *A Deep Plough: Unscrambling Major Post-marxist Texts From Adorno to Zizek*. Canut Intl. Publishers, London, 2011.
–, *Back to Marx: The Philosophical Discourse in the Context of Economics*. Nanjing: Jiangsu People's Publishing House, 1999. English version published by Göttingen University Press, in 2014.
–, *Lenin Revisited. A Post-textological Reading of His Philosophical Notes*. Jiangsu People's Publishing House, 2008. English version by Canut Intl. Publishers, London, 2011.
–, *Selected Works of Zhang Yibing*. Guilin: Guangxi Normal University Press, 1999.
–, *The Impossible Truth of Being: Mirror of Lacan's Philosophy*, The Commercial Press, 2006.
–, *The Subjective Dimension of Marxist Historical Dialectics*. Nanjing: Nanjing University Press, 2002, English version by Canut Intl. Publishers, London 2012.
    Žižek, Slavoj. *The Sublime Object of Ideology*. London: Verso Books, 1997.

ABOUT THE AUTHOR

Zhang Yibin, whose pen name is Zhang Yibing, was born in 1956 in Nanjing, a main city in Jiangsu Province, China. He graduated from the Department of Philosophy at Nanjing University in China in 1981. He is now the Vice Chancellor of Nanjing University; one of the prominent leaders of Association of Dialectical Materialism of China; dean of the Academy of Marxism and director of the Research Center of Social History of Marxism at Nanjing University, works as professor and doctoral tutor in the Department of Philosophy. He is one of rare scholars in China focusing on textological research He has written numerous articles for Chinese academic journals. His main books include: *The Broken Wing of Reason-Philosophical Critique of Western Marxism*. Nanjing: Nanjing Publishing House, 1990; *The Past and Present of Marxist Philosophy*. Nanjing: Nanjing University Press, 1992; Selected Works of Zhang Yibing. Guilin: Guangxi Normal University Press, 1999 and 2009; *Back to Marx: The Change of Philosophical Discourse in the Context of Economics*, Nanjing: Jiangsu People's Publishing House, 1999; Co-authored by Sun Bokui and Zhang Yibing. *Approaching Marx*. Nanjing: Jiangsu People's Publishing House, 2001; *Atonal Dialectical Imagination: A Textological Reading of Adorno's "Negative Dialectic"*. The Joint Publishing Company, 2001; *A Textological Reading of Althusser. Problematic, Symptomatic Reading and Ideology.* Central Compilation and Translation Press, 2003; *A Deep Plough: Unscrambling Major Post-marxist Texts*. Volume I and II published by China Renmin University Press, 2004-2008; *Contra Baudrillard.* Nanjing Publishing House, 2008; *The Subjective Dimension of Marxist Historical Dialectics*. Nanjing: Nanjing University Press, 2002; *The Impossible Real of Being: Imago of Lacanian Philosophy.* The Commercial Press, 2006; *Back to Lenin: A Post-textological Reading of His "Philosophical Notes".* Jiangsu People's Press, 2008; *The History of the Understanding of Capitalism*, 5 volumes (Co authored with Zhang Liang, Hu Daping). Nanjing: Jiangsu Renmin Press, 2009.

His following books were later translated into English and Turkish by Canut Intl. Publishers and Kalkedon Publishing, *A Deep Plough: Unscrambling Major Post-marxist Texts, Volume II: From Adorno to Zizek*, 2010; *The Subjective Dimension of Marxist Historical Dialectics*, English version by Canut Intl. London, 2010; *Lenin Revisited: His Entire Thinking Process on Marxist Philosophy: A Post-textological Reading on Philosophical Notes*, Canut Intl. London 2011; *Back to Marx: The Change of Philosophical Discourse in the Context of Economics.* English version published by Göttingen University Press, 2014; *Alhusser Revisited. Problematic, Symptomatic Reading, ISA and History of Marxism*, English version published by Canut Intl. Publishers London, 2014.

INDEX

A

Academic memory 24, 25, 27, 43, 63, 64, 79, 88, 94, 101, 103, 106, 107, 117, 123, 124, 127, 131, 134, 136, 139, 148, 169, 186

Advertisement 77, 88, 89

B

Bataille 15, 17, 19, 42, 44, 46, 49, 50, 52, 53, 55, 56, 57, 58, 59, 60, 61, 62, 63, 68, 70, 71, 80, 93, 94, 95, 96, 100, 101, 102, 124, 126, 128, 129, 131, 132, 150, 165, 166, 178, 186, 192, 194, 204, 206, 209, 213, 218, 236, 239, 244, 250, 256, 262, 267, 268, 269, 270, 271, 272, 276, 278, 279, 282, 287, 294, 312, 321, 326, 339, 340, 345, 352, 354, 383

Baudrillard 5, 15, 16, 17, 18, 19, 20, 21, 22, 23, 32, 33, 35, 42, 43, 44, 45, 46, 47, 49, 50, 53, 55, 56, 57, 58, 62, 63, 64, 65, 66, 68, 69, 70, 71, 72, 73, 74, 75, 76, 77, 78, 79, 80, 81, 83, 84, 85, 86, 87, 88, 89, 90, 91, 92, 93, 94, 95, 96, 99, 100, 101, 102, 103, 104, 105, 106, 107, 108, 109, 110, 111, 112, 113, 114, 115, 116, 117, 118, 119, 120, 121, 122, 123, 124, 125, 126, 128, 129, 130, 131, 132, 133, 134, 135, 136, 137, 138,

139, 140, 141, 142, 143, 144, 146, 147, 148, 149, 150, 151,
152, 153, 154, 155, 156, 157, 158, 159, 160, 161, 162, 163,
164, 165, 166, 167, 169, 170, 171, 172, 173, 174, 175, 176,
177, 178, 179, 180, 181, 182, 183, 184, 185, 186, 187, 188,
189, 191, 192, 193, 194, 195, 196, 197, 198, 199, 201, 202,
203, 204, 205, 206, 207, 208, 209, 210, 211, 212, 213, 215,
216, 217, 218, 219, 221, 222, 223, 224, 225, 226, 227, 228,
229, 230, 231, 232, 233, 234, 235, 236, 237, 238, 239, 243,
244, 245, 246, 247, 248, 249, 250, 251, 252, 253, 254, 255,
256, 257, 258, 259, 260, 261, 262, 263, 264, 265, 266, 267,
268, 269, 270, 271, 272, 273, 274, 275, 276, 277, 278, 279,
281, 282, 283, 284, 285, 286, 287, 289, 290, 291, 292, 293,
294, 295, 297, 298, 299, 300, 301, 302, 303, 304, 305, 306,
307, 308, 309, 310, 311, 312, 313, 314, 315, 316, 317, 319,
320, 321, 322, 323, 324, 325, 326, 327, 328, 329, 330, 331,
332, 333, 334, 335, 336, 337, 338, 339, 340, 341, 342, 343,
344, 345, 346, 347, 348, 349, 350, 351, 352, 353, 354, 355,
356, 357, 358, 359, 360, 361, 362, 363, 365, 366, 367, 368,
369, 370, 371, 372, 373, 374, 375, 376, 377, 378, 379, 380,
381, 382, 383, 384, 385, 386, 387, 388, 389, 390, 391, 392,
393, 394, 395, 396, 397, 398, 399, 400, 401, 402, 403, 404,
405, 406, 407, 408, 409, 410, 411, 412, 413, 414, 415, 416,
417, 418, 419, 420, 421, 422, 423, 424, 425, 426, 427, 428,
429, 430, 431, 432, 433, 434, 435, 436, 437, 438, 439, 441,
442, 443, 444, 445, 447, 448, 450, 452, 453, 454, 455, 456,
457, 458
Benveniste 230, 231, 232
Big dialectics 320

C

Chapin 107
City of Gradov 61
Configurating 28, 33, 34, 35, 37, 39
Consumption 7, 19, 52, 60, 74, 75, 76, 77, 78, 79, 80, 81, 82, 83,
84, 85, 88, 89, 90, 91, 92, 94, 95, 97, 100, 102, 106, 115, 116,
117, 118, 119, 120, 121, 122, 123, 124, 125, 126, 127, 128,
129, 130, 131, 132, 133, 134, 135, 136, 137, 138, 139, 140,
141, 142, 143, 144, 145, 146, 150, 157, 159, 160, 164, 169,

173, 177, 178, 179, 180, 181, 186, 187, 188, 193, 194, 211,
212, 222, 225, 227, 231, 251, 263, 269, 277, 278, 280, 291,
293, 301, 315, 321, 341, 355, 356, 359, 360, 361, 367, 369,
382, 385, 392, 401, 411
Cool Memories 16, 46, 86, 89, 90, 92, 95, 106, 110, 140, 381, 434,
435, 436, 438, 443, 447, 456, 458
Counterfeit 111, 419, 420, 421, 422, 423, 424, 426, 427, 428, 433

D

Death 43, 45, 57, 71, 340, 442, 447
Debord 18, 19, 20, 24, 42, 49, 63, 76, 78, 79, 89, 96, 104, 106,
122, 142, 147, 165, 177, 188, 231, 276, 315, 357, 395
Differential practice of the object 99, 106
Durkheim 50

E

Exchange value 21, 80, 83, 94, 100, 101, 102, 103, 112, 123, 127,
128, 131, 132, 135, 142, 144, 146, 148, 151, 152, 153, 159,
160, 163, 166, 175, 176, 177, 178, 179, 180, 183, 184, 185,
186, 192, 193, 194, 195, 196, 197, 198, 199, 202, 203, 204,
205, 206, 207, 209, 211, 212, 213, 214, 215, 216, 217, 218,
222, 226, 228, 229, 231, 233, 234, 235, 236, 247, 249, 259,
266, 267, 268, 269, 270, 273, 275, 278, 285, 286, 292, 297,
301, 309, 321, 322, 340, 352, 356, 360, 366, 367, 368, 439,
441, 449

F

Fashion logic 133
Fetishism 20, 146, 147, 148, 149, 150, 151, 152, 153, 154, 155,
156, 157, 158, 159, 160, 161, 162, 163, 164, 165, 166, 182,
183, 187, 199, 204, 206, 213, 217, 228, 229, 276, 297, 436
For a Critique of the Political Economy of the Sign 16, 20, 42, 44,
45, 46, 49, 65, 83, 84, 87, 92, 94, 95, 96, 100, 102, 104, 105,
107, 111, 115, 122, 124, 125, 135, 137, 139, 141, 142, 143,
148, 150, 153, 162, 164, 166, 170, 173, 177, 182, 186, 187,
191, 197, 201, 203, 205, 207, 212, 216, 222, 223, 225, 230,
232, 233, 234, 236, 300, 309, 358, 366, 368, 370, 371, 427,
432

G

Gestell 45, 62, 64, 78, 206, 209, 211, 214

H

Heidegger 18, 27, 29, 31, 32, 33, 35, 42, 43, 58, 60, 63, 66, 68, 70,
71, 76, 78, 88, 101, 106, 122, 124, 125, 205, 206, 209, 210,
214, 218, 231, 260, 267, 282, 284, 308, 309, 312, 323, 357,
375, 389, 423
Hess 27, 35, 37, 38, 185

I

I differentiate, therefore I am 172
Implosion 324, 444, 445
I produce, therefore I am. 21, 278

K

Kristeva 25, 245, 247, 269, 270, 271, 272

L

Labour power 22, 144, 160, 164, 225, 247, 248, 249, 252, 253,
256, 258, 266, 269, 274, 276, 277, 282, 283, 284, 290, 291,
292, 293, 294, 301, 326, 337, 338, 339, 345, 388, 395, 398,
399, 400, 402, 415
Labour shaping 28, 33, 34, 36, 39, 128, 156, 218
Lacan 25, 33, 42, 44, 56, 59, 65, 79, 85, 122, 123, 124, 125, 130,
134, 136, 137, 138, 139, 140, 158, 162, 171, 172, 197, 215,
237, 238, 239, 248, 249, 276, 308, 309, 360, 368, 406, 409,
416, 433, 451, 452, 453
Lefebvre 15, 18, 19, 42, 49, 63, 76, 96, 232, 233, 285, 371
Levi-Strauss 239
List 37, 38, 253
Logical homogeneity 44

M

MARQUE 125
Mauss 15, 17, 19, 42, 44, 46, 49, 50, 51, 52, 53, 54, 55, 56, 57, 59,
60, 61, 62, 63, 64, 65, 67, 68, 69, 71, 80, 93, 94, 95, 96, 100,

101, 102, 103, 124, 126, 128, 129, 131, 132, 136, 150, 166, 192, 194, 204, 206, 209, 213, 218, 236, 238, 244, 247, 256, 262, 263, 267, 268, 269, 272, 276, 278, 279, 282, 287, 307, 312, 321, 326, 339, 340, 345, 350, 352, 353, 354, 383, 418

Mode 21, 22, 25, 26, 28, 31, 39, 40, 41, 42, 54, 61, 72, 99, 102, 104, 106, 109, 144, 145, 148, 149, 153, 162, 172, 176, 181, 183, 189, 201, 203, 207, 213, 218, 219, 222, 223, 228, 244, 247, 248, 250, 251, 253, 255, 258, 259, 260, 262, 263, 264, 265, 268, 269, 272, 273, 279, 282, 283, 284, 285, 286, 287, 299, 300, 304, 310, 311, 315, 320, 321, 322, 326, 327, 328, 329, 331, 334, 335, 336, 337, 339, 342, 343, 344, 345, 346, 348, 349, 350, 351, 354, 356, 357, 359, 361, 362, 365, 371, 375, 376, 377, 378, 379, 382, 383, 384, 389, 394, 395, 403, 410, 412, 425, 430, 438, 444

Modelling 19, 20, 29, 39, 41, 66, 71, 78, 81, 87, 91, 93, 99, 102, 104, 105, 106, 108, 109, 122, 123, 124, 126, 127, 128, 131, 135, 143, 146, 148, 150, 153, 158, 163, 165, 172, 173, 175, 176, 184, 191, 192, 193, 196, 198, 201, 223, 226, 419, 430, 432, 443, 444, 449

Monkey anatomy 335, 346

Murder trilogy 20, 21, 23, 128

N

Nature 20, 21, 23, 30, 32, 33, 35, 37, 38, 39, 44, 51, 52, 55, 59, 69, 70, 71, 92, 111, 113, 116, 138, 157, 159, 162, 163, 165, 175, 179, 195, 204, 210, 214, 218, 227, 235, 249, 253, 254, 256, 257, 258, 260, 261, 262, 263, 265, 271, 274, 277, 278, 279, 280, 281, 282, 285, 290, 295, 296, 300, 301, 302, 305, 307, 308, 309, 310, 311, 312, 313, 314, 315, 316, 317, 319, 320, 321, 322, 332, 337, 340, 341, 345, 350, 353, 356, 357, 359, 361, 367, 368, 369, 370, 372, 374, 375, 382, 383, 389, 390, 400, 407, 408, 410, 411, 415, 417, 421, 422, 423, 424, 425, 426, 427, 428, 430, 431, 433, 436, 438, 439, 441, 448, 449, 450, 451, 452

O

Ordering 22, 25, 26, 28, 33, 35, 36, 39, 45, 46, 65, 68, 70, 72, 75, 76, 93, 99, 100, 102, 112, 129, 132, 137, 153, 158, 163, 172,

175, 178, 179, 181, 183, 188, 191, 211, 228, 229, 367, 410, 426, 428

Other 5, 16, 19, 25, 26, 42, 45, 80, 123, 124, 126, 129, 136, 137, 138, 139, 140, 239, 276, 333, 336, 360, 403, 418, 451, 457

P

Pattern formation 430

Political Economy of the Sign 20, 43, 45, 46, 97, 100, 148, 169, 221, 222, 439, 449

Postmodern 16, 68, 73, 172, 210, 236, 292, 363, 372, 373, 381, 414, 447, 448, 449, 450, 452, 453, 454

Potlatch 52, 53, 54, 59, 101, 263, 340

Production ordering 28, 36, 39

R

Readiness-to-hand 31, 63, 66, 101, 106, 205, 206, 284, 321

Reality 18, 30, 36, 37, 39, 40, 44, 54, 57, 62, 84, 90, 92, 112, 124, 127, 129, 134, 136, 138, 149, 154, 163, 171, 173, 174, 180, 182, 209, 215, 218, 222, 224, 226, 227, 228, 230, 231, 232, 233, 234, 237, 251, 260, 264, 295, 298, 301, 303, 305, 306, 308, 309, 311, 320, 322, 337, 338, 349, 351, 353, 356, 357, 358, 359, 360, 361, 362, 363, 367, 368, 372, 373, 377, 380, 381, 382, 390, 391, 392, 393, 406, 409, 414, 417, 422, 424, 426, 428, 431, 432, 433, 434, 436, 437, 440, 442, 451, 452, 454, 455

Relation configurating 33, 34, 35

S

Sacred world 57, 61

Sade 56, 57, 59, 256, 272, 278

Sahlins 52, 55, 62, 66, 93, 96, 251, 282, 298, 315, 326, 344

Saussure 106, 107, 127, 130, 131, 133, 134, 139, 140, 141, 169, 171, 181, 184, 197, 215, 228, 229, 230, 237, 295, 359, 366, 369, 401, 422, 427, 450

Series 15, 17, 34, 43, 45, 56, 62, 71, 72, 73, 74, 75, 77, 78, 79, 83, 108, 124, 134, 140, 143, 169, 171, 172, 173, 174, 176, 177, 181, 182, 191, 194, 326, 380, 424, 427, 428, 429, 430, 431

Simulacra 16, 23, 43, 45, 72, 73, 111, 188, 198, 241, 372, 415,

419, 420, 422, 424, 426, 427, 428, 429, 430, 431, 432, 433, 434, 436, 437, 438, 440, 444, 447, 449, 456, 457

Simulation 16, 111, 241, 404, 405, 406, 411, 413, 419, 431, 433, 437, 444

Structural value 366, 369, 370, 374, 386, 407, 408, 412, 449

Super-Big 176, 177, 179

Symbol 44, 45, 60, 65, 66, 68, 80, 85, 94, 102, 121, 123, 124, 125, 127, 128, 131, 133, 134, 142, 144, 156, 164, 165, 166, 211, 229, 230, 241, 363, 365, 370, 409, 418, 445

Symbolic exchange 43, 45, 65, 128, 198, 199, 418

Symbolic Exchange and Death 16, 17, 20, 22, 42, 43, 44, 46, 67, 70, 71, 72, 85, 102, 111, 132, 154, 161, 173, 188, 195, 199, 215, 233, 359, 365, 367, 372, 373, 381, 387, 405, 407, 410, 411, 419, 420, 421, 426, 427, 428, 431, 432, 434, 436, 437, 439, 443, 444, 449

T

The Consumer Society 16, 18, 19, 42, 44, 45, 46, 49, 62, 75, 77, 79, 80, 81, 84, 86, 87, 88, 90, 91, 92, 93, 96, 100, 102, 113, 144, 157, 160, 173, 300, 371, 439

The Gift 50, 52, 57, 307

The Mirror of Production 16, 17, 20, 21, 43, 44, 46, 49, 70, 93, 96, 103, 125, 148, 152, 155, 161, 201, 202, 217, 243, 244, 246, 248, 250, 251, 257, 258, 261, 265, 266, 270, 271, 273, 274, 275, 277, 283, 284, 286, 291, 294, 300, 301, 304, 305, 306, 307, 308, 312, 314, 315, 319, 320, 323, 325, 326, 330, 333, 336, 338, 340, 342, 345, 356, 360, 361, 363, 365, 371, 374, 375, 376, 380, 402, 404

The System of Objects 18, 19, 24, 35, 42, 44, 45, 46, 49, 62, 63, 64, 65, 66, 68, 69, 70, 71, 73, 74, 75, 76, 77, 78, 80, 81, 84, 88, 91, 96, 100, 101, 105, 106, 112, 143, 157, 173, 304, 371, 430

U

Use value 198, 204, 205, 208, 209, 215, 216, 217, 218

V

Value 30, 56, 59, 97, 100, 186, 192, 201, 202, 209, 213, 218, 235, 241, 270, 273, 365

Veblen 42, 84, 102, 103, 141, 142, 164, 183, 186, 187, 432

www.ingramcontent.com/pod-product-compliance
Lightning Source LLC
Chambersburg PA
CBHW031136020426
42333CB00013B/404